The Sociology of Aging

A Social Problems Perspective

Duane A. Matcha

Siena College

ALLYN AND BACON

Boston • London • Toronto • Sydney • Tokyo • Singapore

To my spouse and children—
Bonnie, Lisa, and Annie—
and to my parents,
George and Stella Matcha

Editor-in-Chief, Social Sciences: Karen Hanson
Editorial Assistant: Jennifer Jacobson
Marketing Manager: Joyce Nilsen
Editorial-Production Service: Electronic Publishing Services Inc.
Manufacturing Buyer: Megan Cochran
Cover Administrator: Suzanne Harbison

Copyright © 1997 by Allyn & Bacon
A Viacom Company
Needham Heights, Massachusetts 02194

Library of Congress Cataloging-in-Publication Data

Matcha, Duane A.
    The sociology of aging : a social problems perspective / Duane A. Matcha.
       p. cm.
    Includes bibliographical references and index.
    ISBN 0-205-16468-4 (pbk.)
      1. Gerontology—United States.   2. Aged—United States.
I. Title.
HQ1064.U5M395   1996   96-13107
305.26´0973—dc20   CIP

Printed in the United States of America
10 9 8 7 6 5 4 3 2 1   01 00 99 98 97 96

Photo Credits:

Photo credits are found on page 270, which should be considered an extension of the copyright page.

Contents

Preface

The Sociology of Aging: A Social Problems Perspective explores the contextual dimension of growing old in American society today. It constructs a relationship between the process of aging, its societal definitions and their consequences, and thus a sociology of aging. The incorporation of a social problems approach provides a conceptual framework within which such a relationship can be explored. Within this book, a *social problems approach* refers to a critical examination of social forces that impinge on the aging process. It is not the intent of this approach to consider the aging process or the aged a social problem. Instead, the social problems are the divisive images of growing old, created by the institutional structures of society, as well as the myriad patterns of inequality of gender, race, and economics that are compounded in old age.

To understand aging within a societal context, *The Sociology of Aging* incorporates a multiplicity of theoretical perspectives found in basic sociological literature and in social gerontology. Although such theoretical perspectives offer a plethora of explanations, emphasis will be on a political economy/ critical perspective. Thus the social condition of any group within society must be understood within the framework of its ability to exercise economic and political power. However, because it is also necessary to ensure a theoretical balance, the text is grounded in all the traditional theoretical arguments of sociology and gerontology. The following is an overview of its organization and content.

Chapter 1 provides an introduction, that explains the social problems perspective that will be employed in addition to a brief but concise coverage of various research methods and designs. Chapter 2 presents a broad-based historical account of aging. A more specific description of the aging process as experienced in the United States is also presented. The chapter introduces two explanations of population aging: demographic transition theory and modernization theory. With an appreciation of the demographics of aging, the reader is then exposed to various sociological explanations of the aging process. Chapter 3 explains the basic theoretical frameworks found in sociology as well as in gerontology, and the reader is encouraged to create links between research techniques and theoretical explanations. Chapter 4 connects the aging process to basic sociological concepts. Beginning with Chapter 5 the aging process is examined within the larger social structure, first in relation to a number of specific societal institutions, including the family (Chapter 5), economics (Chapter 6), health care (Chapter 7), and politics (Chapter 8), and second, in relation to significant social arrangements, including gender, race, and ethnicity (Chapter 9), living arrangements (Chapter 10), victimization (Chapter 11), and death and dying (Chapter 12). Finally, Chapter 13 offers an assessment of current social policy toward aging as well as future implications of these policies.

ACKNOWLEDGMENTS

A number of people have contributed to the completion of this book. I would like to thank Daniel J. Klenow, North Dakota State University; Brenda J. Moretta, Our Lady of the Lake, San Antonio; and Karen A. Roberto, University of North Colorado. Their comments have proved invaluable in the writing of this text. I would also like to thank the Siena College library staff, who have been most helpful and understanding of my constant demands. Karen Hanson and the staff at Allyn and Bacon must also be recognized for their assistance and encouragement.

Chapter 1

Growing Older

A Sociological Explanation

Old age, in short, is sociologically interesting for what people make of it,
whether they honor the grand old man, or despise the mean old fogey.
—GERTH & MILLS, 1953, P. 16

Imagine that today is your 65th birthday. How would you describe this day relative to any other day? How would you assess your physical well-being, financial status, or family relations? During the spring semester of 1991 some of my students were asked to respond to these and other questions relating to one's perception of being old. The results were not surprising. The students identified the day as significant because, in their view, it was either the beginning of the retirement period or a day of reflection. Gender differences were particularly evident regarding the image of being old. Based on their responses, it was concluded that "the students' interpretation of this event and its resultant consequences is a reinforcement of the social construction of aging which provides the image from which to develop their aged self. . . . Our response to this view is an indication of its importance as a societal issue, and the extent to which it has been internalized and reinforced on the individual level" (Matcha, 1993, p. 17). It is believed that these findings are consistent with a way of thinking in our society about the aging process. Our understanding of the aging process is grounded primarily in our own personal experiences. Our interaction with grandparents or other significant elderly in our social environment provides a generalized image of growing old. As a result, the larger social "other" of elderly is constructed from individual experiences. Seldom do we encounter the diversity that exists within this heterogeneous category. The consequence is that on the individual level we progress forever forward, advancing chronologically and accepting the consequences of biological maturity. Seldom do we recognize that aging is a process involving social forces. Thus we celebrate birthdays as markers of time relative to those around us. Based on our chronological age, we construct a set of physical and social expectations for ourselves that are consistent with our definition of being older. Lost, however, within the welter of our daily efforts to accept the outcome of biological advancement is the inevitable impact of the social environment within which we age.

The purpose of this chapter is to establish the conceptual framework within which the book will be presented. We will discuss a number of basic concepts that will be used throughout the book. We will also construct the relationship between the sociology of aging and social problems. Finally, we will present a basic introduction to research methods. We begin by asking (and answering) some basic conceptual questions.

Aging: A Definition

Aging is an ongoing biological, psychological, and sociological process involving the individual and the structural characteristics of the social system within which it occurs. This book will concentrate exclusively on the sociological. Such a discipline-specific approach allows the reader to examine and understand the process as one component within the larger dimension of social gerontology.

Some cross-cultural examples of aging using the sociological perspective are presented here: In Mali, "a social system which is dominated by elders, older persons naturally hold most powers, and as a result set up structures that enable them to design, execute and control the way in which decisions are implemented" (Traore, 1985, p. 16). In France, "the boundaries of old age are being blurred, and there is a strained contrast between the images that these persons have of themselves and the image that society offers to them" (Guillemard,

1986, pp. 13–25). In Botswana and Namibia, "no ceremonies mark the onset of old age (or menopause), but all elders (including those without children) do bear the honorific 'na' in their names, which means 'old,' 'big,' or 'great.' No ritual occasion marks the moment when one becomes 'na,' usually in one's mid to late forties" (Rosenberg, 1990, p. 21). In the United States, "an individual is only as old as he feels, but how he feels is in large part a function of how the society about him expects him to feel and act" (Breen, 1960, p. 149).

The one intertwining theme throughout these examples is that of having the power to control the means by which aging is defined. It is within this context that the elderly exist, not only in the United States but throughout the world. Thus we can more precisely state that as a sociological concept, *sociological aging* is a process defining appropriate behavior patterns constructed from the expectations and belief systems of the structural characteristics of society. Now that we have defined aging, the next question is, How do we study this process? As with any construction project, the foundation must first be established. In the study of aging, the foundation is called social gerontology.

Social Gerontology

As a scientific discipline, *social gerontology* is relatively young. The discipline evolved throughout the 20th century into a significant and specialized area of study. Tibbitts (1960, p. 14) referred to it as "a many faceted and complex field of study." Before a discussion of its historical development, it is necessary to define what we mean by social gerontology. Koller (1968, p. 4) defines it as "the study of the impact of aging upon individuals and society and the subsequent reactions of individuals and society to aging." The academic breadth of social gerontology is captured by McPherson (1990, p. 17), who defines it "as the interdisciplinary discovery of knowledge by those affiliated with the biological sciences, clinical medicine, and the behavioral and social sciences and the application of this knowledge by social planners and practitioners in the field of human services." Regarding definitions, it is instructive to consider Achenbaum and Levin's (1989, p. 395) concern that "what constitutes gerontology's scope and purpose is often a matter of who is speaking and how the issues are framed." Thus gerontology, like any concept, is socially constructed. While definitions provide a basis for understanding the content of a concept, one must also examine the history within which it was developed. The defining moments in this brief history are chronicled by McPherson (1990, pp. 15–16).

Most research identifies Charles S. Minot's *The Problems of Age, Growth, and Death* (1908), Elie Metchnikoff's *The Prolongation of Life* (1908), and Raymond Pearl's *The Biology of Death* (1922) as the beginning of a systematic study of aging. In addition, works by G. Stanley Hall, *Senescence, the Second Half of Life* (1922), E.V. Cowdry, *Problems of Ageing* (1939), and Leo W. Simmons, *The Role of the Aged in Primitive Societies* (1945), further established the legitimacy of aging research.

The emergence of the term *gerontology* can be traced to N. Rybnikov in 1929 (Strieb & Orbach, 1967). However, according to Schwartz, Snyder, and Peterson (1984, p. 9), "Cowdry is considered by some to be the 'founding father' of modern gerontology." In 1940 gerontology became institutionalized with the appointment of Edward J. Stieglitz as head of the Unit on Gerontology in the National Institute of Health (Strieb & Orbach, 1967). The 1945 charter of the Gerontological Society of America identified two broad goals of this new organization. According to Achenbaum (1987, p. 21), "this new Society was to promote multi-disciplinary research in a variety of established fields of inquiry that utilized both theory and empirical data to broaden the frontiers of knowledge. On the other hand, its founders hoped to translate research into practice in order to deal with the 'problems' of aging." The society has grown from its initial 80 members to 5,929 as of July 1995. Social gerontology was quickly established in applicable subfields such as medicine, psychology, sociology, economics, politics, demographics, and social work (Koller, 1968). Consequently, social gerontology has emerged, on the one hand, as a free-standing discipline. However, it is also viewed as a rubric for various fields of study as they embark on their discipline-specific attempts to explore the phenomena of the aging process. The *Journals of Gerontology* and *The Gerontologist,* as the official journals of the Gerontological Society of America, reflect the need for an allocation of space as the investigation of aging becomes increasingly diverse. It is the subfield of the sociology of aging that is the focus of this book.

Figure 1–1 provides a historical excursion through the development of social gerontology. The stages represent the progressive development of an area of specialization (McPherson, 1990).

The Sociology of Aging

Sociology is the scientific study of human behavior in the social environment. The *sociology of aging* is the scientific study of the reciprocal relationship between the society and those defined as aged by that society. Although the sociology of aging and social gerontology appear to be similar by definition, they are distinct. Social gerontology is a multidisciplinary perspective, whereas the sociology of aging assumes a discipline-specific approach and interpretation. The study of aging from a sociological perspective utilizes concepts and theoretical frameworks applicable to those defined as aged. For example, one possible area of research would be the status of those who are aged as well as the roles they engage in within society. If we accept this definition of the sociology of aging, then the reciprocal nature of this relationship is that one's position, or status, is determined by the society. Thus being defined as aged may result in a decline in status (Cowgill & Holmes, 1972; Cowgill, 1974) as one's society modernizes. One could, however, argue that the elderly were never accorded higher status in more primitive societies. Instead, status was determined by social class position rather than age.

Historical Roots   As one of a number of subfields of social gerontology, the sociology of aging is clearly differentiated from the other discipline-specific areas of study. Although the emergence of social gerontology was influenced by sociology, the sociology of aging was possible only as a consequence of the development of social gerontology (Streib & Orbach, 1967). An early review of the significant works in the sociology of aging is presented by Shanas (1971); a more introspective glimpse into its development is provided by Riley (1987).

The Present and the Future   The sociology of aging has not established itself as clearly as other disciplines, notably psychology and biology. The problem is not the inability of sociology to articulate its unique contribution. Rather, it is the conceptual overlap between social gerontology and the sociology of aging. This is not to suggest that other disciplines do not

**FIGURE 1–1   A Time Line Depicting the Development of the Field of
                Social Gerontology Since 1940**

Date	Event

The Normal Stage (up to 1945)

1940   Publication of the journal *Geriatrics*

The Network Stage (1945–1960)

1945   L. Simmons, *The Role of the Aged in Primitive Society.*

A major review of the anthropological literature on the status and treatment of the elderly in primitive societies. It showed a negative relationship between status and the growth of technology in society.

1945   The Gerontological Society of America was established and held annual meetings thereafter to promote the scientific study of aging from multidisciplinary perspectives and to stimulate communication among scientists, researchers, teachers, and professionals (see Achenbaum, 1987).

1945   The first issue of the *Journal of Gerontology* was published.

1946   The American Psychological Association added a "Maturity and Old Age" section.

1948   O. Pollak, *Social Adjustment in Old Age.* A significant study that shifted the focus from the problems to the process of aging. It also identified the University of Chicago as a leading research center in social gerontology.

1948   The International Association of Gerontology was founded in Liege, Belgium.

1952   The Gerontological Society organized a "Psychology and Social Sciences" section. This reflected the growing interest in and acceptance of this perspective for the study of aging phenomena.

1953   R. Havighurst and R. Albrecht, *Older People.*

1959   L. Cain (ed.), The Sociology of Aging: A Trend Report and Bibliography. *Current Sociology.*

1959–1960   (a) J. Birren (ed.), *Handbook of Aging and the Individual: Psychological and Biological Aspects*

(b) C. Tibbits (ed.), *Handbook of Social Gerontology: Societal Aspects of Aging*

(c) E. Burgess (ed.), *Aging in Western Societies*

These handbooks summarized the state of knowledge in gerontology in the late 1950s.

The Cluster Stage (1961–1975)

1961   The *Gerontologist:* a second journal published by the Gerontological Society to focus on the more applied and professional interests of those working with and for the aged.

1961   E. Cumming and W. Henry, *Growing Old: The Process of Disengagement.* The first attempt to develop a social gerontological theory to explain satisfaction or adjustment in the later years.

1961   First White House Conference on Aging. These conferences are held every 10 years in the United States to draw scientists and professional workers together to make recommendations for consideration by Congress.

1965   A. Rose and W. Peterson (eds.), *Older People and Their Social World.*

1967   E. Youmans, *Older Rural Americans.* One of the few studies to consider aging in a rural context.

1968   M. Riley and A. Foner (eds.), *Aging and Society. Volume One: An Inventory of Research Findings.* This landmark volume presented and interpreted the empirical findings of social science research to this date.

1968   E. Shanas et al., *Older People in Three Industrial Societies.* A cross-national comparative study of the social situation of older people in Denmark, Great Britain, and the United States.

1968   B. Neugarten (ed.), *Middle Age and Aging: A Reader in Social Psychology.* The first collection of readings on the social psychology of aging.

1969   R. Havihurst et al., *Adjustment to Retirement: A Cross-National Study.*

continued

**FIGURE 1–1   A Time Line Depicting the Development of the Field of
Social Gerontology Since 1940** *Continued*

Date	Event
1969	M. Riley et al. (eds.), *Aging and Society. Volume Two: Aging and the Professions.* A statement of the concerns and involvement of a number of professions in the care of the aging and aged.
1970	E. Palmore, *Normal Aging: Reports from the Duke Longitudinal Studies,* 1955–1969. The first interdisciplinary longitudinal study.
1972	M. Riley et al., *Aging and Society. Volume Three: A Sociology of Age Stratification.* Presents a model of aging that stresses the interaction between history and the social structure as it affects various age cohorts.
1972	D. Cowgill and L. Holmes (eds.), *Aging and Modernization*
1972	R. Atchley, *The Social Forces in Later Life: An Introduction to Social Gerontology.* The first textbook written for students enrolled in an undergraduate course on social gerontology.
1972	Canadian Association on Gerontology founded.
1974	National Institute on Aging established in the United States to promote research on all facets of gerontology.

The Specialty Stage (1975–)

Date	Event
1975	R. Rapaport and R. Rapaport (eds.), *Leisure and the Family Life Cycle.* The first examination of leisure within the family context across the life cycle.
1975	Association for Gerontology in Higher Education formed to facilitate leadership development for training programs which were being established in universities and colleges in the United States.
1976–1977	J. Schulz, *The Economics of Aging.* A comprehensive economic analysis of the aging process. Three new handbooks were published which represented the state of knowledge up to the mid-1970s. These were revised in 1985 and 1990.
	(a) R. Binstock and E. Shanas (eds.), *Handbook of Aging and the Social Sciences* (1976)
	(b) J. Birren and W. Schaie (eds.), *Handbook of the Psychology of Aging* (1977)
	(c) C. Finch and L. Hayflick (eds.), *Handbook of the Biology of Aging* (1977)
1979	*Research on Aging: A Quarterly Journal of Social Gerontology* was first published.
1980	V. Marshall, *Aging in Canada: Social Perspectives.* This was the first reader presenting a collection of articles pertaining to aging and the aged in Canada. A second edition was published in 1987.
1982	*Canadian Journal on Aging* was first published.
1983	*Aging as a Social Process.* The first textbook on aging published in Canada.
1986	N. Chappell, L. Strain, and A. Blandford, *Aging and Health Care: A Social Perspective*
1986	S. McDaniel, *Canada's Aging Population.* This monograph launched the Butterworth series, *Perspectives on Individual and Population Aging.*
1987	G. Maddox et al. (eds.), *The Encyclopedia of Aging*
1987	*Journal of Aging Studies* was first published.
1988	D. Harris (ed.), *Dictionary of Gerontology*
1988	G. Fennell et al., *The Sociology of Old Age.* A critical analysis of aging in Great Britain.
1989	*Journal of Women and Aging* was first published.
1990	The third editions in the *Handbook of Aging* series were published; and *Abstracts in Social Gerontology* was first published.

contribute to the advancement of social gerontology. Instead, it indicates the special influence of the sociology of aging to the continued development of social gerontology. The following quotation from Streib and Orbach (1967, p. 636) illustrates this ongoing relationship:

> In considering the future outlook of social gerontology and the sociology of aging, it seems likely, first, that there will be greater development of theoretical approaches to deal with the problems of human aging, and these will be more infused with sociological perspectives. Second, sociological instruction will become more and more a core of training for professional personnel engaged in carrying out practical programs and formulating policies in the field at all levels. Third, sociologists will continue to be involved at all levels with the development of academic training, research, and policy making. Finally, the development of a specific sociology of aging will be part of the broader development of social gerontology.

Based on this quotation, it is evident that the sociology of aging is alive and well. As a discipline it continues to investigate social phenomena associated with the aging process. This investigative process is influenced by a historical assumption: that aging is a social problem. Although most would agree that aging is *not* a social problem, we need to remember that how we interpret this assumption will influence how we explain the aging process. But first, what is a social problem?

The Definition of a Social Problem

Numerous definitions of a social problem exist. The following definitions illustrate the diversity of thought regarding the basic criteria of a social problem. However, we will utilize the argument put forth by Roberts (1978) as most applicable to the sociology of aging. Consider the following definitions:

> The definition of social problems often rests on the ability to have one's definition of a social problem accepted. (Hadden & Lester, 1976, p. 27)

> Societies selectively dignify troubles and misery with the designation "social problems" when three conditions are met: 1) A basic societal value is challenged; 2) the problem appears to be avoidable; and 3) there is the possibility of social consensus about the procedures for correcting the perceived difficulty. (Maddox, 1978, p. 28)

> A social problem exists in a humanistic sense when the institutional arrangements of a society (1) threaten human survival, (2) promote mystification or manipulation through the maintenance of ignorance, (3) limit the social productivity of the individual, and (4) fragment the person from important sides of his or her humanness (e.g., ethics, sense of belonging, a sense of selfhood). (Roberts, 1978, p. 17)

How do these definitions apply to aging? Although these definitions may not agree on the criteria by which social problems are to be determined, they do suggest a common thread: the influence of others in determining what constitutes a social problem. In particular, the criteria identified by Roberts (1978) is applicable to the sociology of aging. His four criteria will be addressed in greater detail shortly.

Please remember that, although we will be constructing our argument around a particular definition of social problems, it is important that you remain aware of the complexities and (in)ability to construct explanations of aging.

Aging and Social Problems: The Connection

Throughout much of this century aging had been considered a social problem within society (Achenbaum, 1978, 1985; Fischer, 1978). Today, few would argue in support of such a relationship. The impetus for this temporal change has been a variation in the source of the problem. An example of this variation is offered by Maddox (1978, pp. 28–29), who identifies three sources of social problems: "the individual, . . . the organization of society . . . and social preferences and power." This book supports the argument that the organization of society and social preferences and power are the primary sources of social problems.

The work of C. Wright Mills is particularly instructive when attempting to understand the relationship between aging and social problems. Mills (1959) constructed the *sociological imagination* as a way of understanding social phenomena.

According to Mills (1959), the sociological imagination provides its user with the ability to distinguish between "personal troubles" and "public issues." Mills (1959, pp. 8–9) states that "troubles occur within the character of the individual. . . . A trouble is a private matter: values cherished by an individual are felt to be threatened." "Issues have to do with matters that transcend these local environments of the individual and the range of his inner life. An issue is a public matter. . . . An issue, in fact, often involves a crisis in institutional arrangements."

Given his use of the concepts, how can we apply Mills to an understanding of the aging process? Consider the following example. Chronological aging is an individual process. As one person experiences the consequences of turning age 65 or beyond, that is a personal trouble. The individual attempts to grasp the meanings associated with this chronological achievement. The individual feels obligated to defend this new status relative to the expectations of others in society. The individual is also expected to understand that the responses of others to this status is the result of his or her growing old. As a result, the older person believes that he or she must create an explanation as well as a justification for behavior. In other words, growing old is an individual problem that must be addressed individually.

Aging becomes a social issue when the criteria, defining for whom the chronological benchmarks are intended, are understood as maintaining existing societal inequalities. This awareness results in a reexamination of one's aging as it is defined within society. One then realizes that it is not one's chronological age but rather the structural constraints of society that creates aging as a public issue and, ultimately, a social problem. As a derivative of the sociological imagination, Estes (1992, pp. 49–50) refers to a "gerontological imagination" as a "quality of mind which enables us to use—but not be seduced by—our techniques and technology: it requires the ability to reason with the fresh insight that accompanies a reflexive (often skeptical and critical) perspective on one's own discipline and its reigning paradigm(s)."

Theoretically, the relationship between the sociology of aging and social problems is examined on the micro/macro levels of analysis. Not mutually exclusive, the two levels are capable of complimenting the deficiencies inherent in the other. The micro level of analysis identifies various consequences of growing old on the individual and prescribes adaptation as a necessary means of survival. This approach found support in the early theoretical arguments of disengagement theory and activity theory. (An extensive discussion of these theories can be found in Chapter 3.) The second level of analysis in the study of age as a social problem is the macro level. This approach argues that rather than viewing the individual as the unit of analysis, the problems of aging can best be examined from a societal level of analysis. (The theories associated with this approach are also addressed in Chapter 3.)

An introduction to the relationship between sociological theory and aging is presented by Passuth and Bengtson (1988, p. 333), who state that "while early social gerontological theories focused primarily on individual difficulties in adjusting to old age, later perspectives have taken into account broader issues regarding social aspects of age and aging." It is the connection between these broader issues and aging that is central to this book. It is important to remember that growing old is not the issue, but rather that growing old has been socially constructed as the problem.

As a precursor to the research section of this chapter and Chapter 3, Table 1–1 identifies theoretical frameworks of aging and areas of research by theoretical levels of analysis.

The relationship between the sociology of aging and social problems is complex. The four factors identified earlier by Roberts (1978) illustrate the extent to which this relationship is intertwined within the larger society. It is instructive to examine these factors individually and determine how the aging process is related to them. According to Roberts (1978), the

TABLE 1–1   Research Topics and Theoretical Perspectives Common to the Sociology of Aging

	Exemplary Topics	Salient Theories

Microsociology of aging	Life events
	Personal autonomy and
	  dependency
	Role adjustment
	  (retirement, widowhood)
	Social interaction
		Activity
		Age stratification
		Disengagement
		Exchange
		Phenomenology
		Social breakdown/
		  competence
		Subcultural

Macrosociology of aging	Cross-national comparisons
	Demographic change
	Generational relations
	Organizational analysis
	  (health, labor)
	Government policy
		Age stratification
		Conflict
		Modernization
		Political economy
		  (sociology) of
		  aging

Source: Ferraro, Kenneth F. (ed.). 1990. *Gerontology: Perspectives and Issues.* Copyright © Springer Publishing Company, Inc., New York 10012. Used by permission.

first point argues that "a social problem exists when institutional arrangements threaten aggregates of human survival" (p. 9). How do such arrangements threaten the survival of the elderly in society? Consider the ongoing health care debate. One of the central issues involves the amount of health care dollars spent on the elderly, particularly in the last month of life. Such a debate questions the legitimacy of access by the elderly to the resources of the society. In essence, the elderly are at risk for survival.

His second point states that "a social problem may be said to exist when institutional arrangements promote mystification or dominance through ignorance" (1978, p. 9). This is perhaps the most insidious aspect because the truth of the aging process is being distorted by those with the ability to construct an image of growing older. This point will be examined in the next section on the social construction of age as a social problem. Chapter 4 will also address this point.

According to the third point, "a social problem emerges when institutional arrangements limit social productivity for the individual" (1978, p. 10). As a society we value work. Thus we are defined by our occupational status. For the elderly, retirement as a newly acquired status is generally viewed as a reward for prior investment of time and effort. However, the value of being retired may diminish as increased emphasis is given to remaining a productive member of society.

The fourth point states that "a social problem occurs when institutional arrangements 'fragment' or separate the person from essential aspects of his or her humanness" (1978, p. 11). This means removing the individual from those parts of his or her life that help create a feeling of wholeness for the individual. Among the elderly this is evident in the relationships they experience daily as they traverse the bureaucracies that fragment them from themselves. This occurs as the elderly are removed from decision-making roles and are assumed to be dependent on the larger society for their needs. The elderly are supported as an age category by a variety of institutional structures that have been created for their "benefit." As a result, the elderly are segregated from themselves as human beings and from others in the larger society. For example, consider programs that provide a service (benefit) to the elderly but do not engage those receiving the service in determining its need or value to the recipient.

These four factors provide an excellent framework within which the relationship between the sociology of aging and social problems can be explained. It is evident that simply growing older does not constitute a social problem. Rather, aging becomes a social problem when those with the ability to define it as a problem do so. "Those with the ability" refers to individuals with the economic, political, or social power to influence societal perceptions and expectations about the aged and the aging process. As a result, the image and the treatment of aging as a social problem is socially constructed. It is to this section that we will now turn as we continue to establish the framework within which the sociology of aging can be studied.

The Social Construction of Age as a Social Problem

One purpose of this chapter has been to introduce students to some of the basic concepts of the sociology of aging. These concepts are useful as "handles" because they provide us with concrete connections between our personal experiences and a viable explanation of those experiences. For example, you should understand the concept of aging as a process emerging out of expectations established within the institutional structures of society. You should also understand by now that one explanation of what constitutes a social problem is that a select segment of society has defined others as a problem. The underlying concept connecting these interpretations of age and social problems is that of *power.* Although various definitions exist, perhaps the most common is that power is the ability to get someone to do something they would rather not do. Consider the classroom. In your sociology of aging class, the professor can dictate how many exams the student will take, when they will be given, and how long the research paper will be. The professor has the power to make others (the students) do what he or she wants. Relative to this book, the social reality of what constitutes aging and a social problem is constructed by those in society with the power to impose their definition(s) on others. The societal response to these definitions creates a reality (Estes, 1979) from which we evaluate aging and social problems. This is illustrated by Estes (1982, p. 574) when she states that "definitions of the 'social problem' of old age and of the appropriate policy solutions for this problem have reflected the ups and downs of the U.S. economy and the shifting bases of political power during the past thirty years."

A number of interrelated factors contribute to the emergence of the social construction of age. In addition to age, other characteristics include the following:

> *Social class*—this concept has numerous definitions. In relation to the sociology of aging, social class refers to the economic position of those defined as old relative to the larger society.
>
> *Gender*—women, regardless of age, have been victims of the larger social structure. Elderly women represent the culmination of structural bias (that is, social security).
>
> *Race*—exploitation of people of color also exists within the larger social structure. The elderly minority also represent the consequences of decades-long structural bias (economic segregation).

This argument is, broadly speaking, referred to as the political economy of aging. We will address the specifics of this perspective as well as other theoretical frameworks in greater detail in Chapter 3. As a cautionary note, please understand that it is not my intent to endorse a specific theoretical interpretation to the sociology of aging. Rather, numerous theoretical arguments will be incorporated throughout the book. It is my belief, however, that a political economy perspective provides additional interpretative power, adding to a more inclusive explanation of the sociology of aging. Whatever the explanation, it should always be grounded in empirical evidence gathered through the application of the research process.

The Importance of Research

This section will examine the significance of conducting research in the sociology of aging. Earlier in the chapter we defined the sociology of aging as "the scientific study" of aging. This means that information gathered through the scientific process must be distinguished from information gained primarily through personal experience.Essentially, the scientific process involves the interrelationship of a series of specific factors. This is not to suggest that our personal experiences of the elderly are irrelevant. Rather, the knowledge that we gain from personal experiences is gathered and interpreted quite differently from knowledge gained through the scientific process. It is only through the application of the scientific process that we can fully appreciate the significance of the aging process. Sanders (1976, p. 1) suggests that sociologists are similar to detectives in that both "formulate theories and develop methods in an attempt to answer two general questions: 'why did it happen?' and 'In what circumstances is it likely to happen again?'—that is, to explain and predict." We will now address not only the *why* of doing research in the sociology of aging but also the *how* of the research method.

Why should we conduct research on aging? What can we learn about aging that we already do not know? Why study this age category when we already know that the only characteristic they have in common is their chronological age? The list of questions that we could raise regarding the role of research in aging is virtually endless. But think about these questions. Without the advantage of scientific research, what would we know about the aging process? We would only have our individual experiences of aging. Although these experiences are significant within the context in which they occur, they do not help us understand why others may have very different experiences with the aging process. However, when we engage in systematic data gathering, we are investigating the collective experiences of all those respondents with whom we define as part of the research. The question of why we conduct research in the sociology of aging can be answered by stating that the scientific process is the foundation upon which knowledge is based. The second question of how research is conducted requires an examination of a number of fundamental concepts. We begin with the most fundamental concept: the *research method.*

The research method can be defined as "the study of ways of understanding the world. It is an absolutely essential set of skills, insights, and tools needed to answer intelligently any but the simplest questions" (Singleton, Straits, Straits, & McAllister, 1988, p. 3). Although the use of the research method involves a number of specific steps, it is not the intent of this book to explore in detail all the nuances of conducting research. Instead, the purpose of this section is to introduce the student to the practical application of research methods in the sociology of aging.

Before we examine the application of the various research designs to the aging process, it is necessary to explain a number of relevant concepts. Although many of these concepts may not be new to you, the context within which they are being applied may very well be. A *variable* is defined as "something that is thought to influence (or to be influenced by) a particular state of being in something else" (Hoover, 1988, p. 19). For example, age has been identified (by some) as an important variable in the rising cost of health care. In the process of measuring whether age is related to increased health care costs, two additional concepts are pertinent: reliability and validity. *Reliability* "is concerned with questions of stability and consistency" (Singleton et al., 1988, p. 111). *Validity* involves "the extent to which an empirical measure adequately reflects the real meaning of the concept under consideration" (Babbie, 1989, p. 111). In other words, is the age of a person a reliable indicator of increasing health care costs? Is the cost of health care a valid indicator of the level of care provided by a health care system?

Research is usually identified as consisting of two types: cross-sectional and longitudinal. *Cross-sectional* research of the aged generally involves a comparison of age groups at a single point in time. The groups are then compared in terms of their responses to specific variables identified by the researcher. This type of research examines age differences. Most research in the sociology of aging (and sociology in general) is of this type. It is less expensive and more accessible to the researcher. Think of this type of research as a snapshot. You have captured a specific moment in the life of your subjects. Although appropriate, this type does not fully address the aging process. The reason is that as a process, aging involves a historical sequence of events. Examining those events at a single point in time may not adequately explain the process.

The second type of research is referred to as longitudinal. *Longitudinal* research involves the continued examination of the same individuals (or groups) over an extended period of time. This type of research involves changes over time. A classic example of this is the Duke Longitudinal Studies begun in 1955. This method is time-consuming and costly and involves the potential to lose subjects over time (because of death or refusal to continue participation). The advantage of such a method is obvious. The researcher can study the ongoing influence of the aging process on his or her subjects. Unfortunately, few researchers currently have the funds available to engage in this type of research. One variation of longitudinal research involves an examination of an age cohort. An age cohort consists of a group of individuals who, because of their similar age, have similar life experiences. As a result, we can study the cohort effect, which is "the impact a particular historical event has on a group of individuals" (Bengtson, 1973, p. 11). Utilizing this conceptual technique, we can better understand why such variation appears to exist among the elderly population. Table 1–2 illustrates the different age periods at which significant events occurred for cohorts born at the beginning of several decades.

By examining age cohorts we realize that the elderly born at different points in time were influenced by these events differently. For example, an individual born in 1900 experienced World War I as a teenager, the "roaring twenties" as a young adult, the Depression in the early prime of adulthood, and World War II as a middle-aged adult. The individual born in 1900 turned 65 as Medicare was signed into law, thus providing health care financing for retirement. An individual born in 1930 did not experience World War I and was a young child during the Depression; this individual was a young teenager during World War II but a prime candidate for military service during the Korean conflict. After Korea, the individual was a young adult entering the economic boom period of the 1950s. By middle age, this individual was experiencing the 1970s and a changing economic climate. Today, this individual (and others in this cohort) have experienced the economic uncertainty of the recent past. As a result of the changing employment structure, this individual may feel quite different about retirement at age 65, the economy, and the role of government than someone born in 1900. The analysis of age cohorts is a useful tool in understanding the behavior of a particular age group relative to other age groups.

Methods of Conducting Research

The method of conducting research that is most frequently used by sociologists is the *survey*. A survey is a useful method of gathering data from a large number of respondents. The

TABLE 1–2   Age at Significant Historical Events

Year of Birth (1994)	World War I (1914–1917)	The Great Depression (1929–1936)	World War II (1941–1945)	Medicare Enacted (1965)	Today
1900	14–17	29–36	41–45	65	94
1910	4–7	19–26	31–35	55	84
1920	—	9–16	21–25	45	74
1930	—	1–6	11–15	35	64
1940	—	—	1–5	25	54

Louis Harris survey of 1975 is an example of the value of the survey method to aging research. A more recent example of survey research is the work of Rowland (1992). This research consisted of a survey questionnaire administered to over 900 respondents in five countries who were living alone. The respondents "were asked to respond to questions about their life and living arrangements, daily activities, social and family contacts, work, life satisfaction, family and informal support, access to and use of health care services, and attitudes toward health services and the health system" (Rowland, 1992, p. 206). A brief profile and comparison of health care attitudes among elderly in the five countries is presented in Table 1–3.

Table 1–3 reveals a number of significant differences. To begin, the elderly in the United States are better educated than elderly in Canada, Great Britain, Germany, and Japan. On the other hand, compared to elderly in these other nations, the elderly in the United States are more concerned about their economic well-being. However, American elderly also share some commonalities with their Canadian and European counterparts. For example, the distribution of American elderly on the basis of their sex and age is similar to what is generally found in other Western industrialized nations.

Surveys are generally conducted via mail or over the telephone. Respondents to a survey represent a *sample* of the larger targeted *population*. For example, assume that a researcher is interested in determining the effect of social class position on the health status of the elderly (defined as aged 65 and over) in New York City. The population would consist of all persons aged 65 and over in New York City. The sample should reflect the characteristics of the population. Thus, if 12 percent of the elderly are below the poverty line, the sample should reflect that segment of the population. Again, if 60 percent of the elderly in New York City are women, the sample should reflect this particular characteristic. The sample is a representation of the larger population from which it is drawn (Babbie, 1989). The next question is, How are you going to conduct the survey? Telephone surveys allow the researcher to contact a large number of people in a short period of time. Although slower, surveys conducted through the mail allow the researcher to ask more sensitive questions (Babbie, 1989).

As with all research designs, advantages and disadvantages of the survey method can be identified. The major advantage of this method to the sociology of aging is its consistency in the construction and implementation of the research instrument. As a result, respondents' attitudes toward specific aging issues can be evaluated knowing that all respondents were given the same questions and opportunity to respond. A disadvantage of the survey is an inability to know whether the respondents were truthful in their answers.

TABLE 1–3   Population Profile of the Elderly in Five Nations, 1991

	United States	Canada	Great Britain	West Germany	Japan
Total population age 65 and over (millions)	30.4	2.8	8.9	9.7	12.3
Age					
65–74	61%	60%	56%	52%	63%
75–84	32	33	35	41	34
85 and older	7	6	8	7	4
Sex					
Male	42	42	40	34	41
Female	58	58	60	66	59
Education					
< high school	43	61	76	74	87
Completed high school	33	15	5	6	4
Post-high school	24	24	19	20	9
Economic well-being					
Somewhat/very difficult to meet expenses	31	25	38	21	15
not very difficult to meet expenses	69	75	62	79	58

Source: Rowland, (Fall, 1992). A five-nation perspective on the elderly. *Health Affairs,* 205–215. Used with permission.

A second method of conducting aging research is the *experiment*. Although not utilized extensively by sociologists, this method offers an opportunity to examine the more individual aspects of the aging process such as learning and memory. The experimental method is shown in Figure 1–2.

There are three components that characterize the experiment. The first component consists of the experimental and control group. Placement in the groups is by random selection. The difference is that members of the experimental group will be exposed to the independent variable (X), whereas members in the control group will not. The second component includes the independent and dependent variables. In an expected relationship, the independent variable is the "cause" of the dependent variable. Conversely, the dependent variable is the presumed "effect." In a research setting you are attempting to explain or predict the dependent variable through the manipulation of the independent variable (Singleton et al., 1988). The third component consists of the pretest and posttest. Ideally, if the experimental and control groups are randomly selected, a pretest of the dependent variable should result in relatively similar scores between the experimental and control groups. However, after the independent variable is administered to the experimental group, the posttest should reflect outcome differences between the experimental and control groups. If statistically significant differences exist between the pretest and posttest scores and all

FIGURE 1–2   **The Experimental Method**

		Independent variable	Dependent variable	
Pretest	experimental group 0	X	0	Posttest
	control group 0		0	

other contributing variables have been controlled, one could then conclude that the independent variable influenced the dependent variable.

Like the survey, the experimental method has its advantages and disadvantages. An advantage of this method is the control over the conditions within which the research occurs. A particular disadvantage may be the lack of generalizability from such research. Because the participants in such research generally are not representative of the larger population, it is difficult to generalize the findings to the larger population.

A third method of conducting research involves the use of what is referred to as qualitative methodology or field research. This type of research differs from the survey and the experiment in that the researcher goes into the field to obtain a more intimate understanding of those being studied. Rather than asking a large number of people a standard set of questions with the same possible responses, the researcher attempts "to see the world from the subject's own frame of reference" (Singleton et al., 1988, p. 296). (See, for example, the work of Arlie Hochschild [1973], *The Unexpected Community.*) Employing the field research approach, a researcher in the sociology of aging could seek employment in a nursing home to study how staff provide care to the residents (see, for example, Stannard [1973]). In order to gather information, there are a number of techniques available to the researcher. In the case of a nursing home, the researcher could use unstructured interviews with staff as well as residents. This technique allows for "an interaction between an interviewer and a respondent in which the interviewer has a general plan of inquiry but not a specific set of questions that must be asked in particular words and in a particular order" (Babbie, 1989, p. 270). The researcher must also determine his or her level of involvement with the group under study. The researcher can become a *complete participant,* a *participant-as-observer,* an *observer-as-participant,* or a *complete observer.* Applying these methods to the nursing home example, a complete participant would not divulge his or her identity as a researcher to anyone on the staff of the nursing home. The researcher performs the tasks for which he or she was hired. This would give the researcher an insider's view of the institution and the interactions that occur. A classic example of this is Arlie Hochschild's work *The Unexpected Community* (1973). In the participant-as-observer role, the researcher would still perform tasks for which he or she was hired. However, the nursing home staff would know that the person was also engaged in research. As an observer-as-participant, the researcher would not participate as a worker in the nursing home. Instead, the researcher would interact with staff and residents, conduct interviews, and observe interactions within the home. Finally, as a complete observer the researcher is completely removed from participating with those under study (Babbie, 1989). In the example of the nursing home, the researcher would be like a fly on the wall, observing but not interacting with the subjects.

Further illustration of how field research can be applied to the study of aging is found in such works as Rosenberg (1990) and Coles (1990). The following is an example of the value of field research:

One women in her early sixties, who owns many cattle, has been observed to be among the loudest of complainers, denouncing all and sundry for their failure to share. One day, while following an anthropologist back and forth while he was packing up camp, she delivered a blistering tirade against his hard-heartedness. Back and forth from tent to truck they trudged, the anthropologist silent, carrying bundles of goods, Nuhka on his heels yelling at him. Suddenly, she stopped, and like a scene in a Brecht play, she stepped out of character, altered the tone of her voice, and calmly said, "we have to talk this way. It's our custom." Then she stepped back into character and resumed her attack. (Rosenberg, 1990, p. 24)

An advantage of field research is the wealth of information contained in the material gathered. Compared to the survey and the experiment, this method allows the researcher to develop fully an understanding of the lives of those under study. A disadvantage is the inability to generalize the findings to other groups. Another problem is the potential for the researcher as complete participant to "go native"; that is, the researcher loses objectivity by identifying with the group under study.

A fourth method of conducting research is called *content analysis.* Content analysis is a systematic investigation of selected pieces of information. This information can exist in print form or in an electronic medium such as television. The researcher "counts" the occurrences of the particular information. For example, I conducted a content analysis of obituary notices by examining the obituary notices of those aged 65 and over at the time of death (Matcha, 1994–95). I was interested in the historical dimension of the notice. By categorizing information contained in the obituary notice, variables such as gender, marital status at time of death, average age at marriage, length of marriage, average length of widowhood, average number of surviving children and grandchildren, and average age at death could be compared. In other words, family and marital patterns occurring at the end of the 19th century and early 20th century in the region covered by that particular newspaper could be examined. This method of research is not meant to trivialize the all-too-significant events in the lives of people. Rather, in the case of the obituary notice, "it is a descriptive instrument of the collective socio-cultural characteristics of a geographical region. On the individual level, the obituary notice serves as one's social footnote in history" (Matcha, 1994–95, p. 137). Table 1–4 illustrates how such information can be categorized for the purpose of analysis.

An advantage of content analysis is the fact that it is unobtrusive. That is, the data can be collected without interfering in the lives of, or even establishing contact with, those under investigation. The problem with such an approach, however, is the reliance on the information collected. In the case of an obituary notice, for example, the researcher must rely on the accuracy of information provided by relatives to the newspaper.

The final research design is that of *secondary analysis.* Secondary analysis involves the manipulation and analysis of data that have already been gathered. For example, the General Social Survey provides researchers with a yearly survey of American attitudes toward a variety of issues. The United States Census Bureau also conducts research on a number of topics. These data are then made available to researchers. For specific research on aging,

TABLE 1–4   Average Age at Death for Decade of Birth

	Average Age at Death	
	Women	Men
Decade of Birth		
1890–1899	93.6	93.4
	(103)	(48)
1900–1909	82.9	84.4
	(268)	(187)
1910–1919	75.1	75.8
	(186)	(235)
1920–1926[a]	67.5	67.4
	(61)	(117)

[a]Data collection occurred in 1990–1991. Thus 1926 would be the last year in the decade for a person to be born and listed as age 65.
Source: Duane A. Matcha. 1994–95. "Obituary Analysis of Early 20th Century Marriage and Family Patterns in Northwest Ohio." *OMEGA.* Vol. 30(2): 121–130. Copyright © 1994 Baywood Publishing Co., Inc.

you may wish to investigate the multiplicity of data sets available through ICPSR (Inter-university Consortium for Political and Social Research) located at the University of Michigan.

One obvious advantage of secondary analysis is that large numbers of cases can be accessed without having to conduct the original research. This saves the researcher considerable expense. A serious disadvantage is that of validity. In other words, does "the question that was asked (originally) provide a valid measure of the variable you want to analyze" (Babbie, 1989, p. 257)?

The Importance of Research Revisited

Think about your individual experiences and knowledge of aging. How did you gather this information? Was it scientific? Can you generalize such knowledge to the larger aged population? The purpose of this section was to acquaint you with the research process and to illustrate the importance of research to the sociology of aging. Although the elderly are a diverse population, they, like all of us, are influenced by social forces. It is the purpose of research to examine the why and the how of such relationships.

At this point you are perhaps cognizant of the fact that the sociology of aging is not what you envisioned when you opened this book. This is meant as a compliment and a challenge. As you continue reading, you will hopefully discover more about growing old. But first we must make a connection to the past. It is only through an understanding of history that we can grasp the significance of the present.

Critical Connection: The Importance of History

From my undergraduate years I remember one history professor giving a lecture on the Spanish-American War. This particular professor's lectures were always more than the usual "names, places, and dates." He made history alive and meaningful. After the lecture, I better understood the reasons why we became involved in the war, the myths and reality of Theodore Roosevelt, and the tragedy of war itself. This is the importance of history. It preserves for future reference the context of an event. Although each one of us may interpret the event differently, the event itself is a fact.

What did America learn from the Spanish-American War? One very important lesson was not to believe everything you read or heard. This is also quite true about the sociology of aging. We hear a number of "facts" about the elderly in American society today, such as the following:

- The increasing cost of health care today is the result of a growing aged population.
- The elderly today are really quite well off financially but continue to demand more, thus draining the younger generations of needed economic resources.
- The elderly have greater political clout than other age groups because they vote as a bloc.
- The elderly have always been considered a social problem in American society.

Are these statements facts? Are they grounded in a historical knowledge of the aged population? Or are they beliefs, based on "common sense"? It is important to differentiate what we know for a fact from what we think is true. According to some these statements are true, whereas to others the answer is no or a qualified "yes, but." What would you say? What is the basis of your answer?

This is why we must begin our study of the sociology of aging with a history lesson. What do we know, empirically, about the elderly in American history? Using your knowledge of research and a historical accounting of the presence of the aged population, we can now begin to piece together a more accurate description of the aged population in the United States. History, then, is our frame of reference for reality.

Chapter Review

Students should have some means by which they can assess their understanding of material just read. Following are a number of questions addressing some of the major points of this chapter. These questions require more than rote memorization of material. They are intended to elicit a critical analysis of the material. As you progress through the chapters you will discover that the questions are designed as "building blocks." That is, what you have learned in Chapter 1 will help in analyzing and answering questions in later chapters.

1. From the definition of aging, what are some of the expectations and belief systems of American society that are used to construct our understanding of aging? Using the examples given at the beginning of the chapter, how do we differ from developing nations?

2. Give an example of how the sociology of aging can be applied. This is not a question of research but rather one of conceptualization.
3. Using an example not given in the chapter, apply Mills to an understanding of the aging process.
4. Is aging a social problem? Use the material in this chapter to support your answer.
5. What is the social reality of aging in contemporary American society?
6. You have just received $50,000 to study gender roles among aging couples. What would you hypothesize? What would be your independent and dependent variables? What research design would you use? (You can recycle this question by changing the variables and trying again.)
7. Using Table 1–2 as a guide, construct another chart identifying the influence of the cohort effect. Using your knowledge of history, explain the cohort differences.

Glossary

Age cohort   An age cohort consists of a group of individuals who, because of similar year of birth, have similar life experiences.

Aging   Aging is a social process that is constructed from the expectations and belief systems of the structural characteristics of society.

Complete observer   A method of conducting field research in which the researcher is completely removed from the group under study. The researcher is an unobtrusive observer of group behavior.

Complete participant   A method of conducting field research in which the researcher is fully engaged as a member of the group being studied. The members of the group are unaware of the researcher's role.

Content analysis   This is a method of conducting research that involves a systematic investigation of selected pieces of information generally found in the print or electronic media.

Cross-sectional research   Relative to aging research, this approach involves a comparison of age groups at a single point in time.

Dependent variable   In a relationship, this is the "effect" produced by the independent variable. In research one attempts to explain or predict the dependent variable by manipulating the independent variable.

Experiment   A method of conducting research that involves a carefully controlled environment in which an independent variable is tested on an experimental group in an effort to determine its influence.

Independent variable   In a relationship, this is the "cause" of the dependent variable. *See* Dependent variable.

Longitudinal research   This type of research involves an ongoing examination of the same individuals (or groups) over an extended period of time.

Observer-as-participant   A method of conducting field research in which the researcher does not participate as a member of the group under study. Rather, the researcher observes group interaction and conducts interviews with group members.

Participant-as-observer   A method of conducting field research in which the researcher is fully involved with the group under study. The group is also aware of the role of the researcher.

Population   This is the total pool of eligibles as defined by the research, for example, all residents of Albany, New York, aged 65 and over.

Power   This can be thought of as the ability to get someone to do something they would rather not do.

Reliability   In research, this refers to consistency. That is, can you rely on the instrument to give you the same information time after time?

Role   An expected set of behaviors relative to others.

Sample   A subset of the population. The sample should reflect the characteristics of the population.

Scientific process   An ongoing cycle involving four points: defining the problem, constructing hypotheses, testing hypotheses, and analysis and conclusion.

Secondary analysis   Research involving the manipulation and analysis of data already collected.

Social gerontology   An interdisciplinary area of study that examines aging primarily from a biological, psychological, and sociological perspective.

Sociological imagination   A way of thinking about social life. According to C. Wright Mills, this allows its user to distinguish between "personal troubles" and "public issues."

Sociology of aging   The scientific study of the reciprocal influence between the society and those defined as aged by that society.

Status   This is a position that one occupies in a set of relationships.

Survey   A method of conducting research that involves the use of questionnaires. These questionnaires provide the researcher with a standard set of possible responses from those surveyed and are administered in person, through the mail, or over the telephone.

Validity   In research this refers to whether the instrument is measuring what it is intended to measure.

Variable   Any factor that influences or is influenced by something else.

Suggested Reading

Babbie, E. (1989). *The practice of social research* (5th ed.). Belmont, CA: Wadsworth.
An excellent introductory research methods text. Babbie has a comfortable style that engages even the most research- or math-anxious student.

Binstock, R. H., & George, L. K. (Eds.). (1990). *Handbook of aging and the social sciences* (3rd ed.). New York: Van Nostrand Reinhold.
This should be required reading for all interested in the sociology of aging. The handbook provides the reader with that which is current in the field.

Hochschild, A. R. (1978). *The unexpected community.* Berkeley, CA: University of Berkeley Press.
This is an insightful examination of an old age community. The student not only may enjoy the personal experiences of the residents but will also appreciate the value of field research.

Mills, C. W. (1959). *The sociological imagination.* New York: Oxford University Press.
Although Mills does not address the sociology of aging, he provides the reader with a new way of thinking about society, the individual, and their ongoing reciprocal relationship. The development of the sociological imagination gives the student of the sociology of aging a framework for viewing the relationship between age and society.

Simmons, L. (1945). *The role of the aged in primitive society.* New Haven, CT: Yale University Press.
This is a classic in the social gerontology literature. This (or any of the other classics identified in the chapter) provides the student with a glimpse at the early days of the development of the discipline.

Sokolovsky, J. (Ed.). (1990). *The cultural context of aging.* New York: Bergin and Garvey.
This is an excellent reader. As the title indicates, the reader will be treated to a cross-cultural examination of aging. The articles force the reader to reexamine American cultural values as they apply to the aging process.

Tibbitts, C. (Ed.). 1960. *Handbook of social gerontology.* Chicago: University of Chicago Press.
This also is a classic in the emergence of social gerontology. This book gives the student a basis for comparison of what was considered important then to the topics of today.

Readers are also encouraged to check their college or university library for journal holdings. Although a growing number of journals exist, look for the basic ones first, such as *Aging, The Gerontologist,* the *Journals of Gerontology, Generations,* and *The Social Security Bulletin.*

References

Achenbaum, W. A. (1978). *Old age in the New Land.* Baltimore: The Johns Hopkins University Press.

Achenbaum, W. A. (1985). Societal perceptions of aging and the aged. In R. H. Binstock & E. Shanas (Eds.), *Handbook of aging and the social sciences* (2nd ed.). New York: Van Nostrand Reinhold.

Achenbaum, W. A. (1987). Restructuring GSA's history. *The Gerontologist, 21*(1), 21–29.

Achenbaum, W. A., & Levin, J. S. (1989). What does gerontology mean? *The Gerontologist 29*(3), 393–400.

Babbie, E. (1989). *The practice of social research* (5th ed.). Belmont, CA: Wadsworth.

Bengtson, V. L. (1973). *The social psychology of aging.* Indianapolis, IN: Bobbs-Merrill.

Breen, L. Z. (1960). The aging individual. In C. Tibbitts (Ed.), *Handbook of social gerontology.* Chicago: University of Chicago Press.

Coles, C. (1990). The older woman in Hausa society: Power and authority in urban Nigeria. In J. Sokolovsky (Ed.), *The cultural context of aging.* New York: Bergin and Garvey.

Cowdry, E. V. (1939). *Problems of ageing.* Baltimore: Williams and Wilkins.

Cowgill, D. O. (1974). Aging and modernization: A review of the theory. In J. F. Gubrium (Ed.), *Late life: Communities and environmental policy.* Springfield, IL: Charles C. Thomas.

Cowgill, D. O., & Holmes, L. D. (1972). *Aging and modernization.* New York: Appleton-Century-Crofts.

Estes, C. L. (1979). *The aging enterprise.* San Francisco: Jossey-Bass.

Estes, C. L. (1982). Austerity and aging in the United States: 1980 and beyond. *International Journal of Health Services 12*(4), 573–584.

Estes, C. L. (1992). The gerontological imagination: Social influences on the development of gerontology, 1945–present. *International Journal of Aging and Human Development 35*(1), 49–65.

Ferraro, K. F. (1990). Sociology of aging: The micro-macro link. In K. F. Ferraro (Ed.), *Gerontology.* New York: Springer.

Fischer, D. H. (1978). *Growing old in America.* New York: Oxford University Press.

Gerth, H., & Mills, C. W. (1953). *Character and social structure.* New York: Harcourt, Brace & World.

Guillemard, A. M. (1986). State, society and older age policy in France: From 1945 to the current crisis. *Social Science and Medicine 23*(12), 1319–1326.

Hadden, S. C., & Lester, M. (1976). Looking at society's troubles: The sociology of social problems. In D. H. Zimmerman, D. L. Wieder, & S. Zimmerman (Eds.), *Understanding social problems.* New York: Praeger.

Hall, G. S. (1922). *Senescence, the second half of life.* New York: Appleton.

Hochschild, A. R. (1973). *The unexpected community.* Berkeley, CA: University of California Press.

Hoover, K. R. (1988). *The elements of social scientific thinking.* New York: St. Martin's Press.

Koller, M. R. (1968). *Social gerontology.* New York: Random House.

McPherson, B. D. (1990). *Aging as a social process* (2nd ed.). Toronto: Butterworths.

Maddox, G. L. (1978). The social and cultural context of aging. In G. Usdin & C. J. Hofling (Eds.), *Aging: The process and the people.* New York: Brunner and Mazel.

Matcha, D. A. (1993). An examination of life at age 65: Student responses to the self evaluation aging survey. Paper presented at the annual meeting of the North Central Sociological Association, Toledo, OH.

Matcha, D. A. (1994–95). Obituary analysis of early 20th century marriage and family patterns in northwest Ohio. *OMEGA 30*(2), 129–138.

Metchnikoff, E. (1908). *The prolongation of life.* New York: Putnam.

Mills, C. W. (1959). *The sociological imagination.* New York: Oxford University Press.

Minot, C. S. (1908). *The problems of age, growth, and death.* New York: Putnam.

Passuth, P. M., & Bengtson, V. L. (1988). Sociological theories of aging: Current perspectives and future directions. In J. E. Birren & V. L. Bengtson (Eds.), *Emergent theories of aging.* New York: Springer.

Pearl, R. (1922). *The biology of death.* Philadelphia: J. B. Lippincott.

Riley, M. W. (1987). On the significance of age in sociology. *American Sociological Review 52,* 1–14.

Roberts, R. E. (1978). *Social problems.* St. Louis: Mosby.

Rosenberg, H. G. (1990). Complaint discourse, aging, and caregiving among the !Kung San of Botswana. In J. Sokolovsky (Ed.), *The cultural context of aging.* New York: Bergin and Garvey.

Rowland, D. (1992, Fall). A five-nation perspective on the elderly. *Health Affairs,* 205–215.

Sanders, W. B. (1976). *The sociologist as detective: An introduction to research methods.* New York: Praeger.

Schwartz, A. N., Snyder, C. L., & Peterson, J. A. (1984). *Aging and life: An introduction to gerontology* (2nd ed.). New York: Holt, Rinehart and Winston.

Shanas, E. (1971, Spring). The sociology of aging and the aged. *Sociological Quarterly 12,* 159–176.

Simmons, L. W. (1945). *The role of the aged in primitive societies.* New Haven, CT: Yale University Press.

Singleton, R., Jr., Straits, B. C., Straits, M. M., & McAllister, R. J. (1988). *Approaches to social research.* New York: Oxford University Press.

Stannard, C. I. (1973). Old folks and dirty work: The social conditions for patient abuse in a nursing home. *Social Problems 20*(3), 329–342.

Streib, G. F., & Orbach, H. L. (1967). Aging. In P. F. Lazarfeld, W. M. Sewell, & H. L. Wilensky (Eds.), *The uses of sociology.* New York: Basic Books.

Tibbitts, C. (1960). Origin, scope, and fields of social gerontology. In C. Tibbitts (Ed.), *Handbook of social gerontology.* Chicago: University of Chicago Press.

Traore, G. (1985). A profile of the elderly in Mali. *African Gerontology 3,* 11–23.

Chapter 2

Two Realities

Demography and Aging

Although the problem of old age is one of power, it arises only within the body of the ruling classes. Until the nineteenth century there was never any mention of the "aged poor"; there were not many of them, for longevity was only possible among the privileged classes; the aged poor represented nothing whatsoever. History, like literature, passes them over in total silence. Old age is revealed, and then only to a certain degree, within the privileged classes alone.

—BEAUVOIR, 1972, P. 89

This chapter addresses two fundamental characteristics of the sociology of aging: the historical context of aging and the distribution of population on the basis of age. Many students question the relevance of such material. "Why should I care what happens in (fill in the country)?" or "Why should I care what happened (x) number of years ago?" Rather than trying to defend why you should care, I would instead challenge you to answer the following question. If you know the answer, congratulations. If not, perhaps you need to find out why.

The question is this: Identify the three factors responsible for a dramatic change in the status of American elderly during the early 19th century. Explain why they became significant. (Hint: industrialization and urbanization are incorrect.) You will find the answer in this chapter.

This challenge is not a cheap trick to induce you to read the chapter (you will find the answer on pages 33–34). Instead, it is intended to sensitize you to the historical and demographic changes within American society. Once you discover the answer, you will also realize the significance that sociology brings to an understanding of the aging process.

This chapter will explore the historical development of aging in American society. We will examine current population and future trends in developing and developed nations. We will also examine the viability of two theoretical attempts to explain the changing status of the elderly in developing societies. The chapter begins with a historical overview of aging in the Western world.

The History of Aging

Contemporary American elderly are characterized as involved in physical activities, engaged within the community as well as with friends, and intimately connected to family. This portrait of youthful aging, complete with the requisite energy necessary, creates an illusion that growing older does not mean becoming older. This positive image is of recent origin. Today, it is no longer just the "famous" elderly who are celebrated for their late-life accomplishments. Increasingly, the more "average" citizen is represented in the media. For example, the Albany, New York, *Times Union* (January 1, 1994) reported that an 86-year-old man recently passed the oral exam for his Ph.D. proposal ("Senior Student," 1994). It is commonplace today to hear of elderly volunteering their time in service to others. The elderly today are also pursuing activities they did not have the time (or money) for when younger. In other words, an increasing number of elderly are continuing to remain actively involved in the larger society. This recent phenomenon is helping to "democratize" the aging process. That is, "successful aging" is no longer the domain of the rich and famous. Historically, the elderly have not always enjoyed such opportunity.

Aging in Premodern Society

An examination of aging in premodern societies is problematic because evidence regarding length of life and composition of the age structure is incomplete (Cowgill, 1986). Although hard data may be lacking, serious scholarly attempts at detailing the conditions of old age in premodern times do exist (Freeman, 1979; Minois, 1989). For example, Freeman believes that "at least nine periods in the scientific knowledge of old age from the beginning of recorded history to the present can be defined in the last 5000 years" (1979, p. 16). These periods range from the archaic period to the modern age of aging. Covey (1992) addresses the historical definitions of old age from ancient Greece to the middle ages to colonial America. A more detailed account of the elderly within premodern societies can be found in Minois (1989).

Minois (1989) examines the history of aging from antiquity to the 16th century. According to Minois, the elderly were honored as well as despised, depending on the culture and the conditions. The oldest known recording of an elderly person describing his condition is that of Ptah Hotep, a scribe. The following is his statement made some 4,500 years ago.

> O sovereign my Lord! Oldness has come; old age has descended. Feebleness has arrived; dotage is here anew. The heart sleeps wearily every day. The eyes are weak, the ears are deaf, the strength is disappearing because of weariness of heart, and the mouth is silent and cannot speak. The heart is forgetful and cannot recall yesterday. The bone suffers old age. God is become evil. All taste is gone. What old age does to men is evil in every respect. (Pritchard, 1955, p. 412)

The lamentations of old age have since persisted. Although old age was a period in which physical deterioration occurred, it is believed that the people of antiquity had a better grasp of their chronological age than their counterparts in the medieval world. The elderly (primarily the males) were generally respected and accorded a high status. For example, Minois (1989) states that in the age of antiquity, elderly men were commonly given positions in the institutional structures of their society. Put into perspective, Minois (1989) points out, however, that "the golden age never was, neither for the old nor for anyone else. But, compared to the conditions of existence of the age, the conditions of the old in the Middle East of antiquity seem to have been relatively bearable" (p. 24).

Not only during the period of antiquity but throughout history the elderly male maintained a position of relative importance within the larger society. During the nomadic period of the Hebraic World the elderly men were considered leaders. However, their position began to erode in the 7th century BC. For example, the term *elder* lost its designation of old. Instead, *elder* referred to someone of importance. The elderly were soon left with little but their weaknesses as old men.

Among the Greeks, old age was viewed as a period of decay. Only among the Spartans were the elderly honored. Within the Roman world, the elderly constituted a greater percentage of the total population than during the Greek period. Initially, Roman law provided the elderly male with an extraordinary amount of authority within the family structure. Such power created an environment fraught with intergenerational conflict. Over time, such authority held by the elderly male began to wane.

Moving forward, Minois (1989) describes the conditions among the elderly throughout the early middle ages and beyond. Along with a greater institutional awareness of aging, the elderly began to view their age negatively, by rounding off their age to the lower tenth. In 1348 the bubonic plague entered Europe. Within three years over one third of the total population had been lost to the plague. The elderly, however, were more fortunate than the population in general. They were less likely to die from the plague. As a result, the elderly increased numerically and as a percentage of the population. As a result, the role of the elderly was strengthened during the 14th and 15th centuries. An indication of this change is the use of the term *retirement,* which became increasingly common among the wealthy by the end of the middle ages. By the 16th century, however, Shakespeare was giving new meaning to aging. In his most famous description of human development he pointed out the following:

> All the world's a stage,
> And all the men and women merely players;
> They have their exits and their entrances:
> And one man in his time plays many parts.
> His acts being seven ages. At first the infant,
> Mewling and puking in the nurse's arms.
> And the whining school-boy, with his satchel
> And shining morning face, creeping like a snail
> Unwillingly to school. And then the lover,
> Sighing like furnace, with a woeful ballad
> Made to his mistress' eyebrow. Then a soldier.
> Full of strange oaths and bearded like the pard,
> Jealous in honour, sudden and quick in quarrel,
> Seeking the bubble reputation
> Even in the cannon's mouth. And then the justice,
> In fair round belly with good capon lined,
> With eyes severe and beard of formal cut,
> Full of wise saws and modern instances;
> and so he plays his part. The sixth age shifts
> Into the lean and slipper'd pantaloon,
> With spectacles on nose and pouch on side,
> His faithful hose, well saved, a world too wide
> for his shrunk shank; and his big manly voice,
> Turning again toward childish treble, pipes
> And whistles in his sound. Last scene of all,
> That ends this strange eventful history,
> Is second childishness and mere oblivion,
> sans teeth, sans eyes, sans taste, sans everything.

The 16th century was also a turning point in life expectancy for men and women. Among the aristocratic class, life expectancy for women was greater than for men. This was a reversal from the past when men had outlived women.

Based on his historical analysis of the elderly, Minois (1989) suggests a number of factors that have been instrumental in defining the social status of the elderly throughout history. These factors, along with a brief statement regarding the historical relationship between age and status, are given below.

1. *Their physical frailty:* As conditions in society deteriorated, the status of the elderly diminished.
2. *The knowledge and experience due to long life:* The greater the reliance by a society on the oral tradition, the kinder they were to the elderly.

3. *Their altered features:* The greater the influence of physical beauty in society, the lower the status of the elderly.

4. *Increasing number of kin:* Societies that had extended and patriarchal families were kinder to old age because they provided support to their dependent members.

5. *The accumulation of worldly goods:* Societies that had movable wealth allowed older people a greater role.

6. *Periods of transition:* Transition periods were less kind to the elderly. This resulted in upheaval, and an unsettled environment for all, but especially for the elderly.

7. *Attitude toward the old:* There has never been a golden age for the old. However, it is always better to be rich and old than poor and old.

8. *Retirement:* This did not exist except for a few privileged wealthy.

9. *The model old person:* The more the model is idealized the more demanding and cruel is the society (Minois, 1989, pp. 304–307).

Moving forward, we will next examine aging in modern societies, that is, societies that are in some stage of the industrial period.

Aging in Modern Societies

The transition to modern societies has not brought about significant change in the position of the elderly. By virtually all historical accounts, the status of the elderly has remained relatively low. An examination of life as an older person in France and in England is illustrated in works by Stearns (1982) and Quadagno (1982). These works provide evidence that the status of the elderly did not increase as these societies progressed through the industrial revolution and into the 20th century. The following is an example of the dilemma confronting the elderly in France:

> The elderly were believed to have lost all their good sense, which is why no one would listen to them anyway. If they acted old, it was noted in the 1860s, everyone shunned them, and if they acted young everyone laughed at them. (Stearns, 1976, p. 30)

In France, according to Stearns (1976), the elderly remained relegated to a dependent status until the mid-20th century. One factor, however, was significant among the aged population: social class. Stearns (1976) points out that aging in the 1800s and 1900s was class based. That is, the aging process was understood differently within the working class compared to the middle class. Within the working class "the concept of aging itself was foreign: one lived, deteriorated a bit, and died" (Stearns, 1976, p. 42).

In England the experience of the elderly was similar, yet distinct. The belief that with industrialization the elderly were removed from the immediate family structure has been reexamined. Anderson (1972) found in 19th-century England that coresidence between the elderly and family was relatively common. In fact, this practice was more common in urban than in rural areas.

As in France, the consequences of growing old in 19th-century England were class based. Quadagno (1982, p. 22) states that "people in the past retired when they had the resources, either land or wealth, to do so. Those who continued to work did so out of financial necessity rather than out of desire." Among those remaining in the labor force, job opportunities were not abundant, and the pay was low. Working-class elderly were likely to end up on poor relief. As Quadagno (1982) suggests, however, the position of the elderly throughout the industrialization period should not be considered any worse than during earlier periods. Walker (1982) suggests that the increasing dependence of the elderly on society is socially constructed. According to Walker (1982, p. 121), "political, financial and to a large extent physical dependency are a function of the social organisation and distribution of resources, status and power."

Based on the historical evidence, it appears that the aging process in the past was viewed in much the same way as today. That is, it is not just age but one's social position as an aged person that influences the societal response. One could argue that many of the "problems" of aging today and in the past are class based. Power, as a social resource, appears significant when assessing the relative position of the elderly within any social period in history. As long as the elderly are relegated to a secondary social position, the image of aging and the resultant consequences will continue to be negative.

In addition to a historical accounting of aging, we can also examine aging within the context of population change within the larger society. We will examine two explanations of aging relative to the broader social changes in society. They include the demographic transition and modernization theory. Although popular explanations, they have come under increasing criticism for their ethnocentric interpretations of development.

Demographic Transition

The *demographic transition* describes the movement within a society from a condition of high birth and death rates to one of low birth and death rates. In this process, birth and death rates begin at relatively high levels. With birth rates slightly higher than death rates, population growth is slow. As the society develops, death rates begin to decline while birth rates remain high. It is during this period that a demographic transition occurs. Because of the differential between rates, rapid population growth occurs. Eventually, birth rates also decline to a level commensurate with death rates. At this point, slow or no population growth exists within the society. This concept was first introduced by Warren Thompson (1929). The demographic transition has been used to explain population increases in Western Europe and the United States. However, it would be a mistake to assume that it will apply to all countries experiencing societal development today. The demographic transition has been criticized for its ethnocentric view of the world. Such criticism is based on the argument that "if this is what happened to the developed countries, why should it not also happen to other countries that are not so advanced?" (Weeks, 1989, p. 75). The demographic transition is illustrated in Figure 2–1.

What is the impact of the demographic transition on the elderly population? Initially, the percentage of the population defined as elderly would decrease. On the other hand, the percentage of the population defined as young would increase. Over time, as this "population bulge" ages, the number and percentage of those considered elderly would increase.

A recent example of this process is Japan. Japan's transition from high to low birth and death rates was later than that of the United States but was quite rapid (Martin, 1989). In the process, Japan's population increased from 56 million in 1920 to 117 million in 1980. The rate of growth among the elderly during this period was less dramatic, increasing from 5.3

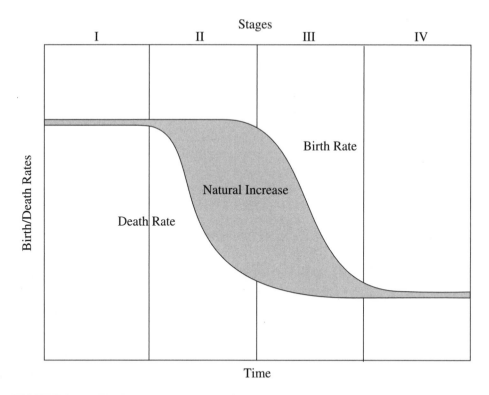

FIGURE 2–1   The Demographic Transition
Source: Reprinted with permission: Joseph A. McFalls, Jr., 1991, "Population: A Lively Introduction," *Population Bulletin,* vol. 46, no. 2 (October): 33.

percent of the population in 1920 to 9.0 percent in 1980 (International Encyclopedia of Population, 1982). However, the rate of growth among the elderly in Japan will accelerate in the 21st century. Table 2–1 illustrates this expected rate of growth. Between 1990 and 2025 the percentage of the population aged 65 and over is expected to increase by 130 percent.

At present, the elderly in Japan constitute a smaller proportion of the population than in the United States (10.8 percent in Japan compared to 12.5 percent in the United States) (U.S. Bureau of the Census, 1992). However, by the turn of the century, Japan will have a greater percentage of its population over the age of 65 than the United States. In fact, Japan will soon "have one of the most elderly populations on earth" (Martin, 1989, p. 7).

Later in this chapter we will examine the expected growth of the elderly in a number of developed and developing nations. You will have an opportunity at that time to reexamine the viability of the demographic transition. But first we will address the argument put forth by modernization theory.

Modernization Theory

Modernization theory was first proposed by Cowgill and Holmes (1972) and later revised by Cowgill (1974). Essentially, this theory asserts that as a society develops (modernizes),

TABLE 2–1   **Percentage of Population Aged 65 and Over in Japan: 1990–2025**

	1990	2010	2025
Percent of total Population	11.8%	21.3%	26.7%

Source: U.S. Bureau of the Census. (1992). International population reports, p. 25, 92-3, *An Aging World II.* Appendix A. Washington, DC: U.S. Government Printing Office.

the status of the elderly within that society will decline. The criteria that define the process of modernization include health technology, economic technology, urbanization, and education. It is expected that the movement from a rural, agrarian-based society to an urban, technology-based system will create fundamental change in the status of the elderly. For example, modernization theory would argue that increasing levels of technology create changes in the type of work available. Increased levels of technology in the workplace also require increased levels of education by the workforce. Generally, those workers most skilled in the utilization of the technology are likely to be younger members of the society. The consequence for older workers is a devaluation of their work skills and of status. Older workers are then expected to retire from the world of work. However, in a technologically developing society, work is valued, whereas nonwork is not. As a result, the status of the elderly is diminished. A diagram of the relationship between the criteria that define the process of modernization and the intervening variables is presented in Figure 2–2.

Support for the theory has been mixed. Cowgill (1986) continues to defend the theory, although with some qualifications. Some suggest that the status of the elderly is best represented as a "J-curve" (Palmore & Manton, 1974), whereas others point out that the elderly were never revered in a "golden age" of aging (Quadagno, 1982; Stearns, 1982; Minois, 1989). An example of this position can be found in the previous section on the history of the elderly. In a recent paper I examined the application of modernization on the status of the elderly (Matcha, 1994). Focusing primarily on health status, it was determined that increased survival rates, juxtaposed with a decreasing economic position, creates an age-related dependence and, ultimately, decreased status. This occurs as the level of economic well-being of the society increases. It was concluded that "such loss of status . . . is more a consequence of economics and politics than of history or demographics" (Matcha, 1994, p. 7). It would appear that, intuitively, modernization theory answers the basic question regarding the status of the aged in a changing world. The demographic transition also appears as a logical representation of population growth and readjustment. Although these arguments may have their detractors, it does not mean that they should be abandoned. The problem with modernization theory and the demographic transition is their inability to examine the influence of power within the social structure of a society. It is within this context that the social construction of aging occurs. The criteria that define "old" as well as the images, expectations, and opportunities are established by those within the larger social structure who have the social and economic power to enforce their interpretation. The result is a definition of aging as a social problem. The reader should be able to identify several instances in the previous material as

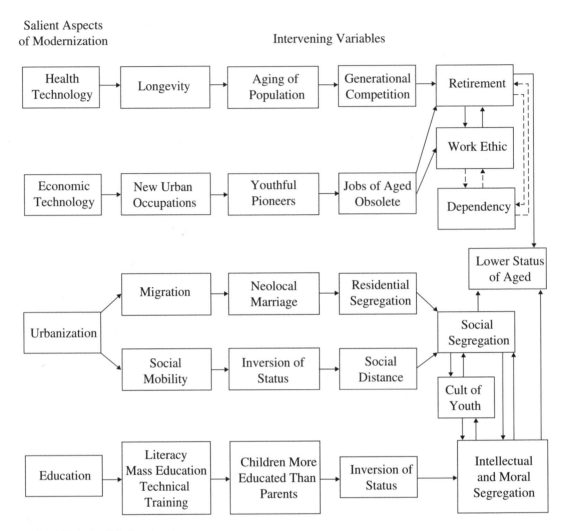

FIGURE 2–2   Modernization

Source: From Donald O. Cowgill, Aging and Modernization: A Revision of the Theory. In J. F. Gubrium (Ed.), *Late Life: Communities and Environmental Policy,* 1974, Courtesy of Charles C. Thomas, publisher, Springfield, IL.

examples. We will now turn our attention to an examination of aging within the United States. This section will focus exclusively on a historical explanation. Later, we will discuss the demographics of aging in the United States and throughout the world.

Aging in America: A Historical View

The position of the elderly throughout American history has varied. For example, in colonial America they were believed to be objects of veneration by earlier generations. Later, beginning in the early 19th century, they became objects of contempt. The following section will address this changing relationship.

A very serious problem in this area is the paucity of material. The two primary sources of information are *Growing Old in America* (1978) by David Fischer and *Old Age in the New Land* (1978) by W. Andrew Achenbaum. Although other material has been published, these two works are the cornerstones of historical investigation of aging.

Any discussion of aging in America invariably begins with a debate over the "golden age" of aging in colonial America. It is important to be aware of the diversity of thought that exists on this issue. One of the supporters of the golden-age period is David Fischer (1978). Fischer argues that between 1607 and 1820 the elderly in America were respected (venerated). Achieving an advanced age was believed to be quite rare during this historical period. As a result, the number of elderly was quite small. A small population, combined with strong religious beliefs regarding respect toward the elderly, enhanced the position of the elderly. Quantitative evidence during this period indicates the inconsistency in available census data. Fischer (1978, p. 47) presents data from a New Hampshire census in 1773 showing men aged 60 and over ranging from 2.0 to 5.5 percent of the county population. According to Laslett (1977) the elderly composed a somewhat higher percentage of the population. Of the 385 residents in Bedford and New Rochelle in 1698, 5.7 percent were aged 60 and over (p. 186).

The argument against this period as a "golden age" is based on the fact that it was less age and more one's social class that influenced respect from others. Fischer (1978, p. 60) points out that "to be old and poor and outcast in Early America was certainly not to be venerated, but rather to be despised." This interpretation is supported by Stearns (1982, pp. 9–10), who suggests that "the golden age approach implicitly emphasizes those elderly who had enough property or physical vigor to retain some real control over their lot—as seems to have been disproportionately the case in colonial America."

An examination of some comparative data provides further evidence against the golden-age concept. This concept is built on the premise that the elderly were a demographic rarity in colonial America. If this golden-age period existed throughout preindustrial Western society (as has been suggested), then similar percentages of elderly should be expected in other countries. According to data compiled by Peter Laslett (1977), that was not the case. Laslett (1977) states that 11.6 percent of the population in Venice, Italy, in 1691–1700 was aged 60 or over. Between 1761 and 1790 in Japan, 11.7 percent of the population was aged 60 and over. Finally, in 1729 in Iceland, 14.7 percent of the population was aged 60 and over. These numbers call into question the relationship between the concept of a golden age of aging and the demographic reality of the elderly in a society.

Moving forward in the history of aging in America, Fischer identifies 1770–1820 as an era of transition. It is during this era that the elderly began to lose whatever status they had enjoyed. The reasons are not all that obvious. This chapter began with a challenge; here is the answer. Fischer argues that it was neither urbanization nor industrialization that brought about the eventual demise of status among the elderly in the United States. Instead, it was the emergence of three political and economic ideals.

The first was "a radical expansion of the idea of equality . . . of condition, . . . of legal status, . . . of social obligation, . . . of cultural manners, . . . of political rights" (Fischer, 1978, p. 109). The status of the elderly had been based on their position in a hierarchical relationship. The ideal of equality reduced their level of importance relative to other age groups (Fischer, 1978).

The second was "an extension of the ancient idea of liberty" (Fischer, 1978, p. 109). The emergence of this ideal undermined the communal nature of age relationships. One result was an alteration of generational obligations.

The third factor was that "the inequality of wealth distribution began to grow" (Fischer, 1978, p. 110). This was the result of changes in the market and economic systems. This change was tied to the increasing belief in equality across generations.

This period of transition for American elderly resulted in a changing societal perception of aging. Age, rather than being venerated, was viewed with contempt. Although the exact historical date is unclear (Fischer uses 1820, whereas Achenbaum identifies 1860), the outcome is not.

By the turn of the 20th century, aging was viewed as a social problem. Changing economic opportunities within the workforce created a decreasing need for older workers. The percentage of males over the age of 65 in the labor force declined from 80.6 percent in 1870 to 60.2 percent in 1920 (Achenbaum, 1974, p. 56). The removal of the older worker eventually resulted in an increasing level of dependence by the elderly on society. At the same time, the population of the United States was becoming older. However, at the turn of the century the percentage of the population over the age of 65 was only 4 percent. In addition to the demographic and socioeconomic changes, Americans also believed that "a person's chronological age increasingly determined his or her role in society" (Achenbaum, 1978, p. 114).

The economic hardships of the 1930s and increasing pressure from the Townsend Movement (Dobelstein & Johnson, 1985) helped to bring about "the most important single piece of old age legislation in American history—the Social Security Act" (Fischer, 1978, p. 182). (The Townsend Movement will be discussed in greater detail in later chapters. Briefly, the movement was built on the premise that all elderly should receive monthly allotments from the government with the stipulation that the money be spent.) Although compulsory health and unemployment programs existed in a number of countries by 1935 (Gordon, 1960), passage of the Social Security Act brought about predictions of dire economic and social consequences (Streib & Orbach, 1967). The purpose of the Social Security Act "was to preserve the traditional fabric of America's capitalist and democratic institutions" (Fischer, 1978, p. 183). For example, the act was never intended as the sole source of retirement income for the elderly. Instead, it was believed that older Americans would have other sources of retirement income and that social security was a supplement.

After passage of the Social Security Act the elderly were not an influential force on national issues again until the 1950s (Williamson, Evans, & Powell, 1985). By the mid-1960s passage of Medicare and Medicaid provided universal health insurance for the elderly. Passage of the Older Americans Act (OAA) in 1965 resulted in the creation of the Administration on Aging (AOA) in the same year. Refinements of federal legislation continued throughout the 1960s and 1970s. However, by 1981 the usually constructive White House Conference on Aging became an ideological battleground. The Reagan administration attempted to manipulate the agenda as well as the conferees toward an outcome amenable to a conservative interpretation of the aged in America. According to the final report of the 1981 White House Conference on Aging, emphasis on the problems of the elderly has obscured the single most extraordinary fact about the great majority of the elderly Americans: They are the wealthiest, best-fed, best-housed, healthiest, most self-reliant older population in our history. (Dobelstein & Johnson, 1985, p. 7, from the *Final Report: The 1981 White House Conference on Aging,* 1982, pp. 1, 8)

Is there a common thread that is intertwined among all of this information? The answer is obviously yes. The common thread is that the "social problem" of aging is, historically, constructed by the economic and political forces of the time. What we have, then, is an ongoing historical explanation in which the social problems affecting the elderly are being redefined as existing because of the elderly. Binney and Estes (1988, p. 85) suggest the following:

Blaming the victim has been an American tradition since the Puritans blamed failure on the doctrine of predetermination. The 1980s version of this process finds the elderly . . . being blamed for such societal ills as the global economic crisis endemic to advanced capitalism, the U.S. deficit, the generation gap, the problems of the "sandwich generation" (middle-aged caregivers whose labor is stretched between multiple older and younger generations), the extraordinary rise in health costs, and a multitude of other ills.

Growing older in American society today is, of course, quite different from any other time in history. The difference today is that the demographic shifting of the age pyramid is much more obvious than in the past. This situation is not unique to the United States. Worldwide, particularly among the developed nations, the elderly as an absolute number and as a percentage of the population is increasing. It is to this demographic explanation that we now turn.

Aging Around the World

This section will examine the changing demographic characteristics of a number of countries. The primary interest here is on the movement of the population toward a more mature age. The implications of such change are significant. But first, here is a definition: *Demography* is "the scientific study of population" (Myers, 1990, p. 19). In the past, population aging in developed and developing nations has been quite distinct.

Today, differences are less pronounced. In fact, current trends and future projections indicate that the rate of growth among the elderly population will be greater in the developing nations compared to the developed nations. We will examine some of these differences as we explore population profiles and projections.

Developed Societies

The developed world is an aging world. Within these societies, the elderly have been increasing in total numbers and as a percentage of the population. Their presence is the result of changing sociodemographic characteristics within such countries.

Within the United States, the growth of the aged population has been significant, particularly in the latter half of the 20th century. At the beginning of this century, some 4 percent of the population were aged 65 and over. By 1970 the elderly, as a percentage of the population, more than doubled to 9.8 percent. In the next 20 years, this percentage again increased to 12.6 percent by 1990. According to the U.S. Bureau of the Census (1989) projections, the elderly will continue to grow in absolute numbers and as a percentage of the population. For example, by the year 2000 the elderly will represent 13 percent of the total population. By the year 2020 the elderly will represent 17.7 percent of the total population. The reason for the huge increase in numbers of elderly by 2020 is that the baby-boom generation will reach age 65 beginning in 2011. The percentage of the population aged 65 and over will continue its increase to an eventual 24.5 percent by the year 2080. It is important to remember that all of this is based on the middle series projections by the Census Bureau. In absolute numbers it means that the elderly will increase from 31,559,000 in 1990 to 52,067,000 in 2020 and eventually to 71,631,000 in 2080. Although the 65-and-over population is experiencing rapid growth, it is the oldest old that are the fastest-growing age category. This is the population aged 85 and over. In 1990 they were 1.3 percent of the population. By 2020 they are expected to increase to 2.3 percent of the total population. They will more than double to 5.8 percent of the total population by 2080 (U.S. Bureau of the Census, 1989).

The United States is not alone in this demographic shift toward an older-aged population. Many Western European countries are already experiencing population percentages that are 30 years ahead of the United States. A number of Eastern European nations are also facing growing populations of elderly citizens. These changes are illustrated in Table 2–2. Among the developed nations, Japan will experience the greatest percentage increase among the age 65 and over population. Compare the numbers and percentages for Japan on page 31 of this chapter with the numbers in Table 2–2.

By comparison, during the same time period the projected increase in the elderly population in the United States and Japan is 101 percent and 129 percent, respectively. The population structures of developed nations will continue to become "top heavy" as the elderly progress chronologically. This is best illustrated by a *population pyramid,* which is a graphic

TABLE 2–2   European Population Trends, Persons 65 and Over: 1990, 2010, and 2025

Country	*Percentage of Population Aged 65 and Over*			*Percentage Increase in Population Aged 65 and Over*
	1990	2010	2025	1990–2025
France	14.6	17.2	22.6	65
Germany	15.0	20.4	24.4	66
Norway	16.4	16.4	22.4	40
Sweden	16.0	19.6	23.7	33
United Kingdom	15.7	17.1	21.5	45
Bulgaria	13.0	18.0	22.5	59
Hungary	13.4	16.7	22.4	63
Poland	10.1	13.2	20.3	121

Source: U.S. Bureau of the Census. (1992). International population reports, p. 25, 92-3 (Figure 2.4 and Appendix A, Table 1), *An Aging World II.* Washington, DC: U.S Government Printing Office.

representation of the population on the basis of age and sex (see Figures 2–3*a* and 2–3*b*). It is obvious that as a society matures, the pyramid becomes more of a rectangle. A number of other measures exist that provide valuable data about the society itself and in relation to others.

One statistic that reveals a considerable amount of information regarding the age structure of a nation is the *median age* of its population. In 1990 the median age of the population of the United States was 33.0. By 2025 the median age is expected to increase to 38.5. By contrast, the median age in 1990 in Italy was 36.7 and is expected to increase to 48.4 by the year 2025. Virtually all countries in Western Europe will have populations with a median age of at least 44 by the year 2025 (U.S. Bureau of the Census, 1992). Another indicator of the level of societal development is that of *life expectancy.* Among the established market economies (EMEs), the United States has a life expectancy rate of 75.7 years at birth. By gender, life expectancy is 72.3 for men and 79.0 for women. Life expectancy also differs by race. White males have a life expectancy of 73.2; white females, 79.7; black males, 65.5; and black females, 73.9 (U.S. Bureau of the Census, 1994). Although impressive, the United States ranks below a number of other nations in this area (World Development Report, 1993). We will discuss some of these issues in greater detail in the chapter on health care.

Developing Societies

If developed societies are considered aged today, then it would be safe to argue that developing societies will become increasingly aged in the near future. Although the aged will not constitute the same percentage of the population as in developed nations, enormous increases will be evident. It is important to remember, however, that many of the developing countries have a relatively small number of elderly at the present time. As a result, any increase in the number of elderly will appear as a substantial increase in their percentage of the population. This is not meant to diminish the significance of population shifts in these countries. Rather, it is meant to underscore the need of developing nations to establish appropriate social policy toward their aged citizens. Table 2–3 illustrates the rate of

TABLE 2–3   Population Trends, Persons 65 and Over in Developing Countries: 1990, 2010, 2025

Country	Percentage of Population Aged 65 and Over			Percentage Increase in Population Aged 65 and Over
	1990	2010	2025	1990–2025
Egypt	3.4	3.9	5.6	238
Morocco	4.2	5.4	8.3	250
China	5.8	8.3	13.3	220
Indonesia	3.0	5.9	9.8	414
Columbia	3.9	6.3	11.2	349
Mexico	3.8	5.6	8.3	290

Source: U.S. Bureau of the Census. (1992). International population reports, p. 25, 92-3 (Figure 2.4 and Appendix A, Table 1), *An Aging World II.* Washington, DC: U.S. Government Printing Office.

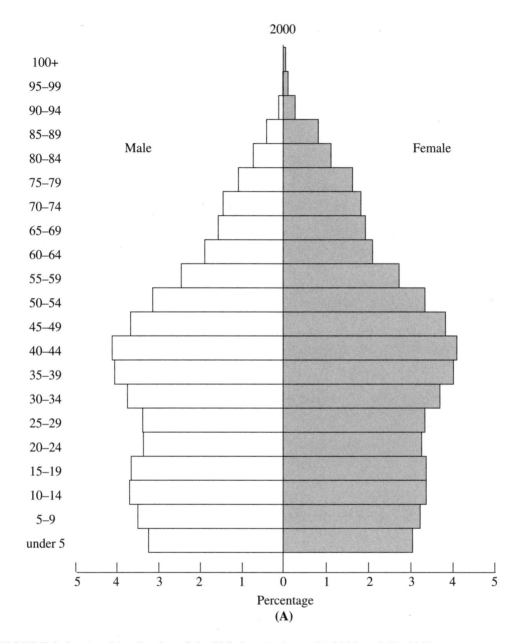

FIGURE 2–3   Age Distribution of the U.S. Population: (A) 2000 and (B) 2030

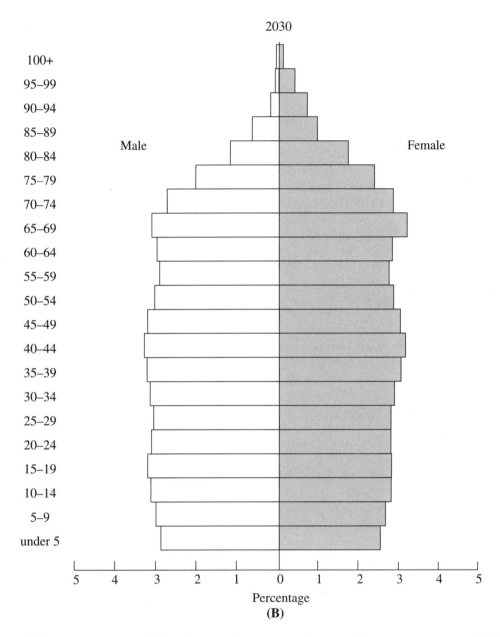

Source: U.S. Bureau of the Census. (1989). *Projections of the population of the United States, by age, sex, and race: 1988 to 2080.* Figure 2. Series P-25, No. 1018. Washington, DC: U.S. Government Printing Office.

growth within a select number of developing nations. Compare the rate of change in Table 2–3 with that of Table 2–2. Such a comparison identifies the changing nature of aging in the world today.

Developing nations are in the process of change. As population pyramids are being restructured, the elderly are emerging as a significant minority in many developing countries. Median age and life expectancy figures indicate population changes. In Tunisia the median age was 20.9 in 1990. By 2025 median age will increase to 34.1 years. In China the median age will increase from 25.5 years in 1990 to 36.7 in 2025. Among many nations of the developing world, life expectancy is also increasing. Because of improved health care and public health services, children who survive can expect to live relatively long lives. As a result, in many of these nations, the elderly are beginning to represent a particular challenge. In many cases, the health care system infrastructure as well as current political and social policy either do not exist or are insufficient to handle the growing needs of this population.

Refer to the section on the demographic transition and modernization theory. Considering the expected shift in population among many developing nations, do you find evidence to support the arguments presented by these two theories?

Cultural Biases

As the world population grows older, attempts to homogenize the aging process become an increasingly serious threat. In other words, there may be attempts by those in power to reduce the significance of cross-cultural differences of aging as political and economic entities worldwide attempt to deal with an increasing number of elderly with a variety of needs. It is important to realize, however, that aging in Western Europe and the United States occurred within a unique cultural context. We must remain cognizant of such distinct aging frameworks as we attempt to interpret the significance of the aging process in developing countries. The experiences of growing older in contemporary Africa, Asia, or Latin America, for example, are particular to the appropriate culture and to the current level of available technology. Their demographic transition or modernization will not, and should not, mirror that of Western Europe or the United States because the historical, political, and economic basis upon which such determinations are made have changed.

Future Prospects

Although history has not been particularly kind to the elderly, the future appears guardedly optimistic. That is, depending on the society, some elderly are realizing an increasing level of status. In the United States there has been a concerted effort to focus on the more positive aspects and outcomes of aging. Such an approach reflects the belief of Palmore and Manton (1974) that the status of the elderly evolves throughout the modernization process. This evolution is described as a J-curve in which status declines during the initial modernization period but eventually increases as modernization is established. For example, it appears that the previously held negative attitudes by younger generations toward the elderly are decreasing. Such change, however, is slow and potentially class based.

Because one's social class position remains as a determinant of status assessment, a new stereotype of the elderly has emerged. That is, many of the elderly are now financially secure and receiving a disproportionate share of the available health and financial resources. If, at the same time, economic opportunity and advancement of younger generations are diminished, the potential for intergenerational conflict is increased. Such images of the elderly reveal how the social problems of aging in American society are socially constructed. Chapter 4 will address this potentially divisive problem.

Critical Connection: The Importance of Numbers

Numbers are deceptively simple. Throughout this chapter we have used numbers to describe an ever-changing aging population. Whereas numbers provide us with a quantitative statement regarding the significance of a social event, the event itself is subject to interpretation by the observer. Within a sociological context, numbers are important because they reduce social events, regardless of cultural or temporal differences, to common empirical facts available for investigation.

A historical or cross-cultural analysis of aging is possible because numbers provide continuity. This means that the age of 65 is the same today as 100 years ago. For purposes of cross-cultural comparisons, 1,000 Americans aged 65 and over today equals 1,000 Japanese aged 65 and over today. The critical factor is ensuring that the numbers being used in one context are, in fact, the same in the other. A sociological explanation of numbers utilizes statistical measures that allow for comparative analysis. Such an approach belies the commonly held belief that aging itself is a social problem by providing evidence contrary to popular opinion. It is through such an interpretation that we attach different meanings to the same numbers.

These interpretations are generally couched within a particular theoretical framework. Chapter 3 addresses the more significant theoretical frameworks within sociology as well as a number of theoretical frameworks associated with the sociology of aging. For example, a social problems perspective on the sociology of aging does not exist as a distinct theoretical argument. However, a social problems approach provides a specific explanation of known empirical facts. Such an explanation, however, may (and does) differ from other theoretical explanations of the same facts. It is to this subjective evaluation of aging that we turn in Chapter 3.

Chapter Review

The following questions are designed to draw on your knowledge of this chapter. You should be able to construct answers based on concrete information as well as conjecture.

1. What was the answer to the question posed at the beginning of the chapter?
2. Evaluate the historical treatment of the elderly. In your own words, explain why being old is viewed with such skepticism, regardless of the time period.

3. If you were 65 years old, which historical period would you like to live in? Explain your answer. Again, if you were 65 years old, which historical period would you not want to live in? Explain your answer.

4. Explain modernization theory and the demographic transition. If they are not appropriate explanations of the changing populations structures of developing nations, what would you suggest as an alternative explanation?

5. Historically, the elderly in America have been identified as a social problem. Do you agree with this assessment? If not, why does this problem persist? If you agree, what characteristics about the elderly continue to create this societal reaction?

6. What are the consequences of an aging society? Think about this on the societal level in terms of such issues as health care, intergenerational problems, and financial concerns.

7. You have been assigned to write an article on the global changes in the elderly population as it relates to the larger population. For purposes of comparison, you decide to examine population changes in two developed and two developing nations. Using library materials, identify the countries and gather the following data: total population, percentage of the population aged 65 and over, median age of the total population, life expectancy, and per capita income.

Based on the data you have collected, what would you conclude? What are the differences between developed and developing nations? (When you go to the library, the World Book and the latest edition of the World Development Report are excellent resource materials. They are found in the reference section. If you are unfamiliar with this area ask the reference librarian for assistance.)

Glossary

Demographic transition A historical explanation of how populations move from a period of high birth and death rates to a period of low birth and death rates. In this process, death rates decline prior to birth rates, creating an increase in the population.

Demography The scientific study of human populations.

Life expectancy The average length of time a person is expected to live, based on their year of birth.

Median age Within a given population, the midpoint in terms of age. One half of the population is older and one half is younger than the median age.

Modernization theory Modernization theory argues that as a society modernizes, the status of the elderly will decline. Modernization is determined on the basis of education, technology, urbanization, and health technology.

Population pyramid A graphic representation of how a particular population is distributed on the basis of age and sex at a given point in time.

Suggested Reading

Achenbaum, W. A. (1978). *Old age in the New Land.* Baltimore: The Johns Hopkins University Press.
This book is considered one of the classics. The author examines the changing role of the elderly in American society.

Cowgill, D. O., & Holmes, L. D. (Eds.). (1972). *Aging and modernization.* New York: Appleton-Century-Crofts.
This book provides a cross-cultural examination of aging. Although dated, the book provides considerable insight into the development of modernization theory.

Fischer, D. H. (1978). *Growing old in America.* New York: Oxford University Press.
Again, this is one of those classic books on aging in America. The author systematically explores the historical development of aging in America.

International Labor Organisation. (1989). *From pyramid to pillar: Population change and social security in Europe.* Geneva: Author.
This book provides extensive coverage of population change among a number of European nations. Some of the changes in the aged population that are examined include income maintenance and health care costs.

Palmore, E. (1975). *The honorable elders.* Durham, NC: Duke University Press.
This book questions the ability of modernization theory and disengagement theory to explain aging in Japan.

References

Achenbaum, W. A. (1974). The obsolescence of old age in America: 1865–1914. *Journal of Social History 8,* 48–62.

Achenbaum, W. A. (1978). *Old age in the New Land.* Baltimore: The Johns Hopkins University Press.

Anderson, M. (1972). Household structure and the Industrial Revolution: Mid-nineteenth century Preston in comparative perspective. In P. Laslett (Ed.), *Household and family in past time* (pp. 215–235). Cambridge: Cambridge University Press.

Beauvoir, S. de. (1972). *The coming of age.* New York: Putnam.

Binney, E. A., & Estes, C. L. (1988). The retreat of the state and its transfer of responsibility: The intergenerational war. *International Journal of Health Services 18*(1), 83–96.

Covey, H. C. (1992). The definitions of the beginning of old age in history. *International Journal of Aging and Human Development 34*(4), 325–337.

Cowgill, D. O. (1974). Aging and modernization: A revision of the theory. In J. F. Gubrium (Ed.), *Late life: Communities and environmental policy.* Springfield, IL: Charles C. Thomas.

Cowgill, D. O. (1986). *Aging around the world.* Belmont, CA: Wadsworth.

Cowgill, D. O., & Holmes, L. D. (1972). *Aging and modernization.* New York: Appleton-Crofts.

Dobelstein, A. W., & Johnson, A. B. (1985). *Serving older adults: Policy, programs, and professional activities.* Englewood Cliffs, NJ: Prentice Hall.

Fischer, D. H. (1978). *Growing old in America.* New York: Oxford University Press.

Freeman, J. T. (1979). *Aging: Its history and literature.* New York: Human Sciences Press.

Gordon, M. S. (1960). Aging and income security. In C. Tibbitts (Ed.), *Handbook of social gerontology.* Chicago: University of Chicago Press.

International Encyclopedia of Population. (1982). New York: The Free Press.

Laslett, P. (1977). *Family life and illicit love in earlier generations.* Cambridge: Cambridge University Press.

McFalls, J. A., Jr. (1991, October). Population: A lively introduction. *Population Bulletin 46*(2), Washington, DC: Population Reference Bureau, pp. 2–38.

Martin, L. G. (1989, July). The graying of Japan. *Population Bulletin 44*(2), Washington, DC: Population Reference Bureau, pp. 5–40.

Matcha, D. A. (1994). *Health and age status of the elderly by level of economic development: An application of modernization theory.* Paper presented at Eastern Sociological Society Meetings, Baltimore, MD, March 17–20.

Minois, G. (1989). *History of old age: From antiquity to the Renaissance.* Chicago: The University of Chicago Press.

Myers, G. C. (1990). Demography of aging. In R. H. Binstock & L. K. George (Eds.), *Handbook of aging and the social sciences* (3rd ed.). San Diego, CA: Academic Press.

Palmore, E. B., & Manton, K. (1974). *Aging and modernization.* New York: Appleton-Century-Crofts.

Pritchard, J. B. (Ed.). (1955). *Ancient Near Eastern texts relating to the Old Testament.* Princeton, NJ: Princeton University Press.

Quadagno, J. (1982). *Aging in early industrial society: Work, family, and social policy in nineteenth century England.* New York: Academic Press.

Senior student. (1994, January 1). *Times Union,* Albany, New York, Section D, pp. 1 and 3.

Stearns, P. (1976). *Old age in European society.* New York: Holmes & Meier.

Stearns, P. (Ed.). (1982). *Old age in preindustrial society.* New York: Holmes and Meier.

Streib, G. F., & Orbach, H. L. (1967). Aging. In P. F. Lazerfeld, W. M. Sewell, & H. L. Wilensky (Eds.), *The uses of sociology.* New York: Basic Books.

Thompson, W. (1929). Population. *American Journal of Sociology 34*(6), 959–975.

U.S. Bureau of the Census. (1989). Current population reports, Series P-25, No. 1018, *Projections of the population of the United States, by age, sex, and race: 1988 to 2080,* by Gregory Spencer. Washington, DC: U.S. Government Printing Office.

U.S. Bureau of the Census. (1992). International population reports, P25, 92-3, *An aging world II.* Washington, DC: U.S. Government Printing Office.

U.S. Bureau of the Census. (1994). *Statistical abstract of the United States.* Washington, DC: U.S. Government Printing Office.

Walker, A. (1982, Summer). Dependency and old age. *Social Policy and Administration 16*(2), 115–135.

Weeks, J. R. (1989). *Population* (4th ed.). Belmont, CA: Wadsworth.

Williamson, J. B., Evans, L., & Powell, L. A. (1985). *The politics of aging.* Springfield, IL: Charles C. Thomas.

World development report. (1993). New York: Oxford University Press.

C h a p t e r 3

The View From the Tower

Theoretical Perspectives

Within the field of sociology of aging, the theoretical perspectives vary greatly with respect to the relative importance given to a number of factors, including consensus, conflict, the self, social structure, and language use. No single theory explains all social phenomena; each focuses on particular aspects of social behavior, offering minimal explanations for other features of social life.
—*PASSUTH & BENGTSON, 1988, P. 334*

As the title of this chapter indicates, we will now examine the theoretical frameworks associated with the sociology of aging. Too often students think of this chapter as either too boring or too abstract to be of any practical value. We hope to change that attitude by demonstrating the importance of theory to our everyday assessment of a phenomenon such as aging. The chapter begins with a brief historical overview of the development of sociology with an emphasis on the emergence of theory. It then examines the major theoretical frameworks found in sociology. Finally, the chapter addresses the major theoretical frameworks associated with the sociology of aging. This process will connect for the reader the broader theoretical arguments of sociology to the discipline-specific arguments found in the sociology of aging.

The significance of theory is its ability to explain social phenomena. For example, imagine that as you walk through the downtown area of your community you encounter a number of homeless elderly living on the street. How would you explain their presence? Would you say that they are lazy? Would you compare them to other elderly in your community whom you would define as "successful"? Would you attribute the economic misfortunes of these elderly to the problems of society? By asking such questions as *how* and *why* you are beginning to think as a theorist. You are attempting to explain social phenomena. Eventually, you will arrive at an explanation as to why a number of homeless elderly are living on the streets of your community. In other words, you will have constructed a theory to explain this phenomenon. This theory, however, is constructed from your interpretation of the phenomenon. I may view the same social phenomenon and construct a very different explanation. Which explanation is correct, yours or mine? Must we choose one over the other? Is one "better" than the other? The answer is no. However, what if I am the mayor of your community, and you are one of some 100,000 residents? Because of my position, will my explanation (theory) be more accepted than yours? Why? Would my position as mayor give me greater credibility? Would my position give me the power to enforce my explanation? All of this does not mean that because I am the mayor I am correct. It may mean that others in the community will accept my explanation and even allow me to enforce my interpretation of the situation. Thus what we eventually believe (and do) regarding the homeless elderly in your community will be determined by someone's theoretical perspective. The significance of this example is the eventual perception that could be created of the homeless elderly in your community (they could be identified as a social problem). If others in similar positions of power accept my theoretical argument, such a perception could have much broader ramifications for the homeless elderly.

This example is meant to sensitize you to the theoretical construction of aging. The addition of a social problems approach creates a framework within which the aging process can be evaluated. Such a scenario is an example of the practical application of theory to the sociology of aging.

This chapter is of particular importance because it provides explanations of the social phenomenon understood as aging within the framework of the larger society. Theoretical explanations, however, have never enjoyed broad support among those interested in aging. With a few exceptions, the theoretical development of the sociology of aging has been virtually nonexistent. Such exceptions occurred in the 1960s, during which time a number of theoretical arguments emerged. A brief, yet succinct, historical accounting of theoretical development can be found in Hendricks (1992). Since the late 1960s, however, a more practical application of the sociology of aging has dominated. As a result, the sociology of aging has been virtually devoid of a strong theoretical grounding. This is not to suggest that theoretical frameworks have not been developed or tested in the past 20 years. Rather, the historical period following the 1960s has been less kind to the study of aging. Changes in the political and economic structure of the 1980s and 1990s have altered societal perceptions and expectations of the elderly. The response has been a resurgence of theoretical explanations and reexamination. These concerns will be constructed and examined in the following pages. But first, we begin with the basics.

Sociology and Social Theory

Sociology and its theoretical arguments developed amid the rubble and unrest that characterized Western Europe during the late 18th and early 19th centuries (Ritzer, 1988). Auguste Comte, a former student of Saint Simon, is acknowledged as the founder of sociology because of his coining the term in 1838. At the time, Comte believed that sociology "was to be concerned with both social statics (existing social structures) and social dynamics (social change) . . . although he felt that social dynamics was more important than social statics" (Ritzer, 1988, p. 13). Sociology as a modern discipline emerged through the works of such classical theorists as Emile Durkheim, Max Weber, and Karl Marx. With the advent of the 20th century, European nations suffered the effects of the World War I and political instability. Sociology soon found comfort within the United States. An era of social reformers attempted to create change amid the ills wrought by rapid industrialization and urbanization. Sociology quickly established itself as a significant intellectual force in 20th-century America. Sociological research provided a wealth of data on a variety of social phenomena. In the process, theoretical explanations emerged in an attempt to explain such action. Historically, the theoretical explanation that has dominated American thought has been structural functionalism. It was only recently (the 1960s) that competing theoretical frameworks such as symbolic interactionism and conflict theory emerged as significant schools of thought. Political and social unrest during the 1960s and 1970s contributed to the development of these competing theoretical explanations of social events. Today sociological theory is not dominated by a single explanation. Instead, there is an eclecticism associated with its application. Albeit brief, the history of Western sociology (and social theory) is an important reminder that the theoretical constructs identified by Comte more than a century and a half ago are still significant.

One definition of *sociological theory* states that it is "a set of assumptions concerning society and social phenomena in reference to their separate societal reality," or, more broadly, "an explanation system of social phenomena" (Kinloch, 1977, pp. 26–27). A number of "explanation systems" exist that attempt to provide the framework within which social phenomena can be explained. First, the major theoretical frameworks in sociology will be briefly examined. We will then turn our attention to the formation of theoretical frameworks in aging. Figure 3–1 illustrates the theoretical connections between sociological theories and theories of aging. We begin with the sociological theories as the foundation for the theories of aging.

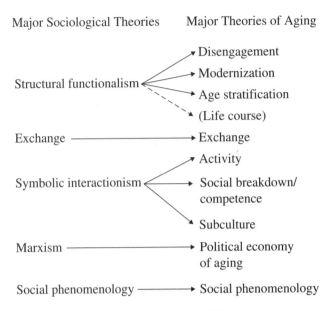

Major Sociological Theories   Major Theories of Aging

FIGURE 3–1   The Influence of Sociological Theories of Aging
Source: Passuth, P. M., & Bengtson, V. L. (1988). Sociological theories of aging: Current perspectives and future directions. In J. E. Birrin & V. L. Bengtson (Eds.), *Emergent theories of aging* (p. 335). Copyright © Springer Publishing Company, Inc., New York 10012. Used by permission.

Sociological Frameworks

Structural Functionalism

Structural functionalism, or *functionalism,* as it is referred to today, is rooted in the works of Comte, Spencer, and Durkheim. Among the frameworks examined here, it is "the oldest and, until recently, the dominant conceptual perspective in sociology" (Turner, 1978, p. 36). It is perhaps easiest to understand functionalism if we examine some of its major concepts. First is that of function, which refers to the consequences attributed to any action. Functions can be manifest or latent (Merton, 1967). That is, a manifest function is an overt or expected function, whereas a latent function is covert or unexpected. For example, a manifest function of retirement is to create work opportunities for younger generations. A latent function of retirement is the creation of a part-time workforce ideally suited for the increasingly transitory jobs available in the economy. The second concept is that of structure. This is the interrelationship of roles at various levels of organization. For functionalists, the level of analysis is generally not at the individual level. Instead, they prefer examining role relationships at the institutional or societal level. Functionalism is also built on the concept of equilibrium. In other words, at whatever level of structure examined, consensus among constituent parts is essential to the maintenance of the system.

Turner, Beeghley, and Powers (1989, p. 472) identify "the basic elements of all functional analysis" as the following:

1. Social systems are composed of interconnected parts.
2. Social systems confront external and internal problems of survival.
3. Such problems of survival can be visualized as the "needs" or "requisites" of the system.
4. Social systems and their constituent parts can only be understood by assessing how a part contributes to meeting the needs or requisites of the systemic whole.

Regarding the study of aging, "functionalist theories see differences based on age as legitimate aspects of the social order. Old age and illness in contemporary society are problems primarily when they disrupt the smooth functioning of society as currently structured" (Estes, Wallace, & Binney, 1989, p. 403). The issue of retirement is a classic example. Why do industrial societies construct retirement systems? Is retirement "functional" for society and the individual? Think of your first career position. Chances are that the position you accept was filled by someone else earlier. Did that person retire? The economic system cannot create a new job for every person wanting to work. Therefore, one method of providing job opportunities for those entering the workforce is to establish a retirement age and remove those already involved. This transition is smooth and causes few disruptions within the larger society. The preceding example clearly defines the functionalist perspective relative to the aging process.

Symbolic Interactionism

Quite unlike the other major theories, symbolic interactionism, or simply *interactionism,* emphasizes "how the process of interaction mediates between the attributes of the individual and society" (Turner, Beeghley, & Powers, 1989, p. 476). This theoretical perspective attempts to understand how humans utilize symbols to communicate with others. Turner (1991, p. 394) captures the essence of interactionism in the following:

> Humans create and use symbols. They communicate with symbols. They interact through role-taking, which involves the reading of symbols emitted by others. What makes them unique as a species—the existence of mind and self—arises out of interaction. Conversely, the emergence of these capacities allows for the interactions that form the basis of society.

Turner has constructed the core of interactionism, but we are left once again with a need to define concepts. The most basic is that of the symbol. A symbol is anything that is given meaning. A wedding, flowers, paper, and the flag are all symbols. When the meaning that is attached to a symbol is shared, the symbol becomes socially significant. That is, a common explanation is attached. As a result, social interaction emerges. For example, why do you stand when the national anthem is played? Why do you stop when the traffic light turns red? As Skidmore points out, "people react to the behavior of others, but they act on the basis of communicated intentions" (1979, p. 192).

Craib (1992, p. 87) identifies three of Blumer's (1969) basic assumptions of symbolic interactionism:

1. Human beings act toward things on the basis of the meanings that the things have for them.
2. These meanings are the product of social interaction in human society.

3. These meanings are modified and handled through an interpretative process that is used by each individual in dealing with the signs each encounters.

Relative to the sociology of aging, "interactionist concepts show how the elderly work to create meaningful lives and to make the most out of their situations" (Estes et al., 1989, p. 404). For example, the knowledge associated with growing older emerges from interaction with others.

Conflict Theory

Present-day *conflict theory* has its roots in the writings of Karl Marx. Marx is of particular importance to sociology because of his analysis of such concepts as alienation and social class explained through the relationship between one's economic position and normative behavior. First, alienation refers to a feeling of removal from that which one does or is. Generally, this is in reference to the world of work. However, one can become alienated from others in a relationship and even from oneself. This concept is of particular importance to the elderly as they, and society, attempt to define the retirement role. (A more thorough explanation is presented in Chapter 6.) Alienation also exists in a more pernicious form: the theoretical argument of disengagement theory, which will be discussed in greater detail later in this chapter.

In addition to alienation, Marx argued that one's social class position is perhaps the most significant indicator of one's ability and potential opportunity. Broadly speaking, a person was either a member of the bourgeoisie (the property owners) or the proletariat (the workers). The belief that one's economic position determined one's social and normative behavior is of particular importance to the elderly. It is this idea that connects the sociology of aging to that of social problems. For example, some 30 ago it was believed that because the elderly were poor (economically), they were in need of assistance from the government. As a consequence, the War on Poverty in the 1960s provided various programs designed to meet various social, psychological, and physical needs. The result has been a significant reduction in the percentage of the elderly below the official poverty line. However, these programs also created a relationship of dependence. That is, it is now assumed that if a person is old, he or she is in need of assistance from others. Thus age has become equated with dependence. Some elderly, because of physical or mental health, are in need of assistance. But this is true of some members of all age categories. Age itself does not create the dependence. Unfortunately in today's society, there is a growing acceptance that age-based dependence is a natural consequence of the aging process. If younger generations believe that such an inevitable outcome is a financial burden to them, their attitude toward the elderly may become increasingly negative. Acceptance of this belief could thus result in increased intergenerational conflict. At the other end of the financial spectrum is the erroneous perception that the elderly live in relative comfort in a beachside resort, with more than enough money relative to their needs, and are wasting precious health care dollars. This argument also influences our image of what we believe about the economic conditions of the elderly. Finally, a number of basic assumptions exist regarding conflict theory:

1. All social systems reveal inequalities in the distribution of scarce and valuable resources.
2. Such inequalities inevitably and inexorably create conflicts of interest among system units.
3. Such conflicts of interest will, over time, generate overt conflict among those who possess, and those who do not possess, valuable resources.
4. These conflicts will result in reorganization of the social system, creating new patterns of inequality that will serve as the next fulcrum for conflict and change. (Turner et al., 1989, p. 473)

Exchange Theory

Exchange theory has its roots in classic economics and in behavioral psychology. Within classical economics, the label *utilitarianism* offers a particular perspective on human relations. The term suggests that "humans are viewed as rationally seeking to maximize their material benefits, or utility, from transactions or exchanges with others in a free and competitive marketplace" (Turner, 1991, p. 285). On the other hand, exchange theory is grounded in the work of George Homans. Homans (1974) applied a behaviorist interpretation to individual behavior by identifying a series of propositions. A discussion of all five propositions is beyond the scope of this book. However, a brief explanation of the first proposition illustrates the influence of behaviorism. According to Homans, the success proposition states that "for all actions taken by persons, the more often a particular action of a person is rewarded, the more likely the person is to perform that action" (Homans, 1974, p. 16). Studying for exams is a most appropriate example. Suppose you ask a particular classmate for assistance regarding your next sociology of aging exam. If the information given by that classmate was beneficial when you took the exam, what are you likely to do when you prepare for the next exam? You will once again ask that classmate for assistance. Now put yourself in the position of the classmate. If I paid you $10 to help me with the sociology of aging exam, would you be willing to tutor me for the next exam? Yes, particularly if rewarded.

Exchange theory is a most appropriate explanation of the sociology of aging. Dowd (1975, p. 590) states that "from an exchange theory perspective, then, the problems of aging are essentially problems of *decreasing power resources.*" In other words, as one ages the value of resources available for exchange is diminished. And because of age the availability of resources is limited, and therefore so is my power. Within the context of exchange theory, resources range from the expected, such as money and skills, to qualities such as esteem and compliance (Dowd, 1975). Exchange theory provides a unique perspective that is particularly instructive when attempting to explain social phenomena.

How have these sociological theories influenced the development of theories of aging? The next section explores the dominant sociological theories of aging.

Gerontological Frameworks

Gerontological frameworks, attempting to provide explanations of human and social behavior, developed later than general sociology. The emergence of gerontological frameworks, however, reflects the dominant paradigms of sociology. This book will focus primarily on those theories that are considered to be the traditional "core" of social gerontology.

Disengagement Theory

Disengagement theory was first articulated in an article by Cumming, Dean, Newell, and McCaffrey (1960) and was later formalized by Cumming and Henry (1961) in their seminal work, *Growing Old.* The theory is based on the Kansas City study that involved 275 middle- and older-aged individuals who were in good financial and physical health. The ostensible basis of this theory is that a linear relationship exists between age and disengagement. That is, as one ages, the disengagement becomes greater. Disengagement is the removal from previous activities. Thus, as one ages, the roles once engaged in (such as work) are set aside in favor of a reduced level of expectation between the individual and the society. Disengagement ultimately ends with the death of the individual. Relative to the aging process, Cumming and Henry (1961, pp. 14–15) state that the process is

> an inevitable mutual withdrawal or disengagement, resulting in decreased interaction between the aging person and others in the social system he belongs to. The process may be initiated by the individual or by others in the situation. . . . When the aging process is complete, the equilibrium which existed in middle life between the individual and his society has given way to a new equilibrium characterized by a greater distance and an altered type of relationship.

According to Cumming and Henry (1961), the process of disengagement involves three basic tenets. The first is that the process of disengagement is mutual. That is, society and the individual are in a constant state of negotiation over the disengagement process. Throughout this relationship the level of satisfaction experienced by the individual declines. An increase in the level of satisfaction occurs once the individual has completely disengaged and reestablishes a sense of equilibrium.

The second tenet is that the disengagement process is universal. Cumming and Henry (1961) argued that such withdrawal occurs across cultures. Third, the process is believed to be inevitable. That is, disengagement will occur regardless of the individual or the position that he or she holds. Since its pronouncement, attempts at replication of the theory and its various components has not proved successful. Rather than age as the central independent variable, others have suggested variables such as "poor health, widowhood" (Hochschild, 1975, p. 563), "perceived imminence of death, or economic hardship" (McPherson, 1990, p. 137) and sociostructural variables (Matcha, 1985). Although flawed, the theory has provided the impetus for continued theoretical development. Remember that Cumming et al. (1960, p. 23) began their paper by noting that "we have no social-psychological theories of aging." They were embarking on a journey in which questions of why and how may have been asked, but not in any systematic fashion. They provided the first of many possible explanations of the aging process.

How applicable is disengagement theory today? Can you think of examples that would support (or not support) the argument presented by Cumming and Henry? How would disengagement theory explain the numbers of homeless elderly living in the downtown section of your community? In order to answer this question properly you need to refer to Chapter 1 and the section on research. You first need data that can be interpreted. What type of research would you conduct? Would you use a cross-sectional or longitudinal approach? Once you decide that, which research design would be most appropriate? Would you conduct a survey of the homeless elderly or engage in participant observation? Could you conduct an experiment? If you are attempting to explain this social phenomenon from a disengagement perspective you would probably conduct a survey.

What questions would you ask in the survey? Remember that you are attempting to understand why there are a large number of homeless elderly living in your downtown. What is it about disengagement theory that you are trying to elicit from your respondents? You will continually be asked these questions as we progress through the remainder of the chapter. The purpose of these questions is twofold: First, it is to demonstrate the connection between theory and research; second, it is to illustrate the significance of research to our everyday understanding of social phenomena.

Activity Theory

Technically, activity theory was the first theory of aging developed in the United States. *Activity theory* has its origins in the work of Cavan, Burgess, Havighurst, and Goldhamer (1949) and, in particular, Havighurst and Albrecht (1953). Although its origins precede that of disengagement theory, the theory was formalized in reaction to the emergence of disengagement theory. Whereas disengagement theory is grounded in the functionalist argument, activity theory developed out of the symbolic interactionist perspective.

Essentially, activity theory attempts to address the relationship between roles, self-concept, activity, and life satisfaction. The theory states that as one ages, rather than being removed (as disengagement theory would argue) from roles, we take on new roles that maintain a sense of continuity. The continued engagement of the individual within society helps to preserve his or her self-concept and maintain a high level of life satisfaction. Individuals are "successfully aging" if they maintain their prior activity level.

The theory sounds deceptively simple. In fact, there is an intuitive belief in the theory because of its implicit connection to such basic American values as independence and individuality. As with disengagement theory, activity theory has also experienced a lack of empirical support. Proponents of activity theory would disagree with such an assessment as attempts have been made to establish an empirical base of support. However, Havighurst (1968, p. 23) argues that "neither the activity nor the disengagement theory is satisfactory, since neither deals, except peripherally, with the issue of personality differences." Havighurst (1968, p. 23) is suggesting that although levels of activity and satisfaction are important, the type of personality exhibited by the older person "seems to be the pivotal dimension in describing patterns of aging and in predicting relationships between level of activity and life satisfaction."

Twenty years after the initial work of Havighurst and Albrecht (1953), Lemon, Bengtson, and Peterson (1972) attempted to establish the empirical base necessary for the support of the theory. They began by identifying four postulates that address the relationship between activity and life satisfaction:

1. The greater the role loss, the less the activity one is likely to engage in.
2. The greater the activity, the more role support one is likely to receive.
3. The more role support one receives, the more positive one's self-concept is likely to be.
4. The more positive one's self-concept, the greater one's life satisfaction is likely to be.
   (Lemon et al., 1972, p. 515)

In addition to the four postulates, the authors constructed a number of theorems and a series of hypotheses. Based on the data, the authors concluded that support for the basic relationship between activity and life satisfaction was not supported. The most significant relationship was "that participation in an informal friendship group appears to be an important correlate of life satisfaction" (Lemon et al., 1972, p. 519). A replication of this research was conducted by Longino and Kart (1982), who provide evidence supporting the predictive capability of activity theory. The continued interest in disengagement theory and activity theory is demonstrated by a recent article by Khullar and Reynolds (1990). Examining the viability of the two theories, the authors concluded that statistical evidence supports the existence of activity theory but not disengagement.

Return to the questions asked on pages 52–53. Replace disengagement theory with activity theory. What questions would you ask? What research design would be most appropriate? Are the types of questions you would ask from an activity theory approach different from those asked from a disengagement approach? One would expect differences in the questions. At this point you should begin to appreciate the significance of theory as an explanation of social phenomena. We will continue to prompt you with these questions at the end of each theoretical perspective discussed in the chapter.

The theoretical debate continues, but it is no longer confined to disengagement and activity theory. There has been a proliferation of theory, primarily in the 1960s and early 1970s. However, the last decade has witnessed the growth of theory as a reaction to social and political circumstances of the elderly within society. The interest in theory has shifted somewhat from a social-psychological approach popular earlier (that is, activity theory, subculture theory) to a more structural interpretation today (social stratification, political economy of aging).

Subculture Theory

Grounded in the symbolic interactionist perspective, *subculture theory* has its origins in the work of Arnold Rose (1965). This theory argues that the elderly constitute a subculture within the larger American culture. Rose (1965) believed that an aged subculture is possible because the elderly have strong attachments to other elderly and that the elderly are, to an extent, excluded from interaction with others in society.

Rose (1965, pp. 4–6) suggests that a number of trends were occurring that would increase the likelihood of a subculture. As a precaution, note that these trends were identified 30 years ago. How relevant are they today?

Trends

1. The growth in the number and percent of elderly in the population.
2. The health of those reaching age 65 has improved. As a result, older people are more capable of creating a subculture.
3. Because of increased levels of health, when the elderly become ill, they are more likely to experience chronic diseases costing more.
4. Self-segregating migration patterns. That is, some elderly move to retirement communities, while others are left behind in rural communities when younger members move out.

5. Increasing rate of retirement and decreasing rate of self-employment.
6. As the economic conditions of the elderly increase, they have the time and money to do the things they want. Such activity eventually becomes part of the subculture.
7. Social programs for the elderly provide the environment for the formation of subcultures.
8. Because of migration, economics, and changes in society, the elderly are more likely to live alone rather than with adult children.

In addition to these trends, Rose (1965) argues that some differentiation may exist within aging subcultures. That is, one's social class or type of community may increase or decrease the likelihood of subcultural formation. Rose suggests that the more affluent and better educated would be less likely to establish subcultural formations because of continued contact with others. In much the same way, elderly residing in age-integrated small towns or in the suburbs are less likely to create aged subcultures.

Finally, Rose (1965, p. 13) identifies what he terms "aging group consciousness," where "some older people have begun to think of themselves as members of an aging group." Rose believed that the trends identified earlier are instrumental in the emergence of this group consciousness. A possible link between the subcultural explanation and activity theory was investigated by McClelland (1982). Figure 3–2 is a representation of his argument.

McClelland (1982) argued that the four central variables formed a causal chain. The variables begin with social activity as the necessary condition for the others. From social activity, the second link is social adequacy. The third link is self-conception, and life satisfaction is the endpoint. McClelland assumed that the central variables would be influenced by the background variables. Subculture theory is related to this argument by way of

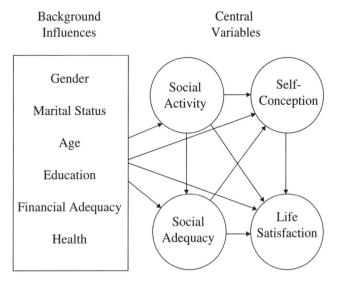

FIGURE 3–2 Proposed Path Model Combining Aged Subculture and Activity Theory
Source: Mclelland, K. A. (1982). Self-conception and life satisfaction: Integrating aged subculture and activity theory. *Journal of Gerontology, 37*(6), 723–732. Copyright © The Gerontological Society of America.

attitudinal values. McClelland (1982, p. 725) assumed "that attitudinal values about other old people may have an effect on the relationship between social activity and the other central variables in this analysis."

McClelland concludes by noting that all four central variables are related to the model. More specifically, he states that "self-conception has been shown to be very strongly dependent on social activity and to have, in turn, a significant effect on life satisfaction" (1982, p. 730). Finally, McClelland suggests further examination of subculture theory, particularly the influence of aging group consciousness. How would subculture theory explain the number of elderly homeless in your community? Ask yourself the same questions as before and address the issue of the research design. This should be easy by now. Can you recognize any patterns of (dis)similarity between the theoretical frameworks and the types of questions you would ask?

Social Breakdown/Competence

A third theoretical perspective constructed within the symbolic interactionist mode, *social breakdown/competence* offers a more pragmatic interpretation of aged behavior. Grounded in the tradition of labeling theory, this perspective is best understood by examining Figures 3–3 and 3–4. The perspective is an extension of work by Zusman (1966) with Kuypers and Bengtson (1973) applying the original stages to the aging process.

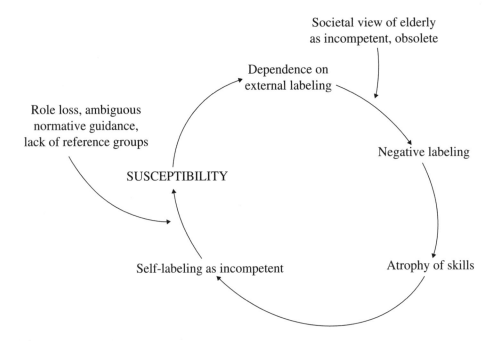

FIGURE 3–3   Social Breakdown Syndrome
Source: Kuypers, J. A., & Bengtson, V. L. (1973). Social breakdown and competence: A model of normal aging. *Human Development, 16,* 181–201. Used with permission. S Karger AG, Basel.

In Figure 3–3 (the social breakdown syndrome), stage 1 reflects the difficulty of growing older in society. According to Bengtson (1973, p. 47), the elderly experience "role loss, vague or inappropriate normative information, and lack of reference groups . . . [which] serve to deprive the individual of feedback concerning who he is." The second stage reinforces the negativity of the first. The elderly, feeling socially impotent, accept the stereotypical (and negative) labels associated with being old. In the third stage, the elderly act on these stereotypic images of being old. The consequence is a loss of the knowledge necessary to function independently. Finally, in the fourth stage, the individual, believing that he or she is inadequate, creates the conditions for another cycle of the social breakdown syndrome. According to Kuypers and Bengtson, this syndrome can be eliminated and replaced with the social reconstruction syndrome (illustrated in Figure 3–4).

The social reconstruction syndrome is expected to develop in response to a series of external inputs. These inputs consist of (1) a freeing of the individual from economic entrapment (that is, removal of the presumed relationship between the concept of "productive" and self-worth); (2) improved conditions of caring (environmental, economic, and medical); and (3) an empowerment of the elderly (allowing the elderly to engage in personal self-determination).

How would the social breakdown/reconstruction syndrome address the question of homeless elderly in your community? Is there a particular research design that would be more appropriate as you apply this theory?

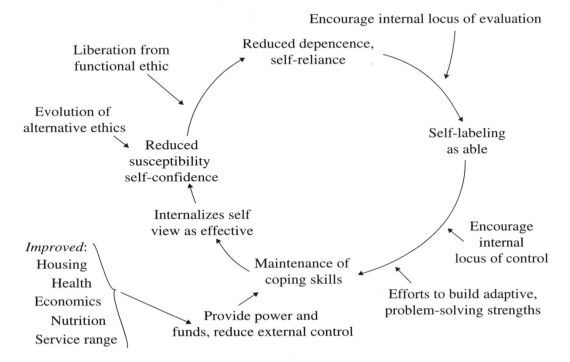

FIGURE 3–4   Social Reconstruction Syndrome
Source: Kuypers, J. A., & Bengtson, V. L. (1973). Social breakdown and competence: A model of normal aging. *Human Development, 16,* 181–201. Used with permission. S Karger AG, Basel.

Continuity Theory

Continuity theory offers an analysis of "normal" aging (we will discuss the meaning attached to this later in this section). Incorporated in this approach is what Atchley (1989) refers to as internal and external continuity. Atchley (1989, p. 183) states that

> a central premise of Continuity Theory is that, in making adaptive choices, middle-aged and older adults attempt to preserve and maintain existing internal and external structures and that they prefer to accomplish this objective by using continuity (that is, applying familiar strategies in familiar arenas of life).

Continuity theory addresses aging as an evolutionary, dynamic process in which change is inevitable and necessary. At issue is this: How do people respond to changes in their daily lives and in the larger society? This theory argues that we use internal and external continuity to maintain stability as a result of our ongoing experiences. Internal continuity involves knowledge of oneself, or, as Atchley (1989) points out, it requires memory. Conversely, the absence of internal continuity would predictably cause considerable distress. For example, an individual with Alzheimer's disease will drift between periods of lucidity and periods of complete memory loss. The inability to construct a self-identity thwarts development of current or future activity. As one ages, the necessity for internal continuity is of increasing significance. On the other hand, external continuity involves the more structured physical environment and social relationships that define our behavior.

Before progressing forward in our discussion of internal and external continuity, we want to return to the comment about "normal aging" made earlier. Atchley describes "normally aging people" as

> independent adults [who] . . . can successfully meet their needs for income, housing, health care, nutrition, clothing, transportation, and recreation. They lead active, satisfying, and purposeful lives that involve adequate networks of longstanding social relationships.

Those elderly unable to provide for themselves because of physical or economic inability experience what Atchley (1989) describes as "pathological aging." As a result, "Continuity Theory is not very helpful in understanding the external reality of pathological aging" (Atchley, 1989, p. 184).

Returning to the central concepts associated with continuity theory, it appears that this theory is applicable within rather well-defined outcome situations. It is argued that internal continuity persists, despite changes within the daily routines of life. This personality remains relatively constant, because once an identity is established, we tend to find ways to support who we are. In terms of external continuity, the existence of a routine is not a problem because it minimizes conflict. That is, we know what to do and what to expect relative to the physical and social structure of the community in which we live. For example, if you move to a new community, you need to start over in terms of finding where things are (banks, shopping, doctors, dentists, and so on). Not only is the physical environment different, but you must establish new social roles. Although one's social and physical environment is not static, some change is not viewed as upsetting to the individual.

An in-depth analysis of continuity theory by Fox (1981–1982) supports the broad arguments put forth by its proponents, but with reservations. Fox (1981–1982, p. 104) points out that "there appears to be some support for a continuity perspective, at least when measurement remains diffuse and general." How would continuity theory explain the large number of homeless elderly living in the downtown area of your community? What research design would be most appropriate with this theoretical framework? Before you answer these questions, reread this section. What would continuity theory say about the scenario? Is this theory applicable?

Social Stratification Theory

Moving from the symbolic interactionist and labeling orientations, we will conclude this chapter with two theories that view aging from a macrosociological (societal-level) perspective. Previous theoretical perspectives were primarily from a microsociological (individual-level) perspective.

Social stratification theory has its origins in the writings of Matilda White Riley (1971) and Riley, Johnson, and Foner (1972). Essentially, this theoretical perspective argues that age stratification can be examined in much the same way as such sociological concepts as social class and social mobility. Riley (1971) posits four questions central to social stratification and then restates the questions in a manner appropriate to an examination of age and aging. We will concern ourselves only with the questions related to aging.

The first question, extrapolated from Mannheim (1952), asks the following: "[H]ow does an individual's location within the changing age structure of a given society influence his behavior and attitude?" (Riley, 1971, p. 80). There are two explanations to this question. The first is concerned with the concept of life course stage. In other words, where you are chronologically provides an understanding of your experiences vis-à-vis others in an earlier or later life course stage. For example, 65-year-olds have experiences (retirement, possible death of spouse) different from those at age 25. The second explanation concerns one's period in history. The concept associated with this explanation is that of cohort, or those born during the same time period. Those born during the same time period have similar experiences as a result of their unique position relative to the occurrence of historical events.

The second question is more of a statement with an explanation. Riley (1971, p. 81) suggests that the analogy "points to the utility of exploring relationships both between and within age strata." She argues that "people's positive or negative feelings and actions toward each other are channeled through the age structure of the particular society. Thus a sociology of age stratification." Riley utilizes the caregiving relationship between generations as an example. She suggests that if we are to understand the elderly, we must examine society as being age differentiated. Different age strata have different experiences and expectations. With regard to material caregiving, she notes that support is sequential rather than reciprocal, that is, the parent generation giving to the children. Elderly should not view the lack of material support from their children as a sign of disrespect. Rather, such behavior is indicative of intergenerational support patterns.

The third question concerns the mobility of individuals as they progress from one age stratum to the next. Riley argues that although similarities exist between age and social mobility, they are still rather distinct concepts. In particular, she points out that social mobility occurs among a select category of the population. That is, not all members of a society will move up or down the social class ladder. However, age mobility is "universal, unidirectional, and irreversible" (Riley, 1971, p. 83).

The fourth question is a compilation of the preceding questions. If the first three questions can be answered, what impact will they have on society? Society is continually influenced by the changes brought about by one age cohort from another. It is instructive to remember that age strata reflect variation in experience and expectation. As Riley states, "changes in societal age strata can be interpreted as the shifting composite of cohorts who, themselves affected by differing historical backgrounds, have aged in different ways" (1971, p. 85).

Again, ask yourself the following questions regarding social stratification theory. Is this an appropriate theory in attempting to address the number of homeless elderly living in your community? If social stratification theory is appropriate, which research design would you utilize?

The Political Economy of Aging

Most appropriately, we began this section by examining the emergence of theoretical frameworks as explanations of the aging process. We will complete this section by discussing one of the more recent frameworks.

The *political economy of aging* has its origins in conflict theory. This perspective examines aging as occurring within an economic and political context. As such, it "emphasizes the broad implications of economic life for the aged and for society's treatment of the elderly. . . . [It assumes] that old age can only be understood in the context of problems and issues of the larger social order" (Estes, 1991, p. 19). According to this perspective, we need to look beyond aging as a cause of societal problems and conditions and instead examine aging as a consequence of institutional structures and an unequal distribution of power. The process of aging is interconnected with the broader features of society such as the state, social class, and gender (Estes, 1991). The political economy of aging draws on a number of intellectual sources in an attempt to better understand the societal as well as individual treatment of the aging population.

As an example of the intellectual diversity involved in this perspective, recall the discussion of the historical view of aging in America in Chapter 2. According to numerous authors, the elderly have been considered a social problem in the United States throughout the 20th century. Explanations exist regarding why the elderly were viewed with such little regard. One plausible answer would identify a series of economic changes that occurred during the time period under investigation. That is, the elderly changed from productive workers within society to a nonproductive status because of institutionalized retirement. The workforce also changed from self-employed to working for someone else. As a result, the worker (and eventually the older worker) lost (primarily) his or her decision-making independence. This was even more problematic for an aging female population. Denied access to the work environment, particularly the primary labor market, women suffered a dual economic hardship. On the one hand, they received less pay than their male counterparts (and still do), and when then could retire they received less because of their earnings.

If a woman remained in the home, she was dependent on the male's retirement income. An expected outcome is that as elderly women get older (and more likely to be widowed), their poverty rate increases.

In addition to a structural analysis of aging, the political economy perspective attempts to understand how labels are created and attached to the elderly. These labels generally convey a negative image of the elderly (we will address the issue of image in much greater detail in Chapter 4). One persistent label today concerns the economic position of the elderly. Once viewed as poor, the current image portrays the elderly as relatively well off and enjoying "the good life" while younger generations suffer economic hardships. These images, which are socially created, negatively affect the elderly. Such an image "homogenizes" the elderly rather than portraying their diversity (Minkler, 1991). The political economy of aging, then, examines the social, political, economic, and historical contexts within which aging occurs. It is within such contexts that we fully understand how the aging process is constructed within a society.

According to Estes (1991, p. 31), the following are basic to the political economy of aging:

- The social structure shapes how older individuals are perceived and how they perceive themselves, affecting their sense of worth and power.
- Attributional labels applied to the elderly not only shape the experience of old age, but also societal decisions concerning public policy for the elderly.
- Social policy and the politics of aging mirror the inequalities in social structure and the outcomes of power struggles around those structured arrangements. As such, policy is neither neutral nor quixotic; it reflects the advantage and disadvantage of capital and labor, whites and nonwhites, and men and women in society.
- Social policy reflects the dominant ideologies and belief systems that enforce, bolster, and extend the structure of advantage and disadvantage in the larger economic, political, and social order.

How would the political economy of aging address the issue of homeless elderly living in your community? What research design would be appropriate with this perspective? What kinds of questions would you ask if you used this perspective compared to other perspectives?

Critical Connection: What We Believe Is What We See

What was your answer to the number of homeless elderly living in the downtown area of your community? How did you arrive at that answer? Naturally you applied a theory or a number of theories in order to construct an answer. Now that you can answer why there are homeless elderly living in your community, take another look at them. Describe them. What adjectives do you employ in your description? Now that you can "see" these elderly in their particular circumstance, you begin to attach labels to them. It is now much easier to pick out one of these individuals and say that whatever characteristics you attach to that person now apply to all of them. Congratulations! You now understand the concept of stereotyping. Theories provide the framework around which we construct our beliefs and (eventual) responses to people.

Earlier we had stated that neither your nor my interpretation of this phenomenon is correct. But then we qualified that by supposing that I was the mayor. Although my interpretation does not become any more correct, it may be granted greater legitimacy. If we label these homeless elderly as a social problem to the community, they will be defined and treated as a problem. The "social problem" of aging then is socially constructed by those with the economic and political power to make the label stick.

Now, how did we arrive at our interpretation of the homeless elderly? Where did we gather the information that shaped my thought processes and eventual decision? To begin, we have been influenced by various agents of socialization as well as the social structure of society. Thus the influence of others shapes not only our sense of self but our perception of others as well. Chapter 4 examines these key elements of the aging process.

Chapter Review

Throughout this chapter we have been addressing questions of theoretical content and application. As a result, the need for additional questions here is limited.

1. Compare and contrast the functionalist argument with that of conflict theory.
2. Briefly explain how each of the following theories would explain the homeless elderly in your community.

Functionalism	Conflict
Interactionism	Exchange
Disengagement	Activity
Subculture	Continuity
Social breakdown/competence	Social stratification
Political economy	

3. You have received a $1 million grant to study nursing home residents (who are primarily elderly). Construct a hypothesis and identify the research design you would use and the theoretical argument that will frame your research and assist in analyzing your findings. You can recycle this question by creating a new scenario.

Glossary

Activity theory   This theoretical perspective argues that one's age, level of activity, and level of life satisfaction are interrelated. In essence, as we age we attempt to sustain a level of activity consistent with the past. The ability to do so increases our level of life satisfaction.

Conflict theory   With roots in the work of Karl Marx, this perspective argues that conflict between groups with competing interests is inevitable. A consequence is economic and political inequality understood through such concepts as social class and alienation.

Continuity theory   This perspective argues that we attempt to maintain consistent patterns of activity throughout our lifetime. According to its proponents, we do so through the use of internal and external continuity.

Disengagement theory   A functionalist argument, this perspective argues that as we age there is an inevitable, mutual, and universal disengagement between the individual and society. Activity levels are reduced and life satisfaction declines. It is argued that life satisfaction will increase, however, once a new equilibrium is established.

Exchange theory   An outgrowth of behavioral psychology and classical economics, this perspective suggests that behavior is dependent on a variation of previous outcomes and potential rewards. Behavior occurs as a result of negotiation between actors.

Functionalism   Considered the oldest theoretical perspective, functionalism is based on an interrelationship of components that operate to maintain equilibrium. In addition to the key concept of function, structure and equilibrium are also important.

Interactionism   This theoretical perspective is built on mediated meanings that arise out of an interactive process between actors and the society in which they live.

Political economy of aging   Grounded in the conflict tradition, this approach suggests that the institutional structures of society construct the context within which aging is evaluated.

Social breakdown/competence   A variation on the symbolic interactionist perspective, this approach argues that the loss of normative evaluations of self with age creates a cycle of personal despair and structural dislocation. An infusion of external inputs creates the conditions within which the elderly assume control over circumstances that affect their life.

Social stratification theory   This perspective argues that age stratification can be examined through the use of concepts understood in social stratification. These concepts are social class and mobility.

Sociological theory   A systematic process for the purpose of explaining social phenomena.

Subculture theory   Established within the interactionist perspective, this approach argues that the elderly are a subculture because of their close affiliation with other elderly and because the elderly are, to an extent, excluded from interactions with others.

Suggested Reading

There are a number of books that devote some segment to one theory or a number of theories of aging. The following books provide an introduction to the topic. Many of these readings are the primary source of the theory.

Bengtson, V. L. (1973). *The social psychology of aging.* Indianapolis: Bobbs-Merrill.
A very short, readable book. Bengtson outlines the social breakdown syndrome and the social reconstruction syndrome from earlier work. He also discusses disengagement theory and activity theory.

Birren, J. E., & Bengtson, V. L. (Eds.). (1988). *Emergent theories in aging.* New York: Springer.
The chapter by Passuth and Bengtson is particularly relevant. The authors construct the relationship between sociological theories and sociological theories of aging.

Cumming, E., & Henry, W. (1961). *Growing old.* New York: Basic Books.
This is the book that formally introduced theory to the sociology of aging. This is "must reading" for anyone interested in aging.

Havighurst, R. J., & Albrecht, R. (1953). *Older people.* New York: Longman's, Green.
A pivotal work in the establishment of activity theory. Although predating Growing Old, *it is not a formalized construction of the theoretical perspective. It is also "must reading" for those interested in aging.*

Kart, C. S., & Manard, B. B. (Eds.). (1981). *Aging in America* (2nd ed.). Sherman Oaks, CA: Alfred.
Part 1 of this book offers a number of theoretical perspectives from the original sources. Don't overlook the rest of the book, either.

Minkler, M., & Estes, C. L. (Eds.). (1991). *Critical perspectives on aging: The political and moral economy of growing old.* Amityville, NY: Baywood.

Chapter 2 provides an excellent coverage of the political economy of aging. Although other books exist, this is one of the most recent and covers a number of related areas.

Riley, M. W., Johnson, M., & Foner, A. (1972). *Aging and society, volume three: A sociology of age stratification.* New York: Russell Sage.

As the title suggests, this book provides the conceptual framework for the development of age stratification theory.

Rose, A. M., & Peterson, W. A. (Eds.). (1965). *Older people and their social world.* Philadelphia: F. A. Davis.

The chapter by Arnold Rose called "Subculture of Aging: A Framework for Research in Social Gerontology" established the framework for the subculture perspective.

References

Atchley, R. C. (1989). A continuity theory of normal aging. *Gerontologist, 29*(2), 183–190.

Bengtson, V. L. (1973). *The social psychology of aging.* Indianapolis: Bobbs-Merrill.

Blumer, H. (1969). *Symbolic interactionism: Perspectives and method.* Englewood Cliffs, NJ: Prentice-Hall.

Cavan, R. S., Burgess, E. W., Havighurst, R. J., & Goldhamer, H. (1949). *Personal adjustments in old age.* Chicago: Science Research Associates.

Craib, I. (1992). *Modern social theory.* New York: St. Martin's.

Cumming, E., Dean, L. R., Newell, D. S., & McCaffrey, I. (1960). Disengagement—A tentative theory of aging. *Sociometry, 23,* 23–35.

Cumming, E., & Henry, W. (1961). *Growing old.* New York: Basic Books.

Dowd, J. J. (1975). Aging as exchange: A preface to theory. *Journal of Gerontology, 30*(5), 584–594.

Estes, C. L. (1991). The new political economy of aging: Introduction and critique. In M. Minkler & C. L. Estes (Eds.), *Critical perspectives on aging: The political and moral economy of growing old.* Amityville, NY: Baywood.

Estes, C. L., Wallace, S. P., & Binney, E. A. (1989). Health, aging, and medical sociology. In H. E. Freeman & S. Levine (Eds.), *Handbook of medical sociology* (4th ed.). Englewood Cliffs, NJ: Prentice Hall.

Fox, J. H. (1981–1982). Perspectives on the continuity perspective. *International Journal of Aging and Human Development, 14*(2), 97–115.

Havighurst, R. J. (1968, Spring). Personality patterns of aging. *The Gerontologist, 8*(1), Part II, 20–23.

Havighurst, R. J., & Albrecht, R. (1953). *Older people.* New York: Longman's, Green.

Hendricks, J. (1992). Generations and the generation of theory in social gerontology. *International Journal of Aging and Human Development, 35*(1), 31–47.

Hochschild, A. R. (1975, October). Disengagement theory: A critique and proposal. *American Sociological Review, 40,* 553–569.

Homans, G. C. (1974). *Social behavior: Its elementary forms* (rev. ed.). New York: Harcourt Brace Jovanovich.

Khullar, G., & Reynolds, B. C. (1990, Spring). Quality of life and activity: A test of the activity-versus-disengagement theories. *International Review of Modern Sociology, 20,* 33–68.

Kinloch, G. C. (1977). *Sociological theory: Its development and major paradigms.* New York: McGraw-Hill.

Kuypers, J. A., & Bengtson, V. L. (1973). Social breakdown and competence. *Human Development, 16,* 181–201.

Lemon, B. W., Bengtson, V. L., & Peterson, J. A. (1972). An exploration of the activity theory of aging: Activity types and life satisfaction among in-movers to a retirement community. *Journal of Gerontology, 27*(4), 511–523.

Longino, C. F., & Kart, C. S. (1982). Explicating activity theory: A formal replication. *Journal of Gerontology, 37*(6), 713–722.

Mannheim, K. (1952). The problem of generations. In P. Kecskemeti (Ed. and Trans.), *Essays on the society of knowledge.* London: Routlege & Kegan Paul.

Matcha, D. A. (1985). *Determinants of disengagement among nursing home residents.* Unpublished doctoral dissertation, Purdue University, West Lafayette, Indiana.

McClelland, K. A. (1982). Self-conception and life satisfaction: Integrating aged subculture and activity theory. *Journal of Gerontology, 37*(6), 723–732.

McPherson, B. D. (1990). *Aging as a social process* (2nd ed.). Toronto: Butterworths.

Merton, R. K. (1967). *On theoretical sociology.* New York: The Free Press.

Minkler, M. (1991). Overview. In M. Minkler & C. L. Estes (Eds.), *Critical perspectives on aging: The political and moral economy of growing old.* Amityville, NY: Baywood.

Passuth, P. M., & Bengtson, V. L. (1988). Sociological theories of aging: Current perspectives and future directions. In J. E. Birren & V. L. Bengtson (Eds.), *Emergent theories of aging.* New York: Springer.

Riley, M. W. (1971, Spring). Social gerontology and the age stratification of society. *Gerontologist, 11,* 79–87.

Riley, M. W., Johnson, M., & Foner, A. (1972). *Aging and society, volume three: A sociology of age stratification.* New York: Russell Sage.

Ritzer, G. (1988). *Sociological theory* (2nd ed.). New York: Alfred A. Knopf.

Rose, A. M. (1965). The subculture of the aging: A framework for research in social gerontology. In A. M. Rose & W. A. Peterson (Eds.), *Older people and their social world.* Philadelphia: F. A. Davis.

Skidmore, W. (1979). *Theoretical thinking in sociology* (2nd ed.). London: Cambridge University Press.

Turner, J. H. (1978). *The structure of sociological theory* (rev. ed.). Homewood, IL: Dorsey.

Turner, J. H. (1991). *The structure of sociological theory* (5th ed.). Belmont, CA: Wadsworth.

Turner, J. H., Beeghley, L., & Powers, C. H. (1989). *The emergence of sociological theory* (2nd ed.). Belmont, CA: Wadsworth.

Zusman, J. (1966). Some explanations of the changing appearance of psychotic patients: Antecedents of the social breakdown syndrome concept. *Milbank Memorial Fund Quarterly, 64,* 363–394.

Chapter *4*

Society, Socialization, and Stereotypes

Age affects which roles are open or closed to an individual, and which social networks and cultural norms will offer certain opportunities or impose certain demands. Age is built into the changing organization of institutions and roles through expectations of how roles are to be performed, and through sanctions for role performance.

—RILEY & RILEY, 1986, P. 57

We are constantly being influenced by the images, words, and behaviors of the world around us. At times, however, we become oblivious to the nuances of a television commercial, an advertisement in the newspaper, or the suggestion of another person. We engage in such behavior because it is impossible to absorb all of the information that bombards us on a regular basis. We also filter out that which we consider irrelevant, unimportant, or possibly disturbing to our sense of self. Although we like to consider ourselves individuals who are unique in development and character, who we are and what we do is constantly being shaped by the structural forces that exist in our temporal social context. For example, consider for a moment your daily routine. Although we are all individuals in the sense that we have a name and biography distinct from others, our behavior and our attitudes are influenced by a myriad of social elements. How have family members influenced your beliefs? How have the media shaped your taste in music? What do you know about growing old? Where did you learn respect or contempt toward older people?

The first three chapters discussed the process of growing old within a variety of different contexts. For example, we can study aging as a specific age category that can be researched or from which sociological theories can be constructed. We also know that aging exists within a historical context. This chapter, however, examines aging in relation to the society in which we live.

The Structure of Society

All societies are constructed within a framework consisting of a number of basic elements. The purpose of structure is to ensure that the society functions in a manner consistent with the expectations of members at that juncture of its historical and social development.

Consider the following example.

Suppose you lived in a society in which all members believed in complete individualism with no ties to anyone else. Because of this belief, all work necessary for individual survival would be conducted by each individual. Who would do what? Who would pick up your trash on Wednesday morning, or deliver the morning newspaper, or drive the metro bus? How would such a society function?

Such a society could not last because it lacks the basic rules and structure necessary for simple human survival. There is nothing wrong with being an individual. We need to remember, however, that individuals live in a society that consists of rules that regulate how we behave and what we eventually come to believe. All of this structure is influenced by such criteria as income, education, and age. Social structure will evolve historically depending on the particular characteristics of the population. The following concepts provide a blueprint as we try to understand the structure of society and how we fit into its construction.

Roles

By definition, *roles* are expectations of behavior in relation to others. Kando (1977, p. 9) states that a "role refers to a pattern of behavior that is linked to a particular social position." The problem with roles is that they are always in the process of change. That is, role relationships are dynamic. My role relative to you today may be different tomorrow. Additionally, the expectations associated with a particular role undergo societal reevaluation. When my spouse and I were married, we were going to live what we thought to be the "typical" family life with four children, a Cape Cod home with a white picket fence, a station wagon in the driveway, and a dog named Spot. I would be the sole breadwinner and she would stay home, performing the expressive roles. In reality, we have two children, live in a California ranch, and are both deeply committed to our academic careers. What happened? Role opportunities changed and we changed the performance of our roles.

More specific to this book, how do roles apply to aging? What expectations are placed on someone who is older? What roles are available? Is old age a "roleless role," as suggested by Burgess (1960, p. 20)? The answer to this last question is no. Although the elderly may not have as many roles available to them as in their earlier years, roles do exist. The reason that the availability of roles diminishes with age is, to a great extent, a function of society's withdrawing opportunities for role involvement or the elderly person's voluntarily withdrawing from a particular role performance. Often an older person would welcome continued involvement but is denied the access by others because of age. This is not to suggest that all elderly want to remain active in previous roles as they age. Rather, the point here is that the elderly should be accorded the same privilege as other age groups by being allowed to decide which roles they wish to engage in and the level of their involvement. Such mutuality would reduce the dependence of the elderly on others because it provides the elderly an opportunity to make decisions that affect their lives and to do so on their own terms.

Status

According to Rosow (1974, p. 2) there are "seven major institutional factors [that] govern the status of older people in all societies." They include (1) property ownership, (2) strategic knowledge, (3) productivity, (4) mutual dependence, (5) tradition and religion, (6) kinship and family, and (7) community life (Rosow, 1974, pp. 3–7). *Status* refers to a position that one occupies in society. There are two types of statuses: ascribed and achieved. According to Kammeyer, Ritzer, and Yetman (1994, p. 96), "an *ascribed status* is one into which individuals move or are placed, irrespective of their efforts or capacities. . . . In contrast, an *achieved status* is one that people acquire through their own efforts." Relative to the aging process, the distinction is particularly important. Chronological age is an ascribed status. A volunteer at the local hospital, a Ph.D. candidate, and a voluntarily retired person are all examples of an achieved status. These are positions that the individuals acquired through their efforts. However, notice how a potentially achieved status can change to an ascribed status. If a person is dismissed from a job at the age of 64, one year prior to voluntary retirement (an achieved status), the person is now unemployed (an ascribed status). Too often the elderly are moved by others into a status (such as nursing home resident) that they either do not want or do not need. Particularly within American culture, removal from the status of worker places the individual in an unproductive status. The consequence is dependency. Walker (1982, p. 121) argues that "political, financial and to a large extent physical dependency are a function of the social organisation and distribution of resources, status and power."

Groups

Within sociology, the concept of group is of particular importance. A *group* can be defined as "two or more people who interact with other members of the group over an extended period of time, forming more or less ordered and lasting relationships" (Kerbo, 1989, p. 115). One's family is the classic example of a (primary) group. In addition, we establish membership in groups at work, at social organizations (referred to as secondary groups), and through our religious affiliation, to name a few. Maintenance of group membership is crucial for the well-being of the elderly. Because the significance of group membership for the elderly will be explored beginning in Chapter 5, we will briefly address the issue here. Unfortunately, if the elderly are denied status opportunities because of age, membership in current or potentially new groups is lost. Thus the elderly become victims of a social structure that limits their social and economic opportunities and defines the nature of their relationships with others. This brings us to our final concept establishing social structure, that of institutions.

Institutions

By definition, an *institution* refers to "a system of statuses, roles, groups, and behavioral patterns that satisfies a basic human need and is necessary for the survival of a society" (Doob, 1991, p. 98). The basic social institutions include the family, the educational system, the economic and political systems, health care, and religion. Each one is constructed from the unique cultural imperatives as well as the social structure of a society (Kerbo, 1989). One could say that the characteristics of an institution at a given point in time reflect the nature of the society in which they are located. How do these social institutions relate to the elderly? The social institutions of the family, economics, and the political system directly affect the work opportunities of the elderly. We will address the role of these institutions in considerable detail in subsequent chapters. For now, a brief example is presented. We are all members of some family of orientation (the family we are born into) and possibly a member of a family of procreation (the family we create). As we grow older, our position (status), relative to other members in the family, will change. And, as a result, so will our roles. For example, the structure of society directly affects the aging process. As a society, one of our central values is that of work (the economic institution). We provide the elderly an opportunity to retire and collect whatever private pensions they have established. In addition, the political institution provides economic benefits in the form of Social Security. However, there is a growing belief among younger members of society that after contributing a substantial amount of money, they will be left with very little in the Social Security program. Thus intergenerational conflicts (the institution of the family) are of increasing concern to the elderly and to those who study this process.

Institutional consequences of growing older are already evident in our society. The elderly are accorded a lower status because of their age, the roles available to them are limited, and although institutional support exists, it is decreasing. How have we (as a society) developed such negative attitudes and behavior about aging and those experiencing the process? To answer this question we need to examine one of the most basic concepts in sociology: socialization.

The Influence of Society

Socialization Over the Life Span

Socialization is the process of creating a social being from a biological being. This process begins at birth and ends with the death of the individual. Throughout one's life, significant others define for us the norms, values, and roles that are considered central to what we believe and do. Eventually, as we incorporate these norms and values in our life, we transmit what we have come to believe to others. We also learn to believe and act on the basis of this information. This does not mean that we cannot change, because we do. It implies that socialization creates a framework within which we learn to function. These significant others that define the socialization process are referred to as agents of socialization. Some agents of socialization include the family, the religious community, the educational system, and the media.

Briefly, socialization occurs as others respond to and evaluate us on the basis of our ascribed statuses such as sex and age or achieved statuses such as college graduate or retiree. The expectations and attitudes of others toward us on the basis of some position we occupy provide a basis for a self-evaluation of who we are. Throughout the process of interaction, we learn the norms and values of others. It is within this continued social interaction that we construct a sense of *self.* According to Charon (1985, p. 66), "the self is an object that the actor acts toward." The self emerges through the interaction process and the evaluations of others. An example of this process is the socialization to old age that occurs throughout one's lifetime. The self consists of two components: the *I* and the *me.* The I is the impulsive, creative part of self. It is the part of self that Atchley (1987, p. 68) refers to as "the entity that is aware of its own existence and the world around it." On the other hand, the me is "what I think and feel about myself as the object of my own attention" (Atchley, 1987, p. 68).

The agents of socialization are a significant influence in the development of self and the image that is created throughout the socialization process. For example, consider how the media portray the elderly. What words exist in your vocabulary that are derogatory of the elderly? What are the first three words in your mind when you hear the word *old?* When I ask students in class if they would like to be 60, 70, or 80 years old they invariable say no because of what they believe to be true of older people. All of this has to do with the development of attitudes. Basically, an *attitude* refers to a liking or disliking of someone or something. Historically, the attitude of younger people toward the elderly had been reported to be negative. More recent research indicates an increasingly positive attitude (Aday, Simms, & Evans, 1991; Austin, 1985; Barrow, 1989). However, many have already been socialized to those qualities they believe constitute old age. If, throughout life, a person is continually presented with a negative image of growing old, then that person will likely believe that of his or her own aging process (Estes, 1979). Unfortunately, as people accept the stereotypes that are constructed, they will behave accordingly as they age (Furstenberg, 1989). The consequence is a reinforcement of the aged stereotypes that exist within society. It is to this influence of society that we now turn.

Stereotypes of Aging: A Consequence

How Stereotypes Are Defined

How often have you heard the phrase "you drive like an old person"? What does that mean? How do "older people" drive compared to those in your age category? Do they all drive the same? If you are a young adult, should we assume that you drive the same way as other young adults? In particular, if you are a young adult male, should we stay off the highway because all young adult males are drunk drivers? You would probably say that that is unfair, that I am *stereotyping* you (and you are right). In other words, stereotypes are "exaggerations of reality that are applied to entire groups of people" (Levin, 1989, p. 81). How did you arrive at the stereotype regarding the driving habits of older people? Did you conduct research or read the research findings of others? Or was this the outcome of personal observation of a few elderly drivers when you were in a hurry? Regardless of the circumstance, we develop stereotypes of others. Unfortunately for those labeled, it is not what they have done as much as it is what those attaching the stereotype believe. The question is, How can we construct such negative evaluations without empirical support? Estes, Swan, and Gerard (1984, p. 25) provide an explanation:

> The conceptualization of old age, as well as the potential of the aged for securing power are "socially" created in that they are not determined solely by objective facts. Rather, they are created by: (1) the interpretation and ordering of perceptions of those facts into paradigms; and (2) the power and influence of the perceivers and interpreters of the data.

How Stereotypes Are Constructed and Perpetuated

It should be obvious by now that stereotypes can be insidious constructs that reinforce a negative evaluation of some category of the population. Stereotypes can provide an exaggerated and deceptively simple image of the population they characterize. Often stereotypes are constructed out of a generalized ignorance and misguided fear. For example, the elderly are often stereotyped because they are living reminders of our own mortality (Brigham, 1986). Stereotyping all elderly as frail and physically and mentally incompetent provides for an age-based comparison of ability. That is, if being old means that which has been created from the stereotype, then being younger represents a lack of those qualities. How are stereotypes perpetuated? If stereotypes represent images that are not only negative but false, why do they continue? From the perspective of Brubaker and Powers (1976), stereotypes represent the subjective conditions of one's past development as well as objective indicators as significant indexes of how old age will be viewed. Brubaker and Powers (1976) developed a model depicting the variables involved and the linkages between them that eventually result in stereotyping of the elderly. Their model is presented in Figure 4–1.

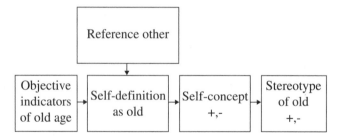

FIGURE 4–1   Stereotyping the Elderly: A Model
Source: Brubaker, T. H., & Powers, E. A. (1976). The stereotype of "old": A review and alternative approach. *Journal of Gerontology, 31*(4), 441–447. Copyright © The Gerontological Association of America.

Relative to their model, Brubaker and Powers (1976, p. 445) believe the following:

1. Aged persons who have a more positive stereotype of old age will not have a negative self-concept if they subjectively define themselves as old.
2. Objective indicators of the aged status influence subjective definitions of oneself as old. . . . The loss of certain roles (worker or husband) and the acquisition of others (retiree or grandfather) are indicators that he is no longer young or middle-aged.
3. A subjective self-definition as old does not necessarily result in a negative stereotype of old age or negative self-concept. The self-concept formed at an earlier age determines whether negative or positive stereotype of old age is accepted . . . whether the person accepts positive or negative elements of the stereotypes of old age depends upon the previous self-concept. If an individual's self-concept has been positive, positive elements of the stereotype of old will be accepted and the individual will hold a positive self-concept. If the previous self-concept was negative, negative elements of the stereotype of old will be accepted and thereby produce a negative self-definition.

Although significant, such an argument does not adequately address the role of society in relation to our belief in and use of stereotypes. This is what Comfort (1976, p. 9) would refer to as sociogenic aging, or "the role which society imposes on people as they reach a certain chronological age." This argument will be addressed in the following section on power.

The Influence of Power

Who is most likely to engage in the use of stereotypes? Think of this question in terms of power. Remember that, broadly speaking, power is the ability to get someone to do something he or she would rather not do. If you do not have power or access to it, are you likely to construct and use stereotypes? Probably not. Rather, a person with the power to apply a stereotype and make it "stick" to someone else would be a more likely candidate. As Vander Zanden (1987, p. 438) states, "power decides which party will be able to translate its social values into the accepted standards for defining situations, and which can make these standards stick through the manipulation of rewards and the imposition of penalties." If we have power, we do not need to learn about others but only to respond to what we believe to be true about them. Consider some popular stereotypes of the elderly; slow, forgetful, senile, asexual. How many exist about young people, the poor, minorities, or women? How many stereotypes can you think of that apply to the middle class, the wealthy, or those in positions of power? Although stereotypes may exist, they do not "stick" the same way when applied by the less powerful.

Power is significant because of the initial unequal relationship that creates the conditions for outcome differentials. This differential reinforces the inequality between actors. If a person has power over another because of status or resources, then the less powerful are vulnerable to the demands and expectations of the powerful. This is of particular consequence if the person with power engages in the use of stereotypes to assert control. For example, if a person believes that the medical community is wasting health care dollars on the elderly (who have lived, in their mind, a full life), that person may attempt to reallocate the distribution of funds or influence public policy using age as the criteria. Power exists within a variety of contexts. We will examine three areas within which power influences our use of stereotypes. These areas include economic power, political power, and the media.

Economic   Applied to the elderly, the concept of economic power is particularly significant. Many elderly find themselves in a precarious position because of their dependency on others for economic survival. This reliance creates an unequal relationship that places the elderly person and his or her needs at the discretion of others. Stereotyping occurs when those with economic power attach negative labels to the elderly and the aging process. Because of a structured dependency between the elderly and the economic system, the issue of cost and accountability arises. A classic example of this relationship involves the continuing treatment of the elderly as a social problem within the larger society (Arber & Ginn, 1991; Estes, 1979). Beginning in the 1930s with the emergence of Social Security, the federal government symbolically assumed a degree of social responsibility toward the elderly. Moving forward, the advent of social programs in the 1960s defined the elderly as in need of assistance from various levels of government through programs established to "help" them (Estes, 1979), thus establishing the stereotype of a dependent aging population. Throughout this period, the relationship between the elderly and the government was paternalistic, with the elderly assumed to be a homogeneous category of the population. The Social Security "crisis" of the 1970s questioned the viability of the system for future generations. Blame for the potential insolvency of the Social Security system was placed on the elderly. The aged population was stereotyped as increasingly well-off financially and at the expense of younger generations (Butler, 1990). The compassionate stereotype of the elderly as being poor and in need of assistance had changed. The elderly were now stereotyped as wealthy, politically powerful, and continuing to cost society even more (Binstock, 1983, 1984).

The emergence of the 1980s witnessed another intergenerational issue: health care costs. The amount of health care dollars spent on the elderly during their last year of life is consistently identified as one of the main reasons for rising health care costs (Fuchs, 1984). In addition, chronological age has become the basis for determining social and economic worth. Avorn (1984, p. 1297), analyzing issues of productivity and cost-benefit analysis, states that the human-capital approach would argue that "it is not cost effective to implement programs that care for the elderly." According to the human-capital argument, the economic worth of males and females by chronological age drops precipitously beginning around age 60 (Avorn, 1984, p. 1297, citing Dolan et al., 1980). The issue of cost is also raised by Callahan (1986, p. 327–328), who questions, "What is the proper—or at least the acceptable—proportion of public resources that should be devoted to the elderly, both in relationship to the health needs of other age groups and to other social requirements as a whole?" Relative to economic power, this is a particularly interesting question. Callahan uses the term *public resources,* suggesting that if one is capable of paying through the private sector, the issue is moot. Secondly, what other category of the population has been singled out and questioned regarding its use of the health care system? Should (could) we add low-birth-weight babies in this category? Perhaps victims of violent crimes who do not have health insurance? What about young people who drink and drive, causing death and injury to others?

If growing older can be placed within such a negative context (that is, associating aging with the economic problems plaguing the nation), negative stereotyping of the aging process will continue to be a problem. Unfortunately, as has been demonstrated, this argument has support. Those with the power define the economic opportunities (and potential stereotypes) for the elderly and the future.

Political   The use of political power is best illustrated in an article by Slava Lubomudrov (1987). The author conducted a content analysis of specific congressional committee and subcommittee hearings and the congressional record. The purpose of the research was to "ascertain whether the senator's or representative's image of the aging, conveyed by his or her statement or speech, expressed only stereotypes about the aging or whether it conveyed information that did not overgeneralize or stereotype the elderly" (Lubomudrov, 1987, p. 78). The senators and representatives engaged in the use of compassionate or negative stereotypes as well as the more recent misperceptions identified as positive stereotypes. Lubomudrov found that legislators who were members of select committees addressing issues relevant to the elderly were less likely to include stereotypes in their statements or speeches. If they made stereotypic statements, they were more likely to be of the compassionate (or negative) type identified earlier by Binstock (1983). Thus, according to Lubomudrov (1987, p. 80), "political support for the aging appears greatest among legislators who express misperceptions about the aging." This study suggests that those in positions of political power exercise that power without being fully aware of the constituents they are supporting. Lack of knowledge of one's constituents can have negative repercussions. In 1988 Congress passed legislation, which was ultimately signed by President Reagan, that authorized sweeping changes in Medicare. This legislation was the Medicare Catastrophic Care Act (MCCA). Essentially, the act "was intended to reduce the potential for financial ruin in the event of a 'catastrophic' illness for an individual on Medicare" (Street, 1993, p. 435). Although initially supported by various interest groups and some senior citizen organizations, the act was repealed in less than a year and a half. Various explanations exist as to why the act did not receive the expected support. Street (1993), in a comprehensive examination of the act and its history, provides an explanation: "For the first time, the cost of Medicare coverage was based on a person's income. This was intolerable to a segment of the elderly population—precisely the segment of the elderly population whose resources and backgrounds were conducive to political mobilization, and who would have to pay—and was the catalyst to their opposition of MCCA" (Street, 1993, p. 440). This change from support to nonsupport demonstrates the increasing diversity of the aging population within the United States. Essentially, upper-middle-class and upper-class elderly would have provided payment for support of this legislation. Such social class differences illustrate "that not all the elderly are represented in one powerful and forceful constituency" (Torres-Gill, 1992, p. 84).

Media   The power of the media to engage in aged stereotyping is evident. Current television programming involving elderly actors and actresses is virtually nonexistent when compared to other age categories. And the roles that do exist perpetuate the stereotypic images of the elderly. However, what exists today is considered an improvement from even the last decade (Bell, 1992). From a list established by the Gray Panthers, Davis and Davis (1985) identify some of the stereotypic characteristics to look for in television programming. These characteristics include the following:

> *Appearance:* The face is blank and expressionless, and the body is always bent over and infirm.
>
> *Clothing:* Ill-fitting garments.
>
> *Speech:* Halting and high pitched.
>
> *Personality:* The dominant characteristics are stubbornness, rigidity, and forgetfulness. The "rocking chair" image predominates. (Davis & Davis, 1985, p. 56)

Media research on the elderly over the past 20 years has produced rather mixed findings that are more negative than positive (Vasil & Wass, 1993). For example, the elderly are underrepresented in prime time television, and when depicted they are given stereotypic roles. In addition, elderly women experienced two negative stereotypes (one for being elderly and one for being female) (Vasil & Wass, 1993). Beyond prime time, Elliot (1984) explored the extent to which the elderly were portrayed in daily soap operas. The percentage of roles available to elderly actors and actresses were minimal. Elliot also reported gender differences in television programming. For example, "older males are more likely than older females to engage in the behaviors of looking and listening, making statements, and problem solving. Older females are more likely to be nurturant and to be verbally aggressive" (Elliot, 1984, p. 631).

Another component of television programming is that of Saturday morning cartoons. Again, the extent to which the elderly are portrayed is minimal. Bishop and Krause (1984, p. 93) reported that the elderly are not central characters, and that "remarks [made during the cartoon] generally reflect the dominant stereotypes of American society about aging and old age."

The ability of the media to construct images that others (such as lawmakers) accept gives incredible power to the media, particularly television. We have also come full circle. We began this chapter with an assumption that we are influenced by the world around us. We have taken a quick look at that world and realized the significant impact it has on what we see and what we believe about what we see. Without realizing it, we often construct images of others from fragmented and incomplete pictures given to us in the course of our daily interaction.

Stereotyping the Elderly

Positive Outcomes   After reading this chapter it may seem difficult to believe, but stereotypes can produce positive images. Earlier, Lubomudrov (1987) identified a number of positive stereotypes of the elderly used by members of Congress. Binstock (1983) identified the emergence of "positive" stereotypes of the elderly beginning in the later 1970s. These stereotypes developed largely in reaction to the earlier compassionate stereotypes that had been used to portray the elderly. As a conscientious student of the sociology of aging, remember that a positive stereotype is still a stereotype. When the elderly today are stereotyped as being well-off financially, others, such as legislators, are potentially affected. Legislators utilize images that have been constructed for them as they engage in decision making. A result of their positive stereotype may be to increase the cost paid by the elderly toward the maintenance of programs such as Medicare (because the image is one of elderly who are financially capable of paying more). Such action negatively affects the financial resources of many elderly. Thus the use of positive stereotypes does not address the fundamental problem of ageism in our society. Justification of the use of stereotypes on the argument that they are positive is to remain ignorant of the consequences of such behavior. As long as we continue to treat people differentially on the basis of age, we will not move beyond the stereotypic impressions that we construct as a result.

Negative Outcomes   When a segment of the population is stereotyped, the negative outcomes are particularly devastating. On the individual level, one's sense of self is questioned. Who we are is construed by others as of less value because of our chronological age. It is perhaps little wonder that we do not look forward to decade birthdays because they signify our placement within that decade and, thus, as being older. We carry with us the socialization process and realize the negative evaluations constructed earlier and wonder if they now apply to us (Walker, 1990). As Arber and Ginn (1991, p. 35) point out, "the stereotyping of elderly people profoundly affects the way they are perceived and consequently treated, both at the societal level and as individuals in everyday interactions." On the societal level, negative stereotyping creates an inequality between categories of the population. Negative stereotyping creates a *definition of the situation* of the aging process for the elderly. That is, what they (the elderly) define as real (being older and fitting the negative stereotype) is real in its consequences. The consequence is an acceptance of the stereotypes and the concomitant behavior. The influence of negative stereotypes is ongoing. Exhibiting the negative stereotypes reinforces social definitions and establishes generational distinctions based on chronological age.

Critical Connection: What We See Is Socially Constructed

In our efforts to describe an "elderly" person we create in our mind an image of someone with a particular set of characteristics. But where did we acquire this information? Much of our knowledge of the elderly and the aging process is rooted in our family history. As we learn the norms and values from our family of orientation, we gather insight into the meaning of old age. What do you know of your grandparents? Can you describe their physical characteristics? What about their behavior? How much of what you believe about aging is grounded in your assessment of your grandparents? We use what we know to construct images of the larger group. In Chapter 1 we made reference to the difference between individual experience and scientific research. At that time you may have wondered why we made such a distinction. Hopefully by now you understand. It is through the individual assessment that stereotypes are constructed to apply to the larger age category. The inclusion of scientific evidence, on the other hand, requires a systematic examination of aging not only from your perspective but from that of many others.

Remember that the family is the most influential agent in the socialization process. As a result, our interaction with grandparents or other elderly members of our extended family creates an image for us of what constitutes aging. In addition, the position of the family within society will influence the likelihood of particular experiences. For example, the economic position of the family influences the health status of its members. Also, if the family is a member of a minority group, its level of opportunity will generally be less. Thus one's experiences relative to the elderly will vary depending on one's position in the social structure of society. It is to that we now turn. The remainder of this book will address the influence of the structural components on the aging process and the reciprocal nature of the relationship.

Chapter Review

This chapter began by examining the world in which we live. We understand this world very superficially. As a result, we need to question what we know and what we see. This ties in with the earlier chapters by attaching significance to the importance of research, theory, and history. In addition, it is important to understand the institutional structures of the society and their impact on our beliefs and behaviors. The following questions are meant to elicit responses by building on the cumulative knowledge base you have acquired through the first four chapters of this book.

1. Identify a status and a series of roles associated with that status that you believe are applicable to the elderly.
2. What research design would you use to examine the validity of the status and roles just identified?
3. Identify a stereotype associated with aging. Using library material, research the stereotype. Write up your findings and discuss what can be done to change the stereotype.

4. Ask five friends to write down the first 10 words that come to mind when they hear the word *old*. Categorize their findings using content analysis. What did you discover? How ageist are your friends?

5. Watch television during the daytime. Log the number of elderly actors in the daily soap operas and in the commercials. Observe prime time television. Again, log the number of elderly actors in programs and in commercials. Identify their behavior. Are they portrayed stereotypically? Are men or women more likely to be stereotyped?

Glossary

Achieved status   A position in society that one holds because of some personal accomplishment of the individual.

Ascribed status   A position in society attributable to some personal characteristic of the individual.

Attitude   A way of thinking in which we evaluate others negatively or positively.

Definition of the situation   According to W. I. Thomas (1928, p. 572), "if men define situations as real, they are real in their consequence."

Group   The basic unit of analysis in sociology. A group consists of two or more individuals engaged in interaction. Groups can be primary (family) or secondary (work environment).

Institution   A component in the structure of society that includes a specific set of norms, roles, and values built around some basic human activity.

Role   This is an expectation of behavior relative to others with whom you interact. Roles are constantly being modified depending on the circumstances of the interaction and are related to the status one currently occupies.

Self   This is the object we act toward to define who we are. The self emerges out of the socialization process and develops from the roles we perform.

Socialization   The lifetime process whereby others in society are actively involved in transforming humans into social beings.

Status   This is a position that one occupies in society at given point in time.

Stereotype   A stereotype is an exaggeration of a quality that is attributed to a particular category of the population.

Suggested Reading

Binstock, R. H. (1983). The aged as scapegoat. *Gerontologist, 23*(2), 136–143.
Binstock outlines the changes that have occurred in aging stereotypes. He makes a forceful argument regarding the potential consequences of the new "positive" stereotypes currently being applied to the elderly. Binstock also addresses what needs to be done to reduce problems of stereotyping.

Gerbner, G., Gross, L., Signorielli, N., & Morgan, M. (1980, Winter). Aging with television: Images on television drama and conceptions of social reality. *Journal of Communication, 30,* 37–49.

This article provides insight into the early stages of media research of the elderly.

Rosow, I. (1974). *Socialization to old age.* Berkeley: University of California Press.
This is one of the classics. Rosow provides an exploration of the social psychology of aging. This is a must-read book for any serious student of aging.

Tuckman, J., & Lorge, I. (1953). Attitudes toward old people. *Journal of Social Psychology, 37,* 249–260.

The need for a historical context is always present. This article provides an introductory examination of attitude research in the field of aging.

Vasil, L., & Wass, H. (1993). Portrayal of the elderly in the media: A literature review and implications for educational gerontologists. *Educational Gerontology, 19,* 71–85.

As evident in the title of the article, this is a relatively current assessment of the literature. It is an excellent resource guide for anyone interested in media bias and aging.

References

Aday, R. H., Simms, C. R., & Evans, E. (1991, September). Youth's attitudes toward the elderly: The impact of intergenerational partners. *Journal of Applied Gerontology, 10*(3), 372–384.

Arber, S., & Ginn, J. (1991). *Gender and later life: A sociological analysis of resources and constraints.* Newbury Park, CA: Sage.

Atchley, R. C. (1987). *Aging: Continuity and change* (2nd ed.). Belmont, CA: Wadsworth.

Austin, D. R. (1985). Attitudes toward old age: A hierarchical study. *Gerontologist, 25*(4), 431–434.

Avorn, J. (1984). Benefit and cost analysis in geriatric care. *New England Journal of Medicine, 310*(20), 1294–1301.

Barrow, G. M. (1989). *Aging, the individual, and society* (4th ed.). St. Paul, MN: West.

Bell, J. (1992). In search of a discourse on aging: The elderly on television. *Gerontologist, 32*(3), 305–311.

Binstock, R. H. (1983). The aged as scapegoat. *Gerontologist, 23*(2), 136–143.

Binstock, R. H. (1984). Reframing the agenda of policies on aging. In M. Minkler and C. L. Estes (Eds.), *Readings in the political economy of aging.* Amityville, NY: Baywood.

Bishop, J. M., & Krause, D. R. (1984). Depictions of aging and old age on Saturday morning television. *Gerontologist, 24*(1), 91–94.

Brigham, J. C. (1986). *Social psychology.* Boston: Little, Brown & Company.

Brubaker, T. H., & Powers, E. A. (1976). The stereotype of "old": A review and alternative approach. *Journal of Gerontology, 31*(4), 441–447.

Burgess, E. W. (1960). Aging in Western culture. In E. W. Burgess (Ed.), *Aging in Western societies: A comparative survey.* Chicago: University of Chicago Press.

Butler, R. N. (1990). A disease called ageism. *Journal of the American Geriatric Society, 38,* 178–180.

Callahan, D. (1986). Health care in the aging society: A moral dilemma. In A. Pifer & L. Bronte (Eds.), *Our aging society: Paradox and promise.* New York: Norton.

Charon, J. M. (1985). *Symbolic interactionism* (2nd ed.). Englewood Cliffs, NJ: Prentice-Hall.

Comfort, A. (1976). *A good age.* New York: Crown.

Davis, R. H., & Davis, J. A. (1985). *TV's image of the elderly.* Lexington, MA: Lexington.

Doob, C. B. (1991). *Sociology: An introduction* (3rd ed.). Fort Worth: Holt, Rinehart and Winston.

Elliot, J. (1984). The daytime television drama portrayal of older adults. *Geronologist, 24*(6), 628–633.

Estes, C. L. (1979). *The aging enterprise.* San Francisco: Jossey-Bass.

Estes, C. L., Swan, J. H., & Gerard, L. E. (1984). Dominant and competing paradigms in gerontology: Towards a political economy of aging. In M. Minkler & C. L. Estes (Eds.), *Readings in the political economy of aging.* Amityville, NY: Baywood.

Fuchs, V. R. (1984). Though much is taken: Reflections on aging, health, and medical care. *Milbank Quarterly, 62*(2), 143–166.

Furstenberg, A. L. (1989, May). Older people's age self-concept. *Social Casework: The Journal of Contemporary Social Work, 70*(5), 268–275.

Kammeyer, K. C. W., Ritzer, G., & Yetman, N. R. (1994). *Sociology: Experiencing changing Societies* (6th ed.). Boston: Allyn & Bacon.

Kando, T. M. (1977). *Social interaction.* St. Louis: Mosby.

Kerbo, H. R. (1989). *Sociology: Social structure and social conflict.* New York: Macmillan.

Levin, W. C. (1989). Age stereotyping: College student evaluations. In H. Cox (Ed.), *Annual editions: Aging* (6th ed., pp. 78–82). Guilford, CT: Dushkin.

Lubomudrov, S. (1987). Congressional perceptions of the elderly: The use of stereotypes in the legislative process. *Gerontologist, 27*(1), 77–81.

Riley, M. W., & Riley, J. W., Jr. (1986). Longevity and social structure: The potential of the added years. In A. Pifer & L. Bronte (Eds.), *Our aging society: Paradox and promise.* New York: Norton.

Rosow, I. (1974). *Socialization to old age.* Berkeley: University of California Press.

Street, D. (1993). Maintaining the status quo: The impact of old-age interest groups on the Medicare Catastrophic Coverage Act of 1988. *Social Problems, 40*(4), 431–444.

Thomas, W. I. (1928). *The child in America: Behavior problems and programs.* New York: Knopf.

Torres-Gill, F. M. (1992). *The new aging: Politics and change in America.* New York: Auburn House.

Vander Zanden, J. W. (1987). *Social psychology* (4th ed.). New York: Random House.

Vasil, L., & Wass, H. (1993). Portrayal of the elderly in the media: A literature review and implications for educational gerontologists. *Educational Gerontology, 19,* 71–85.

Walker, A. (1982). Dependency and old age. *Social Policy and Administration, 16*(2), 115–135.

Walker, S. N. (1990). Promoting healthy aging. In K. F. Ferraro (Ed.), *Gerontology: Perspectives and issues.* New York: Springer.

Family Relationships Among the Elderly

[T]he "everyday family" . . . consists of persons who may or may not be related by blood or marriage, with whom one interacts on a regular basis and from whom one receives love, and solidarity. Sexual intimacy may occur but is not requisite. Such individuals usually reside in the same community or neighborhood, which permits frequent face-to-face interaction. It is a family to which one turns when one has a problem, and it is with those family members that one likes to spend work or leisure time. The notion of an everyday family as a support system for the elderly is viable and potentially useful.
—SUSSMAN, 1985, P. 424

In Chapter 4 we discovered the significance of others in our daily life. This chapter will examine those others who are significant to the aging process in a familial and community context. Subsequent chapters will address the significance of the structural characteristics of society relative to the elderly. Here, however, we will address the interpersonal relationships in which the elderly engage. Figure 5–1 clearly illustrates the interrelationship between three major resource areas and how they relate to the elderly. This figure is particularly useful in visualizing the interconnections between this chapter and the following chapters on economics, health, and minority status.

In an analysis of their diagram, Arber and Ginn (1991, p. 68) assert that "the individual's gender, class and race influence the likelihood of possessing each type of resource." These variables will be addressed in further detail in subsequent chapters.

To begin, interpersonal relationships exist on a variety of levels. On one level, we may have a friend with whom we share our innermost secrets. On another level, we may have friends who serve a more functional purpose such as a golfing buddy or a tennis mate. On a rather different level, we have acquaintances with whom we may discuss our work or the events of the day but never interact beyond that level. On an intimate level we may experience a love relationship that may be sexual, romantic, platonic, companionate, or any combination. All of these levels of relationships exist and are as appropriate to the elderly as they are to anyone else. Remember: the elderly are as heterogeneous in their interpersonal behavior as any other age category. Unfortunately, the consequences of today's relationships can be as deadly for the elderly as they are for the young or middle-aged. We will examine the sexual relationship between aging partners and the increasing number of AIDS cases being reported among the elderly. We begin this chapter with the spousal relationship and gradually expand to the larger community in which they live.

Family Relationships

This section will examine the roles and statuses available to the elderly as they interact with family members in a social environment. Throughout the chapter we will address a number of issues associated with family relationships. Perhaps the issue of greatest concern is the belief that the elderly have been abandoned by the contemporary family. Other issues involve the adult parent–adult child relationship as well as the relationship between the grandparent and grandchild. For example, we will examine the importance of the informal family network juxtaposed with the changing demographics of the family. We will also address the satisfaction of the grandparent role in society today. Intimately connected to the grandparent role is the relationship between grandparents and grandchildren.

Throughout the chapter we will dispel those societal myths of elderly behavior within family and nonfamily relationships that perpetuate stereotypic beliefs about aging (see Shanas & Sussman, 1981, for a brief but thorough identification of these myths). The reader should always be cognizant of the distinction between reality and myth associated with aged relationships. It is this continued portrayal of myth as fact that perpetuates aging as a social problem.

We begin our view of family relationships with the dyadic relationship of the elderly couple. We will work our way through the family structure, expanding our investigation to the other family members in the process.

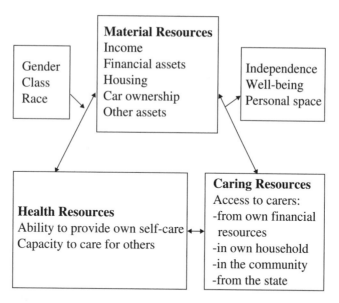

FIGURE 5–1   The Resource Triangle
Source: Reprinted from Sara Arber and Jay Ginn. *Gender and Later Life,* Copyright 1991. P. 68. By permission of Sage Publications Ltd., London.

Spouse

As with all aspects of family life, spousal relationships of all ages are changing. Changes in interpersonal relationships are the result of broad-based societal level changes and cultural beliefs that have restructured role opportunity and expectations. The movement of women into the paid labor market is perhaps one of the most significant societal level changes in decades. Although a minority of women have always been a part of the paid workforce, it has been the integration of women into the primary labor market of male-dominated occupations that has changed the world of work and the world of relationships. Concomitantly, we read and hear about the increasing number of men involved in the caregiver role as well as the work role. The significance of these changes will become evident within the next 20 years as the baby boom generation begins to turn age 65 in the year 2011. The future holds great excitement, but what do we know about today?

Let's look at some numbers. What percentage of the elderly are married, widowed, divorced? Table 5–1 provides a profile of the marital status of elderly women and men.

It is evident from Table 5–1 that elderly men are more likely to have a living spouse than elderly women. On the other hand, elderly women are more likely to be widowed. Thus men die married and women die widowed. Whereas the percentages in Table 5–1 reflect the total aged population, Table 5–2 identifies the percentage of men and women who are married or widowed at three different chronological age periods.

It is evident from Table 5–2 that as one ages, the likelihood of remaining married decreases. This is particularly true for elderly women. Among the elderly who are married, what do we know about their marital relationships? This question will give you an opportunity to apply the research skills that you developed in Chapter 1.

TABLE 5–1 Marital Status of Persons 65 Years Old and Over

	Men	Women
Married	76.8%	42.2%
Widowed	14.3%	47.6%
Single (never married)	4.4%	4.4%
Divorced	4.5%	5.8%
	100%	100%

Source: U.S. Bureau of the Census. (1994). *Statistical abstract of the United States, 1994* (114th ed.). Table 48. Washington, DC: U.S. Government Printing Office.

We begin with the concept of cohort analysis and apply it to an understanding of marriage relationships (Hess & Waring, 1983). Examining marriage relationships of people who are at least 65 means looking at people who were born in 1930 or earlier (using 1995 as the base year). What do we know about their historical experiences, and how would that influence their attitude toward marriage and marital roles? A person who is age 65 today experienced early childhood during the Depression, was too young to fight in World War II, but perhaps participated in the Korean conflict. This person married in the late 1940s or early 1950s. This was an expansion period in which jobs (for some) were available and prosperity prevailed. This was a period of time that is often referred to as the "golden era of the family" because of the emphasis on nuclear family, stability, and very well-defined gender roles. Men were expected to work outside the home, and women performed work roles within the home. Now, as our 65-year-old male retires from work today, our 65-year-old female is still likely to be considered primarily responsible for household roles. The children have been raised and are independent of the parents. If the couple maintains earlier marital role segregation, then marital roles of this aging couple are probably quite rigid. As they enter their "golden years" they are quite likely engaged in a gender-specific role relationship. Thus their spousal relationship today is likely to be the same today as in the past (Stoller & Cutler, 1992). There is considerable disagreement regarding role relationships in later life. Some would argue that with age there is greater role relaxation, allowing for a more mutually based relationship (for example, see Hess & Waring, 1983; Brubaker, 1985). This scenario, as descriptive of any cohort of the elderly, would question what a couple considers necessary in their definition of satisfaction with the marriage arrangement. One possible explanation lies with the argument of Christensen and Johnsen (1971, p. 459), who suggest that "satisfaction in the later years is related not to any particular type of marital role relationship, amount of family interaction, or amount of income. It is more related to the feelings of self-worth the aging couple is able to maintain." Spousal relationships among the elderly are complex. The role expectations of aging continue to change, thus challenging those couples entering this period of their life.

Implicit throughout this discussion is an aged stereotype that the elderly are inflexible in the performance of their roles. In other words, older people are "set in their ways." Think

TABLE 5–2   Marital Status and Age by Sex: 1992

	Men			*Women*		
	65–74	75–84	85+	65–74	75–84	85+
Married	77.1%	71.6%	50.1%	51.4%	28.6%	9.5%
Widowed	10.2%	19.9%	41.9%	35.9%	60.5%	80.8%

Source: Living arrangements of the elderly. (1993). *Profiles of America's elderly.* POP/93-2. Washington, DC: U.S. Bureau of the Census.

about this statement. Why is it more likely to be applied to the elderly? Could the same be said of individuals of all ages? For example, final exam period provides a wealth of evidence that young people are rather inflexible in their role as test-takers. When students enter to take a final exam, many are carrying more than books and notes. Some students wear their good-luck hat or T-shirt or place some trinket on their desk. Are these students set in their ways? Would they be upset if told to remove that hat or good-luck piece? Of course they would. We all engage in behavior that is consistent because it is comfortable, safe, and convenient, and it can be time saving. We all construct routines in our lives. This does not mean that our lives are boring. By having a routine, we are aware of where we are and what needs to be done. Routine means predictability, and we are all creatures of habit. What worked earlier is believed to work again. If it is predictable, we do not have to worry about it. We feel better about ourselves as well. The elderly, as well as other age groups, are performing marital roles in which they feel comfortable. Christensen and Johnsen (1971) would argue that if the couple agreed on the division and performance of the marital roles, and they are satisfied with the arrangement, the relationship is successful.

Although marital satisfaction may be difficult to describe, numerous researchers have attempted to measure it. One of the more consistent findings is that a U-shaped relationship exists between stage of the life cycle and level of marital satisfaction. According to this argument, marital satisfaction is relatively high at the beginning of the marriage relationship. With the birth of the first child, marital satisfaction begins to decline. Although the degree of decline is slight, it nonetheless is evident. This decline continues until the last child is ready to leave home. With the independence of the last child, marital satisfaction begins its upward swing (Rollins & Feldman, 1970). One minor modification to this U-shape pattern of marital satisfaction suggests that the satisfaction of the husband declines slightly after his retirement and then returns to its original level after adjustment to this new status. As the increasing number of dual-career relationships today begin to retire in the 21st century, it will be significant to note their later-life patterns of marital satisfaction relative to those already reported.

Another significant pattern among married couples of all ages is that of divorce. Although divorce among the elderly is relatively rare, it is expected to increase in the next century (Bengtson & Silverstein, 1993). One explanation for the low divorce rate among the elderly is that if a person invests 40 to 50 years of life in a relationship with another person, he or she is likely to find something good with the other person. Otherwise, divorce would suggest that the years spent together were of little value, thus devaluing both partners.

Another explanation for the lower rates of divorce among the elderly is provided by Gilford (1991, p. 39):

> It seems obvious that older spouses are happy in their long-term marriages; otherwise, it is reasonable to assume, they would have divorced along the way. However, these couples exchanged marriage vows at a time when social pressures ruled out divorce as an alternative to an unhappy marriage.

Regardless of the reason, divorce in later life, compared with other age periods, creates an even greater economic hardship for women (Arendell & Estes, 1991). This is particularly true if women have performed the traditional roles of housewife and mother and have not been employed outside the home. Women in this situation find their economic opportunities extremely limited, and, with age, the potential for remarriage decreases, particularly for women (Brubaker, 1985). Remarriage for women is difficult because the sex ratio of men to women decreases with age. That is, as one ages, the number of available men per 100 women continues to decline. According to Brubaker (1985), divorce among the elderly can be classified into three broad categories based on age and frequency of divorce:

1. The career divorced involves elderly, divorced in their early or middle years and never remarried. . . . Since they have raised their children, many enter later life with the support of younger generations as is characteristic of many married elderly.
2. The newly divorced . . . are men and women [who] have been married for many years, and after the children leave home . . . obtain a divorce.
3. The serial divorced . . . (are) older men and women [who] have married and divorced several times during their lifetimes. (Brubaker, 1985, pp. 107–108)

One consequence of the increasing rate of divorce in the United States is reduced intergenerational contact. The lack of intergenerational contact may emerge because of decreased feelings of *filial responsibility,* that is, the "adult children's feelings that they should help their elderly parents" (Brubaker, 1985, p. 51). For example, because of divorce by parents, adult children, or both, intergenerational contact and subsequent expectations of economic and emotional support (filial responsibility) may be affected. We will examine the relationship between elderly parents and their children later in this chapter.

Before we proceed to the next section on children, we will examine the sexual relationship between elderly adults. We will then examine the problem of AIDS among the elderly.

One of the unfortunate consequences of age stereotyping is the image of older people as asexual. As a society we believe that as one ages, interest in being sexual is less appropriate (Zopf, 1986). Until recently, research efforts in this area have been limited. What we know about sexuality and later life is drawn primarily from the works of Masters and Johnson (1966, 1970) and the Duke Longitudinal Study (Volumes I, II, and III) (Palmore, 1970, 1974, 1985).

Based on the research, sexual activity declines with age (Busse & Maddox, 1985). However, sexual activity among all elderly couples does not stop, although one "major reason for decreases in sexual relations among older people in general is widowhood, an experience particularly common among women" (Reiss & Lee, 1988, p. 384). Among couples still married, the reason cited most often for discontinuing sexual activity was "the attitudes or physical condition of the male partner" (George & Weiler, 1985, p. 17). Remaining sexually active can (and often does) continue into the seventh decade of life and beyond (Zopf, 1986). Table 5–3 illustrates the extent of sexual activity among three age groups over a 6-year period. Although the data indicate decreased sexual activity with age, a significant minority of the elderly maintain an active sex life. This is particularly true for men, because they are more likely to be married. Remember: as women age, the chances of being widowed increase.

All of the information just presented is based on research of aging couples. However, sexual activity among the elderly is not confined exclusively to monogamous marital relationships. There is a problem in the lack of research among other types of relationships. What we do know, however, is that sexual activity among single elderly (widowed, divorced, living alone) is much lower than for marrieds.

Many elderly engage in heterosexual relationships, but other elderly engage in homosexual and lesbian relationships. In keeping with the estimates of the general population, a significant minority of the elderly population are gay or lesbian. Doress and Siegal (1987) state that 10 percent or more of elderly women are lesbian. That same percentage is generally applied to the rate of homosexuality within the male population. Although research of gay and lesbian elderly is quite limited, the reader should remember that, as a group, elderly gays and lesbians are as diverse as their heterosexual counterparts. For example, consider the work of Copper (1987), who discusses feelings of growing older in the lesbian community as well as reactions of younger lesbians toward older lesbians. Pope and Schulz (1991) present research findings that challenge the stereotypic image of the aging gay male. In their research, Pope and Schulz (1991) discovered that although homosexual activity decreased with age, the level of enjoyment was not related to age. Friend (1990, p. 243), in a review of the literature, points out that although the "images of older lesbian and gay people available in our culture are negative," the opposite is true regarding research findings. Adelman (1991, p. 21) reports that among aging gay and lesbian respondents, "high life satisfaction, low self-criticism, and few psychosomatic complaints constitute the pattern of adjustment related to being 'very' satisfied with being gay; the reverse pattern of adjustment is related to being 'less than very' satisfied with being gay."

Regardless of age and sexual orientation, a consequence of sexual relationships is the very real threat of AIDS (as well as other forms of transmission). Although considerable AIDS research has been conducted on younger age categories in the population, there is a minimal amount of research data available on the elderly (Levy & Albrecht, 1989). As a result, the use of the term *elderly* within the discussion of AIDS must be clarified. For example, the National Center for Health Statistics (1993) uses age 60 and over as the upper end of the reporting spectrum. Based on this age categorization, the elderly represented 3 percent of the cumulative number of AIDS cases as of 1992. A disturbing trend is that for those over the age of 60 the incidence rate in 1985 was 2.5 percent. By 1992 the incidence rate increased to 3.2 percent for those over the age of 60. Using age 50 and over, Riley (1989) notes that there were some 1,000 known cases of AIDS among those aged 50 and over per year. Those aged 50 and over have consistently registered some 10 percent of the AIDS cases per year. Just over half of these cases were the result of blood transfusions (Stine, 1993), and 27 percent were the result of homosexual or IV drug use transmission. Catania

TABLE 5–3   Distribution of Sexual Activity Patterns over Six Years of Study[a]

	Age at start of study year		
	<56	56–65	<65
		(percentages)	
Men			
Stable activity	66.6%	63.5%	42.4%
No activity to some activity	1.6	2.7	9.1
Increasing activity	3.2	1.4	0.0
Some activity to no activity	4.8	6.8	18.2
Decreasing activity	11.1	8.1	3.0
Continuously absent	0.0	9.5	12.1
Other	12.7	8.1	15.2
Women			
Stable activity	61.4%	55.6%	33.3%
No activity to some activity	1.8	2.8	0.0
Increasing activity	1.8	0.0	0.0
Some activity to no activity	5.3	22.2	33.3
Decreasing activity	10.5	8.3	0.0
Continuously absent	5.3	5.5	33.3
Other	14.0	5.5	0.0

[a]The percentages are rounded to one decimal place; consequently, the column totals may depart slightly from 100 percent.
Source: George, L. K., & Weiler, S. J. (1985). Sexuality in middle and late life. In E. Palmore et al. (Eds.) *Normal aging III: Reports from the Duke Longitudinal Studies, 1975–1984* (pp. 12–19). Durham, NC: Duke University Press. Reprinted with permission.

et al. (1989, p. 374) report that "homosexual and bisexual men represented the largest segment of the AIDS case load for older people between 1982 and 1987." Catania et al. (1989) also point to a steady increase in the reported number of heterosexual transmitted cases of AIDS among the elderly. Catania et al. (1989, p. 377) identify a number of methods by which HIV transmission may occur among the elderly. Two methods include a "decreased immune system function with age and post-menopausal vaginal changes." Another reason why the elderly were identified as being at risk is because of blood transfusions, which, in the past, were linked with the transmission of the HIV virus. The unsuspecting elderly victim would then pass the virus on to his or her sexual partner (Catania et al., 1989). Testing of blood for the HIV virus is now routine, thus reducing the threat of infection. Although precautions now exist, the elderly are still more likely than any other age group to undergo surgery, thus placing them at continued risk for exposure to the AIDS virus. As a result, AIDS among the elderly is an area that will require considerable research in the near future.

Beyond the intimacy of the spousal/lover relationship, another level of interaction exists for the elderly. This is the relationship between the elderly parent and their adult child(ren). The next section will examine this changing relationship.

Children

Perhaps the greatest myth associated with aging is that elderly parents have been abandoned by their adult children. The myth is based on the premise that as adult children mature, they will move away from the family in search of career opportunities and financial independence. In addition, the nuclear family, necessary in the modern and postmodern society, necessitates creating isolated individual family units independent of other kin members. Although such an argument appears logical, it does not represent most adult parent–adult child relationships. In reality, at least one adult child lives in fairly close proximity and maintains regular contact with elderly parents (Shanas, 1961; Adams, 1970, provides an excellent review of early research). Research over the past 30 years has supported the argument of continued intergenerational relations, thus putting to rest any doubt that the elderly are isolated from their families. Demographic and gender role changes within younger generations, however, are legitimate areas of concern (Treas, 1977). First, as the number of children per family decreases, the likelihood of available children to provide care to elderly parents is diminished. A second factor in this changing relationship between adult parent and adult child is the dynamic quality of role opportunities for women. In the past, women have generally been assigned the primary caregiver and care-provider role to elderly parents. As women continue to enter the world of work, their ability to provide familial assistance diminishes. At the same time, increasing longevity is expanding the number of generations that generally exist at any given point in time. The consequence of this intergenerational structure is what Bengtson and Silverstein (1993) refer to as the *"beanpole family."* That is, families today are having fewer children but are living longer.

While the structure of family relations is changing, Mancini and Blieszner (1989, p. 282) argue that "the character of the relationship that parents and children had earlier in life is likely to affect that of the later years." It is also important to remember that these roles "are among the least clearly defined" (Mutran & Reitzes, 1990, p. 149).

Riley and Riley (1993, p. 188) suggest that "four major changes have been transforming the nature of the parent-child relationship:"

1. The *power* balance has changed, now that for most of their lives parents and offspring are status equals.
2. Property and material resources are no longer the dominant base of the relationship, now that support from the state and other institutions enhances the independence of the old.
3. The heterogeneity of contemporary families in *age* (hence also in cohort membership) reduces the traditional "age gap" as a source of potential contention and conflict.
4. The many *alternative forms* of relationships available today diffuse the traditional primary focus on the intergenerational connection.

The most basic issue in this discussion of intergenerational relationships is that of interactional quality and quantity. As mentioned earlier, considerable documentation exists in support of intergenerational contact. However, the meaning of such contact for the adult child as well as the aging parent has become the focus of considerable debate. An early assessment of this issue is provided by Troll (1971, p. 278), who argues that residential proximity does not guarantee interaction. Presumably, people who live near each other see each other frequently, but they may not be in any kind of intimate or meaningful contact. If the chief reason for this renewed physical closeness is obligation and concern, much of the visiting may be little more than monitoring: the children taking turns to see how mother is rather than truly communicating with her. Until more qualitative measures are used, this question will be unanswered.

Mancini and Bleiszner (1989, p. 280) provide a more recent assessment of the quality-versus-quantity debate. Citing a number of studies, they concluded that since the early 1970s "research . . . has also failed to find an important relationship between simple contact and well-being." One explanation for this apparent nonrelationship is given by Reiss and Lee (1988, p. 395). They suggest that "the quality of the parent-child relationship, and the patterns of support and assistance exchanged between the generations, may be more important in explaining this fact." A number of specific areas within which patterns of support and assistance exist include that of health, living arrangements, finances, and attitudes toward the elderly (Johnson & Bursk, 1977). We will briefly explore these areas.

The health status of the elderly parent(s) will dramatically influence the type and quality of the relationship with adult children (Stahl & Potts, 1985). This is particularly evident in terms of social class. Research of the relationship between social class and health among the elderly exists but is not particularly extensive in the United States (Arber & Ginn, 1991). What we do know is that one's social class is related not only to health status (Longino, Warheit, & Green, 1989), but also to the type of caregiving provided (Haber, 1989). Thus, as the health of the elderly parent deteriorates, he or she becomes increasingly dependent on the adult child(ren) for support and assistance. The potential consequences are intergenerational problems. These difficulties arise because of familial expectations placed on the adult child regarding the type and amount of care necessary. If the adult child is unable to provide the increased time and resources to assist the aging parent, the adult child–aging parent relationship may ultimately suffer. Although it is still generally true that the adult child primarily responsible is a daughter or daughter-in-law (Haber, 1989), it is also increasingly true that she is also employed outside the home. This change in the working patterns of women in the past 30 years has had an impact on the availability of women to engage in full-time caregiving responsibilities. Demographically, the United States is beginning to experience two population consequences. Not only are the elderly increasing as a percentage of the population, but the number of available children to provide support and assistance continues to shrink because of decreased birth rates. In addition, the elderly are living longer. Increased life expectancy results in potentially greater health problems, particularly as the elderly move from being "young-old" (generally up to age 74) to becoming "old-old" (75 and over). Consider the following example: A 50-year-old female is the adult child of a 70- to 75-year-old parent (generally the mother). At the same time, this 50-year-old adult child is also the mother of 20- to 25-year-old children. The demands placed on this 50-year-old can be significant. On the one hand, the needs of the aging parent require the adult child to remain actively engaged in providing care to the parent. At the same time, the 50-year-old is a parent to young adults who are in need of emotional and financial assistance as they attempt to enter college and the world of work. Such 50-year-olds are referred to as the "sandwich generation" because they are caught between competing demands of two generations.

The second area within which intergenerational patterns of support and assistance exist is that of living arrangements.

Johnson and Bursk (1977, p. 92) suggest that this indicator consists of "questions of privacy, whether close friends live nearby, convenience to transportation, reason for moving to the present location, fearfulness in the home, and general attitude toward the surroundings." Rather than attempting to generalize from individual explanations of living arrangements, we will address this concept within the context of household arrangements. Table 5–4 provides the percentage distribution for four categories of living arrangements.

Although the majority of elderly reside in residences that are independent of their children, others live either with adult children or with other adults. According to Table 5–4, living arrangements depend on the age and sex of the elderly person. That is, as one ages, the likelihood of residing with others increases. Significant differences exist between elderly men and women. When compared with elderly men, elderly women are far more likely to live with relatives or nonrelatives. The reason for this is the result of the demographics of aging. That is, men die at younger ages than women. As a result, surviving males are more likely to have a surviving spouse. The reverse is generally true for elderly women. Because they live longer, they are more likely to be widowed. They are therefore more likely to either live alone or with others. As Siegel (1993, p. 346) points out, "most elderly who live alone are not isolated. The great majority have one or more living children, and one or more living siblings, have frequent contact with their children, siblings, and friends, have lived for a long time in the same house or neighborhood or live in retirement communities, and have telephones that are used for contacts."

Living arrangements are significant because they structure the environment within which the immediate relationship between the adult child and elderly parent exists. This environment is the consequence of the other correlates such as the health status of the elderly parent.

The third correlate of the adult child–elderly parent relationship is that of finances. Relative to this point, I will briefly examine the economic issue of social class and intergenerational relationships. A more thorough (as well as broader) discussion of economic issues will be presented in Chapter 6.

TABLE 5–4   Living Arrangements of Persons 65 and Over (in Percentages)

	Total			*Male*			*Female*		
	65 and over	65–74	75+	65 and over	65–74	75+	65 and over	65–74	75+
Alone	31	25	41	16	13	22	42	34	52
W/spouse	54	63	41	74	77	68	40	51	24
W/other relatives	12	10	16	7	6	8	16	13	21
W/non-relatives	2	2	2	3	3	2	2	2	2

Source: U.S. Bureau of the Census. (1993). *Statistical abstract of the United States, 1993* (113th ed.). Table 71. Washington, DC: U.S. Government Printing Office.

A direct relationship exists between one's social class position and the type of intergenerational relationship experienced between adult children and their aging parents. Furthermore, there is general agreement that middle-class elderly continue to provide more economic support to their children than the reverse. On the other hand, lower-class elderly are more likely to rely on adult children for "direct provision of in-home assistance to parents" (Cantor & Little, 1985, p. 757). The reason for this difference lies in the availability of resources among the elderly. That is, resources tend to be greater among the middle class in old age (Reiss & Lee, 1988). In addition, middle-class adult children, because of economic opportunities, are more likely to engage the paid services of others to perform tasks for elderly parents. This option is increasingly necessary because of the number of adult children remaining in the paid labor force rather than assuming duties associated with the caregiving role of adult child.

The final correlate in the relationship between the adult child and aging parent is that of attitudes toward the elderly. Johnson and Bursk (1977, p. 92) suggest that indicators of this include "questions about the parent's current happiness, the difficulty of his/her life, and general life satisfaction." Such qualitative issues as interpersonal relations reflect a more subjective interpretation of previous life experiences than other correlates. The significance of this variable is provided by Mancini and Blieszner (1989, p. 281), who point out that "several studies have examined how relationship quality covaries with well-being. These studies have looked into communication patterns, the amount of affection and interpersonal conflict, and so on. As expected, these variables were relatively more important for the well-being of the older parent than the contact variables."

The four patterns of support and assistance just presented illustrate the intergenerational complexity of caregiving in today's society. However, there is continued disagreement regarding the motivation and ability to perform such behavior. One issue in particular is that of generational equity (Hewitt & Howe, 1992).

Generational equity is concerned with three broad areas.

1. The first is the magnitude of the coming upward shift in our society's age structure—and the enormous demands this shift will place on our future living standards.
2. The second is society's failure to prepare our economy for the aging of America; instead of saving our resources and investing more in children, we are overconsuming and saddling our children with debts.
3. The third is a political dilemma—how can a democratic society manage income transfers between generations in a way that is equitable to Americans who are young or unborn, those who cannot vote and whose interests are protected only by the sense of stewardship and the instinct for endowment shared by those of us who are older? (Hewitt & Howe, 1992, p. 223)

The generational equity argument predicts that the 1990s will be a period of austerity, particularly for the younger generation. At the same time, the generational equity argument suggests that the elderly could enjoy greater economic involvement if they would delay retirement. The purpose of continued economic involvement of the elderly is to reduce their economic dependency on others.

Essentially, generational equity pits generations against one another in an economic climate within which there are limited positive outcomes. The generational equity argument suggests that the younger generations have not received equitable economic treatment relative to the elderly population. An argument against the generational equity position suggests that intergenerational transfers are not the reason for the demise of patterns of support and assistance. Rather, increased economic competition within the world of work, decreased pay scales, and continued job insecurity are all more significant reasons why younger generations are feeling economically impotent. According to Minkler (1991, p. 78), generational equity "is based on misleading calculations of the relative financial well-being of the elderly vis-a-vis other groups and on questionable assumptions concerning such notions as fairness and differential stake in the common good."

Meanwhile, the *economic dependency ratio* offers a historical perspective that questions population aging as a cause of the current economic concerns. The dependency ratio is defined as the number of workers between the ages of 16 and 64 divided by the number of young people below the age of 16 plus the number of elderly aged 65 and over. The basic argument is that the dependency ratio continues to decrease while service needs of the dependent population continue to rise. In other words, there are fewer workers supporting an increasing number of dependent members of the population. According to Siegel (1993, pp. 442-443),

> In 1965 100 workers supported 154 nonworkers, in 1985 100 workers supported 103 non-workers, and in 2010 100 workers will have to support only about 96 nonworkers. In 2030 100 workers will have to support 112 nonworkers, however. This is about where we were in 1980, but the mix of elderly dependents, other adult dependents, and children will have shifted dramatically. . . .

Placed within a historical context, this shift is illustrated in Table 5–5. According to the table, the dependency ratio for those under the age of 16 was almost five times greater than for those age 65 and over. By 1985 the dependency ratio for those under the age of 16 was slightly more than double that of the age-65-and-over category. By 2030 the dependency ratio for those 16 and younger will be roughly equal to those aged 65 and over. The economic implications of this transition are still unclear. Siegel (1993, p. 444) points out that "public support cost for an elderly person is also greater than that for a child." However, Siegel (1993, p. 445) provides evidence from a German study (Wander, 1978, pp. 57–58) "that the cost of raising a child from birth to age 20 was about one fourth to one third greater than the cost of supporting a person aged 60 or older over his or her remaining lifetime." Nonetheless, Siegel (1993, p. 445) concludes this argument by predicting that "aggregate public support costs for elderly dependents may now already be greater than those for working-age dependents and children combined and will almost certainly be far greater by 2030." There is concern, however, that "the dependent status of many older persons subjects them to a greater degree than younger persons to the social relations of subordination to public and private service agencies that act to reproduce capitalist culture and class relations" (Estes, 1991, p. 25). There is serious question, then, whether the economic dependency "problem" of aging is real or socially constructed.

TABLE 5–5   Economic Dependency Ratio, 1975–1972 and Projected 1995–2005, by Age (per 100 in the labor force)

Year	Total All Ages	Under Age 16	Ages 16–64	Age 65 and Over
1975	126.3	61.4	44.2	20.7
1980	108.9	50.7	37.4	20.8
1985	103.3	47.3	34.2	21.8
1990	98.3	45.8	30.5	22.1
1992	98.4	47.7	28.8	21.9
1995	96.4	46.3	27.7	22.4
2000	92.8	44.9	26.2	21.7
2005	89.7	43.0	25.3	21.4

Note: The economic dependency ratio is the total population not in the labor force per 100 of those in the labor force. *Source:* U.S. Department of Labor. (1994). *The American work force: 1992–2005.* Bulletin 2452, Table 10. Washington, DC: U.S. Bureau of Labor Statistics.

A somewhat more positive assessment of intergenerational relations suggests that although societal demands continue to increase, particularly on adult women, there are encouraging intergenerational expectations for the future (Monk, 1992). For example, the income and educational levels of the elderly are expected to continue rising, allowing an increasing proportion of the elderly to maintain an independent lifestyle. This increasing economic self-reliance, however, will be class specific and dependent on previous economic conditions of the individual. Because women and minorities continue to earn less than their male and white counterparts, women and minority elderly will continue to lag behind elderly white males.

Grandchildren

Perceptions of the grandparent-grandchild relationship consist of myth as well as fact. Myth suggests that there is an idyllic relationship between grandparent(s) who willingly provide unlimited assistance to their grandchildren. In return, grandchildren provide purpose and meaning to the lives of grandparents. This image creates the belief that the elderly look forward to grandparenthood and their newfound social status. Although true for some, "the valued grandparent is an earned and acquired status, involving personal qualities, and not automatically ascribed to the role" (Troll, 1971, p. 279). For some, grandparenthood provides an opportunity to assume new and exciting roles relative to other family members. However, as with other aspects of aging, grandparenthood does not imply a homogeneity of belief or practice. Not all grandparents appreciate the task of rearing or caring for grandchildren. One factor that appears to influence grandparent-grandchild interaction is that of age of grandparent and grandchild. That is, as the grandparents age, they become limited in the range of activities in which they can engage (Roberto & Stroes, 1992). However, according to Gershenson Hodgson (1992), grandchildren do not disassociate with grandparents because of age. Rather, grandchildren maintain contact with grandparents, even as adults. In fact, Gershenson Hodgson (1992, p. 221) reports that "older grandchildren have not terminated their bonds with their grandparents, nor have they maintained these bonds only on an obligatory and ritualistic basis." According to Cherlin and Furstenberg (1986, pp. 53–69) there are three styles of grandparenthood:

1. *Remote.* The remote grandparent generally lives a considerable distance from children and grandchildren. In addition to a physical distance, there is also an emotional distance between the grandparents and their children and grandchildren. Based on these characteristics, approximately 29 percent of grandparents could be classified as remote.
2. *Companionate.* The companionate grandparent is involved but tries not to interfere in the lives of the children and grandchildren. Within this type, grandparents remain intimately connected to family, but from a distance. Cherlin and Furstenberg (1986, p. 60) believe that this type is characterized as "satisfied and loving, but passive and accepting of the limitations of their relationship." Approximately 55 percent of grandparents fit into this category.
3. *Involved.* The involved grandparent is intimately connected to all family members. This type of grandparent engages in activities with grandchildren and offers advice (solicited as well as unsolicited) to children and grandchildren. In addition to functioning at the behavioral level, this type of grandparent interacts on an emotional level as well. These characteristics are representative of 16 percent of grandparents.

The relationship between grandparent and grandchild(ren) is quite different from other kinship bonds. This relationship offers participants an opportunity to establish bonds in which expectations are not significant to the outcome.

If one's spouse or children are unavailable to provide the type of assistance necessary, the elderly have another alternative within the informal support system. They can request assistance and support from their siblings.

Siblings

As with children, one of the problems of receiving assistance and support from siblings is that there are fewer available today than in the past. Because the number of children born per family has decreased, the likelihood of having a sibling available to provide assistance has also decreased. Yet, according to Shanas et al. (1968), elderly women were far more likely to have a living sibling than a living spouse.

The role of the sibling as a caregiver is primarily dependent on the availability of spouse or children. If more immediate family members are unavailable, or if the elderly person is unmarried or alone because of divorce or death of spouse, then sibling help is more likely to be provided. Relative to immediate family members, however, the extent of sibling assistance as a caregiver is minimal (Cicirelli, Coward, & Dwyer, 1992). All of this is not meant to undermine the importance of siblings. Rather, siblings are generally not considered for the caregiver role unless circumstances warrant their involvement. As

Cicirelli et al. (1992) point out, there is a hierarchy within the family, and siblings rank below spouse and children.

In conclusion, the elderly are not being abandoned by their family. Instead, a family member is usually within close proximity to the elderly parent to provide assistance and support when needed. In fact, "families provide up to 80 percent of all home health care for elderly individuals in the United States" (Cantor & Little, 1985, p. 763). Again, another of the myths associated with the elderly does not withstand the scrutiny of research. Beyond the informal support system of the family just presented, the elderly can also rely on services and support from others. In particular, services are provided within the community by various organizations ranging from religious to governmental. It is to this broader context of family through the formal support system that we will next turn our attention. We will also explore an explanation of increased dependency by the elderly on the formal support system.

The Formal and Informal Support System

As discussed earlier, the *informal support system* consists of assistance primarily from family. However, in a case of obvious gender bias, those primarily responsible are female members of the family. This is particularly troublesome among lower-income families. As England, Keigher, Miller, and Linsk (1991, p. 239) point out, "social and individual costs of policies that coerce families into caregiving would fall most heavily on those least able to bear them." In addition to the family, the informal support system also consists of "friends and neighbors. It also includes a widely diverse group of people whose primary relationship to the person in need is not as a helper with personal problems. The beauty operator, barber, maid, bartender, dressmaker, taxi-driver, fellow worker, or any person who has established a relationship over time that provides reciprocal support" (Dobelstein & Johnson, 1985, p. 170).

Informal support consists of a myriad of activities, depending on the needs and ability of the elderly person receiving assistance. Although informal support is the primary source of assistance today, the changing demographic structure of American society and the family in particular will increase the reliance on the formal support system. Figure 5–2 illustrates a clear distinction between the provision of services by informal and formal providers.

In addition to the delineation of services, Figure 5–2 dispels another significant myth of aging: that all elderly are physically impaired. The health status of the elderly will be discussed in greater detail in Chapter 7. For now, however, it is significant to realize that even with the use of broad categorizations of physical competence identified in Figure 5–2, 60 percent of the elderly are not impaired. It is also important to remember that regardless of the health status of the elderly, the role of formal support systems is increasingly significant to the needs of the elderly and affected family members. As a result, there is an increasing integration of formal and informal support services. This means that the formal and informal support systems are working in concert to provide the services necessary so that the elderly are capable of remaining independent, viable members of the community.

The *formal support system* is loosely considered to include "agencies and organizations made up of a range of incorporated or public bodies . . . [with] a corporate structure

5–2   Task Performance Among Formal, Mediating, and Informal Systems of Support by Level of Functional Impairment of the Elderly

Level of Competency	Informal System	Mediating and Formal Systems
Low (frail impaired 10%)	Coresidence Total money management Assistance in home—extensive, light and heavy housekeeping, meals, shopping, etc. Personal care—washing, bathing supervision of medical regimes, etc.	Institututional care Protective service Case management Counseling—older person and/or families, self-help groups Respite service—day hospital, day care, special set-aside beds Homemaker services Home health aides, visiting nurse Meals on wheels
Moderately impaired, 30%	System negotiation Help with financial management Accompanying to medical appointments Assistance in home—more frequent, wider array of tasks, i.e., shopping, occasional meal preparation, light housekeeping	Linkage to services, counseling older person Escort, transportation Friendly visiting Congregate housing Chore service—limited in time and amount
Well Elderly 60% of Population High	Assistance when ill—short term Assistance in home—short term Escort, transportation Advice Gifts, money Visiting, providing affective support	Reduced-fare programs on public transportation Information and referral Assistance with entitlements Cultural and spiritual enrichment programs Socialization, recreation opportunities, i.e., senior center, nutrition, parks

Provider of Service

Source: Cantor, M., & and Little, V. (1985). Aging and social care. Pp. 745-781. In R. H. Binstock & E. Shanas (Eds.), *Handbook of aging and the social sciences* (2nd ed., pp. 745–781). New York: Van Nostrand Reinhold. Used with permission.
Note: The services shown are cumulative, and it is assumed that any services shown in a prior level will continue to be available if appropriate.

FIGURE 5–2   Task Performance Among Formal, Mediating, and Informal Systems of Support by Level of Functional Impairment of the Elderly
Source: Cantor, M., & Little, V. (1985). Aging and social care. In R. H. Binstock & E. Shanas (Eds.), *Handbook of aging and the social sciences* (2nd ed., pp. 745–781). New York: Van Nostrand Reinhold Company. Used with permission.

as a base of organization" (Dobelstein & Johnson, 1985, p. 184). Whether the activity is transportation, in-house nurse visitation, meals on wheels, outreach, or legal services, individuals specialized in providing such assistance carry out these functions within the confines of an organizational structure with formal rules, regulations, hierarchy, and goals. Agencies and organizations that are considered part of the formal support system range from "working as friendly visitors in a nursing home" (Dobelstein & Johnson, 1985, p. 184) to state and national government departments of aging. Within this vast range of helping organizations elderly recipients can find the necessary assistance that will produce favorable results.

Not all in the discipline are as enthusiastic about the positive role of the formal support system. From a critical perspective, formal support systems have rather deleterious outcomes for their recipients. That is, the creation of programs for the elderly fosters their dependence on the program (and thus on the program providers). This dependency emerges when programs and services are defined as age specific and those that qualify are defined as in need. Such programs are created less to provide for the needs of the elderly and more to fit the career opportunities of those providing the services. The consequence of service provision is that elderly client dependency appears as an affirmation of need for the program (Estes, 1981). Specifically, Estes (1981) uses the Older Americans Act as an example of provider-created dependence. She begins by stating that the purpose of the Older Americans Act was to enable "the aged to live independently with adequate income, giving them opportunities for leisure, employment, and decent housing, and making it possible for them to maximize their health and develop their potential" (Estes, 1981, pp. 29–30). Binstock (1991, p. 12) supports that argument when he points out that the intent of the original sponsors of the OAA in Congress was to ensure that "the OAA was to be of service to all older persons, regardless of income status." Estes (1981, p. 24) claims that what has emerged from the OAA has created a rather different interpretation of that task. She states that the OAA

> prescribed solutions to the needs of the elderly fall into several broad service categories—area planning and social services, multipurpose senior centers, and nutrition and employment programs. In general, these services strategies assign to the aged a dependent status and give them little opportunity to reciprocate for services received. In an achievement-oriented society this kind of unilateral dependency is likely to result in a lowered social status for the recipients of services.

Although its goals and methods may be considered questionable by some, the formal support system continues to provide for the needs of the elderly population. It is also important to remember that when examined in a quantitative context, utilization rates of formal support systems relative to the informal system are quite low. Nonetheless, formal support systems are of increasing importance to a growing proportion of the elderly population. A personal example will highlight the positive contributions that formal organizations offer the elderly. The example also identifies the integration of the formal and informal systems. Finally, the example illustrates the concerns addressed from a political economy perspective.

After completing my undergraduate degree, I worked as an outreach worker for a commission on aging. This agency, located in a relatively small community in the upper great plains, was funded through the state office on aging and the federal government. The commission on aging offered a wide range of services primarily to low- and moderate-income elderly in the community. These services included information and referral, congregate meal sites, meals on wheels, contact with legal services, nursing services (blood pressure and the like), transportation, and advocacy. The purpose of the commission was not to replace the informal support system. Rather, the services provided by the commission were intended to assist those elderly who requested assistance because informal support systems either did not exist or were experiencing difficulty in the provision of services.

I spent 2 years working as a direct service provider within this formal support system. An example of the informal and formal support systems working together occurred during two consecutive spring floods. Because of confusion regarding services during the first flood, I identified homes in the flood zone that were occupied by elderly residents. In addition to the name and address of the elderly resident, names and addresses of the nearest living relative were also gathered. The following spring, when flooding was again imminent, the commission had available the names and telephone numbers of elderly who needed to be moved as well as immediate family members to contact so they could evacuate their elderly relative. If family members were unavailable or unable to provide assistance, then reliance on the formal support system was necessary to evacuate the people from their homes to ensure their safety. When the flood threat subsided, those evacuated were returned to their homes either by the commission or family members. This example demonstrates how the informal and formal support systems can work together. This example also demonstrates how formal systems need not denigrate the elderly or create recipient dependence on the provider.

The argument that formal support systems can create recipient dependence is also valid. For example, the congregate meal site program provides elderly with one warm meal 5 days per week. For some, the congregate meal is an opportunity to leave the home or apartment and socialize with others. These elderly are capable of preparing a meal but prefer the company of others when eating. They decide when they wish to attend the meal site. In other words, these elderly are physically and socially independent and utilize the congregate meal site as one of a number of interaction arrangements in their daily life. For others, however, the congregate meal site promotes dependence on the organization providing the meal. This dependence establishes the justification for the continuation of the program and job opportunities for those employed in the program. I am well aware that these meals may represent the primary nutrition for some elderly. The problem is when the meal site is not coupled with efforts to assist at-risk elderly by addressing the economic circumstances that perpetuate their inability to function without the program.

Critical Connection: *It's Who You Know That Counts*

Throughout this chapter we have focused on intergenerational relationships within the context of the term *family*. Although we can all relate to family as a social institution, the importance of that family to the outside world will vary. One of the basic functions of the family is to provide a social identity for its members, in other words, a social status relative to others within the same social environment. As a result, we are all reared within a specific social context with particular norms, values, and contacts with a unique set of others in the world outside our family. Such contacts provide younger members with opportunities that are differentiated on the basis of one's social class position. The consequence is a socially constructed environment of potential social, educational, and work experiences. Access to these opportunities is significant not only in one's early life but throughout one's life experiences. At the time of retirement, what one has accumulated is determined by the work experience and income potential realized throughout the earlier work career.

In relation to intergenerational relations of support and assistance, need and ability are influenced by one's social position. The consequence is the perpetuation of the economic status quo within clearly defined social class indicators. Thus the economics of growing old begin rather early in one's family of orientation. It is within this context that the structure of society itself creates the social conditions within which aging occurs. In other words, aging is differentiated by one's connection to the economic institution and the outcomes associated with available opportunities.

Chapter Review

This chapter addresses a fundamental component in the aging process: the role of family. Briefly, we began this chapter by examining the relationship of the aging couple and discovered that the majority of elderly are married and living with their spouse. Elderly males are more likely to enjoy this arrangement than are elderly women. This occurs because men die at a younger age, leaving women widowed. Integrating information from Chapter 5 with knowledge gained from earlier chapters, answer the following questions.

1. Explain why elderly men are more likely to be married and elderly women are more likely to be widowed.
2. Utilizing cohort analysis, develop possible marital role expectations for elderly couples. Pick at least three different periods of time as your starting points. Identify the age of the couples at present and provide explanations for your interpretation. Are there changes in marital roles? Why?
3. Extrapolating from the material in the chapter, identify some stereotypes of married and unmarried elderly.
4. Although increasing, divorce among the elderly is still relatively rare. Why? Will divorce rates continue to increase among the elderly? To what would you attribute this increase (or decrease)?
5. Why does sexual activity decline among the elderly? To what extent is this decline related to societal stereotyping?
6. If adult children are not abandoning their elderly parent(s), what type of relationship exists? Considering the historical context of aging in America, describe the future adult child—elderly parent relationship.
7. Identify and discuss the four patterns of support and assistance between the adult child and the elderly parent.
8. Describe the relationship between grandparent and grandchildren. Considering the changing demographics, what changes will occur in this relationship?

9. Describe the formal support system. Do you think that the formal support system can provide for the needs of the elderly?
10. Construct a hypothetical situation in which the informal and formal support systems operate in concert for the betterment of the elderly they serve.
11. Evaluate the political economy argument regarding the formal support system. Are there other theories of aging that provide an explanation of the formal support system? Explain how they apply.

Glossary

Beanpole family Family structure today includes an increasing number of generations with fewer members. A visual image is that of a beanpole: tall and skinny.

Economic dependency ratio This ratio combines the age-16-and-under population and those 65 and over into the dependent population divided by the total number between 16 and 65 employed in the labor force.

Filial responsibility The expectation that adult children, rather than a governmental entity, will assume the caregiver role for their aging parents.

Formal support systems Organizations or agencies established around a bureaucratic structure that provide services to elderly clients. Formal systems operate independently of and in concert with informal support systems.

Informal support systems Family, friends, or even neighbors who provide services to the elderly. Distinct from formal systems, the informal system relies on an emotional and familial appeal for need rather than that of efficiency.

Suggested Reading

Copper, B. (1987). *Agism in the lesbian community.* Freedom, CA: Crossing Press.
A short but important book that addresses feelings of growing older within the lesbian community. The author discusses her feelings and the reactions of younger lesbians toward older women.

Doress, P. B., & Siegal, D. L. (1987). *Ourselves, growing older.* New York: Simon and Schuster.
This is an excellent resource guide for women as they grow older. The book covers an array of topics relevant to aging women.

Estes, C. L. (1981). *The aging enterprise.* San Francisco: Jossey-Bass.
The author argues that social policies have not fully addressed the disadvantaged conditions within which many elderly are found. A thought-provoking book that questions the intent of many formal support systems.

Shanas, E. (1961). Living arrangements of older people in the U.S. *Gerontologist, 1,* 27–29.
A classic article that is required reading. The author discounts the prevailing myth of elderly parents being abandoned by their adult children.

Shanas, E., & Sussman, M. B. (Eds). (1977). *Family, bureaucracy, and the elderly.* Durham, NC: Duke University Press.
As the title implies, this book offers the reader a cross-cultural examination of the connections between intergenerational relations and bureaucracy.

Troll, L. E. (1971). The family of later life: A decade review. *Journal of Marriage and the Family, 33*(2), 263–290.
Although dated, this article provides the reader with an early historical account of the research in intergenerational family relations.

References

Adams, B. N. (1970, November). Isolation, function, and beyond: American kinship in the 1960s. *Journal of Marriage and the Family 32,* 575–597.

Adelman, M. (1991). Stigma, gay lifestyles, and adjustment to aging: A study of later-life gay men and lesbians. *Journal of Homosexuality, 20*(3–4), 7–32.

Arber, S., & Ginn, J. (1991). *Gender and later life.* Newbury Park, CA: Sage.

Arendell, T., & Estes, C. L. (1991). Older women in the post-Reagan era. In M. Minkler & C. L. Estes (Eds.), *Critical perspectives on aging: The political and moral economy of growing old.* (pp. 209–226). Amityville, NY: Baywood.

Bengtson, V. L., & Silverstein, M. (1993). Families, aging, and social change: Seven agendas for 21st-century researchers. In G. L. Maddox & M. P. Lawton (Eds.), *Annual review of gerontology and geriatrics: Focus on kinship, aging, and social change* (pp. 15–38). New York: Springer.

Binstock, R. H. (1991, Summer/Fall). From the Great Society to the Aging Society—25 years of the Older Americans Act. *Generations, 15*(3), 11–18.

Brubaker, T. H. (1985). *Later life families.* Beverly Hills, CA: Sage.

Busse, E., & Maddox, G. (1985). *The Duke longitudinal studies of normal aging: 1955–1980.* New York: Springer.

Cantor, M., & Little, V. (1985). Aging and social care. In R. H. Binstock & E. Shanas (Eds.), *Handbook of aging and the social sciences* (2nd ed., pp. 745–781). New York: Van Nostrand Reinhold.

Catania, J. A., Turner, H., Kegeles, S. M., Stall, R., Pollack, L., & Coates, T. J. (1989). Older Americans and AIDS: Transmission risks and primary prevention research needs. *Gerontologist, 29*(3), 373–381.

Cherlin, A. J., & Furstenberg, F. F., Jr. (1986). *The new American grandparent.* New York: Basic Books.

Christensen, H. T., & Johnsen, K. P. (1971). *Marriage and the family* (3rd ed.). New York: The Ronald Press.

Cicirelli, V. G., Coward, R. T., & Dwyer, J. W. (1992, September). Siblings as caregivers for impaired elders. *Research on Aging, 14*(3), 331–350.

Copper, B. (1987). *Ageism in the lesbian community.* Freedom, CA: Crossing Press.

Dobelstein, A. W., & Johnson, A. B. (1985). *Serving older adults: Policy, programs, and professional activities.* Englewood Cliffs, NJ: Prentice-Hall.

Doress, P. B., & Siegal, D. L. (1987). *Ourselves, growing older.* New York: Simon and Schuster.

England, S. E., Keigher, S. M., Miller, B., & Linsk, N. L. (1991). Community care policies and gender justice. In M. Minkler & C. L. Estes (Eds.), *Critical perspectives on aging: The political and moral economy of growing old* (pp. 227–244). Amityville, NY: Baywood.

Estes, C. L. (1981). *The aging enterprise.* San Francisco: Jossey-Bass.

Estes, C. L. (1991). The new political economy of aging: Introduction and critique. In M. Minkler & C. L. Estes (Eds.), *Critical perspectives on aging: The political and moral economy of growing old* (pp. 19–36). Amityville, NY: Baywood.

Friend, R. A. (1990). Older lesbian and gay people: Responding to homophobia. *Marriage and Family Review, 14*(3–4), 241–263.

George, L. K., & Weiler, S. J. (1985). Sexuality in middle and late life. In E. Palmore (Ed.), *Normal aging III* (pp. 12–19). Durham, NC: Duke University Press.

Gershenson Hodgson, L. (1992). Adult grandchildren and their grandparents: The enduring bond. *International Journal of Aging and Human Development, 34*(3), 209–225.

Gilford, R. (1991). Marriages in later life. In H. Cox (Ed.), *Aging* (7th ed., pp. 37–41). Guilford, CT: Dushkin.

Haber, D. (1989). *Health care for an aging society.* New York: Hemisphere.

Hess, B. B., & Waring, J. M. (1983). Changing patterns of aging and family bonds in later life. In A. S. Skolnick & J. H. Skolnick (Eds.), *Family in transition* (4th ed., pp. 521–537). Boston: Little, Brown and Company.

Hewitt, P. S., & Howe, N. (1992). Generational equity and the future of generational politics. In H. Cox (Ed.), *Aging* (8th ed., pp. 233–236). Guilford, CT: Dushkin.

Johnson, E. S., & Bursk, B. J. (1977). Relationships between the elderly and their adult children. *Gerontologist, 17*(1), 90–96.

Levy, J. A., & Albrecht, G. L. (1989). A review of research on sexual and AIDS-related attitudes and behaviors. In M. W. Riley, M. G. Ory, & D. Zablotsky (Eds.), *AIDS in an aging society* (pp. 39–59). New York: Springer.

Longino, C. F., Jr., Warheit, G. J., & Green, J. A. (1989). Class, aging, and health. In K. S. Markides (Ed.), *Aging and health: Perspectives on gender, race, ethnicity, and class* (pp. 79–109). Newbury Park, CA: Sage.

Mancini, J. A., & Blieszner, R. (1989, May). Aging parents and adult children: Research themes in intergenerational relations. *Journal of Marriage and the Family, 51,* 275–290.

Masters, W., & Johnson, V. (1966). *Human sexual response.* Boston: Little, Brown.

Masters, W., & Johnson, V. (1970). *Human sexual inadequacy.* Boston: Little, Brown.

Minkler, M. (1991). "Generational equity" and the new victim blaming. In M. Minkler & C. L. Estes (Eds.), *Critical perspectives on aging: The political and moral economy of growing old* (pp. 67–80). Amityville, NY: Baywood.

Monk, A. (1992). Aging, generational continuity, and filial support. In H. Cox (Ed.), *Aging* (8th ed., pp. 199–205). Guilford, CT: Dushkin.

Mutran, E., & Reitzes, D. C. (1990). Intergenerational exchange relationships in the aging family. In K. F. Ferraro (Ed.), *Gerontology: Perspectives and issues* (pp. 149–161). New York: Springer.

National Center for Health Statistics. (1993). *Health United States, 1992.* Hyattsville, MD: Public Health Service.

Palmore, E. (1970). *Normal aging.* Durham, NC: Duke University Press.

Palmore, E. (1974). *Normal aging II.* Durham, NC: Duke University Press.

Palmore, E. (1985). *Normal aging III.* Durham, NC: Duke University Press.

Pope, M., & Schulz, R. (1991). Sexual attitudes and behavior in midlife and aging homosexual males. *Journal of Homosexuality, 20*(3–4), 169–177.

Reiss, I. L., & Lee, G. R. (1988). *Family systems in America* (4th ed.). New York: Holt, Rinehart and Winston.

Riley, M. W. (1989). AIDS and older people: The overlooked segment of the population. In M. W. Riley, M. G. Ory, & D. Zablotsky (Eds.), *AIDS in an aging society* (pp. 3–26). New York: Springer.

Riley, M. W., & Riley, J. W., Jr. (1993). Connections: Kin and cohort. In V. L. Bengtson & W. A.

Achenbaum (Eds.), *The changing contract across generations* (pp. 169–189). New York: Aldine DeGruyter.

Roberto, K. A., & Stroes, J. (1992). Grandchildren and grandparents: Roles, influences, and relationships. *International Journal of Aging and Human Development, 34*(3), 227–239.

Rollins, B. C., & Feldman, H. (1970). Marital satisfaction over the family life cycle. *Journal of Marriage and the Family, 32*(1), 20–28.

Shanas, E. (1961). Living arrangements of older people in the United States. *Gerontologist, 1,* 27–29.

Shanas, E., & Sussman, M. B. (1981). The family in later life: Social structure and social policy. In J. G. March (Ed.), *Aging: Stability and change in the family* (pp. 211–231). New York: Academic Press.

Shanas, E., Townsend, P., Wedderburn, D., Friis, H., Mihhoj, P., & Stehouwer, J. (1968). *Older people in three industrial societies.* New York: Atherton Press.

Siegel, J. S. (1993). *A generation of change: A profile of America's older population.* New York: Russell Sage Foundation.

Stahl, S. M., & Potts, M. K. (1985). Social support and chronic disease: A propositional inventory. In W. A. Peterson & J. Quadagno (Eds.), *Social bonds in later life: Aging and interdependence* (pp. 305–323). Beverly Hills, CA: Sage.

Stine, G. J. (1993). *Acquired immune deficiency syndrome.* Englewood Cliffs, NJ: Prentice Hall.

Stoller, E. P., & Cutler, S. J. (1992). The impact of gender on configurations of care among married elderly couples. *Research on Aging, 14*(3), 313–330.

Sussman, M. B. (1985). The family life of old people. In R. H. Binstock & E. Shanas (Eds.), *Handbook of aging and the social sciences* (2nd ed., pp. 415–449). New York: Van Nostrand Reinhold.

Treas, J. (1977). Family support systems for the aged: Some social and demographic considerations. *Gerontologist, 17,* 486–491.

Troll, L. E. (1971). The family in later life: A decade review. *Journal of Marriage and the Family, 33*(2), 263–290.

U.S. Bureau of the Census. (1993). Living arrangements of the elderly. *Profiles of America's elderly.* Washington, DC.

U.S. Bureau of the Census. (1993). *Statistical abstract of the United States: 1993* (113th ed.). Washington, DC.

U.S. Bureau of the Census. (1994). *Statistical abstract of the United States: 1994* (114th ed.). Washington, DC.

U.S. Department of Labor. (1994). *The American work force: 1992–2005.* Bulletin 2452. Bureau of Labor Statistics, Washington DC.

Wander, H. (1978). Zero population growth now: The lessons from Europe. In T. J. Epenshade & W. J. Serow (Eds.), *The economic consequences of slowing population growth* (pp. 57–58). New York: Academic Press.

Zopf, P. E., Jr. (1986). *America's older population.* Houston: Cap and Gown Press.

Chapter 6

Aging in a Changing Economy

Just as the present reflects the past, it also determines the future. The options for work and retirement in late adulthood, with their implications for income adequacy or inadequacy three or four decades from now, will be largely determined by current and future decisions in the private and public sectors. Careful thought should therefore be given now to ways of improving economic security mechanisms in order to provide better options regarding work and retirement in old age; that is, a better future for an aging society.
—CHEN, 1988, P. 190

Every day the print and electronic media report the effects of a changing economic climate in the United States. We continue to read and hear about corporations laying off thousands of their employees or permanently closing their factory gates in favor of cheaper labor in less developed nations. As a result, the current economic climate is highly unstable and expectedly unpredictable. American workers have discovered that loyalty to the company is not always reciprocal. Nor does increased worker productivity guarantee continued employment. As a result, this is a particularly difficult economic period for American workers.

These economic difficulties have produced mixed results for the mature worker. (As used throughout this chapter, the term *mature worker* refers to a person aged 40 or over who is engaged in the world of work.) When companies idle workers, it is generally easier for a younger worker to move and find new employment. Mature workers, being less mobile, are more likely to remain in the area. Because they do not relocate, mature workers are therefore more likely to be recalled if the company begins rehiring (Sandell & Baldwin, 1990). At the same time, mature workers experience increased difficulty in reemployment because of their age (Hutchens, 1993). Attempting to start over at age 55 or 60 is extremely difficult. An equivalent position is unlikely to exist, leaving the unemployed older worker with little choice but to accept lower-paying wages with lowered expectations of Social Security benefits. In addition, private pensions are increasingly the responsibility of the worker rather than a benefit of the workplace. Considering the current wage level for many, saving for one's retirement years is not easy.

The consequences of the current economic conditions extend far beyond the present. As young and middle-aged workers are forced to seek employment elsewhere and company loyalty fades, workers are becoming increasingly more cynical of the economic system and those who benefit from it. In particular, there is an increasing intergenerational tension between the younger and the mature workers. There is a misplaced belief on the part of younger workers that the elderly are responsible for the current economic difficulties (Estes, 1981; Farrell, Palmer, Atchison, & Andelman, 1994). This misplaced belief is grounded in a misunderstanding of the Social Security system and the societal construction of aging as an economic social problem.

Historically, growing old generally did not mean leaving the world of work. Instead, the elderly remained wedded to their work until they died or turned the property over to a son (Levine, 1988). Whereas the past offered little assurance of life outside the work world, the present offers little assurance of continuation in the work world. Examining this chapter within the context of a social problems approach, you will understand the significance of issues raised in previous chapters. For example, in Chapter 5 the provision of care to family members was disproportionately the role of women. The stereotypic expectation explicit in the work world is that it is a man's world.

This chapter is about more than the world of work. It is about removal from work, the lack of work, and the inability to earn enough money not to be poor. We will examine the problem of poverty among the elderly, particularly in light of the myth that all elderly today are wealthy. The social construction of aging as a social problem is interwoven throughout the chapter.

The World of Work

Within American society, the significance of work is well established. Historically, males were socialized to enter the world of work. Today, socialization to the world of work has becoming increasingly gender neutral. Serious economic differentiation between men and women remains a contemporary problem. This socialization occurs as children engage in various career performances during play. These performances begin early in life when children model themselves after their parents, eventually progressing to a wider repertoire involving other significant figures in their lives.

We unofficially enter the world of work when we are given household tasks to perform in exchange for an allowance. Although these tasks are, for the most part, gender specific, they introduce us to the expectations of others relative to our performance. Eventually, we broaden our work experience beyond the family. It is generally at this point that most young people enter the official world of work. We usually begin this phase with part-time employment during the summer. Once we enter this world of official work, we are likely to remain in it for at least four decades. Although the number of elderly remaining in the labor force has declined, the percentage remain significant. Table 6–1 identifies labor force participation rates for elderly men and women. Two significant trends are evident in Table 6–1. The first is that the rate of participation in the labor force continues to decrease among the elderly. The second trend is that the rate of labor force participation between men and women has been decreasing. Greater involvement of women in the world of work has helped to shift this trend toward parity in the workplace.

Depending on gender, one will, on average, hold between 10 and 12 different jobs throughout one's lifetime (Mitchell, 1993). These job changes may be voluntary or involuntary. When they are voluntary, they are generally the result of increased specialization or skill acquisition on the part of the worker. Job changes have resulted in an increased rate of mobility among Americans. Although the rate of mobility has declined in the recent past, we nonetheless are still willing to relocate for economic reasons. Relocation continues to create ramifications for family obligations (see Chapter 5).

TABLE 6–1   Civilian Labor Force Participation Rates for Men and Women Aged 65 and Over, 1970–2005

	1970	1980	1985	1990	1991	2000	2005
Male	26.8	19.0	15.8	16.4	15.8	15.8	16.0
Female	9.7	8.1	7.3	8.7	8.6	8.6	8.8
Rate of labor force participation: men to women	2.76	2.35	2.16	1.89	1.83	1.83	1.82

Source: U.S. Bureau of the Census. (1992). *Statistical abstract of the United States: 1992* (112th ed.). Table 609. Washington, DC: U.S. Government Printing Office.

When job changes are involuntary, they are generally the result of *worker dislocation.* In other words, the worker is laid off from work and forced to find employment elsewhere. Those workers who remain unemployed because of plant closing or other structural change in the economy are referred to as "dislocated workers" (Maynard, 1990). Recent events on the national and international level have created conditions that enhance the prospect of economic uncertainty. The fluidity of the job market is becoming an all-too-familiar consequence of the world of work today.

The Changing Job Market

Two hundred years ago, the vast majority of Americans were self-employed, primarily in agriculture. One hundred years ago, the emergence of an industrial manufacturing base created a demand for a new workforce that would work for someone else and for a wage. Today, less than 5 percent of the workforce is in agriculture, and less than 20 percent is in manufacturing. The job market today involves primarily service-sector employment.

To appreciate fully the historical changes occurring in the job market, complete the following exercise. If you live in a relatively urban area, read the obituaries of those aged 65 and over. Identify the occupation of the deceased. What percentage of the men were retired from factories, mills, or other forms of manufacturing formerly located in your hometown or surrounding area? Many of these facilities had been the lifeblood of the local community, but because of changing technology needs they were closed. Do the same thing for elderly women. What percentage of women were employed at that time? In what type of work were women most likely to be found?

The changing job market can be particularly troublesome for the mature worker (those aged 40 and over). The federal government recognizes those aged 40 and over as complainants in *age discrimination* lawsuits. We will discuss this problem in greater detail in a later section. For now, it is important to realize that there has been a steady increase in the number of age discrimination lawsuits brought before the court system in the last 25 years (Hale, 1990). A number of interrelated factors provide a partial explanation. Throughout the 1970s the baby boom generation continued to enter the world of work at a time when job opportunities were not keeping pace with the number of applicants. At the same time, the economy was experiencing "stagflation." This term refers to rising rates of inflation during a period of zero growth in the economy. The 1980s gave rise to "trickle-down economics." This approach argued that if the individuals who run the corporations receive substantial tax advantages, they will have more money to spend and hire more workers because of increased consumer demand. Instead, corporations used the tax breaks to engage in takeovers of other corporations. Mergers and acquisitions became standard fare during this period. When companies merge or one buys out another, there is usually an overlapping of jobs resulting in redundancy. This attitude of economic Darwinism continues to permeate the world of work. As a consequence, mature workers have been as vulnerable as their younger co-workers to layoffs and firings. The fate of mature workers appears to be related to factors such as their level of skill training, their willingness to engage in retraining, their level of education, and their willingness to remain in the local area. Mature workers were more likely to be recalled after a layoff because of their job seniority (Sandell & Baldwin, 1990). However, research findings also indicate that mature workers are less likely to find comparable salary positions after being laid off from their present position (Sandell & Baldwin, 1990). Thus age discrimination lawsuits by the mature worker became a tool to ensure equal opportunity in the workplace. During this period of time (roughly from the latter 1970s to the present) the job market continued to experience significant change. Companies continue to "downsize" through layoffs while the positions that remain demand an increased knowledge of technology. The computerization of the workplace has created less demand for the types of experiences identified with the mature worker. As a result, the status of mature workers relative to their younger counterparts has declined during this period of time. As Schor (1992, p. 28) states,

> According to a 1990 survey of men between the ages of fifty-five and sixty-four who were out of the labor force, almost half (45%) would prefer to have jobs, a far larger percentage than has previously been recognized. Mandatory retirement and pressures to take early leave have led many unwillingly out of the world of work. Plant closing, corporate restructuring, and ageism have contributed to their difficulties in finding re-employment.

Factors such as the changing demographic structure of society, the effect of the changing job market, and the increased competition for available positions have created an increased feeling of alienation among the mature workforce. *Alienation* refers to "a condition in which men are dominated by forces of their own creation, which confront them as alien powers" (Coser, 1977, p. 50). More specifically, Coser (1977, p. 51) states that "alienation in the domain of work has a fourfold aspect: Man is alienated from the objects he produces, from the process of production, from himself, and from the community of his fellows."

The concept of alienation is particularly applicable to the mature worker. As the workplace becomes increasingly impersonal and competitive, and when knowledge associated with increasing age is devalued, the mature worker becomes even more alienated toward the production of goods or services. Alienation occurs because the mature worker is evaluated on the basis of age and productivity, thus creating a feeling of dissonance. That is, if mature workers attempt to deny their age, they become alienated from who they are. In essence, they are denying their own existence. However, if they deny their ability to be productive because of their age, they alienate themselves from the one societal process that produces their social status. At issue then is which is more valuable to the mature worker, their age or social position. Social position generally emerges victorious. The key point to remember in all of this is that the dichotomy between age and productivity is socially created. That is, increasing age and level of economic productivity need not be mutually exclusive. They become mutually exclusive when they are manufactured as distinct elements incapable of coexistence. What has been created is yet another myth of aging that argues that mature workers cannot be productive workers.

Not all mature workers experience such difficulty. As with any age group, employment opportunities and experiences differ for mature workers depending on their occupation (Hayward, Hardy, & Grady, 1989). For example, Williamson, Munley, and Evans (1980, p. 150) point out that "those persons who perceive their jobs as alienating, and thus as something to be eagerly relinquished in favor of retirement, are often those whose jobs have least prepared them for the self-direction so useful to leisure activities and retirement." We will continue to examine this issue in the next section.

Age and Occupational Status

Occupational status can be defined as the social and economic position one occupies in society as a result of the work performed. One's occupational status influences various employment conditions. For example, one's occupational status is linked to the likelihood of continued employment (Sandell & Baldwin, 1990), the transition from worker to retiree, the potential for unemployment, and the level of economic condition one may expect (Torres-Gill, 1992; Pampel & Hardy, 1994). This is because the occupation itself influences the opportunity structure for the elderly person. That is, professional job holders are provided greater latitude in decision making and enjoy considerable independence. Work allows them the freedom to explore new ideas and interact with others in the process of work (Zopf, 1986). On the other hand, blue-collar workers are generally not provided similar opportunities to make job-related decisions. They are expected to follow the orders of others in the completion of their task. As a result, levels of job satisfaction are generally lower among workers in low-status occupations (Maccoby & Terzi, 1989).

Although most elderly are no longer in the workforce, a small minority remain. The occupational distribution of this segment of the workforce is presented in Table 6–2.

Occupational areas in which the elderly tend to continue employment beyond age 65 are generally in the areas of "service, trade, and agriculture" (Matras, 1990, p. 223). Based on the numbers presented in Table 6–2, this trend is evident for elderly women as well.

The desire to remain active in the workplace is a decision made by the worker. It is also a decision made by those who own the workplace. When we discuss the concept of work, we cannot do so without exploring the role of the owners of the world of work.

TABLE 6–2 Employment of Persons Aged 65 and Over by Major Industry Group and by Sex: 1991

Industry	Men	Women
Agriculture	234,000	34,000
Mining	9,000	2,000
Construction	105,000	18,000
Manufacturing	203,000	106,000
Transportation, communications, and other public utilities	96,000	27,000
Trade	389,000	344,000
Financial, insurance, and real estate	151,000	96,000
Services	666,000	774,000
Public administration	70,000	59,000
Total	1,923,000	1,460,000

Source: U.S. Department of Labor, Bureau of Labor Statistics. N.d. Unpublished data from the Current Population Survey. Washington, DC.

Control of the Workplace and Decision Making

Thus far we have been discussing the role of the aging worker vis-à-vis the economic institution. Implicit within this argument is that the mature worker is just that: a person who is employed in a position and paid by others for the products or services that are produced. The elderly, however, are a rather diverse population. Not only do the elderly work for others, but they are also the owners of businesses. Economic decision making is increasingly becoming a function of all age groups, including the elderly. Occupational decision making by the elderly will continue to increase as the baby boom generation reaches age 65 beginning in the year 2011.

Most mature workers, however, do not enjoy such decision-making power. Instead, they are subject to age-graded treatment that negatively affects their economic well-being. In other words, they are being discriminated against on the basis of their age.

Age Discrimination

Increasingly, mature workers experience discriminatory practices within the workplace. The following scenarios illustrate the subtle (and not so subtle) forms of age discrimination.

> Joe has been employed as a district manager for the last 20 years with the same company. He started with the company directly out of college, working in the sales department. Eventually, promotions lead him to his current position. He has been with the company for over 40 years now and expects to retire next year. This morning he is called into the vice president's office and is told that he is being fired because the company is downsizing and cannot afford "dead wood" at his level. Because he is fired, he loses 40 years of retirement investment with the company.

> Pete has been employed as an assembly line worker at a local manufacturing plant for the past 35 years. Although the work is physical, Pete has been able to maintain a consistent level of productivity. The company has begun to modernize the plant by adding technological tools to do some of the work. The supervisor informed Pete that his position will require an increased level of technological ability. As a result, his position will be assigned to a younger worker who "understands" computers. Pete is told he can either take a lower-status position on the line or leave.

In the past, age discrimination in the workplace could exist in any number of behaviors. Kendig (1979, pp. 302–303) identifies the following:

1. Dismissal of older employees without cause
2. Involuntary retirement on an individual basis and not agreed on as a condition of employment
3. Maximum age limitations for initial employment within an organization with little or no supporting justification for such a requirement
4. Limitations placed on promotion or training based on age
5. Consideration of only younger employees for certain positions without valid occupational reasons for doing so

Age discrimination is a serious problem. The number of age discrimination lawsuits filed with the Equal Employment Opportunity Commission (EEOC) has increased in the past 10 years. According to Table 6–3, the number of cases reported to the EEOC has increased from some 15,000 in 1984 to 17,000 in 1994. The consequence of age discrimination is a diminution of self-esteem among those elderly attempting to remain engaged in the larger world of work.

Age discrimination in the workplace is illegal. In 1967 the federal government passed the Age Discrimination in Employment Act. This act "is intended to promote employment of older people based on ability rather than age to prohibit discrimination" (Torres-Gill, 1992, p. 50). Originally, the ADEA only protected workers aged 40–65 who were employed in firms with more than 25 employees (Rich & Baum, 1984). The act was first amended in 1974. At that time, governmental employees at all levels were included (Rich & Baum, 1984). A 1978 amendment "extended protection against age discrimination to nonfederal employees up to age 69 and eliminated the upper age limit entirely for employees of the federal government" (Schulz, Borowski, & Crown, 1991, p. 153). In 1986 mandatory retirement was abolished for virtually all employees, although some exceptions "are justified and legally acceptable when the employer can show that age is a bona fide occupational qualification reasonably necessary to the normal operations of a business. . . . Organizational practices, such as setting maximum age limits on hiring, must be substantiated with proof that age requirements are essential for the protection of the public or allowed on the basis of some reasonable factors other than age, such as physical fitness" (Sterns, Matheson, & Schwartz, 1990, p. 166).

Initially, concern had been expressed that as the age of retirement was removed, large numbers of older workers would remain in the labor force. That fear was never realized (Morrison, 1986). In fact, the median age at retirement continues to decrease (see Table 6–4 on page 117 for specific ages). Unfortunately, age discrimination is difficult to identify and even more difficult to prosecute. As a result, mature workers face an uncertain future. On the one hand, there is a projected shortage of workers in the near term. However, the areas within which workers will be needed does not match particularly well with the areas in which many mature workers are found. This employment mismatch will continue and will be exacerbated by the continuing low wage rate paid to an increasing number of workers.

Age discrimination in the workplace is the result of a number of societal-level factors. First, and perhaps most basic, is that of economics. As corporations continue to reduce their workforce, they will attempt to eliminate those employees who are the most expensive (Hale, 1990). In a period of economic Darwinism, the mature worker is considered expendable. The mature worker is also considered less prepared for the changing technological advances occurring in the workplace. Second, there is a growing intolerance toward aging workers. As younger workers question the future viability of the Social Security system, the current recipients become easy scapegoats. Third, demographic changes will occur as a result of population aging. For example, the baby boom generation will begin to turn 65 in the year 2011. If, at that point, the economy is unable to support an increasing number of elderly who need to remain in the workforce, intergenerational conflict over the availability of jobs may emerge. Fourth, discrimination will continue because the value associated with aging continues to decline in American society.

TABLE 6–3   Age Discrimination Suits: 1984–1994

	1984	1986	1990	1992	1994
Federal (EEOC)	15,614	17,443	14,526	19,350	17,009

Source: Equal Employment Opportunity Commission (EEOC).
Washington, DC. 1995.

Age discrimination occurs as a result of any one of these factors. Thus, not only is the status of the elderly devalued in American society, but the availability of economic role opportunities is also limited. Increasingly, the mature worker is left with few occupational options. One available option is that of retirement, which will be addressed in the next section.

The Meaning of Retirement

How do you define *retirement?* The word evokes a plethora of definitions that attempt to address the intricacies associated with the concept. Two definitions provide the reader with the range associated with the term. According to Parnes and Less (1985, p. 57), "*retirement* [italics in original] implies complete cessation of all labor market activity at some reasonably advanced age." This definition is particularly vague regarding a point at which activity will cease. At the same time, the definition is quite specific regarding the level of work activity necessary to differentiate between employed and retired. Atchley (1976, p. 1) defines retirement as

> a condition in which an individual is forced or allowed to be and is employed less than full-time (whatever that may mean in his particular job) and in which his income is derived at least in part from a retirement pension earned through prior years of service as a job holder. Both of these conditions must be met for an individual to be retired.

Atchley's definition suggests that retirement is a process rather than an event. Atchley also implies a level of work activity that qualifies as retired. Finally, Atchley includes income received as a result of previous employment as a condition of retirement. These definitions certainly do not exhaust the range of interpretations available. These definitions do, however, provide an example of criteria required (or expected) in defining retirement.

We will examine retirement within a variety of social contexts. That is, retirement is a process that begins early in one's work life and culminates in a benchmark day in which one's social status is redefined by a ceremony honoring workplace disengagement, which results in a period of readjustment to a life consisting primarily of noneconomic activity. Retirement is also a societal response to the vagaries of an economic system in which a modicum of support is provided the elderly. Retirement is also a social redefinition of the social status of an aging individual. Throughout all of this, retirement is a socially constructed demarcation date utilized in a potentially discriminatory manner toward the elderly. We begin our examination of retirement with a brief historical sketch of retirement and the pension system in American history. We will then explore the demographics of retirement and the future of the Social Security system. Finally, we will examine retirement as a social process, within the time line constructed by Atchley (1976).

With the emergence of industrialization in Europe and the United States, the nature of the world of work changed. In Germany, Otto von Bismarck established the first national pension system in 1889. With the age of retirement originally set at 70, few workers qualified for benefits because they generally did not live that long. The age of retirement was later reduced to 65 in the early 1900s (Levine, 1988).

Retirement in America has been noted as far back as 1713 (Haber, 1978). According to Levine (1988) public pensions date back to at least the Civil War. Levine (1988, p. 21) notes that "there were both state and federal pensions for veterans of every American war. . . ." Within the private sector of the economy, American Express proposed a pension plan in 1875 (Williamson, Shindul, & Evans, 1985). In 1884 the Baltimore and Ohio Railroad implemented the first pension plan (Levine, 1988). The eventual transformation of the worker from engagement in the paid labor market to the status of nonemployment had begun. Haber (1978, p. 77) suggests that

> what was new to the late 19th century was the growing demand by a wide variety of companies that their workers automatically retire at some specific, predetermined age. This arbitrary separation of the old from the young had a significant effect upon the life of every aging worker, both in terms of his own self-image and in the way he was perceived by others.

Relative to retirement, it is important to realize that at the beginning of the 20th century the ratio of men to women at age 65 was approximately 1 to 1. Today that ratio has declined to approximately 65 males for every 100 females (Meier & Boyle Torrey, 1982). The reasons cited by Meier and Boyle Torrey (1982, p. 66) for the 1-to-1 ratio include "the large immigration of males in the 19th century and the high mortality of women in the childbearing years." During this period of time, the majority of men aged 65 and over remained engaged in the workforce. Older workers were beginning to experience the effects of industrialization, however, as jobs became more difficult to maintain (Meier & Boyle Torrey, 1982). It would appear that the emergence of private and eventually public pension systems provided a mechanism through which room could be made in the expanding industrial workplace for an influx of younger workers. Today, because of decreasing sex ratios, retirement income increasingly provides economic support to elderly women who are widows of retired men. As these differences in mortality rates between elderly men and women remain, social policy will continue to shape the meaning of pensions and retirement.

The dawn of the 20th century in the United States brought forth a most infamous speech by Dr. Osler, who was leaving Johns Hopkins for Oxford. In his presentation on February 22, 1905, Osler outlined two ideas. His first point addresses the issue of old age. His second point is of particular interest here because he quite emphatically argues for the retirement of those over the age of 60. In order to provide the reader with the image he created of age, an extended excerpt of his presentation follows.

I have two fixed ideas well known to my friends, harmless obsessions with which I some-times bore them, but which have a direct bearing on this important problem. The first is the comparative uselessness of men above forty years of age. This may seem shocking, and yet read aright the world's history bears out the statement. Take the sum of human achievement in action, in science, in art, in literature—subtract the work of the men above forty, and while we should miss great treasures, even priceless treasures, we would practically be where we are to-day. It is difficult to name a great and far-reaching conquest of the mind which has not been given to the world by a man on whose back the sun was still shining. The effective, moving, vitalizing work of the world is done between the ages of twenty-five and forty—these golden years of plenty, the anabolic or constructive period, in which there is always a balance in the mental bank and the credit is still good. In the science and art of medicine young or comparatively young men have made every advance of the first rank. . . .

My second fixed idea is the uselessness of men above sixty years of age, and the incal-culable benefit it would be in commercial, political and in professional life if, as a matter of course, men stopped work at this age. . . . As it can be maintained that all the great advances have come from men under forty, so the history of the world shows that a very large proportion of the evils may be traced to the sexagenarians—nearly all the great mis-takes politically and socially, all of the worst poems, most of the bad pictures, a majority of the bad novels, not a few of the bad sermons and speeches. (Osler, 1932, pp. 381–383)

An inevitable outrage ensued regarding his age-specific comments. He was vilified as an enemy of the aged, whereas others (those under age 25) considered his rationality as essential in a new age of work (Graebner, 1980).

In addition to the age-graded rationality of Osler, the 20th century also ushered in the application of pension plans into government as well as private industry. Among federal employees, the first piece of legislation addressing retirement was signed into law in 1920 (Graebner, 1980). The most significant piece of federal legislation regarding retirement was the Social Security Act of 1935. The passage and signing of this legislation culminat-ed a lengthy debate regarding the role of government, particularly during a time of severe economic crisis. In response to increasing pressure for more radical reform, President Roo-sevelt signed the Social Security Act into law in 1935 (Wallace, Williamson, Lung, & Powell, 1991).

During the Great Depression of the 1930s, various schemes were created to revitalize the economy. One idea gained significant support among the elderly. It was referred to as the Townsend plan. Francis Townsend was a physician living in California during the Depression. After losing his position with a local health department, he began writing let-ters to the local newspaper in which he outlined the reason for the Depression and a unique method to cure the problem (Fischer, 1978). Basically, the Depression was the result of "excess production." Townsend argued that what was needed was "an old age pension (supported by a sales tax) of $150 a month for everyone over sixty" (Fischer, 1978, p. 180). The pension would be provided on the condition that the elderly person (then aged 60) would spend all of the money every month. The idea is that increasing the supply of money would facilitate growth in other segments of the economy. Eventually, the Townsend plan had some 3.5 million followers nationwide (Fischer, 1978). Although federal efforts to implement his program failed, the national sentiment that emerged in support of his ideas laid the groundwork for the emergence of the Social Security Act of 1935.

As the Great Depression ended, world events forewarned the United States of its impending responsibilities to the global community. The American entry into World War II resulted in the departure of many eligible males from the workforce. The departure of these men created an increased need for workers throughout the occupational structure. Throughout World War II women assumed a significant role in the labor market. In addition, the elderly remained a viable segment of the labor force. It was not until after World War II that increased rates of retirement were noted, as servicemen returned home in search of civilian work.

The number of private pension plans, and concomitantly the number of workers covered, remained relatively small until the 1940s. Workers covered by pensions were generally located in "railroad, banking, and public utility sectors of the economy" (Clark, 1990, p. 76). Even as late as 1950, only one-fourth of private-sector workers were covered by a pension. This increased to over 50 percent in the mid-1980s (Clark, 1990). Today the availability of pension income is dependent on marital status. For example, 61 percent of elderly couples reported receiving pension income. However, only 52 percent of unmarried men and 42 percent of unmarried women reported pension income (*Social Security Bulletin,* 1994).

Retirement and an accompanying pension plan may become less of a workplace reality in the future. Many corporations today are reducing their commitment to pension plans as a component of the benefits package for their workers. As a result, an increasing number of workers are forced to establish their own pension fund through the use of 401(k)s. There is serious question whether these individuals will have enough money set aside to provide for their needs upon retirement (Woods, 1989). The lack of retirement income in the future increases the risk of intergenerational dependency. In addition to the lack of private financial resources available at the time of retirement, the retirement event is occurring at an increasingly younger age for American workers (Gendell & Siegel, 1992). Comparing labor force participation rates between 1965 and 1985, Hayward, Crimmins, and Wray (1994, p. S220) point out that "retirement as a status clearly increased in popularity." Table 6–4 chronicles the changing median age at retirement for men and women in the United States.

According to the data in Table 6–4, American men and women are retiring at increasingly younger ages. Along with an increasing number of retirees, the average monthly Social Security benefit has also increased. In 1970 the average Social Security benefit for retirees aged 62 and over was $118. For a retired worker and wife, the benefit was $199. In 1990 average monthly benefits were $603 and $1,027, respectively (U.S. Bureau of the Census, 1992). This trend has created a serious problem for the Social Security system. As a result, the age of full retirement will gradually increase to 66 in 2009 and 67 in 2027 (Leonesio, 1993). The reason for increasing the age at retirement is to ensure the viability of the Social Security system. If workers remain employed longer, they continue to pay money into the system rather than retire and receive money from the system (Siegel, 1993). Fears of the Social Security system being bankrupt are exaggerated; yet realistic concerns exists as the baby boomers prepare to enter retirement.

The Social Security system obtains its funds from two sources: "the Federal Old-Age and Survivors Insurance (OASI) Trust Fund, which pays retirement and survivors benefits, and the Federal Disability Insurance (DI) Trust Fund, which pays benefits after a worker becomes disabled" (*Social Security Bulletin,* 1994, p. 53).

TABLE 6–4 **Median Age at Retirement, for Men and Women by Sex, for Selected Years, 1950–55 to 2000–05**

Period	Men	Women
1950–1955	66.9	67.7
1960–1965	65.2	64.6
1970–1975	63.4	63.0
1980–1985	62.8	62.7
1990–1995[a]	62.7	62.6
2000–2005[b]	61.7	61.2

[a]Actual 1990 data and projected 1995 data.
[b]Projected data.
Source: Gendell, M., & Siegel, J. S. (1992, July).
Trends in retirement age by sex, 1950–2005. *Monthly Labor Review,* p. 27.

At the present time, these two trust funds have very different futures. According to projections, the Disability Insurance trust fund will be exhausted sometime during 1995 unless adjustments are made. Meanwhile, the Old Age and Survivors Insurance is considered solvent. However, "the year of exhaustion for the OASI Trust Fund under intermediate assumptions does not occur until 2036" (*Social Security Bulletin,* 1994, p. 56).

There are two broad social forces at work regarding retirement and the ability of the Social Security system to remain solvent. On the one hand, the Social Security system needs mature workers to remain employed for as long as possible, thus avoiding the necessity of paying out benefits for extended periods of time. On the other hand, American workers continue to remove themselves from the world of work at even earlier ages than in the past. One consequence of these two seemingly intractable forces is an increase in the age at which Social Security benefits will begin (Siegel, 1993). Such age increases are already planned to take effect beginning early in the 21st century. However, these increases may need to be accelerated in an attempt to delay retirement for an increasingly larger number of American workers. A related problem with Social Security is the decreasing public confidence in the system. Chen (1989) points out that public confidence in Social Security decreased from 63 percent in 1975 to 40 percent in 1986. This lack of confidence has decreased not only among the young but the elderly as well. According to Chen (1989), such pessimism is unwarranted. Chen recommends that the workplace be restructured to allow continued employment for an aging workforce.

Aside from purely economic considerations, why do people retire from their jobs (or careers)? Parnes and Less (1985, p. 69) identify four basic reasons:

1. Persons who were involuntarily retired under a mandatory retirement plan (mandatory)
2. Those whose retirement appears from the total record to have been dictated by poor health (health)

3. Individuals whose retirement appears to have been attributable to labor market adversities (discouragement)
4. The remainder; that is, men who appear to have freely chosen retirement (voluntary)

Zopf (1986) further reduces the reasons for retirement into two basic types: involuntary and voluntary. He argues that involuntary retirement occurs when one is required to retire or is laid off from one's job, or because of health or disability. According to Zopf (1986), more than one-half of all retirees are involuntarily retired. According to Zopf (1986) about 45 percent of all retirement is voluntary. The reasons for voluntary retirement differ for men and women and by position in the occupational structure. Men are more likely to retire if they have an adequate pension and to enjoy the free time retirement offers. Women, on the other hand, are more likely to retire if family circumstances warrant. As mentioned in Chapter 5, women are generally the caregiver in an intergenerational relationship. As a result, women are likely to retire in order to spend a greater amount of time assuming the caregiver role and its attendant responsibilities (Zopf, 1986; Hatch, 1987). Henretta, O'Rand, and Chan (1993) examined the influence of gender on the likelihood of spousal retirement and did not discover any significant difference. Palmore, George, and Fillenbaum (1982) argue that when attempting to determine the predictors of retirement, the definition of retirement must be considered. They suggest that predictors of retirement differ depending on the definition of retirement that is being applied. For example, when "retirement is defined objectively as working less than full-time and receiving a pension, then the strongest predictors among those age 65 are structural factors such as SES and job characteristics that increase the incentives or necessity of retirement" (Palmore, George, & Fillenbaum, 1982, p. 741). When retirement is not operationalized, health status is identified as being influential in the decision-making process (Sickles & Taubman, 1986). The influence of health status on the decision to retirement is limited (Ruhm, 1989).

Occupationally, those with the greatest levels of education are the least likely to retire. It is obvious that if one enjoys one's career, and physical exertion is not required for the completion of tasks, retirement is unnecessary. For others, however, who are employed in jobs in which their "educations and opportunities have caused them to be laborers all of their working lives are apt to retire as soon as they can afford to do so, thus escaping the arduous physical demands of their jobs" (Zopf, 1986, p. 173). Research by Ozawa and Wai-on Law (1992) link increased retirement age, voluntary or involuntary retirement, and Social Security benefits. They began by dividing workers in two groups: advantaged and disadvantaged. The distinction between these groups include amount of wages earned, health, level of education, race, sex, and availability of pension. The authors conclude that "the financial implications of the change in the normal retirement age seem detrimental to disadvantaged workers. If the future cohort of advantaged workers work longer than previously, and if the disadvantaged groups of workers cannot work longer for reasons beyond their control, then the dispersion of Social Security benefits will become greater, making the income distribution among retired workers more unequal than it is today" (Ozawa & Wai-on Law, 1992, pp. 48–49).

Thus the income gap between the well-off elderly and the less well-off elderly is expected to continue into retirement. One's occupation, then, is an indication of one's probable involuntary or voluntary retirement and level of economic sufficiency. This is related to what is known as a "dual economic approach" to retirement. Hendricks and McAllister (1983) argue that from a dual-economy approach, one would examine retirees in terms of their former location within the occupational structure. The economic conditions of a retiree are represented by the financial resources and opportunities of the past. A dual-economy approach argues that occupations are located either in the core of the occupational structure or on its periphery. Those in the core have greater access to the resources necessary for retirement. Occupations on the periphery have less access and, as a result, offer fewer benefits. Workers located in core and periphery occupations differ in terms of a number of characteristics. Thus Hendricks and McAllister (1983) argue that less emphasis should be placed on individual differences and greater examination of the structural components that locate workers in this dual-economy retirement.

Knowing who retires and why is significant. This knowledge provides the basis for understanding and developing social policy. It is also important to understand the retirement process as it unfolds throughout life. Throughout this chapter we are, on the one hand, observing the effects of macro-level sociological analysis on behavior, while on the other hand we can engage in a micro-level inspection of the interaction that occurs as a result of such an event. It is to this second level of analysis that we now turn.

Retirement is also a process that involves not only the actor but also those with whom one maintains role relationships. The classic example is that of Atchley (1977), who developed a time-line typology of retirement. The time line is depicted in Figure 6–1.

Atchley (1976) divides the retirement process into two broad areas: preretirement and retirement. In the preretirement stage, the person experiences two phases: the remote and the near. The *remote phase* consists of the very early period of one's work life. For example, when college graduates enter the workforce they are in the remote phase. Many new workers contribute or their company will contribute to a retirement plan. The *near phase* begins when the worker and the workplace begin to plan for the eventual retirement of the worker. This phase will usually entail some type of preretirement counseling of the worker. It is at this point that the worker realizes that his or her official work life will end relatively soon. Expectant retirees play out the new role they will assume in a short period of time.

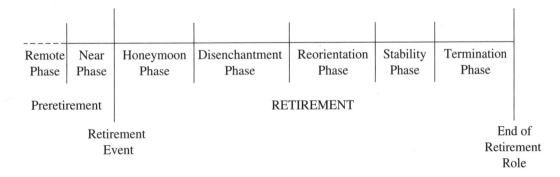

FIGURE 6–1   A Time Line Depicting the Phases of Retirement
Source: Atchley, R. C. (1976). *The sociology of retirement.* Cambridge, MA: Schenkman. Used with permission.

The retirement event is a demarcation between the official world of work and retirement. An office party, an official recognition, or whatever form of public acknowledgment is provided, and the worker is now declared retired. This public pronouncement creates new role opportunities and expectations for the retiree while eliminating previous role obligations. The new retiree enters the *honeymoon phase* of retirement ready to enjoy this newfound freedom from work. The retiree typically engages in a variety of activities he or she did not have time for earlier in life. This is an opportunity to "do it all." Like any honeymoon, the routine soon becomes the new reality. Atchley (1976, p. 68) suggests that "if the individual is able to settle into a routine that provides a satisfying life, then that routine will probably stabilize." For some retirees, however, the next phase comes all to quickly and with unfortunate consequences.

Retirees enter the *disenchantment phase* realizing that their expectations of retirement are not being met. Atchley indicates that research associated with this phase is virtually nonexistent. Essentially, this phase emerges when the reality of retirement is realized. For some, this is inconsequential. For others, however, particularly those with limited income and few available options, this realization can be traumatic.

For some retirees, the *reorientation phase* offers an opportunity to reexamine their experiences and construct a new set of options. It is during this phase that the retiree establishes a routine for living and a realistic outlook on retirement. For some, the transition to the next stage does not occur because they do not acquire or construct the alternatives necessary to establish stability.

The *stability phase* offers an even greater routinization of activity. Such routine, however, should not be considered as an unwillingness to change. Rather, stability implies the ability to address changes as they occur. It is at this point that the retiree has gained control over the retirement process. That is, the person has discovered his or her capabilities and has placed them within a context of personal comfort. Unfortunately, it is during this phase that the physical deterioration begins to impair functional ability.

Finally, the *termination phase* results in the eventual movement from the retirement role to the sick role. As physical deterioration continues, the person is forced to relinquish an increasing number of roles and assume an increasing dependent status. During this phase death generally occurs. For others, death occurs during the stability phase. If death takes place during the stability phase, the older person avoids the continued loss of roles and social status associated with declining health.

Atchley (1976) argues that individuals need not progress through all phases in the order described. He also states that one phase is not a necessary precursor to the next. The process of retirement is quite tenable and is determined by a multiplicity of factors that vary depending on the characteristics of the person involved.

Retirement is a social status available to most elderly. Although the status may not be highly valued within society, retirement at least provides the recipient with a modicum of financial support that provides for emotional security. And yet the reality is that "to be old and retired is generally to be poorer than other members of society" (Hardcastle, 1981, p. 153).

Older workers find themselves in an untenable position. On the one hand, they are encouraged to remain in the labor force in an effort to reduce their impact on the Social Security system. On the other hand, by remaining in the labor force the older worker may experience the consequences of an unstable economic system that cannot accommodate his or her economic needs.

The World of Unemployment

Numerically, there are very few elderly who are unemployed. In 1991 there were 116,000 persons aged 65 and over who were categorized as unemployed. Among the unemployed, 56.9 percent were men and 43.1 percent were women (U.S. Department of Labor, 1992). However, those elderly who are unemployed remain unemployed for longer periods of time relative to younger workers. For example, 37.4 percent of the unemployed elderly were out of work for 15 weeks or more. By comparison, 12.2 percent and 24.7 percent of unemployed workers aged 16–19 and 20–34, respectively, were out of work for 15 or more weeks (U.S. Department of Labor, 1992). Among the elderly who remain employed, fear of deteriorating health is a major concern. Ruchlin and Morris (1992, p. 53), when referring to their sample of older workers aged 66–91, stated that "a deterioration in health status is strongly associated with the likelihood of stopping work." Other reported consequences of unemployment include loss of job skills, "loss of family income, and reduced future pension benefits" (Robinson, Coberly, & Paul, 1985, p. 508).

The unemployment rate of the elderly has been increasing. In 1980 3.1 percent of those aged 65 and over were unemployed. The rate of unemployment among the elderly continued to drop until it reached 2.5 percent in 1987. Since then it has begun to increase, and it stood at 3.8 percent in 1992. This increase is gender based. Among elderly males, unemployment remained relatively stable between 1980 and 1992 (3.1 percent and 3.3 percent). Among elderly females, however, unemployment increased from 3.1 percent in 1980 to 4.5 percent in 1992 (U.S. Bureau of the Census, 1993). Although the rate of unemployment among the elderly remains low relative to other age categories, the numbers are deceiving. Robinson et al. (1985, p. 508) argue that if "the discouraged worker and involuntary early retiree are added to the official count of the unemployed, the problem of unemployment among older workers is much more serious." The next section will broaden this issue and examine the extent of poverty among the elderly population today.

Poverty

Perhaps the most pervasive myth today regarding the elderly is that they are "greedy geezers" who are enjoying life at the financial expense of the younger generations. A recent cover story in *Business Week* (Farrell, Palmer, Atchison, & Andelman, 1994) is a prime example of the current image that has been created of the aging population in the United States. The older American is portrayed as healthy, well-off financially, physically active, and in control of every facet of his or her life. Although this image is an accurate portrayal of some of the elderly, it does not reflect reality for the entire elderly population. Farrell et al. (1994) acknowledge the diversity within the elderly population, but spend virtually the entire article on the "positive forces" affecting the elderly. The descriptive account is augmented by color graphics that identify the expected economic well-being of the baby boom elderly. However, data from the New Beneficiary Data System (NBDS) reveal that "one in nine (respondents) was simultaneously satisfied with their standard of living, in good to excellent health, and never had financial worries" (*Social Security Bulletin,* 1994, p. 69). The phrase that "the best is yet to be" remains largely a poetic, and not a realistic, interpretation of aging for many. Poverty, and the threat of poverty, is a continued reality experienced by a significant minority of the elderly population.

Social Causes and Personal Pain

People are poor when they do not have the economic means to purchase those goods and services necessary for basic human survival. Among the elderly, poverty is the result of a multiplicity of circumstances. These circumstances include growing older, being female, minority status, retirement, and the type of employment prior to retirement. At the same time, the elderly are identified as perhaps the only group that directly benefited from the War on Poverty initiated under President Johnson in the 1960s. In addition, the attachment of cost-of-living adjustments (COLAs) to Social Security benefits has lifted many elderly out of poverty conditions. Poverty among the elderly has been steadily decreasing since the 1960s. In fact, the official poverty rate for those aged 65 and over is now below that of other age groups. Why, then, do we continue to address the issue of poverty among the elderly?

The answer is that the problem of poverty among the elderly has become more narrowly focused but broader in its potential. That is, some categories of the elderly are more likely to be poor than others. At the same time, poverty is a concern felt by virtually all elderly. As the cost of medical care continues to increase, particularly for nursing home care, most elderly remain at risk for poverty status if struck with a major medical condition that would require long-term care. This constant fear of losing their life savings, their home, and their dignity make poverty all that more difficult for most elderly. For many, poverty is not the result of something they have done. Rather, poverty is the result of an economic system that expects financial independence of all, regardless of age. And, as we will discuss in Chapter 7, poverty is the result of a for-profit health care system that expects a generous return on its care of an aging population. Although Medicare provides health care coverage for the elderly, the extent of such coverage is limited. Many elderly are forced to purchase additional insurance to cover the deficiencies inherent within Medicare. The following section will examine the extent to which poverty exists among the elderly and for whom.

The Extent of the Problem

First, we need to examine poverty among the elderly relative to other age groups. Second, we will examine racial differences among the elderly poor. Table 6–5 identifies poverty rates for all age groups by race for 1990.

It is evident that in comparison with other age groups, the elderly are relatively well-off. Overall, the poverty rate for those age 65 and over is below that of the national average. However, differences do exist. By race, elderly blacks are more likely to be in poverty than any other age group except those 16 and under. Among Hispanics, poverty is fairly evenly distributed throughout the life cycle. Elderly whites are more likely to be in poverty than any other age group except those 21 and under.

Table 6–6 identifies the historical changes in poverty rates that have occurred among the elderly by race. As is evident from the data in this table, the poverty rate among the elderly has decreased over the last two decades. Differences in the rate of poverty on the basis of race continue to exist. For example, the percentage of elderly below poverty by race has decreased at different rates. Among elderly whites, the percent in poverty between 1970 and 1990 decreased by 55.3 percent. Among black elderly, the percent in poverty between 1970 and 1990 decreased by 29.1 percent. Thus, although the percentage of the

TABLE 6–5   Poverty Level, by Race and Age: 1990

	Percentage Below Poverty Level			
Age	All Races[a]	White	Black	Hispanic[b]
Total	13.5	10.7	31.9	28.1
Under 16 years old	21.1	16.3	45.6	39.2
16 to 21 years old	16.2	13.0	32.9	29.7
22 to 44 years old	11.0	9.1	24.0	23.0
45 to 54 years old	7.8	6.2	21.1	17.9
55 to 59 years old	9.0	7.4	22.0	18.5
60 to 64 years old	10.3	8.2	27.9	18.1
65 years +	12.2	10.1	33.8	22.5

[a]Includes other races not shown separately.
[b]Hispanic persons may be of any race.
Source: U.S. Bureau of the Census. (1992). *Statistical abstract of the United States: 1992* (112th ed.) Table 720. Washington, DC: U.S. Government Printing Office.

TABLE 6–6   Persons 65 Years Old and Over Below Poverty, by Race: 1970–1990

	Percentage Below Poverty Level			
Race	1970	1979[a]	1985[b]	1990
Person, 65 yr. and over[c]	24.6	15.2	12.6	12.2
White	22.6	13.3	11.0	10.1
Black	47.7	36.3	31.5	33.8
Hispanic[d]	(NA)	26.8	23.9	22.5

[a]Population controls based on 1980 census: see text, section 14.
[b]Beginning 1985, based on revised Hispanic population controls; data not directly comparable with prior years.
[c]Beginning 1979, includes members of unrelated subfamilies not shown separately. For earlier years, unrelated subfamily members are included in the "in families" category.
[d]Hispanic persons may be of any race.
Source: U.S. Bureau of the Census. (1992). *Statistical abstract of the United States: 1992* (112th ed.). Table 721.Washington, DC: U.S. Government Printing Office.

elderly population living below poverty has been decreasing, the rate of decrease has been almost double among white elderly compared to black elderly.

We also know that the rate of poverty increases with the age of the elderly. Thus the poverty rate is 8.2 percent for those aged 65–69, 9.6 percent for those aged 70–74, 13.5 percent for those 75–79, 16.7 percent among those 80–84, and 18.4 percent for those aged 85 and over (Radner, 1991). We also know that women live longer than men. As a result, women are more likely to end up in poverty as they age. Litman (1991) identifies poverty rate differences among white, black, and Hispanic males and females in Table 6–7. The data indicate that regardless of race, elderly women are more likely to be in poverty than elderly men. Race, however, remains a significant variable in the likelihood of poverty among the elderly.

The phrase *feminization of poverty* is applicable not only among younger women but also among elderly women. According to Stone (1989), elderly women are likely to experience the feminization of poverty for the following reasons:

1. *Female dependence.* Within American society, economic differentiation between men and women has resulted in outcomes that have been deleterious for women. It has been a widely held belief that women are economically dependent on men. As a result, national policies such as Social Security have been constructed to maintain that economic disadvantage for women.

2. *Family and work history.* What a worker does prior to age 65 and retirement greatly influences what he or she will receive in benefits. This is addressed more specifically in the next factor.

3. *Division of labor between genders.* Historically, women have been expected to perform the caregiver role, not only toward their children but toward elderly parents as well. With the caregiver role as their primary function, women have had difficulty establishing consistent work records. Too often women interrupt their work career to provide support to other family members. As a result of this sporadic work history, pension benefits are generally lower.

4. *Labor market discrimination.* When women do enter the labor market, they are generally located in occupations that pay lower wages with fewer opportunities for upward mobility. As a result, pension benefits for women are consistently lower because of lower wages upon which the benefits are determined. In addition, sexual discrimination in the workplace can result in lower job performance evaluations, which affect promotion and pay increases.

5. *Spousal impoverishment.* Generally, women live longer than men. The consequence of outliving one's spouse for many elderly woman is that they become economically impoverished because their spouse is institutionalized. The elderly woman is then required to spend down before Medicaid will cover the cost. As a result, the elderly woman is left with few economic resources after the death of a spouse (Stone, 1989).

The economic crises that pervade American society today affect all of us. For young people, the dream of a good job after college is becoming more and more elusive. Among middle-aged workers, the fear of losing the job one now holds is quite real. The elderly must constantly wonder whether the public and private benefits that they are entitled to will continue funding them now that they have retired.

TABLE 6–7   Percent Poor Elderly in 1990, by Age, Sex, Race, and Hispanic Origin: March 1991

	Male			*Female*		
	White	Black	Hispanic	White	Black	Hispanic
65–74	4.5	24.6	18.0	10.2	33.6	22.7
75 and over	7.8	34.4	20.1	17.3	43.9	30.1

Source: Litman, M. (1991). *Poverty in the United States: 1990.* U.S. Bureau of the Census. Current Population Reports, Series P-60, No. 175. Table 5. Washington, DC: U.S. Government Printing Office.

The economics of aging will become even more expensive as the baby boom generation reaches retirement age. We know that based on current statistics, the Social Security Trust Fund is solvent for another 40 years. Maintaining solvency of the fund will require some difficult choices. Should we increase the minimum age at which a person can begin collecting Social Security beyond the age 67 already proposed for the year 2023? Should we increase the percentage of income that is taxed for Social Security benefits? Should we eliminate the upper limit of income that is taxable and tax all earnings, regardless of amount? These are all possible solutions that address the economics of aging. Are there alternative methods of financing retirement? Fischer (1978) presents an interesting alternative. He suggests that the government should provide each newborn with a $4,400 gift that would be placed in an interest-bearing account. This account could not be used until retirement, at which time the person would receive the yearly interest on the amount. According to Fischer, the original $4,400 would grow to $200,000 in 65 years (assuming 6 percent interest). The recipient would then receive the interest on this amount. Again, assuming 6 percent interest, the recipient would be receive $12,000 per year. There are serious flaws with this idea (such as a significant increase in the inflation rate), but Fischer demonstrates the ingenuity necessary to develop answers to the economics of aging. All of these solutions also pose particular political and economic risks. For those in decision-making positions, these are risks that few are willing to take.

Critical Connection: What You Have Determines What You Get

This chapter is the pivotal point in this book. The basis for the economics of aging are grounded in the history, images, and role opportunities that have created what we call the elderly. The consequence of economics is reflected in health and political differences for men and women, whites and minorities. Economic consequences also affect living arrangements, the likelihood of victimization, and how and when we die. Throughout this chapter we have emphasized the importance of economics relative to the aging process. On the one hand, one's social position will intimately influence one's available opportunities.

On the other hand, one's chronological position within society will also influence available economic opportunities. The multiple negative influences of being old and poor is not new to American history. Whatever reverence existed toward the elderly in earlier historical periods was reserved for the wealthy.

We continue to differentiate between elderly based on their financial status. Today, however, we have created an image of aging that consistently portrays those elderly who are financially secure as typical of the population. On the other hand, there has been an elimination of those elderly who are poor or near poor from the public's image. This socially constructed blending of social class and chronological age serves a dual purpose. First, it justifies reductions in services to other elderly as a waste of taxpayer dollars. Second, it legitimates the treatment of poor elderly as the cause, rather than the victim, of their circumstances. The outcome of this social construction of aging and social class is a differentiation of opportunity and influence. For example, the next chapter addresses the health care needs of the elderly. Health outcomes are related to an ability to pay for such services. Essentially, the remainder of this book is a reflection of the economic differences that exist among the elderly in the United States.

Chapter Review

The following questions not only address material in Chapter 6 but also require the reader to synthesize knowledge gained throughout earlier chapters of the book. The reader should attempt to construct answers that reflect more than mere rote responses to information. Instead, use the material as a guide to the future investigation of aging.

1. Why is participation in the labor force decreasing for men and increasing for women? If this trend continues, what are the consequences?
2. The elderly are less willing to relocate than are younger workers. As the number of mature workers increases, what are the consequences for businesses that attempt to relocate?
3. Are mature workers less capable of performing work-related tasks compared to younger workers? If yes, then what should companies do with mature workers if they cannot maintain a defined level of productivity? If no, then what should be the criteria for determining work-related worth?
4. Should employers have a right to decide when an employee is too old to perform the task for which he or she was hired? If you agree, what would you do with the mature workers who will lose their jobs? If you disagree, how will employers maintain profitability as their workforce ages?
5. Should the age at which a worker can receive full Social Security benefits be increased to age 70? If you believe the age should be increased, what are the consequences on the world of work? If you disagree, what should the age be, and why?
6. The elderly are considered to be economically well-off. Numbers indicate, however, that growing older in old age increases the risk of poverty, primarily among women. How would you explain this apparent inconsistency between image and reality?

Glossary

Age discrimination   Differential treatment of a person on the basis of chronological age (for example, firing a person because it is believed that an "older" worker is not as productive as a younger worker).

Age Discrimination in Employment Act (ADEA)   A federal law, passed in 1967 and subsequently amended in 1974, 1978, and 1986. The act makes it illegal to discriminate on the basis of an employee's age.

Alienation   When applied to the world of work, alienation exists when the worker loses control over the work performed and is removed from the processes that define the work and the worker.

Disenchantment phase   The second phase in the retirement process constructed by Atchley (1976). This phase occurs when retirement as a social reality is realized. It is in this phase that some retirees realize that their expectations of retirement are not being met. As a consequence, they are disappointed with the options available to them.

Dual-economy approach   This approach argues that occupations are located either in the core or the periphery of the occupational structure. Occupations in the core are better paying, offer greater benefits, and generally provide more access to resources necessary for retirement.

Equal Employment Opportunity Commission (EEOC)   The federal agency responsible for handling claims of age discrimination.

Feminization of poverty   Applied to elderly women, the fact that as women age, they increase the likelihood of poverty. This is the result of a number of societal level factors, such as pay differentials between men and women.

Honeymoon phase   According to Atchley (1976), this is the first phase after the retirement event. In this phase, most retirees have an opportunity to engage in various activities that they did not have time for earlier in life.

Involuntary retirement   This is generally forced on a person because of external circumstances such as job loss, health, or physical disability.

Mature worker   This is a person aged 40 or over employed in the paid workforce.

Near phase   This is the second phase in the preretirement period outlined by Atchley (1976). Here the worker is relatively close to retirement and begins to prepare for the event.

Occupational status   This is the position one occupies within society as a result of one's occupation.

Remote phase   This is the initial phase in the retirement process constructed by Atchley (1976). This phase begins when the person is initially employed and establishes benefit packages that provide for retirement at some point in the future.

Reorientation phase   During this phase of the retirement process constructed by Atchley (1976), the retiree is likely to reexamine his or her previous experiences and establish a new set of options consistent with current reality.

Retirement   A range of definitions exist. Here the term implies the termination of paid employment and the acquisition of benefits from public or private sources that the retiree is entitled to as a condition of previous employment.

Social Security   Federal legislation signed into law in 1935 by President Roosevelt. The legislation is the basis for the current Social Security system. See Chapter 8 for further information.

Stability phase   Within the retirement process constructed by Atchley (1976), this phase represents control over the routine of retirement. The retiree has established a comfortable existence based on a realistic assessment of his or her capabilities.

Termination phase   The final phase in the retirement process. Within this phase the individual moves from the retirement role to the sick role.

Townsend plan   So-called because of its leader, Francis Townsend, who proposed the plan during the Depression of the 1930s. The plan argued for a direct payment to all those over the age of 60. The only stipulation was that the recipients would be required to spend all of the money every month. It was believed that increasing the supply of money in the country would stimulate growth in the economy.

Voluntary retirement   When a worker decides to retire, based on reasons other than health, disability, or forced economic circumstances.

Worker dislocation   Because of structural changes in the work world (such as a plant closing or relocation), a worker is involuntarily unemployed.

Suggested Reading

Atchley, R. C. (1976). *The sociology of retirement.* New York: Wiley.
  Atchley offers the reader insight into the process of retirement. This is a classic in the sociology of aging and should be read by anyone who is seriously considering a career in the field.

Graebner, W. (1980). *A history of retirement.* New Haven, CT: Yale University Press.
  A superb examination of a multifaceted issue. Graebner addresses retirement within a historical context. The reader is provided a glimpse into the social and historical factors that shaped one of the most important events of the modern-day work environment.

Levine, M. L. (1988). *Age discrimination and the mandatory retirement controversy.* Baltimore: Johns Hopkins University Press.
  This is a social policy book that explores the myriad of issues associated with mandatory retirement. The book is quite helpful to those interested in making connections among policy issues affecting the elderly.

References

Atchley, R. C. (1976). *The sociology of retirement.* Cambridge, MA: Schenkman.

Chen, Y.-P. (1988). Better options for work and retirement: Some suggestions for improving economic security mechanisms for old age. In G. L. Maddox & M. P. Lawton (Eds.), *Varieties of aging (annual review of gerontology and geriatrics)* (vol. 8, pp. 189–216). New York: Springer.

Chen, Y.-P. (1989). Low confidence in Social Security is not warranted. *Journal of Aging and Social Policy, 1*(1/2), 103–129.

Clark, R. L. (1990). Pensions in an aging society. In I. Bluestone, R. J. V. Montgomery, & J. D. Owen (Eds.), *The aging of the American work force* (pp. 75–100). Detroit: Wayne State University Press.

Coser, L. A. (1977). *Masters of sociological thought* (2nd ed.). New York: Harcourt Brace Jovanovich.

Equal Employment Opportunity Commission. (1995). *Age Discrimination in Employment Act (ADEA) statistics.* Washington, DC: Author.

Estes, C. L. (1981). *The aging enterprise.* San Francisco: Jossey-Bass.

Farrell, C., Palmer, A. T., Atchison, S., & Andelman, B. (1994, September 12). The economics of aging: Why the growing number of elderly won't bankrupt America. *Business Week,* pp. 60–68.

Fischer, D. H. (1978). *Growing old in America.* New York: Oxford University Press.

Gendell, M., & Siegel, J. S. (1992). Trends in retirement age by sex, 1950–2005. *Monthly Labor Review, 115*(7), 22–29.

Graebner, W. (1980). *A history of retirement.* New Haven, CT: Yale University Press.

Haber, C. (1978). Mandatory retirement in nineteenth-century America: The conceptual basis for a new work cycle. *Journal of Social History, 18,* 77–96.

Hale, N. (1990). *The older worker: Effective strategies for management and human resource development.* San Francisco: Jossey-Bass.

Hardcastle, D. A. (1981). Getting along after retirement: An economic inquiry. In F. J. Berghorn & D. E. Schafer (Eds.), *The dynamics of aging* (pp. 151–168). Boulder, CO: Westview Press.

Hatch, L. R. (1987). Research on men's and women's retirement attitudes: Implications for retirement policy. In E. F. Borgatta & R. J. V. Montgomery (Eds.), *Critical issues in aging policy* (pp. 129–157). Newbury Park, CA: Sage.

Hayward, M. D., Crimmins, E. M., & Wray, L. A. (1994). The relationship between retirement life cycle changes and older men's labor force participation rates. *Journal of Gerontology, 49*(5), S219–S230.

Hayward, M. D., Hardy, M. A., & Grady, W. R. (1989). Labor force withdrawal patterns among older men in the United States. *Social Science Quarterly, 70*(2), 425–448.

Hendricks, J., & McAllister, C. (1983). An alternative perspective on retirement: A dual economic approach. *Ageing and Society, 3*(3), 279–299.

Henretta, J. C., O'Rand, A. M., & Chan, C. G. (1993). Gender differences in employment after spouse's retirement. *Research on Aging, 15*(2), 148–169.

Hutchens, R. M. (1993). Restricted job opportunities and the older worker. In O. S. Mitchell (Ed.), *As the workforce ages: Costs, benefits and policy challenges* (pp. 81–102). Ithaca, NY: ILR Press.

Kendig, W. L. (1979). The problem of age discrimination in employment. In J. Hendricks & C. D. Hendricks (Eds.), *Dimensions of aging* (pp. 300–303). Cambridge, MA: Winthrop.

Leonesio, M. V. (1993). Social Security and older workers. In O. S. Mitchell (Ed.), *As the workforce ages: Costs, benefits, and policy challenges* (pp. 183–204). Ithaca, NY: ILR Press.

Levine, M. L. (1988). *Age discrimination and the mandatory retirement controversy.* Baltimore: Johns Hopkins University Press.

Litman, M. (1991). Poverty in the United States: 1990. U.S. Bureau of the Census, Current Population Reports, Series P-60, No. 175. Table 5. Washington, DC: U.S. Government Printing Office.

Maccoby, M., & Terzi, K. A. (1989). What happened to the work ethic? In A. R. Gini & T. J. Sullivan (Eds.), *It comes with the territory: An inquiry concerning work and the person* (pp. 65–77). New York: Random House.

Matras, J. (1990). *Dependency, obligations, and entitlements: A new sociology of aging, the life course, and the elderly.* Englewood Cliffs, NJ: Prentice-Hall.

Maynard, O. P. (1990). Investing in experience: Job barriers to older workers in Michigan. In I. Bluestone, R. J. V. Montgomery, & J. D. Owen (Eds.), *The aging of the American work force* (pp. 379–388). Detroit, MI: Wayne State University Press.

Meier, E. L., & Torrey, B. B. (1982). Demographic change and retirement age policy. In M. H. Morrison (Ed.), *Economics of aging: The future of retirement* (pp. 61–97). New York: Van Nostrand Reinhold.

Mitchell. O. S. (1993). As the workforce ages. In O. S. Mitchell (Ed.), *As the workforce ages: Costs, benefits and policy challenges* (pp. 3–15). Ithaca, NY: ILR Press.

Morrison, M. H. (1986). Work and retirement in an older society. In A. Pifer & L. Bronte (Eds.), *Our aging society* (pp. 341–365). New York: Norton.

Osler, W. (1932). *AEQUANIMITAS: With other addresses to medical students, nurses and practitioners of medicine* (3rd ed.). Philadelphia: Blakiston.

Ozawa, M. N., & Wai-on Law, S. (1992). Reported reasons for retirement: A study of recently retired workers. *Journal of Aging and Social Policy, 4*(3/4), 35–51.

Palmore, E. B., George, L. K., & Fillenbaum, G. G. (1982). Predictors of retirement. *Journal of Gerontology, 37*(6), 733–742.

Pampel, F. C., & Hardy, M. (1994). Status maintenance and change during old age. *Social Forces, 73*(1), 289–314.

Parnes, H. S., & Less, L. J. (1985). The volume and pattern of retirements, 1966–1981. In H. S. Parnes et al. (Eds.), *Retirement among American men* (pp. 57–77). Lexington, MA: D.C. Heath Publishing.

Radner, D. B. (1991). Changes in the incomes of age groups, 1984–89. *Social Security Bulletin, 54*(12).

Rich, B. M., & Baum, M. (1984). *The aging: A guide to public policy.* Pittsburgh, PA: University of Pittsburgh Press.

Robinson, P. K., Coberly, S., & Paul, C. E. (1985). Work and retirement. In R. H. Binstock & E. Shanas (Eds.), *Handbook of aging and the social sciences* (2nd ed., pp. 503–527). New York: Van Nostrand Reinhold.

Ruchlin, H. S., & Morris, J. N. (1992). Deteriorating health and the cessation of employment among older workers. *Journal of Aging and Health, 4*(1), 43–57.

Ruhm, C. J. (1989). Why older Americans stop working. *Gerontologist, 29*(3), 294–299.

Sandell, S. H., & Baldwin, S. E. (1990). Older workers and employment shifts: Policy responses to displacement. In I. Bluestone, R. J. Montgomery, & J. D. Owen (Eds.), *The aging of the American workforce* (pp. 126–148). Detroit: Wayne State University Press.

Schor, J. B. (1992). *The overworked American.* New York: Basic Books.

Schulz, J. H., Borowski, A., & Crown, W. H. (1991). *Economics of population aging: The "graying" of Australia, Japan, and the United States.* New York: Auburn House.

Sickles, R. C., & Taubman, P. (1986). An analysis of the health and retirement status of the elderly. *Econometrica, 54*(6), 1339–1356.

Siegel, J. S. (1993). *A generation of change: A profile of America's older population.* New York: Russell Sage Foundation.

Social Security Bulletin. (1994). *57*(1).

Sterns, H. L., Matheson, N. K., & Schwartz, L. S. (1990). Work and retirement. In K. F. Ferraro (Ed.), *Gerontology: Perspectives and issues* (pp. 163–178). New York: Springer.

Stone, R. I. (1989). The feminization of poverty among the elderly. *Women's Studies Quarterly, 1–2,* 20–34.

Torres-Gill, F. M. (1992). *The new aging: Politics and change in America.* New York: Auburn House.

U.S. Bureau of the Census. (1992). *Statistical abstract of the United States: 1992* (112th ed.). Washington, DC: U.S. Government Printing Office.

U.S. Bureau of the Census. (1993). *Statistical abstract of the United States: 1993* (113th ed.). Washington, DC: U.S. Government Printing Office.

U.S. Department of Labor. n.d. Bureau of Labor Statistics. Unpublished data from the Current Population Survey. Washington, DC.

U.S. Department of Labor. (1992). *Bureau of Labor Statistics: Employment and earnings.* Washington, DC: U.S. Government Printing Office.

Wallace, S. P., Williamson, J. B., Lung, R. G., & Powell, L. A. (1991). A lamb in wolf's clothing? The reality of senior power and social policy. In M. Minkler & C. L. Estes (Eds.), *Critical perspectives on aging: The political and moral economy of growing old* (pp. 95–114). Amityville, NY: Baywood.

Williamson, J. B., Munley, A., & Evans, L. (1980). *Aging and society: An introduction to social gerontology.* New York: Holt, Rinehart and Winston.

Williamson, J. B., Shindul, J. A., & Evans, L. (1985). *Aging and public policy.* Springfield, IL: Charles C. Thomas.

Woods, J. R. (1989). Pension coverage among private wage and salary workers: Preliminary findings from the 1988 survey of employee benefits. *Social Security Bulletin, 52*(10), 2–19.

Zopf, P. E., Jr. (1986). *America's older population.* Houston: Cap and Gown Press.

$C\ h\ a\ p\ t\ e\ r$ *7*

Aging and Health Care

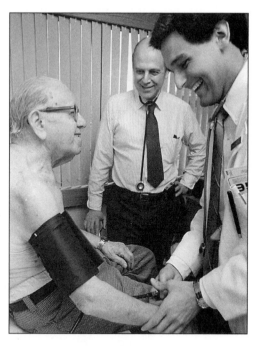

The social construction of aging as illness is consistent with the definition of aging as a problem. Once something has been defined as a problem—be it drug use, teen pregnancy, or old age— government resources are more likely to be committed to the issue. The association between ill health and aging has increased as the major health problem in America has shifted from infectious and acute diseases to chronic disease. This increased importance of chronic illness has shifted the burden of illness from the young to the old since the elderly are more likely to have chronic illnesses.
—ESTES, WALLACE, & BINNEY, 1989, P. 406

Perhaps the most vociferous national debate in recent memory emerged with the election of President Clinton in 1992. This debate involves the current health care system and its need for reform. If (and when) it is passed, health care reform will represent the greatest shift in American social policy since the implementation of Social Security in 1935. The president outlined his health reform package to the American public in 1993 (White House Domestic Policy Council, 1993). Congressional opposition and lobbying from special interest groups have stopped the president's reforms from becoming a reality. In fact, the inability to enact health care reform has now been identified as a key factor in the 1994 Republican congressional victories (Toner, 1994). Only a year earlier Americans were evenly divided (45 percent were in favor, 45 percent were opposed, and 10 percent had no opinion) on President Clinton's health reform measure (Gallup Poll, 1993). Interestingly, the Gallup poll of November 3, 1993, reveals significant age differences regarding attitudes toward the president's health reform agenda. The elderly felt greater insecurity regarding their own health care coverage under President Clinton's proposal. Among all age categories, the elderly were more likely to believe that the total amount of money spent on medical care would increase (Gallup Poll, 1993). Today the American public appears more interested in an incremental approach to reform as a more palatable alternative (Toner, 1994). What is it about the American health care system that creates such strong emotions and fluctuations in public sentiment?

Briefly, the American health care system is unique relative to other nations in the industrialized world (Roemer, 1991). One aspect of this uniqueness is the method of financing and the cost of the health care system. For example, the United States finances the majority (60 percent) of its health care through the private sector. By comparison, other Western industrialized nations finance the majority of their health care through the public sector. The United States also has the most expensive health care system in the world. As of 1994 the United States spent slightly more than $3,000 per capita on health care (Angell, 1993). That amounts to some 14 percent of the gross domestic product (GDP) (Graig, 1993). By comparison, Canada, in 1991, spent $1,915 per capita, or 10 percent of the GDP on health care. Here is one final statistic: In 1990 the United States consumed 41 percent of all the health care dollars spent in the world on health care (World Development Report, 1993).

A second aspect that signifies the unique American health care system is its selectivity of coverage. Again, other industrialized nations provide universal or near-universal health care coverage to their citizens. Within the American health care system, not everyone has access to medical care services, and for those that do, the services are not necessarily equal. According to Swartz (1994, p. 65), "close to a quarter of the nonelderly population are without health insurance sometime during a year."

Our uniqueness in health care has created the most expensive system in the world and yet, it is unable to provide basic coverage to all of its citizens. An inevitable consequence is that "the American public will continue to suffer the effects of a system that perpetuates inequality of access and outcome" (Matcha, 1994a, p. 8).

How does all of this relate to the elderly? First, Davis (1985, p. 730) argues that "the health of the elderly is a good measure of how well a health system works." Second, the elderly, like all others, are health care consumers. Third, the percentage and total number of elderly will continue to increase (see Chapter 2 for specific numbers and percentages).

The consequence, then, is that health care utilization rates by elderly are higher when compared to other age groups. Not surprisingly, the elderly are identified as consuming a disproportionate share of the health care services relative to their percentage of the population. Generally speaking, one-third of health care costs are attributed to service utilization by the elderly (Fuchs, 1984). It is assumed by some that as the numbers and percentage of the elderly continue to increase, there will be a concomitant increase in the cost of health care and the percentage of health care spent on the elderly (Callahan, 1987, 1990). Others (for example, Binstock & Post, 1991; Getzen, 1992) argue that attempting to blame the elderly for the increasing cost of health care is misplaced. This chapter will examine two broad aspects of aging and health. We will first explore the health of the elderly relative to other age groups. In addition, we will examine the health status of the elderly. Whereas these areas present a purely objective analysis of age-related conditions, the second area of discussion in this chapter will examine the "crisis" of health care for the elderly (issues such as cost and health care rationing) and future implications. This chapter will focus on the health of the elderly. Chapter 8 will explain how health care for the elderly is organized.

The Health of the Elderly

When we discuss the health of the elderly, we can define health in two ways: "in terms of the presence or absence of disease, or in terms of how well the older person functions or his general sense of 'well-being'" (Shanas & Maddox, 1985, p. 701). We will address these definitions in the following sections.

Relative to other age groups, the elderly are not as healthy (Townsend & Harel, 1990). As the body ages, it becomes increasingly susceptible to the vicissitudes of daily living (Willits & Crider, 1988). As a result, we begin to experience a general breakdown of the body's ability to respond to an array of acute and chronic diseases (Francis & Smeeding, 1987). However, this is not to say that all elderly experience physical deterioration. Nor should we assume that old age equals sickness (Stahl & Feller, 1990).

Before we proceed, it would be useful to define some of the terminology utilized in this chapter. According to Cockerham (1992, p. 137),

> *disease* is considered an adverse physical state, consisting of a physiological dysfunction within an individual; an *illness* is a subjective state, pertaining to an individual's psychological awareness of having a disease and usually causing that person to modify his or her behavior; while *sickness* is a social state, signifying an impaired social role for those who are ill.

We know that disease rates are generally greater among the elderly than among any other age group. For example, death rates as a result of diseases of heart and cerebrovascular diseases and malignant neoplasms are higher among those aged 65 and over than any other age group (National Center for Health Statistics, 1994). The numbers of deaths attributed to these three diseases are presented in Table 7–1.

This is not to suggest that as we grow older we will automatically become physically disabled. Rather, as we age, we increase the probability of a chronic disease (Haber, 1989).

TABLE 7–1 Death Rates for Diseases of Heart, Cerebrovascular Diseases, and Malignant Neoplasms, by Age: 1989–1991 (per 100,000 Resident Population)

Age	Diseases of Heart	Cerebrovascular Diseases	Malignant Neoplasms
45–54 years	121.1	18.5	157.3
55–64 years	369.3	48.0	450.3
65–74 years	897.0	143.6	869.7
75–84 years	2,291.8	496.6	1,339.3
85 years +	6,717.3	1,625.2	1,738.8

Source: National Center for Health Statistics. (1994). *Health, United States, 1993.* Tables 33, 34, & 35. Hyattsville, MD: Public Health Service.

Keep in mind, however, that "because 'perfect health' is probably unobtainable, individuals lie somewhere on a health continuum" (Stahl & Feller, 1990, p. 22). Fries (1980) suggests that with the elimination of premature deaths, the elderly would experience an extended period of nondebilitating health prior to increased susceptibility. Fries (1980) referred to this as "squaring the curve" or the "rectangular survival curve." This concept is illustrated in Figure 7–1. The health status of the elderly remains relatively constant into old age (assuming age 85 as the outer limit). At this point, the individual is likely to be afflicted with one or more chronic diseases and die within a relatively short period of time (the compression of morbidity and mortality). The consequences of such an approach are significant. According to Fries (1980, p. 133), "death and disability, occurring later, become increasingly unavoidable. The incremental cost of marginal medical benefit inevitably rises. Intervention in the patient without organ reserve will be recognized as futile." The argument put forth by Fries (1980) has created considerable controversy. We will discuss this problem in greater detail later in this chapter.

To understand fully the health of the elderly, we need to examine the historical changes associated with the health of the elderly in the United States. This is perhaps best demonstrated through the use of rates of disease and death by age. Death and dying will be covered in greater detail in Chapter 12. Here we are concerned with specific disease factors and health-utilization measures associated with deteriorating health.

We begin our analysis by examining the primary causes of death today and in the recent past. At the turn of the century, the 10 leading causes of death were generally the result of the body's inability to defend itself from the prevalent infectious diseases. Today, among those aged 65 and over, the leading causes of death in the United States include chronic, long-term diseases. Table 7–2 provides a comparison of the 10 leading causes of death among the elderly in 1980 and 1991. Even within a relatively short time span of 11 years, changes in those diseases leading to increased or decreased risk of death among the elderly are evident.

Changes in the cause of death have also changed the meaning of growing older in society. Previously, "death was almost a random event" (Fries, 1980). Today, death is pri-

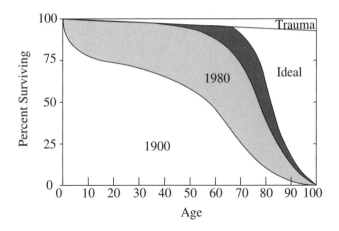

FIGURE 7–1   Rectangularization of Survival
Source: Fries, J. F. (1980). Aging, natural death, and the compression of morbidity. *New England Journal of Medicine, 303*(3), 130–135. Copyright 1980, Massachusetts Medical Society. Reprinted by permission of the *New England Journal of Medicine.*

marily an occurrence within old age. We can examine changes in mortality rates as well as morbidity rates to demonstrate this historical shift.

Morbidity and Mortality Rates

Before we begin, we need to define what we mean by mortality and morbidity. *Mortality* "refers to the number of deaths in a population," whereas *morbidity* "refers to the amount of disease, impairment, and accident in a population" (Weiss & Lonnquist, 1994, pp. 44, 52). Mortality and morbidity rates for a given population are calculated by dividing the number of deaths of disease by the total population under investigation. In order to standardize rates and provide a basis for comparison, the number is then multiplied by 100,000. The following provides an opportunity to test your skills and determine the mortality rate among those aged 65 and over.

> In 1980, 1,341,848 persons aged 65 and over died.
>
> In 1991, there were 1,563,527 deaths among the same age population.
>
> In 1980, there were 25,550,000 persons aged 65 and over in the United States.
>
> In 1991, that number increased to 31,764,000.

Calculate the mortality rate among those aged 65 and over in 1980 and 1991.

Based upon the rates, what can you state regarding changes in mortality in the aged population between 1980 and 1991? You will find the rates in the chapter review at the end of this chapter.

If we disaggregate the elderly population and create three age categories of 65–74, 75–84, and 85 and over, we can compare not only change over time but also the rate of

TABLE 7–2   Leading Causes of Death Among
             Persons Aged 65 and Over: 1980 and 1991

1980	1991
Diseases of heart	Diseases of heart
Malignant neoplasms	Malignant neoplasms
Cerebrovascular diseases	Cerebrovascular diseases
Pneumonia and influenza	Chronic obstructive pulmonary disease
Chronic obstructive pulmonary disease	Pneumonia and influenza
Atherosclerosis	Diabetes mellitus
Diabetes mellitus	Unintentional injuries
Unintentional injuries	Nephritis, nephrotic syndrome, and nephrosis
Nephritis, nephrotic syndrome, and nephrosis	Atherosclerosis
Chronic liver disease and cirrhosis	Septicemia

Source: National Center for Health Statistics. (1994). *Health, United States, 1993.* Table 31. Hyattsville, MD: Public Health Service.

change by age. The data in Table 7–3 illustrate the rate of death per 100,000 population as well as the percentage change between 1980–1982 and 1990–1991. What this means is that the health of the younger elderly has been improving. That is, the death rate among the younger elderly has been decreasing at a rather rapid rate, while as one ages the rate of change in death rates is minimal.

Morbidity rates are calculated by using the same procedure as was just discussed. An examination of morbidity rates among the elderly reveal significant differences between men and women. Table 7–4 provides rates of selected chronic conditions for elderly men and women. The rates also vary by age of the elderly person. According to Rabin (1985, p. 35), "age is the single best indicator of morbidity, and morbidity is the single most important determinant of use of health services."

TABLE 7–3   Death Rates Among Persons Aged
             65 and Over: 1980–1982 and
             1990–1991 (per 100,000 Population)

	1980–1982	1990–1991	% change
65–74	2,929.6	2,650.8	-9.52%
75–84	6,482.6	5,979.2	-7.77%
85+	15,404.8	15,231.2	-1.13%

Source: National Center for Health Statistics. (1994). *Health, United States, 1993.* Table 32. Hyattsville, MD: Public Health Service.

TABLE 7–4 **Prevalence of Selected Chronic Conditions, by Age and Sex: 1992 (per 1,000)**

| | *Male* | | *Female* | |
	65–74	75+	65–74	75+
Condition				
Arthritis	364.8	417.2	508.7	611.2
Visual impairments	96.6	131.9	49.6	99.4
Cataracts	112.5	193.2	137.1	245.2
Hearing impairments	322.3	452.7	204.3	392.9
Tinnitus	95.5	113.7	77.1	84.6
Frequent indigestion	56.0	34.4	43.4	35.7
Diabetes	119.6	96.8	109.2	110.2
Heart conditions	334.7	408.5	220.6	401.2
High blood pressure (hypertension)	341.4	314.7	377.7	374.3

Source: U.S. Bureau of the Census. (1994). *Statistical abstract of the United States: 1994* (114th ed.). Table 208. Washington, DC: U.S. Government Printing Office.

The data in Tables 7–1 through 7–4 and the mortality exercise given earlier demonstrate that death and disease occur most often among those aged 65 and over. The data also reveal that death and disease are most likely among the oldest-old. That is, as one progresses beyond age 65 the likelihood of death and disease increase, particularly beyond age 75. Highly correlated to the increased susceptibility to disease and potential death is the changing health status of the elderly. Siegel (1993, p. 250) argues that based on mortality and morbidity rates, there has been "little or no improvement . . . in the health status of the elderly population during the period 1961–1982."

Changing Health Status

As we age, our health status changes. *Health status* refers to the rating (subjective or objective) we apply to our overall feeling of being healthy. One's health status is directly related to one's level of life satisfaction (Girzadas, Counte, Glandon, & Tancredi, 1993) as well as a variety of biosocial and sociodemographic variables (Pol & Thomas, 1992). As Larson (1978, p. 112) states, "health is the most strongly related to subjective well-being. People who are sick or physically disabled are much less likely to express contentment about their lives." However, "older elderly adults perceive themselves as healthier than younger elderly adults with similar health problems" (Johnson & Wolinsky, 1993, p. 118). Staats et al. (1993, p. 200) provide support for this argument when they report that "age group and health status tend to interact so that older persons in failing health have a more youthful bias than do younger persons in failing health." A persistent problem has been the determination of how health status is being measured. Although dated, an early article by Fanshel and Bush (1970) provides an 11-point continuum upon which health status indicators are located. Fanshel and Bush (1970, p. 1029) argued that "on any given day, there is a distribution of the entire population or target group among the states; all members of the population belong to one and only one state." These points include the following:

1. *Well-being.* The person is not experiencing any of those symptoms that would indicate anything less than complete well-being.
2. *Dissatisfaction.* The person exhibits conditions that reflect a departure from complete well-being. Although minimal, these conditions are nonetheless unacceptable indicators of the level of well-being (for example, dental caries).
3. *Discomfort.* Although symptomatic, the person remains capable of performing routine daily activities.
4. *Disability, minor.* The person is capable of remaining active in daily routines but experiences physical and/or emotional exigency as well as diminished efficiency.
5. *Disability, major.* The person experiences a significant limitation of daily activities and a reduction in their level of efficiency.
6. *Disabled.* Although unable to engage in activities such as work or school, the person is capable of mobility within the community.
7. *Confined.* Generally institutionalized, the person remains ambulatory.
8. *Confined, bedridden.* Regardless of location (such as a nursing home or hospital), the person is confined to bed.
9. *Isolated.* The person is segregated from significant others and activities.
10. *Coma.* Although distinction from death is minimal, the person may experience improvement in level of well-being.
11. *Death.* The person experiences total loss of functional ability with absolutely no probability of improvement in the level of well-being (Fanshel & Bush, 1970).

The question, then, is this: How do the elderly rate their health status? According to the National Center for Health Statistics (1994) the elderly are more likely to rate their health as being fair or poor as compared with younger age groups. These findings hold regardless of sex or race, although African Americans are more evenly distributed in their self-assessment than are whites. Data on self-assessed health status by age, sex, and race are presented in Table 7–5.

Although younger African Americans are more likely to state that their health status is fair or poor, it is the age of the respondent that is most significant. Although gender and race differences are evident, the overwhelming disparity between age groups is a reminder of the subjective nature of health status and the influence of the aging process.

Because of increased morbidity rates, the elderly will have greater contact with the health care system. Table 7–6 presents differences in physician contact by age. As expected, children under the age of 5 have a relatively high mean number of yearly contacts. The mean number of contacts decreases until middle age, when rapid increases occur after age 75.

Table 7–7 presents hospital utilization rates and average length of stay in short-term hospitals by age. The utilization rates remained constant among the elderly but declined

TABLE 7–5   Respondent-Assessed Health Status, According to Selected Characteristics: United States, 1987–1992

Characteristic	*Percent with fair or poor health*					
	1987	1988	1989	1990	1991	1992
Age						
Under 5 years	2.6	3.4	2.6	2.9	2.6	2.9
5–14 years	2.3	2.4	2.3	2.2	2.4	2.8
15–44 years	5.4	5.5	5.6	5.4	5.8	6.4
45–64 years	17.4	17.1	16.1	16.0	16.7	17.2
65 years and over	30.8	29.4	28.5	27.7	29.0	28.7
65–74 years	28.2	26.6	26.3	25.1	26.0	25.7
75 and older	34.9	33.8	32.0	31.7	33.6	33.2
Sex and age						
Male						
Under 15 years	2.5	2.7	2.6	2.6	2.5	2.9
15–44 years	4.5	4.6	4.6	4.5	5.0	5.7
45–64 years	16.6	16.5	15.4	15.5	16.1	16.5
65–74 years	28.9	27.0	27.2	25.0	26.7	26.8
75 years and over	36.0	33.0	33.0	31.7	33.7	33.5
Female						
Under 15 years	2.3	2.8	2.3	2.2	2.4	2.7
15–44 years	6.3	6.4	6.6	6.3	6.6	7.2
45–64 years	18.1	17.6	16.8	16.5	17.2	17.8
65–74 years	27.7	26.4	25.6	25.1	25.5	24.7
75 years and over	34.2	34.3	31.5	31.6	33.5	33.0
Race and Age						
White						
under 15 years	2.0	2.4	2.0	1.9	2.1	2.5
15–44 years	4.6	4.8	4.9	4.8	5.2	5.7
45–64 years	15.6	15.3	14.5	14.6	15.4	15.5
65–74 years	26.8	24.8	24.5	23.9	24.6	24.1
75 years and over	33.2	32.3	30.8	30.7	32.4	31.9
Black						
Under 15 years	4.1	4.6	4.4	4.8	4.5	4.4
15–44 years	10.5	9.9	10.2	9.9	9.7	10.7
45–64 years	32.9	30.9	29.6	28.3	27.2	30.9
65–74 years	42.9	46.8	44.7	38.4	41.2	42.1
75 years and over	52.4	50.8	45.2	42.9	48.2	48.4

Source: National Center for Health Statistics. (1994). *Health, United States, 1993*. Table 71. Hyattsville, MD: Public Health Service.

among other age groups. The average length of hospital stay decreased among all age groups. The elderly require hospitalization and are hospitalized more than other age groups. Considering the increasing rate of chronic disease, such an observation should not be particularly surprising. Although other age groups decreased their median length of stay

TABLE 7–6   Physician Contacts by Sex and Age of Patient: 1992

	Under 5 Years	5–14 Years	15–44 Years	45–64 Years	65–74 Years	75 years and over
Male	7.1	3.5	3.7	6.1	9.2	12.2
Female	6.7	3.3	6.2	8.2	10.1	12.1

Source: National Center for Health Statistics. (1994). *Health, United States, 1993.* Figure 25. Hyattsville, MD: Public Health Service.

in hospitals, the median remained constant among the elderly. The problem appears to be greater hospitalization, not longer lengths of stay among the elderly.

One significant change that occurs with age is an increased limitation on one's activity. Table 7–8 illustrates this change.

Within the elderly population, social class differences exist regarding health status. The next section will examine the perceived and real influence of social class on health status.

TABLE 7–7   **Average Length of Hospital Stay, Hospital Discharge Rates, and Rate of Change, in Nonfederal Short-Stay Hospitals, by Age: 1988–1992**

	Average Length of Hospital Stay				
Age	1988	1990	1991	1992	% Change 1988–1992
Under 15 years[a]	5.0	4.8	4.8	4.9	-2.0
15–44 years	4.7	4.6	4.7	4.3	-8.5
45–64 years	6.8	6.7	6.5	6.3	-7.4
65–74 years	8.4	8.0	8.1	7.7	-8.3
75 years and over	9.3	9.2	9.0	8.7	-6.5
	Hospital Discharges/1000 population				
Age	1988	1990	1991	1992	% Change 1988–1992
Under 15 years[a]	49.2	43.9	45.3	45.2	-8.1
15–44 years	104.0	101.7	99.3	96.0	-7.7
45–64 years	140.5	133.1	132.2	131.0	-6.8
65–74 years	262.8	253.9	264.2	264.5	+0.6
75 years and over	436.5	430.0	443.5	432.6	-0.9

[a]Excludes newborn infants.
Source: National Center for Health Statistics. (1994). *Health, United States, 1993.* Figures 27 and 28. Hyattsville, MD: Public Health Service.

TABLE 7–8   Limitation of Activity Caused by Chronic Conditions, According to Selected Characteristics: United States, 1987 and 1992

	Total with Limitation of Activity		Limited but Not in Major Activity		Limited in Amount or Kind of Major Activity		Unable to Carry on Major Activity	
	1987	1992	1987	1992	1987	1992	1987	1992
Age								
Under 5 years	2.1	2.8	0.7	0.7	1.0	1.4	0.5	0.6
5–14 years	6.2	7.4	1.7	1.9	4.1	5.0	0.4	0.5
15–44 years	8.1	9.9	2.6	3.0	3.4	4.0	2.0	2.9
45–64 years	22.3	22.8	5.6	5.6	8.2	7.8	8.5	9.3
65 years and over	37.5	38.8	14.7	15.6	12.9	12.5	10.0	10.6
65–74 years	34.7	34.4	12.8	13.6	11.3	10.4	10.7	10.4
75 years and over	41.9	45.3	17.7	18.6	15.4	15.7	8.9	11.1
Sex and age								
Male[a]								
Under 15 years	5.5	6.8	1.4	1.8	3.7	4.3	0.4	0.7
15–44 years	8.2	10.2	2.5	2.8	3.4	4.1	2.3	3.3
45–64 years	21.4	21.7	4.4	4.5	6.8	6.7	10.3	10.5
65–74 years	35.4	36.1	12.5	14.3	9.5	9.8	13.4	12.1
75 years and over	39.9	42.5	21.8	22.1	10.7	10.9	7.4	9.4
Female[a]								
Under 15 years	4.0	4.7	1.3	1.2	2.3	3.1	0.4	0.5
15–44 years	7.9	9.6	2.8	3.3	3.4	3.9	1.7	2.5
45–64 years	23.2	23.9	6.6	6.7	9.6	8.9	6.9	8.3
65–74 years	34.1	33.1	13.0	13.1	12.7	11.0	8.4	9.0
75 years and over	43.1	46.9	15.3	16.4	18.0	18.5	9.8	12.0
Race and age								
White[a]								
Under 15 years	4.7	5.6	1.4	1.5	3.0	3.6	0.4	0.5
15–44 years	8.1	9.8	2.8	3.1	3.5	4.1	1.8	2.6
45–64 years	21.5	22.1	5.6	5.7	8.1	7.9	7.8	8.5
65–74 years	34.2	34.0	13.1	13.8	11.1	10.4	10.1	9.8
75 years and over	41.3	44.6	18.0	18.8	14.9	15.3	8.4	10.4
Black[a]								
Under 15 years	5.5	7.3	1.4	1.5	3.5	4.8	0.6	1.1
15–44 years	9.1	11.1	1.8	2.7	3.9	3.7	3.4	4.7
45–64 years	30.9	29.9	5.8	5.2	10.0	7.9	15.0	16.8
65–74 years	41.2	41.4	10.6	13.3	13.2	11.4	17.3	16.6
75 years and over	49.7	53.6	14.8	16.9	20.6	18.7	14.3	18.0

[a]Age adjusted.
Source: National Center for Health Statistics. (1994). *Health, United States, 1993.* Table 69. Hyattsville, MD: Public Health Service.

Social Class and Health Status

Historically, empirical evidence has been relatively clear regarding the relationship between social class and health. We know that as social class position improves, so does health status (Townsend & Harel, 1990; Estes & Rundall, 1992). For example, Johnson and Wolinsky (1993, pp. 118–119) point out that "those with higher levels of education also tend to evaluate their health more positively than . . . those with lower levels of education." Incorporating the effect of race, Johnson (1994, p. 16) states that "a higher occupational level of whites is associated with better perceived health. . . ." On a somewhat different level, Grembowski et al. (1993, pp. 89–90) point out that "self-efficacy, or an individual's perceptions of his of her ability to perform specific health behaviors, greatly influences actual health behavior and health status." House, Kessler, and Herzog (1990, pp. 401–402) state that

> understanding the mechanisms that have generated socioeconomic differences in the relation of age to health at least up to age 75 could provide a basis for substantially improving health and perhaps reducing health-care expenditures by increasingly postponing morbidity and functional limitations into the last years of the human life span.

Inversely, when the socioeconomic status of the elderly person decreases, so does subjective health status (Siegel, 1993). Longino, Warheit, and Green (1989) point out that the relationship between social class and age is dependent on the specific disease. Incorporating the economic circumstances of the elderly, we know that as the elderly age, their socioeconomic position declines. House et al. (1990) suggest that socioeconomic position becomes less influential among the oldest-old. The reason why there is less social class differentiation among the oldest-old is because of the effect of government-sponsored Medicare and the loss of those less healthy prior to older age. The data support the argument that greater health care coverage in early life among all income levels would increase the likelihood of survival into older age regardless of social class position.

Unfortunately, the generalized image of health status, social class, and age contains misconceptions. In the past, the image consisted of financially poor elderly in frail health. Today the image has changed to one of economic prosperity among the elderly, who are in relatively good health (Farrell, Palmer, Atchison, & Andelman, 1994). The September 12, 1994, edition of *Business Week* is but one example of this created dichotomy. It is the effect of these stereotypes on societal assumptions of health service inequality that have created calls for reduced health care coverage of the elderly. It is to the "crisis" of health care coverage that we now turn.

The "Crisis" of Health Care Coverage to the Elderly

The "crisis" of health care coverage to the elderly involves two broad areas: the changing demographic profile of the American population and the rapidly increasing cost of health care costs (Matcha, 1993). First, the changing demographic profile in the United States is known as *population aging*. This means that the population aged 65 and over is increasing as a percentage of the total population (Siegel & Taeuber, 1986). As the elderly increase in total number and as a percentage of the population, the oldest-old (aged 85 and over) are experiencing the most rapid growth rates. The United States is not the only nation experiencing population aging. In fact, the United States is considered a "young" nation when compared with other Western industrialized countries.

Interestingly, it is the changing demographic profile that has become the "crisis" (Callahan, 1987). However, "the recognition, shaping, formulation, and analysis of crises are socially produced by individuals in dominant institutions" (Estes, Wallace, & Binney, 1989, p. 408). In the remaining pages of this chapter we will examine not only the cost of health care, but arguments to reduce the amount of care to the elderly. We will also examine an alternative explanation to the increasing cost of health care.

The Cost of Health Care

Health care costs in the United States are the most expensive in the world. We spend more money, as a percentage of GDP and per capita, on health care than any other nation; yet we experience some of the poorest health outcomes. These outcomes are measured by life expectancy and infant mortality. Table 7–9 provides a comparison of per capita health care expenditure and health expenditure as a percentage of GDP for the United States and a number of other industrialized nations. These data cover the period 1960–1990.

The per capita cost of health care in the United States has been increasing for a period of time. However, the percentage of GDP spent on health care was comparable to that of Canada until the early 1970s. According to Graig (1993, p. 56),

> in 1970, Canadian and American health expenditures were on par with one another at 7.1 and 7.4 percent of GDP respectively. Within the following ten years, however, U.S. expenditures shot up to 9.2 percent of GDP while Canadian expenditures remained steady at 7.4 percent of GDP. Canada kept its health expenditures below 9 percent of GDP throughout the 1980s while U.S. health costs soared beyond 11 percent of GDP.

The divergence of health care costs occurred during a period of time when the percentage of elderly Canadians was growing at a more rapid rate than in the United States. By 1990, 12.5 percent of Americans were aged 65 and over, compared with 11.5 percent of Canadians. In terms of growth of the elderly population, "the resulting percentage increase between 1970 and 1990 in the United States was 21.6%; in Canada 31.3%" (Matcha, 1994b, p. 10). As a result, it is difficult to attribute the increasing cost of health care to an increasing aged population. In fact, Getzen (1992, p. S103) argues that "while it is possible that population aging may increase total national health expenditures, no corroborating evidence for such an effect currently exists, and, if found in subsequent studies, its magnitude is apt to be significantly smaller than has customarily been assumed." The National Center for Health Statistics (1993, p. 6) attributes 9 percent of the increased cost of personal health expenditure to increased population, 54 percent to rising prices, and 37 percent to "changes in the use of kinds of services and supplies."

It is evident that the increasing cost of health care in the United States is the result of economic forces within the current health care system rather than the result of an increasingly aged population. Unfortunately, the image that has been created of the "greedy

TABLE 7–9 Total Health Expenditure as a Percentage of Gross Domestic Product and per Capita Expenditures in Dollars: Selected Countries and Years, 1960–1991

Health Expenditure as a Percentage of GDP

Country	1960	1970	1980	1990	1991[a]
Canada	5.5	7.1	7.4	9.5	10.0
Denmark	3.6	6.1	6.8	6.3	6.5
France	4.2	5.8	7.6	8.8	9.1
Germany	4.8	5.9	8.4	8.3	8.5
Ireland	4.0	5.6	9.2	7.0	7.3
Japan	3.0	4.6	6.6	6.5	6.6
Norway	3.3	5.0	6.6	7.4	7.6
Sweden	4.7	7.2	9.4	8.6	8.6
United Kingdom	3.9	4.5	5.8	6.2	6.6
United States	5.3	7.4	9.2	12.2	13.2

Per Capita Health Expenditure[b]

Country	1960	1970	1980	1990	1991
Canada	109	253	743	1,811	1,915
Denmark	70	212	582	1,051	1,151
France	75	203	698	1,528	1,650
Germany	98	216	811	1,522	1,659
Ireland	38	97	449	748	845
Japan	27	127	517	1,175	1,267
Norway	49	134	549	1,193	1,305
Sweden	94	271	855	1,455	1,443
United Kingdom	79	147	458	985	1,043
United States	143	346	1,063	2,600	2,868

[a]Priliminary figures
[b]Per capita health expenditures for each country have been adjusted to U.S. dollars using gross domestic product purchasing power parities for each year.
Source: Schieber, G.J., Poullier, J.P., Greenwald, L.G.: U.S. health expenditure performance: An International comparison and data update. Health Care Financing Review. Vol. 13, No. 4. HCFA Pub. No. 03331. Health Care Financing Administration. Washington. U.S. Government Printing Office, September 1992; Office of National Health Statistics, Office of the Actuary. National health expenditures, 1991. Health Care Financing Review. Vol. 14, No. 2, HCFA Pub No. 03335. Health Care Financing Administration. Washington. U.S. Government Printing Office, Winter, 1992; unpublished data.

geezer" is more popular and more identifiable. As a result, the elderly, and the growth in the elderly population, is more readily identified as contributing to the "crisis" in health care coverage than the health care system itself. The consequence of this socially created explanation for rising health care costs has been an ongoing debate regarding methods to curb health care usage by the elderly. We now turn to that debate in the following section on health care rationing.

Rationing of Health Care

In the United States, the contemporary origins of health care rationing on the basis of age is usually attributed to a 1983 statement by economist Alan Greenspan. Greenspan questioned whether Medicare coverage of those elderly in their last year of life was worth it. Since then, others have espoused this concept but perhaps none with such notoriety as Richard Lamm, who in 1984 was governor of Colorado. Lamm was purported to have said that the elderly have a "duty to die" (Binstock & Post, 1991). By 1987 two books were published that generated considerable debate within the academic community and in the general population. The work of Smeeding, Battin, Francis, and Landesman (1987) represented articles originally presented at a conference held at the University of Utah. Also in 1987, Daniel Callahan's book *Setting Limits: Medical Goals in an Aging Society* was published. We will examine the rationale associated with the argument that health care should be rationed on the basis of age.

The best source for understanding the rationale for rationing of health care on the basis of age is that of Callahan (1987). He begins by citing the growth in the aging population as well as current and future health care expenditures. He then identifies three complaints that exist regarding the elderly. "The first is that an increasingly large share of health care is going to the elderly in comparison with benefits for children. . . . The second is that a disproportionately large portion of health-care expenditures goes for the care of the dying elderly. . . . The third is that a large and growing proportion of health-care research and technology is devoted to conditions that affect the elderly more than other age groups" (Callahan, 1987, p. 21).

Callahan also explores the intergenerational relationship issue by questioning the ability of American society to focus on communal rather than individual needs. He concludes by identifying three proposals that encompass the basis of his argument. He suggests that, first,

> we desist from pursuing without prudent limits medical goals that combine these features: the beneficiaries are primarily the elderly, indefinite life extension is sought, the costs are high, and the population-wide benefits are slight. . . . The second proposal is that those who work in behalf of the old shift their priorities from simply gaining more for the elderly, whatever the "more" is, toward the development of an integrated perspective on a natural live span, one that knows where the boundaries are. . . . The third proposal is that we try to enter into a pervasive cultural agreement to alter our perception of death as an enemy to be held off at all costs. (Callahan, 1987, pp. 222–223)

These proposals established the framework within which those who subscribe to the rationing argument could base their argument. In addition to the research of the last 10 years, a considerable literature in the ethics and moral implications of societal and individual responsibility has emerged that supports Callahan's original argument. In essence, the rationing argument questions the viability of medicine and the elderly to maintain a quality of life. As a result, how "quality of life" is interpreted could have serious consequences.

One explanation of health care rationing on the basis of age is the human-capital approach. Avorn (1984) outlines the meaning and consequences of this approach to health programs. This approach is analogous to a factory setting in which owners of machinery that is old and less productive are less likely to invest in upkeep and continuation because it is not cost-efficient. As an example of the human-capital argument, Avorn (1984, p. 1297) cites Dolan, Hodgson, and Wun (1980), who calculated the monetary value of life for men and women of various age groups. According to their calculations, the value of human life peaks between ages 30 and 34 and declines thereafter. Table 7–10 illustrates their argument.

According to Dolan et al. (1980), the value of life not only declines after age 34, but monetary values differ between men and women. In fact, women are identified as having greater economic value in old age. The reason for the gender difference is that women remain "productive" by performing domestic roles.

The human-capital approach removes any sense of humanity from interpersonal relations. Instead, it argues that all human behavior can be calculated on a cost-benefit analysis. When the elderly have been removed from the productive process through legislative action, it is not surprising that they would not have a great deal of economic value.

The age-based health care rationing argument assumes that all elderly are consuming a disproportionate share of the health care budget. Thus the elderly as a distinct chronological age group are responsible for the increasing cost of health care. In reality, a small percentage of those aged 65 and over consume a significant proportion of the Medicare budget. It is also true that "most old people are not very sick until the last year of life" (Cassel & Neugarten, 1991, p. 80). Rationing of health care, then, "is a rationally defensible policy only if the alleged scarcity is real and cannot be relieved without introducing still greater injustices" (Battin, 1987, p. 91). It would also appear that "Callahan has provided an 'ethical' solution to a fiscal problem" (Sprott, 1991, p. 123). Given the data, it would appear that health care rationing on the basis of age is not particularly defensible. Rather than age, Getzen (1992, p. S103) suggests that "spending is a result of political and professional choices, rather than the outcome of objective trends in demography, morbidity, technology, or other relentless forces beyond our control."

TABLE 7–10   Value of a Life at Various Ages

Age	Male	Female
20–24	$170,707	$133,238
30–34	$205,062	$130,044
40–44	$180,352	$111,647
50–54	$124,989	$86,268
60–64	$45,169	$53,426
70–74	$9,781	$29,189
80–84	$2,820	$16,787
85 and over	$943	$5,705

Note: Values are expressed in 1977 dollars.
Source: Dorn, T. J., et al. (1980). *Present Values of Expected Lifetime Earnings and Housekeeping Services.* Hyattsville, MD: National Center for Health Statistics.

An alternative explanation to the health care rationing argument is offered through the theoretical construct of the political economy of aging. Rather than blaming the elderly for the increasing cost of the health care system, the political economy perspective would instead examine

> the sociopolitical context in which society views older persons and how this affects the elderly; the sociopolitical and economic causation of illness; the political and economic basis of health policies; the distribution of benefits that affect health; and the relative power of the professions, medical industries, corporations, and banks in framing the life chances of different subgroups of older persons. (Estes, Gerard, Zones, & Swan, 1984, p. 2)

From a political economy perspective, we examine where and how health care services are provided to the elderly. To begin, it is important to understand how the structural components of society determine the health outcomes of various populations.

Health, or the lack of health, does not occur in isolation. Relative to the elderly, Estes et al. (1984) identify three environments within which health care and social services are provided. These include institutional, community, and informal settings. Estes et al. (1984, p. 85) state that "the institutional setting, which is the most restrictive, consumes the lion's share of public funds for the elderly in the United States." Thus the issue that the elderly consume a disproportionate share of the health care dollars is fallacious. Considering that the institutional settings are primarily private (particularly nursing homes), the cost of caring for the elderly has been established by market forces, not demographics. The cost of caring for the elderly is a profitable business for many in the health care profession (Estes & Binney, 1991). Beginning with the passage of Medicare and Medicaid in 1965, the health care profession realized the economic viability of the elderly. Cost of health care increased not because of the elderly but as a result of legislative action that created health care services for the elderly as a lucrative for-profit business. This has been particularly true among the elderly who are capable of paying for services above those provided by Medicare and Medicaid. As Estes, Gerard, Zones, and Swan (1984, p. 12) suggest, "the status, resources, and health of the elderly, and even the trajectory of the aging process itself, are conditioned by one's location in the social structure and the economic and political factors that affect it." Health care is related to an ability to pay (directly or indirectly) for services. It is not always the age of the individual but rather the social status one enjoys that affects one's health status. For example, if Medicare were eliminated, how would the elderly pay for medical care? The well-to-do elderly would pay for the best care as an out-of-pocket expense. The middle class elderly would purchase other insurance policies that would pay much of what Medicare now covers. The poorer elderly would be forced to accept the level of care provided all indigent people. The reality is that health care rationing on the basis of age perpetuates social class differences already in existence within American society (Jahnigen & Binstock, 1991; Schneider, 1993).

Regardless of the explanation given, health care costs continue to increase within society in general and the elderly in particular. Given the fact that health care is currently one-seventh of the GDP, continued growth of health care is not only undesirable but fiscally irresponsible. The problem for some is not how to ration health care but how to reallocate the resources that currently exist. However, even reallocation advocates such as Moody (1992) have a difficult task of convincing the public that reallocation will work. This debate will continue and perhaps become even more divisive as we progress through the decade of the 1990s.

The Future of Health Care for the Elderly

The future of health care for the elderly is not as bright today as in the past. Issues of legitimacy to access, limited national resources, and societal commitment to an aging population permeate the health care debate today. Today the emphasis is on less governmental involvement in the affairs of individual members of society. This diminished role of government has been accompanied by an increased economic responsibility placed on the individual. All of this is quite distinct from earlier policy initiatives. Based on existing legislation, the elderly are provided assurances of societal responsibilities toward them (Davis, 1985). Utilizing the Older Americans Act as a model, Davis (1985, p. 740) presents a number of "principles that reflect the objectives of the Older Americans Act and can serve as a basis for such a health care policy:

1. Adequate health care throughout life is essential to a healthy old age. Health policy for the aged must also ensure the health of the future aged through assurance to children and nonaged adults of access to preventive and acute care services.
2. As one enters old age, health care financing should continue to be universal and comprehensive, with additional benefits tailored to the needs of old age. All aged regardless of income, race, or prior work history should be covered.
3. Comprehensive benefits should include preventive services, treatment for acute and chronic conditions, and assistance in coping with functional limitations. The scope of services covered should be flexible enough to enable the aged to meet their health needs without incurring heavy financial burdens.
4. Choice of care alternatives and maximum independence should be promoted. Choice of living arrangements with supportive services from family, friends, and community should be available.
5. Services should be financed from federal, state, and local tax revenues, philanthropy, and individual contributions. Any financial requirements should not constitute an undue burden on the aged.
6. Cost controls must be included in any comprehensive health care scheme. Incentives should encourage low-cost, high-quality care and program administration.
7. Access to quality care must be assured through monitoring efforts of the existing network of voluntary agencies, senior citizen groups, and community organizations."

These principles enumerate an implicit relationship that existed between society and the aging individual. With regard to health care, the social contract was quite explicit. Society assumed responsibility for the health care needs of the aging population through such programs as Medicare. Although programs such as Medicare are flawed, social responsibility remained as a reminder of increased expectations. Health care for the aged today and in the future is less secure. As the health and health status of the elderly improves relative to other age groups, health policy may reflect a decreasing differentiation on the basis of age. Although health care equity is important, monies once allocated for health care services of the elderly may be reallocated to serve other age populations. The elderly may be faced with decreased rather than increased expectations for health care.

Critical Connection: If I Have My Health I Can Do Anything

The old saying "If I have my health I can do anything" is the most optimistic interpretation of health and offers the greatest range of possible activity available. We know however, that one's health is related to one's social class position in society. As a result, some elderly are limited in what they can do, whereas others remain actively involved in the larger social world in which they live. While the economic position will potentially influence our health status, it is the availability of roles that reflects societal willingness to integrate the elderly into the larger society. As an example of the interrelationship of social status and health as necessary precursors to aged activity, consider the political system.

Ronald Reagan was in his 80s when he completed his second term as president. Many members of Congress are in their 70s and 80s. Supreme Court appointments are made for life. As long as these individuals remain healthy, they can continue to perform their elected or confirmed roles. These individuals also have something else in common; they were all relatively wealthy to first achieve the social status they now enjoy. The result is that the statement "If I have my health I can do anything" is true, but what I do is dependent on my economic position throughout life and in old age.

Although economic position is a significant indicator of political involvement, regardless of one's age, myths abound regarding the political activity of the elderly. In particular, the elderly are assumed to "block vote." That is they use their age as a basis for political commonality. Such a myth homogenizes the elderly rather than attempting to understand their different needs and (in)ability to influence the political system. Chapter 8 will examine the reciprocal role of the elderly in the political process.

Chapter Review

This chapter addresses health care as it applies to the elderly. In addition, economic issues and population changes are also significant factors to understanding the impact of health on the elderly. Such interrelationships are important to the understanding of broader implications associated with the aging process. The following questions are intended to begin connecting these various structural components of society into a coherent explanation of aging.

1. We know that the elderly have the highest rate of death of any age group. We also know that the primary causes of death have changed over the years. Assuming that life expectancy continues to increase (even at a very moderate rate), would you expect the primary causes of death to remain the same? Why?

2. As women assume a greater role in the workplace, will they begin experiencing the same types of health care problems in old age currently experienced by

males? If so, is this result a consequence of the movement of women into the workplace or a function of the workplace?

3. The concept of squaring the curve assumes that individuals will live rather healthy lives until their eighth decade, when they will experience chronic disease(s) and die shortly thereafter, thus a compression of morbidity and mortality into a very short period of time. Do you agree or disagree with this concept? Explain your answer.

4. The mortality rates for the exercise in this chapter are 5,252/100,000 in 1980 and 4,922/100,000 in 1990. What does this mean? Using reference materials, calculate the mortality rate among the elderly for two different countries. Choose a developed and a developing nation. Compare their rates. What would you conclude? Explain your answer.

5. Why do the elderly rate their health status lower than other age groups? Will the health status of the elderly increase or decrease in the near future? Explain your answer.

6. Considering the demographic changes expected in the next 50 years, what is the future of health care for American elderly? Will rationing of health care on the basis of age be necessary in the future? If rationing is necessary, what is the future for the elderly in the United States?

7. Why is rationing of health care on the basis of age such a significant issue in the United States and not in other industrialized nations?

8. Reread the human-capital approach to health care rationing on the basis of age. Construct an argument in support of this approach. Construct an argument against the human-capital approach.

Glossary

Disease   A physiological disorder requiring medical definition and intervention.

Health status   The overall rating (subjective and objective) we apply to our feeling of health.

Illness   An individual's subjective analysis of his or her disease state or health status.

Morbidity   The number or rate of specific disease patterns within a defined population.

Mortality   The number or rate of deaths within a defined population.

Population aging   An observation that a population is getting older and is measured by percentage of the population aged 65 and over.

Sickness   A socially defined role dependent on the medical definition and intervention of a particular disease state.

Suggested Reading

Abraham, L. K. (1993). *Mama might be better off dead.* Chicago: University of Chicago Press.
The author is a journalist who provides a case study analysis of one family and its contact with the health care system.

Binstock, R. H., & Post, S. G. (1991). *Too old for health care? Controversies in medicine, law,* *economics and ethics.* Baltimore: Johns Hopkins University Press.
An excellent series of articles that address numerous issues associated with the health status of the elderly.

Callahan, D. (1987). *Setting limits: Medical goals in an aging society.* New York: Simon and Schuster.

Essential reading for those interested in the argument for health care rationing on the basis of age.

Estes, C. L., Gerard, L. E., Zones, J. S., & Swan, J. H. (1984). *Political economy, health, and aging.* Boston: Little, Brown and Company.

Recommended reading in conjunction with Callahan. This book provides an alternative explanation to the argument for health care rationing on the basis of age.

Ory, M. G., Abeles, R. P., & Lipman, P. D. (1992). *Aging, health, and behavior.* Newbury Park, CA: Sage.

A compilation of research activity addressing the elderly and their health.

In addition to these books, readers are encouraged to peruse the table of contents of *The New England Journal of Medicine* and *The Journal of the American Medical Association* for articles from the medical profession. There are also numerous aging journals to peruse. These include *The Gerontologist, Journals of Gerontology, Research on Aging, Journal of Aging Studies,* and *Generations.* This is not meant as a complete listing but rather as a beginning for those interested in continuing their investigation of the health of the elderly.

References

Angell, M. (1993). How much will health reform cost? *New England Journal of Medicine, 328*(24), 1778–1779.

Avorn, J. (1984). Benefit and cost analysis in geriatric care. *New England Journal of Medicine, 310*(20), 1294–1301.

Battin, M. P. (1987). Age rationing and the just distribution of health care: Is there a duty to die? In T. M. Smeeding, M. P. Battin, L. P. Francis, & B. M. Landesman (Eds.), *Should medical care be rationed by age?* (pp. 69–94). Totowa, NJ: Rowman and Littlefield.

Binstock, R. H., & Post, S. G. (1991). Old age and the rationing of health care. In R. H. Binstock & S. G. Post (Eds.), *Too old for health care?* (pp. 1–12). Baltimore: Johns Hopkins University Press.

Callahan, D. (1987). *Setting limits: Medical goals in an aging society.* New York: Simon and Schuster.

Callahan, D. (1990). *What kind of life: The limits of medical progress.* New York: Simon and Schuster.

Cassel, C. K., & Neugarten, B. L. (1991). The goals of medicine in an aging society. In R. H. Binstock & S. G. Post (Eds.), *Too old for health care? Controversies in medicine, law, economics and ethics* (pp. 75–91). Baltimore: Johns Hopkins University Press.

Cockerham, W. C. (1992). *Medical sociology* (5th ed.). Englewood Cliffs, NJ: Prentice Hall.

Davis, K. (1985). Health care policies and the aged: Observations from the United States. In R. H. Binstock & E. Shanas (Eds.), *Handbook of aging and the social sciences* (2nd ed., pp. 727–744). New York: Van Nostrand Reinhold.

Dolan, T. J., Hodgson, T. A., & Wun, W. M. (1980). Present values of expected lifetime earnings and housekeeping services. Hyattsville, MD: National Center for Health Statistics.

Estes, C. L., & Binney, E. A. (1991). The biomedicalization of aging: Dangers and dilemmas. In M. Minkler & C. L. Estes (Eds.), *Critical perspectives on aging: The political and moral economy of growing old* (pp. 117–134). Amityville, NY: Baywood.

Estes, C. L., Gerard, L. E., Zones, J. S., & Swan, J. H. (1984). *Political economy, health, and aging.* Boston: Little, Brown and Company.

Estes, C. L., & Rundall, T. G. (1992). Social characteristics, social structure, and health in the aging population. In M. G. Ory, R. P. Abeles, & P. D. Lipman (Eds.), *Aging, health, and behavior* (pp. 299–326). Newbury Park, CA: Sage.

Estes, C. L., Wallace, S. P., & Binney, E. A. (1989). Health, aging, and medical sociology. In H. E. Freeman & S. Levine (Eds.), *Handbook of medical sociology* (4th ed., pp. 400–418). Englewood Cliffs, NJ: Prentice Hall.

Fanshel, S., & Bush, J. W. (1970). A health-status index and its application to health service outcomes. *Operations Research, 18,* 1021–1066.

Farrell, C., Palmer, A. T., Atchison, S., & Andelman, B. (1994, September 12). The economics of aging: Why the growing number of elderly won't bankrupt America. *Business Week,* pp. 60–68.

Francis, L. P., & Smeeding, T. M. (1987). Introduction. In T. M. Smeeding, M. P. Battin, L. P. Francis, & B. M. Landesman (Eds.), *Should medical care be rationed by age?* (pp. 1–10). Totowa, NJ: Rowman and Littlefield.

Fries, J. F. (1980). Aging, natural death, and the compression of morbidity. *New England Journal of Medicine, 303*(3), 130–135.

Fuchs, V. R. (1984). "Though much is taken": Reflections on aging, health, and medical care. *Milbank Quarterly, 62*(2), 143–166.

Gallup, G., Jr. (1993, November 3). President Clinton/health care plan. Wilmington, DE: Scholarly Resources.

Getzen, T. E. (1992). Population aging and the growth of health expenditures. *Journal of Gerontology, 47*(3), S98–104.

Girzadas, P. M., Counte, M. A., Glandon, G. L., & Tancredi, D. (1993). An analysis of elderly health and life satisfaction. *Behavior, Health and Aging, 3*(2), 103–117.

Graig, L. A. (1993). *Health of nations: An international perspective on U.S. health care reform.* Washington, DC: Congressional Quarterly.

Grembowski, D., Patrick, D., Diehr, P., Durham, M., Beresford, S., Kay, E., & Hecht, J. (1993, June). Self-efficacy and health behavior among older adults. *Journal of Health and Social Behavior, 34,* 89–104.

Haber, D. (1989). *Health care for an aging society.* New York: Hemisphere.

House, J. S., Kessler, R. C., & Herzog, A. R. (1990). Age, socioeconomic status, and health. *Milbank Quarterly, 68*(3), 383–411.

Jahnigen, D. W., & Binstock, R. H. (1991). Economic and clinical realities. In R. H. Binstock & S. G. Post (Eds.), *Too old for health care? Controversies in medicine, law, economics, and ethics* (pp. 13–43). Baltimore: Johns Hopkins University Press.

Johnson, C. L. (1994). Differential expectations and realities: Race, socioeconomic status and health of the oldest-old. *International Journal of Aging and Human Development, 38*(1), 13–27.

Johnson, R. J., & Wolinsky, F. D. (1993, June). The structure of health status among older adults: Disease, disability, functional limitation, and perceived health. *Journal of Health and Social Behavior, 34,* 105–121.

Larson, R. (1978). Thirty years of research on the subjective well-being of older Americans. *Journal of Gerontology, 33*(1), 109–125.

Longino, C. F., Jr., Warheit, G. J., & Green, J. A. (1989). Class, aging, and health. In K. S. Markides (Ed.), *Aging and health: Perspectives on gender, race, ethnicity, and class* (pp. 79–109). Newbury Park, CA: Sage.

Matcha, D. A. (1993). Rationing of health care on the basis of age: A political economy perspective. Paper presented at the Eastern Sociological Society Annual Meetings, Boston, MA, March 27.

Matcha, D. A. (1994a). In the interest of all: Real health care reform. *New York State Sociological Association Conference Proceedings,* Dowling College, Long Island, NY. Fort Worth, TX: Cyberspace Publications.

Matcha, D. A. (1994b). Aging, health care, and social policy. Poster presentation at the New York State Society on Aging, Albany, NY, October 15.

Moody, H. R. (1992). *Ethics in an aging society.* Baltimore: Johns Hopkins University Press.

National Center for Health Statistics. (1993). *Health, United States, 1992.* Hyattsville, MD: Public Health Service.

National Center for Health Statistics. (1994). *Health, United States, 1993.* Hyattsville, MD: Public Health Service.

Pol, L. G., & Thomas, R. K. (1992). *The demography of health and health care.* New York: Plenum Press.

Rabin, D. L. (1985). Waxing of the gray, waning of the green. In Committee on an Aging Society, *America's aging: Health in an older society* (pp. 28–56). Washington, DC: National Academy Press.

Roemer, M. I. (1991). *National health systems of the world: Vol. 1. The countries.* New York: Oxford University Press.

Schieber, G. J., Poullier, J. P., Greenwald, L. G. (1992, September). U.S. health expenditure performance: An international comparison and data update. *Health Care Financing Review.* Vol. 13, No. 4. HCFA Pub. No. 03331. Health Care

Financing Administration. Washington, DC: U.S. Government Printing Office.

Schneider, E. L. (1993). Changing the debate about health care for the elderly. In G. R. Winslow & J. W. Walters (Eds.), *Facing limits: Ethics and health care for the elderly* (pp. 161–174). Boulder, CO: Westview Press.

Shanas, E., & Maddox, G. L. (1985). Health, health resources, and the utilization of care. In R. H. Binstock & E. Shanas (Eds.), *Handbook of aging and the social sciences* (2nd ed., pp. 696–726). New York: Van Nostrand Reinhold.

Siegel, J. S. (1993). *A generation of change: A profile of America's older population.* New York: Russell Sage Foundation.

Siegel, J. S., & Taeuber, C. M. (1986). Demographic dimensions of an aging population. In A. Pifer & L. Bronte (Eds.), *Our aging society: Paradox and promise* (pp. 79–110). New York: Norton.

Smeeding, T. M., Battin, M. P., Francis, L. P., & Landesman, B. M. (Eds.). (1987). *Should medical care be rationed by age?* Totowa, NJ: Rowman and Littlefield.

Sprott, R. L. (1991). Policy implications and ethical dilemmas posed by an aging population. In F. C. Ludwig (Ed.), *Life span extension: Consequences and open questions* (pp. 120–131). New York: Springer.

Staats, S., Heaphey, K., Miller, D., Partlo, C., Romine, N., & Stubbs, K. (1993). Subjective age and health perceptions of older persons: Maintaining the youthful bias in sickness and in health. *International Journal of Aging and Human Development, 37*(3), 191–203.

Stahl, S. M., & Feller, J. R. (1990). Old equals sick: An ontogenetic fallacy. In S. M. Stahl (Ed.), *The legacy of longevity* (pp. 21–34). Newbury Park, CA: Sage.

Swartz, K. (1994). Dynamics of people without health insurance: Don't let the numbers fool you. *Journal of the American Medical Association, 117*(6), 511–519.

Toner, R. (1994, November 16). Health reform cast as election's bitter pill. *Times Union* (Albany, NY), pp. A1, A9.

Townsend, A., & Harel, Z. (1990). Health vulnerability and service need among the elderly. In Z. Harel, P. Ehrlich, & R. Hubbard (Eds.), *The vulnerable aged: People, services, and policies* (pp. 32–52). New York: Springer.

Weiss, G. L., & Lonnquist, L. E. (1994). *The sociology of health, healing, and illness.* Englewood Cliffs, NJ: Prentice Hall.

White House Domestic Policy Council. (1993). *The President's Health Security Plan.* New York: Random House.

Willits, F. K., & Crider, D. M. (1988). Health rating and life satisfaction in the later middle years. *Journal of Gerontology, 43*(5), S172–176.

World Development Report. (1993). *Investment in health.* New York: Oxford University Press.

Chapter 8

Aging and the Political Process

The aging, long a favored social-welfare constituency in the United States, are in the early stages of being confronted with a series of obstacles which may put their favored status—and its concomitant material and symbolic benefits—in jeopardy. Rapidly rising public policy costs for meeting the needs of an aging population, a nascent but growing reassessment of policy benefits directed toward the elderly, and competitive pressures from other social-welfare constituencies are now threatening two of the aging's longstanding political resources—their singular legitimacy as a policy constituency and their political utility to other actors in the policy process.
—HUDSON, 1978A, P. 428

The passage just cited is as significant today as it was in 1978. As the United States approaches the end of the 20th century, political posturing is expected to diminish many of the earlier advances made on behalf of the elderly. Once sacrosanct programs such as Medicare and Social Security are now openly discussed as potential targets of governmental "downsizing." When the political power that supposedly existed among the elderly shifts from age- to class-based interests, those aged 65 and over will find little in common beyond chronological age. The consequence of differentiation on the basis of class is that "if affluent older Americans split with the low-income elderly over policy issues in the future, the influence of the elderly as a group could be significantly neutralized, as happened in the case of catastrophic health insurance" (Wallace, Williamson, Lung, & Powell, 1991, p. 110).

This chapter will examine the political fortunes and problems of the elderly in American society. We begin with the two greatest achievements in American social policy: Social Security and Medicare. We then shift our focus of attention to the political process itself. We will explore the nature and extent to which political behavior is exhibited by the elderly relative to the larger society. Finally, we will link the elderly to the political system through their involvement with various levels of government. Throughout the chapter the underlying concept is that of power, specifically, the political power to establish goals and objectives experienced by oneself and others. It is the loss of such power that is of concern to present and future generations of American elderly. We begin with the emergence (or at least the perception) of political power among the elderly.

Governmental Attitude and Action

Throughout the history of the United States, the relationship between government and its citizens has been one of benign tolerance. The religious and cultural forces that were basic to the founding of the nation also established an ethos from which such tolerance was legitimated. We will examine two specific historical events that have altered the relationship between society and its citizens.

Social Security

Historically, the signing of Social Security into law in 1935 established the United States as one of the last developed, free-market systems to provide some form of pension coverage to its aging population. Prior to the signing in 1935, some 40 nations had already established pension laws (Epstein, 1928). It is also important to realize that the use of the term *social security* in the United States is unique relative to other nations. Americans identify Social Security with income maintenance, whereas in other nations the term is applicable to a wide range of social and economic services available to a larger population (Myles, 1992).

Why did President Roosevelt sign the Social Security Act into law in 1935? As discussed briefly in Chapter 6, there is a historical context within which Social Security emerged.

That context includes the cultural value of rugged individualism, which required all to provide for their own safety and security (Douglas, 1939). That value was threatened by the Depression of the 1930s. The failure of the economy and the inability of individual states to provide significant support to its citizens were also factors. As Douglas (1939) points out, if states were to remain economically competitive, they would be at a disadvantage if they imposed labor restrictions or taxes that increased the cost of labor relative to other states. However, as the Depression worsened and the numbers of elderly on the dole continued to increase, states in the North and West began to take action (Douglas, 1939). A third variable is usually identified as a significant contributor to the enactment of Social Security. This is the famous Townsend plan discussed briefly in Chapter 6.

The Townsend plan is named after its founder, F. E. Townsend. Townsend was a retired physician who had worked for the Long Beach (California) health office until he was fired in 1933 because of the continued economic depression. Using his own money, he circulated petitions requesting that the federal government adopt two laws:

> the voluntary retirement on a federal monthly pension of $200, of all citizens of good character who were sixty years of age or over, with the provision that the person thus retired would spend the entire $200 within thirty days from its receipt and within the borders of the United States and for goods and services.
>
> The second law called for . . . the financing of the pension roll by means of universal transactional-sales tax of 2 percent. (Roosevelt, 1936, p. 3)

Success of the Townsend plan relied heavily on the rhetoric of its founder. According to Putnam (1970), there were four characteristics of this rhetoric:

1. The plan was always billed as an economic cure-all rather than merely a program to provide handouts for aged Americans.
2. The rhetoric of the plan offered not only economic security but social and psychological security.
3. The rhetoric was a masterly synthesis of political conservatism and radicalism.
4. The rhetoric of the plan was often religious in character and tended to elevate Townsend to godlike stature. (Putnam, 1970, pp. 52-55)

The Townsend plan began in 1934 and attracted a great deal of national attention and support. By early 1935 there were almost half a million members nationwide and petitions with millions of signatures (Douglas, 1939). Although attractive, the Townsend plan was economically flawed. For example, the cost of the plan was estimated at $24 billion, but the 2 percent sales tax would raise less than one-half that amount. Politically, the plan was denounced by both the political left and right, although for very different reasons (Amenta, Carruthers, & Zylan, 1992). The plan was also attacked by President Roosevelt (Douglas, 1939) as age-graded dependence on the government rather than on family. Nonetheless, the plan was introduced in Congress and was soundly defeated.

A second, and less publicized, bill also ultimately influenced the character of Social Security. This was the Lundeen bill. The bill was originally introduced into Congress in 1934 and reintroduced in 1935 by Representative Lundeen of Minnesota (Douglas, 1939). This bill was less generous than the Townsend plan and enjoyed greater legislative support. Essentially, the bill "provided for the payment of unemployment compensation out of the funds of the federal government to all unemployed persons over the age of eighteen years for as long as they were out of work through no fault of their own" (Douglas, 1939, p. 74). The unemployed worker would receive a minimum of $10 per week and $3 for each dependent. The final draft of the bill included not only those who were unemployed but also those "workers and farmers who were unable to work for any reason, whether this inability was caused by sickness, old age, maternity, industrial injury, etc." (Douglas, 1939, p. 75). The Lundeen bill was recommended for passage in the House Committee on Labor. The administration did not support the bill, and it died.

Although the Townsend plan and the Lundeen bill failed to gain congressional and administrative approval, they had an impact on the outcome of the Social Security Act of 1935. (Pratt [1976] disagrees with this assessment by arguing that the Townsend movement came too late to have any real impact on the Social Security legislation.) Nevertheless, President Roosevelt, realizing the increasing worker discontent with the status quo, was interested in legislation that would appease those who wanted significant change in the relationship between the government and the individual. Therefore, in mid-1934 the president established the Committee on Economic Security (Booth, 1973). The committee argued that a Social Security system should not include a disincentive to work or place money in savings for future retirement "and that these [savings] be protected by assurance that bank deposits, private pensions, and other assets would be safeguarded. 'Maximum employment' was identified as the 'first objective of a program of economic security' through public works and related measures. In addition to expansion of public health services, insurance mechanisms should cover the costs of medical care" (Booth, 1973, pp. 8-9).

The committee, however, did not include health insurance in its draft proposal (Starr, 1982) for a number of reasons. These reasons range from the committee's not wanting to overload the program to opposition from the American Medical Association (Douglas, 1939). Debate began in Congress in January 1935. (For a complete text of H.R. 7260, the Text of the Federal Social Security Act, see Douglas [1939, pp. 437-486].) The bill was approved by the House of Representatives and the Senate in early August 1935. The bill was signed into law by President Roosevelt on August 18, 1935 (Douglas, 1939).

Although the Social Security Act contained a number of provisions, the one of greatest importance here is that of old-age benefits. These benefits were based on three basic points: "(1) a national (not state-by-state) system, (2) compulsory for those in covered employments, (3) providing benefits as a matter of right (without regard to individual means or needs)" (Booth, 1973, p. 10). An early provision to old-age benefits brought the spouse and dependents under the social insurance system. This provision was called the Old Age and Survivors Insurance (OASI) (Bernstein & Bernstein, 1988).

Today the old-age benefits provision is known as OASDHI (Old-Age, Survivors', Disability, and Health Insurance). For an historical accounting of Social Security (specifically OASDI), refer to the *Social Security Bulletin,* Annual Statistical Supplement (1993).

Originally, Social Security only covered some 60 percent of those who worked. Today, approximately 95 percent of workers are covered (Bernstein & Bernstein, 1988). Among those not covered include the following:

1. Federal civilian employees hired before 1984
2. Employees of state and local governments who are members of their employer's retirement system and who have not been covered by a voluntary Federal/State Social Security agreement

3. Certain agricultural and domestic workers (U.S. Department of Health and Human Services, 1993a, p. 5).

Although the intention of Social Security was not to provide complete retirement income to the elderly (Rich & Baum, 1984), it has become the sole source of income for a large percentage of retirees. In 1990 Social Security accounted for 51 percent of total median monthly family income among retired workers. Not surprisingly, the percentage of total median monthly family income from Social Security was greater for women than for men. This percentage also increased with the age of the retired worker. For example, among men and women aged 62–64, 37 percent and 39 percent, respectively, of median monthly family income was in the form of Social Security. Among men and women aged 75 and over, 60 percent and 66 percent, respectively, of income came from Social Security. Finally, as family income increased, the percentage of income from Social Security decreased. This means that poor elderly are more likely to rely on Social Security as a source of income than middle- or upper-class elderly. Among the elderly with median family income below $500 per month, 95 percent of income is from Social Security. When family income increases to $1,500–1,999, Social Security accounts for 53 percent of total median income. When median family income is $3,000 or more, Social Security accounts for only 21 percent (*Social Security Bulletin,* 1993). Stated differently, 59 percent of beneficiaries rely on Social Security for at least one-half their income. More specifically, 13 percent rely on Social Security for all of their income, and for another 11 percent Social Security represents 90 to 99 percent of their income. Thus one-fourth of all beneficiaries rely on Social Security as their only source of income (Darnay, 1994).

In addition, the number of recipients has increased from 597,000 retired worker families in 1945 to over 25 million in 1992. According to Table 8–1, the average monthly family benefits have increased from an average of $38.50 in 1945 for a worker and wife to $1,110.50 in 1992 for a worker and wife (*Social Security Bulletin,* 1993).

Increasing Social Security payments and recipients have created a funding problem for Social Security. As a result, governmental pronouncements have questioned the viability of Social Security in the future. However, Social Security enjoys considerable support from the general public (Cook & Barrett, 1988). The success of Social Security led to the eventual emergence of additional programs and initiatives for the elderly, in particular, the Older Americans Act of 1965 and the passage of Medicare, also in 1965 (Williamson, Evans, & Powell, 1982). Binstock (1991) has written an excellent 25-year review of the Older Americans Act. We will now turn our attention to the politics of health care for the elderly.

Medicare/Medicaid

Medicare   The second social policy program to significantly affect the elderly was the 1965 passage of Medicare and Medicaid. Medicare is national health insurance for those aged 65 and over (Torres-Gil, 1992). The program is operated by the Health Care Financing Administration in the Department of Health and Human Services. Medicaid is a federal program operated individually by the states for those individuals who are determined to be income eligible. The basic difference is that Medicare is considered an entitlement program based primarily on age, whereas Medicaid is an entitlement program based on need (Enos & Sultan, 1977). We will examine each one separately as they apply to the elderly.

**TABLE 8–1   OASDI Average Monthly Retired-Worker
Family Benefit: 1945–1992**

| | *Retired Worker Families* | | | |
| | Worker Only | | | Worker and |
	Total	Men	Women	Wife
1945	$ 23.50	$ 24.50	$ 19.50	$ 38.50
1950	42.20	44.60	34.80	71.70
1955	59.10	64.60	49.80	103.50
1960	69.90	79.90	59.60	123.90
1965	80.10	90.50	70.00	141.50
1970	114.20	128.70	101.60	198.90
1975	201.60	225.50	181.80	343.90
1980	333.00	377.10	297.40	566.60
1985	465.80	531.80	412.00	813.90
1990	588.30	671.90	519.10 `	1,026.60
1991	614.70	702.00	542.10	1,071.70
1992	637.80	728.10	562.30	1,110.50

Source: Social Security Bulletin. (1993). Annual statistical supplement.
Table 5.H1. Washington, DC.

Medicare was passed on July 30, 1965, as Title XVIII (Health Insurance for the Aged) of the Social Security Act and took effect 11 months later, on July 1, 1966 (*Social Security Bulletin,* 1993). A history of the provisions since its passage can be found in the 1993 *Social Security Bulletin,* Annual Statistical Supplement.

Earlier in this chapter it was noted that health care coverage was not part of the Social Security Act of 1935. Although President Roosevelt did propose legislation in 1938 addressing health care reform, no action was taken. In 1943 the Wagner-Murray-Dingell bill "proposed a universal, compulsory, and comprehensive approach to national health insurance" (Waitzkin, 1989, p. 476). An attempt by President Truman to revive national health insurance also failed. For some 30 years between the Social Security Act and Medicare, debate over any form of a national health plan identified the sharp divisions that existed in American society. According to Marmor (1973, p. 108), the debate over health care was a reflection of "class conflict, of socialized medicine vs. the voluntary 'American way,' of private enterprise and local control against 'the octopus of the federal government.'" Those opposed to Medicare included the AMA and the conservative coalition in Congress (Derthick, 1979). For an in-depth presentation of the historical and political background within which Medicare eventually emerged, see Poen (1979).

Medicare consists of two parts. The first (Part A) is called *Hospital Insurance Plan.* Under Part A,

Medicare provides 90 days of hospital care per "episode of illness" with an additional 60 day lifetime reserve. An episode of illness begins when a beneficiary enters the hospital and ends after he or she has remained out of the hospital for 60 consecutive days. All services ordinarily provided by a hospital (except for physician services) are covered during the stay. Skilled nursing facility (SNF) care is covered to 100 days if medically necessary and subsequent to a hospitalization; unlimited medically necessary home health visits are also covered. . . . The first 20 days of SNF care are covered in full but days 21–100 involve a $67.50 daily copay (one-eighth the hospital deductible). There is no copay for home health care visits. For the terminally ill with a life expectancy of 6 months or less, Part-A covers hospice care. However, benefit limits and daily coinsurance apply. (Jensen & Morrisey, 1993, p. 189)

Those over the age of 65 are entitled to Part A without paying a monthly premium. Part B is the Supplementary Medical Insurance Plan. This part of Medicare "helps pay for doctors' services, outpatient hospital services, durable medical equipment, and a number of other medical services and supplies that are not covered by the Hospital Insurance part of Medicare" (U.S. Department of Health and Human Services, 1993b, p. 1).

In 1966 there were 19,082,000 elderly enrolled in Part A and 17,736,000 in Part B. By 1992 the numbers had increased to 31,585,000 and 30,713,000, respectively (*Social Security Bulletin,* 1993). The cost of Medicare has increased from $4,737,000,000 in 1967 to approximately $132,256,000,000 in 1992 (National Center for Health Statistics, 1994). Although expenditures are significant, remember that per capita health care expenditures among the elderly in 1987 were $5,360 and that Medicare paid only 44.6 percent of these expenditures (Jensen & Morrisey, 1993). As a result, the health care needs of lower-income elderly are not properly addressed. It is also important to remember that "about 17 percent (of the elderly) account for over 60 percent of Medicare payments" (Cassel & Neugarten, 1991, p. 80). Because Medicare covers less than half the per capita costs for the elderly, those with the money to purchase additional insurance are provided a greater array services and health care opportunities. The American experience of providing universal coverage to a specific segment of the population was well intentioned, but short-sighted in its unwillingness to cover the needs of those it proposed to serve. The politics of aging are less an issue of chronological age and increasingly one of social class position. The influence of social class position taking precedence over commonality with age is best illustrated by the short-lived history of the Medicare Catastrophic Coverage Act of 1988.

The Medicare Catastrophic Coverage Act (MCCA) of 1988 was "the biggest expansion of Medicare since its implementation in 1965" (Street, 1993, p. 431). As the title of the act implies, its purpose was to reduce the financial hardships associated with catastrophic illnesses. These hardships would be reduced by implementing a series of reforms within Medicare and extending services associated with catastrophic illnesses. Initially, MCCA appeared to enjoy broad support. However, the method of paying for the increased services was a significant departure from the past. MCCA was to be funded by a tax primarily on the wealthy elderly. The tax was capped at $800 per person. The idea that upper-income elderly would pay increased taxes to fund a program that would assist primarily lower- and middle-class elderly was not accepted. Middle-class elderly believed they would also be forced to pay the $800. As a result, those elderly most affected financially (or presumed affected) mobilized and vented their displeasure against those in Congress. In October of 1989 the Medicare Catastrophic Coverage Act was repealed by Congress (Street, 1993). Class-based interests of the elderly demonstrate that political power lies with those who have the wealth and influence to alter the affairs of others. As the well-to-do elderly control the health affairs of other elderly, other vested interests control the health affairs of the poor elderly on Medicaid. The result is the creation of the elderly poor as the image of aging as a social problem. This social construction of aging and its images detracts from the more serious problems affecting the elderly such as diminishing social control over life events.

Medicaid   Distinct from Medicare, Medicaid is a needs-based program run by individual states. As a result, there are, in effect, 50 different versions of Medicaid. The elderly poor, if qualified, are eligible for a number of health services. Many of these services are not covered under Medicare (such as long-term care in a nursing home). However, eligibility for Medicaid services requires the person to "spend down" their assets. For example, although Medicare provides limited coverage of nursing home care, Medicaid coverage begins when the elderly person no longer has the assets available to cover the cost of nursing home care. In effect, the elderly must become paupers to qualify for Medicaid assistance.

Medicaid is a federal program that provides for the medically needy of all ages, not just the elderly poor. Over time, the number of elderly receiving Medicaid assistance has decreased as a percentage of all recipients. In 1972 those aged 65 and over constituted 18.6 percent of all recipients. In 1992 the elderly constituted 12.0 percent of all recipients (National Center for Health Statistics, 1994). The number of elderly recipients, however, has increased. In 1972 there were 3,318,000 elderly Medicaid recipients. By 1992 there were 3,749,000 recipients. In addition, the cost of the Medicaid program has increased dramatically. Monies spent on health assistance to the elderly poor increased from just under $2 billion in 1972 to more than $29 billion in 1992. Cost increases were not confined to the elderly. The cost of health care services increased for all recipients. Overall, the Medicaid program increased from $6.3 billion in 1972 to $91.5 billion in 1992. The average amount of Medicaid monies spent on the elderly poor increased from $580 in 1972 to $7,759 in 1992 (*Social Security Bulletin,* 1993). Although considerable amounts of money are spent on the elderly poor, the money is used to pay the salaries of thousands of health care workers. According to Dobelstein and Johnson (1985, p. 124), "most of the Medicaid payments to older people are used to reimburse hospitals, nursing homes, intermediate care homes, and group homes for the prolonged care of older people." Table 8–2 provides a categorical breakdown of how Medicaid monies are spent on the elderly. Note that over two-thirds of Medicaid payments for the elderly were spent on nursing homes.

The politics of health care for the elderly has resulted in attempts to limit services (for example, the concept of health care rationing on the basis of age discussed in Chapter 7). If those who wield political and economic power maintain a myopic view of the aging process, then their attempts to reduce services or force continual justification of need will result in a further erosion of political significance of the elderly. As Williamson, Evans, and Powell (1982, p. 4) point out,

> there appears to be a dialectical relationship between programmatic gains for the elderly and the strength of the opposition to further gains from other groups. The more successful the elderly are in their claims on governmental monies, the less legitimacy they have when they (or their advocates) request additional programs or increases in funding for existing programs.

This view of the aging process is the result of an image of aging that has been created within the media and by those in power (refer to Chapter 4 for a more detailed analysis of

TABLE 8–2   Federal and State Medicaid Payments for the Aged by Service Category, Fiscal Year 1991

Type of Expense	Percentage
Nursing homes	67.3
Home care services[a]	8.0
Prescription drugs	7.2
Inpatient hospital	6.4
Inpatient mental health	4.1
ICF/MR	1.7
Physician services	1.3
Outpatient hospital	1.0
Clinic services	0.5
Other practitioner	0.2
Dental services	0.2
Lab and X-ray	0.2
Rural health clinics	0.0
Other services[b]	1.8

[a]Home care services in this table include home health, personal care services, and home and community-based waiver services.
[b]Other services include payments for unknown service spending, as well as transportation and other related travel services, physical therapy services, occupational therapy, dentures, hospice services, family planning services, and many other services.
Source: Subcommittee on Health and the Environment. (1993). *Medicaid source book: Background data and analysis* (a 1993 Update). Table C-2. Washington, DC: U.S. Government Printing Office. Table originally prepared by the Congressional Research Service based on data contained in *Statistical Report on Medical Care Eligibles, Recipients, Payments, and Services,* HCFA Form 2082.

the social construction of aging). It is the increase in the cost of health care that has concerned many who believe that the elderly are overutilizing the health care system. It is important to remember, however, that if the numbers of elderly have not increased dramatically, then perhaps the increasing cost is the result of rapid growth in the cost of health services within the industry. Rather than blaming the elderly, the real cost culprits are those serving the needs of the elderly. When there is a for-profit health care system and a "captive patient" pool, it is not surprising that health care costs increase. This is the dialectic to which Williamson, Evans, and Powell (1982) were referring. Although the elderly have experienced real gains in health and economic status (Duncan & Smith, 1989), these advances have come with a price. Because commensurate advances have not been made in other population groups, the elderly have been singled out as receiving preferential treatment at the expense of others. Thus, as health care costs rise, the culprit is being identified as the aging population, not the health care system (Hudson, 1978a). All of this is manifested by the political power structure of the United States. We now turn to that structure and examine the role and influence of the elderly.

Who Decides Who Governs?

Political power in the United States is generally explained within two broad theoretical frameworks. First is the *pluralistic* explanation. This approach argues that power is distributed equally among all groups, and that coalitions emerge that exercise power as it applies to a specific special interest. This is the idealistic argument that assumes a democratic interplay among all competing interests. Pluralism also assumes that all competing interests are equal. This is not always true. Finally, pluralism believes that the role of the federal government is to remain neutral. Although case studies may identify specific circumstances within which pluralism actually functioned, it is not the dominant explanation. Estes (1981) argues that pluralism has three major inadequacies:

1. It equates organized representation and interest-group participation with democratic participation of the individual citizen, thereby nullifying the significance of individual (in preference to group) action;
2. It fosters the belief that equal access is provided all relevant parties through interest-group politics and ignores the fact that citizens with important concerns, but who are not organized, are excluded from the political process;
3. It assumes the existence of an underlying value consensus that will make whatever results from the competitive interplay of organized interests congruent within broad areas of value agreement. (Estes, 1981, p. 62)

The second explanation of power and how it is distributed within the United States is that of the *power elite*. This argument is grounded in the work of C. Wright Mills (1956). Essentially, Mills argued that there are three interconnected groups that determine much of what society will do and when and how. This group consists of select members of the executive branch of government, the military, and big business. The result is the concentration of power in the hands of a small number of individuals. For example, a recent study found that the power elite in the United States are still primarily Protestant, although less so today than in the past (Briggs, 1994).

How does this apply to the elderly? Whoever governs has the opportunity to establish social policy. Such policy can influence everything from Social Security to Medicare to the White House Conference on Aging. The elderly, like any other group, are particularly vulnerable to prevailing political forces. The viability of Social Security, Medicare, or Medicaid are all dependent on those elected to office (particularly at the state and national levels), and their political interpretation of the necessity of such programs. As a result, power, or the ability to get someone to do what they would rather not do, is politically significant. Those with political power will influence how the elderly are covered (or not) for basic necessities such as health care or social insurance upon retirement. (Witness the efforts by the 104th Congress regarding attempted changes in Medicare and Medicaid). The second question is, How did these individuals arrive at their positions of power to make such decisions? The (partial) answer is the voters. However, do the elderly participate in the political process as often as other age groups? If the elderly do participate, does their participation differ from other age groups, and if so, how? Finally, what is the significance of the elderly voter relative to the outcome of an election?

Voter Participation Among the Elderly

The elderly generally remain engaged in the political process through the ballot box. Research has confirmed the fact that there is a rather direct relationship between voting and age. Voting percentages generally level off after middle age, however (Glenn & Grimes, 1968; Cutler, 1977). Table 8–3 provides the percentage who reported voting in presidential elections beginning in 1964 through 1992. It is evident that regardless of year, the percentage reporting that they voted increased with age. Voting generally peaks among those aged 45–64 and then fluctuates among those aged 65 and over.

Table 8–4 identifies the percentage of the population that reported voting in congressional election years between 1978 and 1990. Here the relationship between age and percentage reported voting is direct. That is, as age increases, so does the percentage reported voting, regardless of congressional election year.

Voting behaviors vary depending on the characteristic of the elderly. Jirovec and Erich (1992, p. 223) report that among their sample of urban elderly, "homemakers and those who had experienced a decline in their health within the past year" had lower voting records. According to their research, other variables such as income, current health, education, age, and gender were not statistically related to voting activity. Peterson and Somit (1992) found that the health status of elderly (over age 55) women was related to political participation (which included voting). Research by Bazargan, Kang, and Bazargan (1991) identifies not only characteristics of elderly voters but also differences between elderly white and African-American voters. Voting behavior among elderly whites is related to their perceived health status. Among elderly African Americans, life satisfaction is related to the likelihood of voting. Based on the voting records of the November 1988 elections, the educational and income levels of the elderly are significant factors influencing voting behavior. Table 8–5 addresses the percentage of elderly who reported voting by level of education for males and females. As the level of education increases among those aged 65–74, the percentage who reported voting increased. The only deviation was a 0.6 percent

TABLE 8–3   Percent Reported Voted in Presidential Election Years by Age: November 1964–1992

	Presidential Election In Original Year							
	1992	1988	1984	1980	1976	1972	1968	1964
18–24 years	42.8	36.2	40.8	39.9	42.2	49.6	50.4[a]	50.9[a]
25–44 years	58.3	54.0	58.4	58.7	58.7	62.7	66.6	69.0
45–64 years	70.0	67.9	69.8	69.3	68.7	70.8	74.9	75.9
64 years and over	70.1	68.8	67.7	65.1	62.2	63.5	65.8	66.3

[a]Prior to 1972, includes persons 18 to 20 years old in Georgia and Kentucky, 19 and 20 in Alaska, and 20 years old in Hawaii.
Source: U.S. Bureau of the Census. (1993). Current population reports, P20-466, *Voting and Registration in the Election of November 1992,* Table A. Washington, DC: U.S. Government Printing Office.

TABLE 8–4   **Voting-Age Population**
Voting in Congressional
Election Years, 1976–1992[a]

| | *Congressional Election Years* | | | |
	1990	1986	1982	1978
18–20	18	19	20	20
21–24	22	24	28	26
25–34	34	35	40	38
35–44	48	49	52	50
45–64	75	59	62	59
65 and older	77	61	60	56

[a]Data for earlier years can be found in previous editions of *Vital Statistics on American Politics.*
Source: Stanley, H. W., & Niemi, R. G. (1994). *Vital statistics on American politics* (4th ed.). Washington, DC: Congressional Quarterly, Inc. Used with permission.

drop between those with a bachelor's degree and those with an advanced degree. Among elderly males, as their level of education increased, the percentage who reported voting increased. The only exception is between those with a bachelor's degree and an advanced degree. Among elderly females, the relationship is direct. As level of education increases, so does the percentage who vote. Interestingly, the percentage difference between elderly males and females decreases as educational level increases. This would suggest that increasing levels of education act as an equalizer between voting behaviors of men and women. Among elderly aged 75 and over, the relationship between level of education and age is also direct. Among males aged 75 and over, there is a continued increase in the percentage who voted, except among those with a bachelor's degree. Among women aged 75 and over the relationship is direct except for those women with advanced degrees.

Table 8–6 addresses voting differences among the elderly by level of income. Among the elderly aged 65–74, there is a continued increase in the percentage who reported voting except among those earning between $35,000 and $49,999. Among those aged 75 and over, the relationship is not as direct. Voting behavior increases among the lower- and lower-middle-class elderly (income below $25,000). Among middle-class elderly, voting behavior does not appear to be related to income.

We know that the elderly vote, but we also know that certain subgroups of the elderly are more likely to vote than others. Middle- and upper-class elderly (as measured by education and income) are more likely to vote than lower-class elderly. The consequence of this behavior is that issues and their outcomes are more likely to favor those who are actively involved in the political process. The politics of aging is perhaps more appropriately the politics of aging by social class. Thus the voting behavior (and political power) of the elderly is potentially significant, but increasingly within the narrow confines of social class interests (Ginn, 1993).

**TABLE 8–5   Persons Aged 65 and Over Reported Voting,
by Sex and Years of School Completed: 1992**

65–74 Years Old, Percent Reported Voting

Level of Education	Both Sexes	Male	Female
Less than 5th grade	31.2	34.2	27.9
5th to 8th grade	55.4	60.6	50.9
9th to 12th grade (no diploma)	67.4	71.1	64.8
High school graduate	77.9	79.5	76.9
Some college or associate's degree	84.1	85.3	83.0
Bachelor's degree	88.2	89.5	86.7
Advanced degree	87.6	87.8	87.3

75 Years Old and Over Percent Reported Voting

Level of Education	Both Sexes	Male	Female
Less than 5th grade	36.5	47.8	27.6
5th to 8th grade	51.9	59.0	47.6
9th to 12th grade (no diploma)	62.7	71.7	57.4
High School graduate	70.5	76.5	67.5
Some college or associate's degree	77.6	84.0	74.0
Bachelor's degree	81.0	81.4	80.7
Advanced degree	81.9	88.8	72.4

Source: U.S. Bureau of the Census. (1993). Current population reports,
P20-466, *Voting and registration in the election of November 1992.* Table 7.
Washington, DC: U.S. Government Printing Office.

It is evident, however, that the elderly voter contributes to the American political process, although, as Jennings and Markus (1988, p. 315) point out, "the specific modes of participation and their substantive focuses may well change in age-related ways." The question is, How significant is this contribution to political outcomes?

The Significance of the Older Voter: Overstated or Misunderstood?

One of the great myths of the elderly is that they vote as a bloc. On the national level, the elderly are too diverse in opinion, need, and expectation of government to vote effectively as a bloc. Ragan and Davis (1978, p. 53) suggest that "individuals do not become more like each other as they grow older, but rather that the accumulation of complex combinations of environmental and maturational effects results in infinitely varied outcomes in old age."

**TABLE 8–6 Persons Aged 65 and Over
Reported Voting, by Sex and
Family Income: 1992**

	Percentage of Elderly Reported Voting	
Family Income	65–74	75 and Over
Under $5,000	48.8	54.1%
$5,000–$9,999	57.6	54.6
$10,000–$14,999	67.2	64.4
$15,000–$19,999	78.5	68.9
$20,000–$24,999	80.1	75.3
$25,000–$34,999	85.8	67.7
$35,000–$49,999	81.0	67.8
$50,000 and over	86.6	67.9

Source: U.S. Bureau of the Census. (1993). Current population reports, P20-466. *Voting and registration in the election of November 1992.* Table 12. Washington, DC: U.S. Government Printing Office.

The latest example of age *not* being a unifying characteristic is the Medicare Catastrophic Coverage Act of 1988. The program would have benefited lower-income elderly at the expense of the upper-income elderly. The act was repealed when middle-class elderly began to believe that they would be required to pay additional taxes to cover the cost of the program (Wallace et al., 1991).

As a group, the elderly have the numbers to effect political change. We also know that the elderly are also one age group most likely to vote. A legitimate question would be, Why do they not vote as a bloc? One answer is that they do not have a common goal. There is no unifying issue that affects all of the elderly to the extent that they feel threatened. On the one hand, this demonstrates the heterogeneity of the elderly. The elderly are not all alike. They have different interests, needs, and abilities. On the other hand, this is a classic example of why the elderly are losing their political support base. The elderly constitute less of a political threat because they are not a single, unified group. As a result, voting against popular issues or programs supported by the elderly or some of their organizations is easier and politically safer today. However, as Cigler and Swanson (1981, p. 179) suggest, "certain subgroups of the elderly may coalesce around specific issues." This argument is supported by Hudson (1978b, pp. 32–33), who suggests that "nothing binds together members in an organization, or organizations in coalitions, more effectively than common opposition, and that may be the political setting in which older persons and their organizations soon find themselves." Some of the major organizations devoted to promoting the elderly and issues specific to their needs consist of the American Association of Retired Persons (AARP), the National Council of Senior Citizens (NCSC), and the Gray Panthers. The next section offers a brief description of these organizations.

The Elderly in Politics

The elderly not only vote but remain actively involved in the political process of both major parties at all levels. In addition, many elderly continue to work for political causes through organizations established with age-related issues as their basis for existence. We will examine some of the larger and more visible organizations promoting issues affecting the elderly. We will also examine the political changes and dynamics associated with the White House Conference on Aging. Finally, we will explore the role of the elderly at the federal, state, and local levels.

Aging and Powerful

American Association of Retired Persons (AARP)

The AARP was founded in 1958 "as a way of offering the [life] insurance to retired persons who were not former teachers" (Wallace et al., 1991, p. 103). Today the organization has some 30 million members. The organization

> has primarily identified with the issues of concern to white-collar, middle-class, professional-status retirees. In contrast to the more ideologically liberal National Council of Senior Citizens and the radical Gray Panthers, AARP has generally taken nonpartisan stances in national electoral politics. (Wallace et al., 1991, p. 104)

By remaining nonpartisan, the organization has commanded the attention of both Republicans and Democrats as they attempt to curry the favor of the elderly. The lobbying efforts of the AARP extend beyond Washington. The organization operates lobbying efforts in all 50 states as well (Wallace et al., 1991).

The National Council of Senior Citizens (NCSC)

The NCSC is much smaller than the AARP. The National Council of Senior Citizens has a membership of some 4.5 million. The NCSC was founded in the 1960 presidential campaign of John F. Kennedy. Whereas the AARP identifies generally with the white-collar, middle-class elderly, the NCSC recruits its membership primarily from the blue-collar, working-class elderly. Lobbying efforts of the NCSC reflect its constituency (Wallace et al., 1991).

The Gray Panthers

Founded in 1972, the Gray Panthers are quite distinct from the AARP and the NCSC. First, the Gray Panthers are quite small (50,000) when compared with the other age-related organizations just mentioned. Second, compared to the AARP and the NCSC, the Gray Panthers have taken an activist approach to problems encountered by the elderly in the United States. Led by Maggie Kuhn (who died in 1995 at the age of 89), the Panthers have been more militantly engaged in local political issues. Nationally, the Gray Panthers have been an effective force in bringing attention to issues relevant to the elderly (Wallace et al., 1991).

It is evident that organizations devoted to supporting and advancing issues of the elderly are quite diverse in their constituency, philosophy, and tactics. As a result, issues that affect the elderly may be interpreted differently by the various organizations. The consequence is a dilution of the potential voting power of the elderly. Estes (1978, 1979) is critical of such an assumption that "senior power" is not possible and therefore not a threat to those in power. At issue is the construction of reality of aging and the political power they do (or do not) wield. An example of the ongoing changes at the national level is the White House Conference on Aging.

There have been four White House Conferences on Aging. The initial conference was held in 1950. Presidential administrations have had an increasingly difficult time getting delegates to accept their position (Pratt, 1978). Pratt (1978, p. 68) argues "that the declining reliance by administration spokesmen on purely symbolic politics can be traced to the emergence of new advocacy structures—both private voluntary organizations like the American Association of Retired Persons and the National Council of Senior Citizens, and units within the government, such as congressional committees concerned with aging matters." Pratt is speaking only of the 1950, 1961, and 1971 conferences. The 1981 conference was quite different. We will briefly detail each conference to illustrate the historical and social changes associated with each.

The 1950 National Conference on Aging

The initial conference was the result of professionals in the field of aging. Among those working in the field of aging, there was concern over lack of data and adequate coherence and conceptualization of that which did exist. At the same time, the National Health Assembly had identified aging and the problems attendant with the process as complex. In addition, the Truman White House may not have been interested had it not lost its battle with Congress over national health insurance in 1949 (Pratt, 1978). "White House strategists cast about for a way to overcome congressional antipathy. In the process they hit on the aging as an appealing group, regarded by all as both needy and deserving" (Pratt, 1978, p. 68).

In terms of substance, the initial conference accomplished very little. The conference did establish two standards for selection of those who would attend. According to Pratt (1978, p. 69) these standards include the following:

> First, they decided against involving primarily expert-professionals and federal bureaucrats, and instead to invite primarily nongovernmental workers and volunteers active in the field of aging. Second, the planners opted to involve local people primarily, rather than those on the headquarters staffs of various national organizations.

The 1961 White House Conference on Aging

The time period between the initial conference and the 1961 conference represents a significant shift in public knowledge of aging. A special subcommittee on the problems of aging had been established in the United States Senate. Congress was debating efforts to enact Medicare legislation. Although actions to implement Medicare failed, they established the importance assigned to the health needs of the elderly.

The conference was held in January 1961, just weeks before the departure of President Eisenhower and the inauguration of President Kennedy. Eisenhower, opposed to Medicare, did address the conference delegates. His remarks were less partisan and requested attendees to examine all aspects of health care for the elderly. Other administration officials offered similar advice. The chair of the Senate Subcommittee on Aging and the Aged addressed the conference with a plea for accepting Medicare. As a result, Medicare received the endorsement of the conference section on income maintenance (Pratt, 1978).

The 1971 White House Conference on Aging

The 1971 conference was quite unlike the first two. For the first time, the elderly were referred to as a political force. This was also the first conference at which a number of organizations dedicated to the needs of the elderly were actively involved. At the same time, it was believed that the Nixon White House was attempting to control delegate selection at the local level. This would reduce the risk of activists at the conference, thus creating a more harmonious gathering. The conference itself was rife with conflict between the delegates and the White House. President Nixon attempted to appease the conference attendees by addressing some of the more minor and less expensive issues while avoiding the more controversial and expensive needs (Pratt, 1978).

The conference appeared to produce a number of tangible results. According to research, the White House acted on 78 percent of the recommendations identified by the conference. However, Pratt (1978, p. 72) suggests that "from the White House viewpoint, conferences are a means of 'cooling out' malcontents by appearing to deal with their problems; a subtler form of neglect parading under the guise of recognition."

The 1981 White House Conference on Aging

This was perhaps the most acrimonious conference to date. The reasons lie in the tactics utilized by the Reagan White House in an effort to manipulate the conference and its outcomes. First, the White House appointed additional state delegates. For example, the number of delegates from New York State increased by 60 (Dobelstein & Johnson, 1985). Concern over the consequences of "stacking the deck" soon became real as the conference prepared to open. The rules committee changed the recommendation procedure allowing each committee to put forth a recommendation rather than a conference recommendation. In addition, committee chairpersons were selected by the White House. These chairpersons ultimately limited debate and who could submit recommendations.

Conference delegates, in an attempt to keep the Reagan White House from subverting the process and intent of the conference, called on their most ardent supporter, Representative Claude Pepper of Florida (Dobelstein & Johnson, 1985). Representative "Pepper gave an impassioned plea for an open conference, pledged the support of Congress for Social Security, and vowed to attend the session of the committee on economic security, thus setting the stage for the following day's confrontation" (Dobelstein & Johnson, 1985, pp. 9–10). The outcome of the conference was not as ideologically charged as expected.

There was even some signs of optimism among the conferees. "What has not been forgotten, however, are the politics of aging demonstrated by the conference" (Dobelstein & Johnson, 1985, p. 10). This conference demonstrated the fragile nature of politics and its influence of change on those directly affected by its policies.

The 1995 White House Conference on Aging

Four years late, the next conference may be as confrontational as the last. As the 104th Congress prepares to change the structure of the federal government, programs once considered sacrosanct are now being reevaluated. In the spring of 1995, states convened their individual conferences in preparation for the national conference. I was a participant at the New York State Governor's Conference on Aging held in March 1995. For three days, some 400 participants eventually agreed on 57 recommendations and 17 resolutions that would be taken to the White House Conference. I was impressed with the process by which the recommendations and solutions were accomplished. Although each participant began the conference as a member of a defined topic area, the final outcome was the result of a truly democratic process. The White House Conference on Aging took place May 2–5, 1995, with some 2,500 delegates. The final agenda identified "four broad issues. . . . They are: (1) Assuring Comprehensive Health Care Including Long Term Care, (2) Promoting Economic Security, (3) Maximizing Housing and Support Service Options, and (4) Maximizing Options for a Quality of Life" (New York State Governor's Conference on Aging Bulletin, 1995, issue 2, p. 1). The delegates at the White House Conference on Aging eventually adopted 51 resolutions, including opposition to "arbitrary cuts in Medicare and [the opposition to] block granting of the Medicaid program . . . [the preservation of] Social Security and the Older Americans Act . . . [and] universal health care coverage and further development of home and community based long term care services" (New York State Governor's Conference on Aging Bulletin, 1995, issue 3, p. 1). It is my belief that the 1995 White House Conference on Aging maintained the historical tradition of previous conferences. That is, policy issues have been defined that will guide the future discussion of aging in America.

Earlier the statement was made that the elderly do not vote as a bloc in national politics. Although true, the reasons are not always clear. Historically, the elderly have been used for political purposes to advance agendas of both political parties. Meanwhile, as the elderly attempt to influence social policy, they face opponents with far greater political influence (Vinyard, 1978). We are left with serious questions regarding the political future of the aging population in the United States. Potentially, the elderly could emerge as a potent political force in the early to mid-21st century. However, politicians must address the needs of the elderly today. When the baby boom generation reaches age 65 in 2011, the elderly will either become a demographic force for change or an albatross around the collective necks of those in the political system. Either way, the elderly need to make decisions regarding their collective future rather than relying on those in power to create an image of aging that best suits the current political agenda. Instead of allowing those in power to define what aspects of aging constitutes a social problem, the elderly must become involved in the political process and redefine a more accurate portrayal of the elderly in American society. The social problem of aging is a construct of political power and has been used as a means to exploit the elderly and nonelderly for political gain. Estes (1986, p. 132) has captured the essence of this struggle in the following statement:

> A deeply political process of crisis naming, blaming, sorting and shifting has occurred. For the ageing, the potential implications include greater social inequalities; the private purchase of more and more needed health and social care by individuals rather than entitlement to it; increased corporatism of services; the medicalisation and disaggregation (unbundling) of services to increase profitability: and the transference of a growing number of public responsibilities to private families (informalisation).

Levels of Political Involvement

The elderly, as with any age group, are politically involved at all levels of the political process. We will briefly examine the federal, state, and local levels of government as they relate to the elderly. Before we encounter the various levels at which the elderly are politically involved, another myth must be addressed. It is generally assumed that one becomes more politically conservative with age. The research findings generally do not support this relationship. Hudson and Strate (1985, p. 558) conclude that "the effect of aging on the tendency to identify as a conservative, if it exists at all, is probably small." Estes (1978) suggests that other variables, such as educational attainment or the political context within which ideology developed, may confound the presumed relationship. Finally, according the U.S. Bureau of the Census (1992), the elderly are more likely to identify themselves as a weak or strong Republican than younger-aged respondents. However, the elderly are also more likely to identify themselves as a weak or strong Democrat. Although it is evident that the elderly are politically involved, it is not demonstrated that aging causes one to become more politically conservative. We now can turn our attention from ideology to political involvement.

Federal   It is at the federal level that the elderly are most prominent. Examples of elderly at the federal level include former President Reagan, members of the Supreme Court, and a relatively small contingent of Congress. Stanley and Niemi (1994) present data on the age distribution of members of Congress from 1971 to 1993. The problem with their numbers is the age categories they impose. Rather than utilizing age 65 and over, they employ ages 60–69, 70–79, and 80 and over. Based on their categorization, 40 percent of the senators in 1971 were over the age of 60. In 1981 only 20 percent of the senators were aged 60 and over. By 1993 the percentage had increased to 34 percent. In the House of Representatives, 24.9 percent were aged 60 and over in 1971. By 1981 the elderly constituted only 15.4 percent of the House. The percentage of the elderly in the House of Representatives increased to 24.6 percent in 1993.

Examined differently, Uhlenberg (1987) questioned whether the percentage of elderly in the House and Senate is equal to what would be expected, given their increased percentage of the population. The results of Uhlenbergs' (1987) research are presented in Table 8–7.

The findings indicate that percentage differences between actual and expected members of Congress began to decrease in the Senate between 1950 and 1970 but increased dramatically in 1980. In the House, the percentage difference was relatively even in 1950 and decreased in 1960. By 1970, however, the percentage difference began to increase and has continued into 1980. Fears of a gerontocracy being established at the federal level of

TABLE 8–7 Members of the U.S. Senate and House of Representatives Age 65+: 1950–1980

	Senate		House	
	Expected	Actual	Expected	Actual
1950	33%	24%	16%	14%
1960	36	27	9	14
1970	38	29	20	13
1980	42	15	22	9

Source: Uhlenberg, P. R. (1987). Will an aging population lead to increased gerontocracy? *Social Science*, 72(2–4), 206–208. Used with permission.

government would certainly appear to be unfounded. Wiegele, Schubert, and Hines (1990) would disagree with this assessment. They argue that the young-old are potential participants in the governmental process, particularly at the state and local levels.

State   There is a paucity of research on the political participation of the elderly at the state and local levels. As a result, inferences generally provide potential political scenarios rather than empirical fact. Based on the research that does exist, there is concern that age-based interests may begin to dominate the political process at the state and local levels. An example of this is the Adults Only Movement (AOM). The basic premise of Rose (1965) was that the elderly could constitute a subculture if they established a common set of values and created an age consciousness. Increasing the likelihood of a subculture of aging would be physical segregation on the basis of age. Anderson and Anderson (1978) suggest that the presence of adult-only communities in Arizona provide fertile ground for age-based political power. An example is provided by Kastenbaum (1991), who examined election results following the defeat of the latest proposal to make Martin Luther King Day a state holiday. Although the proposal was narrowly defeated in the state, adult-only communities had much higher percentages of "no" votes. Kastenbaum reports that "no" votes ranged from two to four times greater than "yes" votes in adult-only communities.

The consequence of age-based political participation in states with large elderly populations is unclear. Although adult communities may be more likely to engage in homogeneous voter behavior, there does not appear to be any evidence to suggest that such behavior has had significant impact on the outcome of statewide issues.

Local   The impact of political participation by the elderly at the local level is not well defined. Button (1992, p. 793) states that *"the aging were a very significant factor in local school bond issue elections, and they tended to oppose such bonds"* (italics in original). However, Button and Rosenbaum (1990) suggest that although the elderly have the political potential to impose spending restrictions on the local level (by voting against issues), they have not engaged in such age-based voting statewide.

In addition to age, other variables related to the lack of support for local issues include social class, educational level, race, and the migratory nature of an increasing number of elderly. Thus, as the elderly move from northern states to the sunbelt states after retirement, they do not feel connected to local concerns. The potential is to not support school tax increases or increases for local services. This relationship, however, is not firmly established. The potential for political power would appear greater at the local level. Such power, however, may come at the expense of intergenerational and class differences (Button, 1992).

Critical Connection: The Powerful Don't Change; They Just Get Older

Throughout this chapter, the word *power* has been used as the reason that the lives of the many are influenced by the actions of a few. Such action is not new. Historically, the political process in this country has attempted to address the needs of its elderly. Unfortunately, the consequence has been piecemeal social policy intended to alleviate the economic and health care burdens of those growing older. The problem is that those with the political power to affect the long-term outcomes of the elderly do not always address, nor do they understand, the dynamic qualities or the heterogeneity of the elderly population. What those with political power have always understood is that those elderly who vote and have influence in the political process should be rewarded. The result is the maintenance of the status quo among the elderly. The elderly who exercise their power are accorded greater benefits while those elderly with less power are ignored. As a result, age may decline as an indicator of political significance, and social class may increase in importance. In this "politics of exclusion" many elderly are being ignored. For example, we know that problems of poverty continue to exist among the oldest-old, women, minorities, and those elderly living alone. We also know that the elderly poor are less likely to vote than middle- and upper-class elderly. Those with power know how to retain their power as they age. Thus the most economically disenfranchised elderly are also the most politically underserved and the most disadvantaged. The next chapter examines those elderly who have experienced the politics of exclusion.

Chapter Review

Chapter 8 has introduced the dynamic qualities of aging within a political context. Although the elderly constitute a significant percentage of the population, there are questions regarding their ability to affect the political process. Some of the following questions address specific issues presented in the chapter. Other questions explore the contextual nature of aging and the political process.

1. Why did President Roosevelt sign the Social Security Act into law? Identify and discuss only the first two reasons given in the chapter.
2. Discuss the historical development and life of the Townsend plan. Develop an argument that is supportive of the plan and an argument against the plan. Which argument is most persuasive? Explain your answer.

3. Describe the Lundeen bill. Compare and contrast the Townsend plan and the Lundeen bill. Which is most persuasive? Why?

4. Discuss the historical development of Medicare.

5. Are the politics of aging becoming less an issue of chronological age and more one of social class? Explain your answer.

6. Compare and contrast Medicare and Medicaid as they apply to the elderly.

7. Have the elderly lost their political significance? If so, explain why. If they have not, explain why they continue to remain significant.

Glossary

Lundeen bill   A less ambitious bill than the Townsend plan. First proposed in 1934, the Lundeen bill would have paid all unemployed adults over the age of 18 a minimum of $10 per week and $3 per dependent. The bill received some congressional support but was not favored by the Roosevelt administration.

Medicaid   A needs-based federally sponsored health and social service program for the poor administered by individual states. Medicaid primarily covers the cost of nursing home care for the elderly.

Medicare   A federally sponsored health program for everyone over the age of 65. Most elderly must pay for additional health insurance coverage because Medicare covers less than one-half the cost of health care.

Pluralism   The argument that political power exists within multiple groups and organizations within a society. Depending on the issue, these groups and organizations develop coalitions as they attempt to construct a power base that will advance their ideas and agenda. The role of the federal government is that of a neutral third party. Generally speaking, this is an idealistic explanation of the distribution of power in the United States.

Power elite   The argument that political power exists within a very small, defined group of individuals. These individuals are located in the executive branch of government, top military officials, and key leaders of business. Together, the power elite define the existence, direction, and character of social policy in the United States.

Social Security   A government-sponsored program providing a monthly income to those aged 65 and over. This income is dependent on the amount of money earned by the recipient prior to retirement. Workers who retire at age 62 receive a percentage of the what they would have received at age 65.

Townsend plan   An ambitious retirement plan proposed during the Great Depression of the 1930s. The Townsend plan argued that all elderly Americans should receive $200 per month. The only stipulation was that all $200 must be spent, thus providing an infusion of cash into the economy. The Townsend plan was rejected by Congress and President Roosevelt.

Suggested Reading

Poen, M. M. (1979). *Harry S. Truman versus the medical lobby: The genesis of Medicare.* Columbia, MO: University of Missouri Press.
A historical excursion through the political minefield of health care reform. The historical context for contemporary explanations is valuable.

Pratt, H. J. (1976). *The gray lobby.* Chicago: University of Chicago Press.
The author chronicles the significant events in the development of old-age legislation in the United States.

Putnam, J. K. (1970). *Old-age politics in California: From Richardson to Reagan.* Stanford, CA: Stanford University Press.
This book details many of the old-age pension plans developed during the Depression. The reader is provided a historical context within which current issues evolved.

Starr, P. (1982). *The social transformation of American medicine.* New York: Basic Books.

The book does not address only issues of old age. Part Two is particularly significant, as it offers a historical examination of the American health care system. The elderly, as a specific segment of the population, are directly affected by the events presented.

References

Amenta, E., Carruthers, B. G., & Zylan, Y. (1992). A hero for the aged? The Townsend movement, the political mediation model, and U.S. old-age policy, 1934–1950. *American Journal of Sociology, 98*(2), 308–339.

Anderson, W. A., & Anderson, N. D. (1978). The politics of age exclusion: The adults only movement in Arizona. *Gerontologist, 18*(1), 6–12.

Bazargan, M., Kang, T. S., & Bazargan, S. (1991). A multivariate comparison of elderly African Americans' and Caucasians' voting behavior: How do social, health, psychological, and political variables affect their voting? *International Journal of Aging and Human Development, 32*(3), 181–198.

Bernstein, M. C., & Bernstein, J. B. (1988). *Social Security: The system that works.* New York: Basic Books.

Binstock, R. H. (1991, Summer/Fall). From the Great Society to the aging society—25 years of the Older Americans Act. *Generations, 15,* 11–18.

Booth, P. (1973). *Social Security in America.* University of Michigan—Wayne State University: Institute of Labor and Industrial Relations.

Briggs, D. (1994, December 17). Power-elite still largely Protestant, study shows. E1. *Times Union* (Albany, NY), p. E1.

Button, J. W. (1992). A sign of generational conflict: The impact of Florida's aging voters on local school and tax referenda. *Social Science Quarterly, 73*(4), 786–797.

Button, J., & Rosenbaum, W. (1990). Gray power, gray peril, or gray myth? The political impact of the aging in local sunbelt politics. *Social Science Quarterly, 71*(1), 25–38.

Cassel, C. K., & Neugarten, B. L. (1991). The goals of medicine in an aging society. In R. H. Binstock & S. G. Post (Eds.), *Too old for health care? Controversies in medicine, law, economics, and ethics* (pp. 75–91). Baltimore: Johns Hopkins University Press.

Cigler, A. J., & Swanson, C. (1981). Politics and older Americans. In F. J. Berghorn & D. E. Schafer (Eds.), *The dynamics of aging* (pp. 169–193). Boulder, CO: Westview Press.

Cook, F. L., & Barrett, E. J. (1988). Public support for Social Security. *Journal of Aging Studies, 2*(4), 339–356.

Cutler, N. E. (1977). Demographic, social-psychological, and political factors in the politics of aging: A foundation for research in "political gerontology." *American Political Science Review, 71,* 1011–1025.

Darnay, A. J. (Ed.). (1994). *Statistical record of older Americans.* Detroit: Gale Research Inc.

Derthick, M. (1979). *Policymaking for Social Security.* Washington, DC: The Brookings Institution.

Dobelstein, A., & Johnson, A. B. (1985). *Serving older adults: Policy, programs, and professional activities.* Englewood Cliffs, NJ: Prentice-Hall.

Douglas, P. H. (1939). *Social Security in the United States.* New York: McGraw-Hill.

Duncan, G. J., & Smith, K. R. (1989). The rising affluence of the elderly: How far, how fair, and how frail? *Annual Review of Sociology, 15,* 261–289.

Enos, D. D., & Sultan, P. (1977). *The sociology of health care: Social, economic, and political perspectives.* New York: Praeger.

Epstein, A. (1928). *The challenge of the aged.* New York: Vanguard Press.

Estes, C. L. (1978, July/August). Political gerontology. *Society, 15,* 43–49.

Estes, C. L. (1979, Spring). *Sociological Symposium, 26,* 1–27.

Estes, C. L. (1981). *The aging enterprise.* San Francisco: Jossey-Bass.

Estes, C. L. (1986). The politics of ageing in America. *Ageing and Society, 6,* 121–134.

Ginn, J. (1993). Grey power: Age-based organizations' response to structured inequalities. *Critical Social Policy, 13*(2), 23–47.

Glenn, N. D., & Grimes, M. (1968). Aging, voting, and political interest. *American Sociological Review, 33,* 563–575.

Hudson, R. B. (1978a). The "graying" of the federal budget and its consequences for old-age policy. *Gerontologist, 18*(5), 428–474.

Hudson, R. B. (1978b, July/August). Emerging pressures on public policies for the aging. *Society, 15,* 30–33.

Hudson, R. B., & Strate, J. (1985). Aging and political systems. In R. H. Binstock & E. Shanas (Eds.), *Handbook of aging and the social sciences* (pp. 554–585). New York: Van Nostrand Reinhold.

Jennings, M. K., & Markus, G. B. (1988). Political involvement in the later years: A longitudinal survey. *American Journal of Political Science, 30*(2), 302–316.

Jensen, G. A., & Morrisey, G. A. (1993). Health insurance coverage of the Medicare elderly. *Trends in Health Benefits.* Washington, DC: U.S. Department of Labor.

Jirovec, R. L., & Erich, J. A. (1992). The dynamics of political participation among the urban elderly. *Journal of Applied Gerontology, 11*(2), 216–227.

Kastenbaum, R. (1991). Racism and the older voter? Arizona's rejection of a paid holiday to honor Martin Luther King. *International Journal of Aging and Human Development, 32*(3), 199–209.

Marmor, T. R. (1973). *The politics of Medicare.* Chicago: Aldine.

Mills, C. W. (1956). *The power elite.* New York: Oxford University Press.

Myles, J. (1992). Social Security and support of the elderly: The Western experience. In J. F. Gubrium & K. Charmaz (Eds.), *Aging, self, and community: A collection of readings* (pp. 277–293). Greenwich, CT: JAI Press.

National Center for Health Statistics. (1994). *Health, United States, 1993.* Hyattsville, MD: Public Health Service.

New York State Governor's Conference on Aging Bulletin. (1995, April 4). Albany: New York State Office for the Aging.

New York State Governor's Conference on Aging Bulletin. (1995, July 7). Albany: New York State Office for the Aging.

Peterson, S. A., & Somit, A. (1992). Older women: Health and political behavior. *Women and Politics 12*(4), 87–108.

Poen, M. M. (1979). *Harry S. Truman versus the medical lobby: The genesis of Medicare.* Columbia, MO: University of Missouri Press.

Pratt, H. J. (1976). *The gray lobby.* Chicago: University of Chicago Press.

Pratt, H. J. (1978, July/August). Symbolic politics and White House conferences on aging. *Society, 15,* 67–72.

Putnam, J. K. (1970). *Old age politics in California: From Richardson to Reagan.* Stanford, CA: Stanford University Press.

Ragan, P. K., & Davis, W. J. (1978, July/August). The diversity of older voters. *Society, 15,* 50–53.

Rich, B. M., & Baum, M. (1984). *The aging: A guide to public policy.* Pittsburgh: University of Pittsburgh Press.

Roosevelt, N. (1936). *The Townsend Plan: Taxing for sixty.* New York: Doubleday, Doran & Company.

Rose, A. M. (1965). *The subculture of the aging: A framework for research in social gerontology.* In A. M. Rose & W. A. Peterson (Eds.). Philadelphia: F. A. Davis Company.

Social Security Bulletin. (1993). Annual Statistical Supplement. U.S. Department of Health and Human Services. Social Security Administration. Washington, DC.

Stanley, H., & Niemi, R. G. (1994). *Vital statistics on American politics* (4th ed.). Washington, DC: Congressional Quarterly.

Starr, P. (1982). *The social transformation of American medicine.* New York: Basic Books.

Street, D. (1993). Maintaining the status quo: The impact of old-age interest groups on the Medicare Catastrophic Coverage Act of 1988. *Social Problems, 40*(4), 431–444.

Subcommittee on Health and the Environment. (1993). *Medicaid source book: Background data and analysis* (a 1993 update). Washington, DC: U.S. Government Printing Office.

Torres-Gil, F. (1992). *The new aging: Politics and change in America.* New York: Auburn House.

Uhlenberg, P. R. (1987). Will an aging population lead to increased gerontocracy? *Social Science, 72*(2–4), 206–208.

U.S. Bureau of the Census. (1992). *Statistical abstract of the United States: 1992* (112th ed.). Washington, DC: U.S. Government Printing Office.

U.S. Bureau of the Census. (1993). Current population reports, P20–466, *Voting and registration in the election of November 1992.* Washington, DC: U.S. Government Printing Office.

U.S. Department of Health and Human Services. (1993a). *Social Security handbook, 1993* (11th ed.). Social Security Administration, SSA Publication No. 65-008. Washington, DC.

U.S. Department of Health and Human Services. (1993b). *The Medicare 1993 handbook.* Health Care Financing Administration Publication Number HCFA 10050. Baltimore, MD.

Vinyard, D. (1978, July/August). The rediscovery of the elderly. *Society, 15,* 24–29.

Waitzkin, H. (1989). Health policy in the United States: Problems and alternatives. In H. E. Freeman & S. Levine (Eds.), *Handbook of medical sociology* (4th ed., pp. 475–491). Englewood Cliffs, NJ: Prentice-Hall.

Wallace, S. P., Williamson, J. B., Lung, R. G., & Powell, L. A. (1991). A lamb in wolf's clothing? The reality of senior power and social policy. In M. Minkler & C. L. Estes (Eds.), *Critical perspectives on aging: The political and moral economy of growing old* (pp. 95–114). Amityville, NY: Baywood.

Wiegele, T. C., Schubert, J. N., & Hines, S. M., Jr. (1990). Age and political structure: Reflections on gerontocracy. In K. F. Ferraro (Ed.), *Gerontology: Perspectives and issues* (pp. 206–224). New York: Springer.

Williamson, J., Evans, L., & Powell, L. A. (1982). *The politics of aging: Power and policy.* Springfield, IL: Charles C. Thomas.

Chapter **9**

Double Jeopardy/
Triple Jeopardy

*What is unique about today's cohorts of older minorities is that, by and large,
they retain the features of their early socialization: the language, culture,
traditions, and rural life-styles prevalent at the turn of the century. . . .
However, there are significant gaps in the knowledge essential to
understanding the factors affecting future cohorts of minority elderly.*
—TORRES-GIL, 1987, P. 240

> *[T]he reality [is] that other social and economic factors interact with the aging trend's impact on women's lives—forces such as gender and age discrimination, responsibilities for homemaking and children, lack of pay equity, inadequate opportunities or training or retraining in employment, the availability only of part-time employment offering no health or retirement benefits, and divorce or premature widowhood.*
> *—PIFER, 1993, P. 245*

Discrimination within the social process of aging contributes to an ongoing inequality among the elderly. This inequality is quantitative and qualitative. Quantitatively, some elderly groups (white males, for example) consistently have earned more than minority males or females and white women. When retirement benefits are based on previous earning levels, those who made less throughout their lives (and therefore were poorer) continue to be poorer relative to those who earned more. Earning opportunities are tied to occupations, and occupations are related to benefits. Generally speaking, women and minorities are still more likely to work in the secondary labor market. The secondary labor market consists of occupations that pay low wages and offer few benefits, very little upward mobility, and virtually no job security. On the other hand, white males are more likely to work in the primary labor market. The primary labor market consists of occupations offering higher wages, more benefits, increased chance for upward mobility, and greater job security. The consequences of a lifetime of economic differences in opportunity creates differing opportunities in old age. Among the nation's poor are found a disproportionate number of women, minorities (men, but predominantly women), and those who live alone.

Qualitatively, inequality is measured not in terms of dollars earned or current retirement benefits but rather in the experiences associated with growing older. For example, the health status of elderly blacks is consistently lower than that of elderly whites (National Center for Heath Statistics, 1994). Perceived health status differences between elderly males and females is less clear. Elderly males are more likely to identify their health status as excellent or good (Darnay, 1994). Elderly males are also more likely to identify their health status as fair or poor (National Center for Health Statistics, 1994).

These subtle, and not so subtle, forms of inequality are reminders of the consequences associated with the lack of power. The determinants of these social outcomes include gender, race, and ethnicity. This chapter will sensitize the reader to the needs and rights of those who are less powerful, less wealthy, but still aging. If, as suggested in earlier chapters, the image of the elderly continues to be that of "greedy geezers" and program funding is reduced, the poorer elderly will be most affected. Disproportionately, that means women and minority elderly.

This chapter begins with a brief overview of elderly women and minorities. We then establish the significance of experiencing discrimination based on these characteristics. Throughout this chapter the interactive nature of a multiplicity of variables such as income, education, and health as they impact on women and minority elderly are addressed.

The Significance of Sex, Marital Status, Race, and Ethnicity

Aging is a social process. Within society, some groups fare better than others. For example, we know that as people grow older they are more likely to be poor if they are female, single (widowed or divorced), African American, or Hispanic. Why are some groups better off than others? Perhaps the heading of this section is misnamed. Sex, marital status, race, and ethnicity are certainly significant, but it is the societal context within which these variables exist that influences differential outcomes. Consider why women are paid less than men. Is it because men are better or more productive workers? No. Women receive less than men because the social structure supports normative employment practices that constrain women in job acquisition and pay. Thus it is the social stratification of society that perpetuates and reinforces existing social norms. As society differentiates opportunities on the basis of sex, race, or ethnicity, what are the consequences? These outcomes are addressed in the remaining sections of this chapter.

Women and Aging

Double jeopardy involves not only being elderly but being an elderly female. However, a cursory examination of the numbers of elderly who are women would suggest strength in numbers. In 1992 19,240,000 of the 32,285,000 (or 59.6 percent) of the elderly were women (U.S. Bureau of the Census, 1994). More importantly, the percentage of the elderly who are women increases with age. Among the oldest-old (85 and over), women outnumber men 2,349,000 to 909,000. As a percentage, this means that women constitute 72.1 percent of those aged 85 and over (U.S. Bureau of the Census, 1994). We also know from previous chapters that as age increases, so does the likelihood of poverty. We can conclude, then, that poverty is a problem for aging women (Malveaux, 1993). In addition to poverty, elderly women are "vulnerable because of dependence upon public resources and programs to offset social factors such as diminished finances, loss of spouse or family supports, urban relocation, and increased incidence of health problems" (Estes, Gerard, & Clarke, 1984, p. 211). These intertwining social, demographic, economic, and political forces impinge on women as they age. These forces exist within a historical context, which we will briefly explore.

Although women represent a majority of the elderly, they do not have the political or economic power necessary to alter their current circumstances. These experiences are grounded in the historical relationship of men and women (Jacobs, 1993). Unfortunately, there has been little research providing specific historical information regarding elderly women. What is known is that women experienced oppression under the guise of expected social roles and statuses (McDaniel, 1989). As Arendell and Estes (1991, p. 209) state, "the social origins of the disadvantaged status of older women are not mysterious; they reside in the institutional arrangements and processes of the family . . . the labor market and the state and its social policy." For a brief but thorough overview of aging women and the public policies that affect them, see Jorgensen (1989). In addition to the ongoing institutional discrimination just identified, Olson (1988) suggests that sex-role socialization has influenced the circumstances many elderly women currently experience. The aging process, then, is experienced differently depending on gender (Levy, 1988). What do we know about elderly women? Lewis and Butler (1984, p. 201) suggest that a profile of elderly women "means living alone, on a low or poverty-level income, often in substandard housing with inadequate medical care and little chance of employment to supplement resources." Lewis and Butler (1984) provide supporting evidence for their statement, but we already know from previous chapters that the profile they characterize is accurate. For purposes of illustration of their point and as a summation of earlier material, Malveaux (1993) reports that among the elderly poor, 73.8 percent are women and 26.2 percent are men. Furthermore, 8.9 percent of elderly males fall below the poverty line, compared to 15.7 percent of elderly females (U.S. Bureau of the Census, 1994).

We know that these outcomes are historically grounded. The question is, Why has society not attempted to alter the known consequences of being female? We examine this point in the following section.

Feminism Among the Elderly

Are the feminist movement and the aging process compatible? Lewis and Butler (1984) raise this question and attempt to answer by suggesting that they are. They point out that the women's movement could benefit from the absolute numbers that represent potential membership among elderly women. Conversely, the women's movement could benefit elderly women by providing a forum for change and the political influence to effect such change. The reason why the women's movement had not incorporated the needs of elderly women into their cause is because of ageism (Lewis & Butler, 1984). More recently, Gould (1989, p. 196) argues that "as a result of consciousness raising by groups such as the Older Women's League and the National Coalition on Older Women's Issues, aging has now emerged as a major feminist issue." Nonetheless, elderly women were evidently not viewed as being particularly significant to the feminist movement. It is unfortunate because many elderly women could make significant contributions to society in general and to the woman's movement in particular. Many elderly women are free of the burdens of child care or other family responsibilities. They have the time (and for an increasing number, the wealth) to devote to causes (Peterson & Somit, 1992). Relative to other age groups, elderly women are more likely to be registered to vote and actually vote. "They could provide backing for the women's liberation movement and specifically for their own age group problems" (Lewis & Butler, 1984, p. 208). The problem is that even today, elderly women are perceived more in terms of age, not gender. Although a problem in itself, men are generally evaluated on the basis of gender regardless of age. This difference reflects the level of authority and power attached to the elderly on the basis of gender. This is an area within which the women's movement could provide leadership opportunities to elderly women to gain political and economic access as well as some much-needed public exposure to demythesize the aging process. This realization is also significant to younger women who, as they age, realize the basis for societal evaluation of who they are. Feminism is alive and well among many elderly women. The feminist movement must become more adept at realizing the potential and utilizing the skills and knowledge that exists among elderly women.

Before we turn to an examination of elderly minorities, we will first explore the meaning of a phrase that is usually associated with younger women: the *feminization of poverty*. Unfortunately, poverty among women knows no age limit. The data on poverty presented earlier provide a stark picture of the economic differences experienced by elderly men and women.

The Importance of Marital Status

Marital status is important to elderly women. The longer they remained married, the longer they remain out of poverty. Unfortunately, there are two basic demographic factors working against elderly women. First, the male is generally older than the female at the time of marriage. Depending on the period in the 20th century, the age difference has been between 1 and 2 years. Secondly, men have a shorter life expectancy than women. Today, life expectancy for males is approximately 72.3 years; for females, life expectancy is 79.0 years. In other words, there is a difference of 6.7 years in life expectancy between men and women (U.S. Bureau of the Census, 1994). Added to the 2-year age differential at marriage, women can expect to spend up to 9 years as a widow. The economic consequence of this change in marital status is an increasing reliance on government-assisted programs. Thus the longer elderly women live, the greater the likelihood of living in poverty. Marital status of elderly women is also related to their economic condition. Estes et al. (1984, pp. 214–217) identify possible sources of income among the elderly. Consider the gender differences for all of these programs:

1. *Income from assets.* Assets represent a relatively small proportion of the income for perhaps one-half of the elderly. Assets are also tied to previous earnings. Considering that women earn, on average, less than their male counterparts, the likelihood of assets among older women is diminished, and "marital status is a critical factor" (Estes et al., 1984, p. 215).
2. *Private pensions.* Although a vast number of private pension plans exist, women are less likely to be covered than are men. Until recently, women retirees received lower payments than men because of their longer life expectancy.
3. *Social Security.* Among all sources of income for most elderly women, Social Security is the most important. Women earn less than men throughout their lifetime, thus affecting the amount of Social Security received. Historically, Social Security has been biased against women.
4. *Income programs for those over 65.* Eliminated by the Reagan Administration, the minimum Social Security benefit provided subsistence income, primarily for elderly women. Supplemental Security Income (SSI) was established to provide assistance to the elderly and others in need. Intended to supplement those with extremely low incomes, the amount provided varies by state. Among the elderly receiving funds, women over the age of 75 are the prime beneficiaries.

The Feminization of Poverty Among the Elderly

Throughout this chapter one overriding theme has been the economic impoverishment of women. We know from previous chapters that the lack of access to political, economic, and familial power has limited opportunities for women, regardless of age. In fact, among elderly women there is a cumulative effect associated with the absence of power over one's lifetime. As a result, the phrase *feminization of poverty* is applicable not only among younger women but also among elderly women. According to Stone (1989), elderly women are likely to experience the feminization of poverty because of the following:

1. *Female dependence.* Within American society, economic differentiation between men and women has resulted in outcomes that have been deleterious for women. It has been a widely held belief that women are economically dependent on men. As a result, national policies such as Social Security have been constructed to maintain that disadvantage for women.
2. *Family and work history.* What a worker does prior to age 65 and retirement greatly influences what he or she will receive in benefits. This is addressed more specifically in item 3.
3. *The division of labor between genders.* Historically, women have been expected to perform the caregiver role not only toward their children but for elderly parents as well. With the caregiver role as their primary function, women have had difficulty establishing consistent work records. Too often, women interrupt their work career to provide support to other family members. As a result of this sporadic work history, pension benefits are generally lower.
4. *Labor market discrimination.* When women do enter the labor market, they are generally located in occupations that pay lower wages with fewer opportunities for upward mobility. As a result, pension benefits for women are consistently lower because of lower wages upon which the benefits are determined. In addition, sexual discrimination in the workplace can result in lower job performance evaluations, which affect promotion and pay increases.
5. *Spousal impoverishment.* Generally, women live longer than men. The consequences of outliving one's spouse for many elderly women is that they become economically impoverished because their spouse is institutionalized. The elderly woman is required to spend down any savings and assets before Medicaid will cover the cost of extended care. The result is that elderly women are left with few economic resources after the death of a spouse (Stone, 1989).

The double jeopardy experienced by elderly women is exacerbated when racial or ethnic minority status is added to the variable list. The remainder of this chapter will address the added dimension of race and ethnicity in this social equation.

Aging Among Minority Populations

Triple jeopardy means being elderly, female, and a member of a minority group. This section will address the quantitative characteristics of the elderly minority populations as well as the social context within which they age. Before we proceed, it is necessary to clarify some of the concepts that will be utilized throughout this section. First, *race* or *racial group* is "a social group that persons inside or outside the group have decided is important to single out as inferior or superior, typically on the basis of real or alleged physical characteristics subjectively selected" (Feagin & Feagin, 1993, p. 7).

Based on this definition, African Americans, Asian Americans, and Native Americans have all been characterized as inferior racial groups at some point in time in the United States. The physical characteristics used are arbitrarily identified by those in power as the basis for distinction. These characteristics can change depending on the society and the historical period within a society.

The second major concept is that of *ethnicity* or *ethnic group*. Feagin and Feagin (1993, p. 9) define an ethnic group as "a group socially distinguished or set apart, by others or by itself, primarily on the basis of cultural or nationality characteristics." Examples of an ethnic group would include Hispanics, Norwegians, Irish, Bohemians, and Jewish Americans. Again, the powerful group within a society determines the "place" of ethnic groups relative to one another. Throughout American history, various ethnic groups have been singled out for discrimination. For example, the Irish and Eastern Europeans were considered inferior during different periods in American history.

Third is the concept of *minority group*. A minority group refers to "a group of people who, because of their physical or cultural characteristics, are singled out from others in the society in which they live for differential and unequal treatment and who therefore regard themselves as objects of collective discrimination" (Wirth, 1945, p. 347, as quoted in Feagin & Feagin, 1993, p. 10).

Racial and ethnic groups are minority groups. A minority group, however, is not determined by the number within the group. A minority group may receive differential and unequal treatment and be in the majority within the population (for example, in South Africa during apartheid). Instead, minority and majority groups are distinguished on the degree of power exercised.

How do these concepts apply to the elderly? The elderly consist of not only whites but African Americans, Hispanics, Native Americans, and Asian Americans. In fact, the fastest-growing segment of the elderly population is among Hispanic and Asian Americans (Wray, 1991). Minority group representation among the elderly will continue to grow well into the next century. As a result, the image of the elderly as a white female will become less of a reality (Stanford & Yee, 1991). Table 9–1 illustrates the aging population change expected in the near future. As minority elderly increase as a percentage of the overall number, serious consideration will be necessary regarding interpretation of the aging process. No longer will a monolithic white interpretation be credible. A multiracial/ethnic investigation will be necessary to fully appreciate the diversity associated with those engaged in the aging process.

The data indicate significant change ahead regarding the aging population of the United States. At present, minority elderly are financially poorer and in worse health than their elderly white counterparts (Hyde & Torres-Gill, 1991). This interpretation represents the double jeopardy approach to explaining diversity among the elderly. A second interpretation of this diversity suggests that age is a leveler. In other words, differences among the elderly are diminished with age. Thus ethnic and racial minority elderly are not particularly different from white elderly. These approaches represent two broad interpretations of circumstances among an increasingly diverse aging population (Burton, Dilworth-Anderson, & Bengtson, 1991). Throughout this chapter our interpretation reflects a greater belief in the former approach rather than in the latter. The following section on aging among racial and ethnic minorities reinforces the double-triple jeopardy interpretation of aging. Consider the following: "the most pronounced findings that demonstrate how racism, sexism, and ageism affect choices throughout the life cycle, are those related to the poverty status of nonwhite females. Older minority women constitute the poorest segment of American society" (Gould, 1989, p. 202).

TABLE 9–1   Projected Population Distribution of the Population Aged 65 and Over: 1992–2025

	Percentage of the Total Number of Elderly			
	1995	2000	2010	2025
White Non-Hispanics	85.3%	85.3%	80.5%	76.1%
Non-Hispanic Black	7.9%	7.9%	8.2%	8.9%
Hispanic origin[a]	4.6%	4.6%	7.3%	9.8%
Non-Hispanic American Indian, Eskimo, Aleut	0.4%	0.4%	0.5%	0.5%
Non-Hispanic Asian, Pacific Islander	1.9%	1.9%	3.6%	4.6%

[a]Persons of Hispanic origin may be of any race.
Source: U.S. Bureau of the Census. (1990). *Statistical abstract of the United States, 1994* (114th ed.). Table 24. Washington, DC: U.S. Government Printing Office.

African Americans

African American elderly currently constitute 7.9 percent of the total elderly population. This percentage is expected to increase slowly to 8.9 percent by the year 2025. In general, African American elderly are poorer than any other minority (National Caucus and Center on Black Aged, Inc., 1987). Harlow and McDonald (1991, p. 237) found that "aging in Black America today means aging in place—near or below poverty, with multiple chronic conditions and functional impairments." Research by Ford, Haug, Jones, Roy, and Folmar (1990) also confirmed the continued disadvantaged income status of African-American elderly. More specifically, African-American elderly women are the poorest population of any minority elderly in the United States. Malveaux (1993) reports that although black women constitute 5.04 percent of the total elderly, they comprise 15.69 percent of the poor elderly. Stated differently, 32.7 percent of elderly black women between the ages of 65 and 74 are below the poverty line. Furthermore, 42.0 percent of elderly black women aged 75 and over are below the poverty line (Malveaux, 1993). Wilson-Ford (1990) identifies a number of factors that contribute to the poverty of African-American elderly women. These factors include income, Social Security, private pensions, widowhood, education, and labor force participation. The contribution of these factors to the economic impoverishment of elderly black women is discussed in the following section on discrimination. As Wilson-Ford (1990, p. 17) states, "poverty among older Black women does not occur because of age, but rather the roots of poverty stem from lifelong patterns of disadvantaged status that come to fruition when they are old." This statement highlights the significance of *discrimination* and *prejudice* in social relations. Discrimination is the unequal treatment of members of one group relative to other groups. Prejudice is an attitude (generally negative) toward members of some group. In the above statement by Wilson-Ford, African-American elderly women are described as victims of individual and institutional discrimination. In other words, they have been treated as second-class citizens by being offered less pay and fewer job opportunities and have been relegated to a lowered social standing because of the color of their skin. Over a lifetime, the cumulative effects of prejudice and discrimination become painfully obvious. The extent to which poverty and ill health exist among minority elderly in general, and African-American elderly women in particular, is evidence of a disadvantaged status.

Finally, although African-American women who are poor represent a greater percentage than whites and Hispanics, living alone cuts across racial and ethnic boundaries. Among elderly African-American women, 60 percent who are poor live alone.

Throughout this discussion, it must be remembered that African Americans are not a monolithic group. Approximately one-third of African Americans belong to the "middle class" of America. Among African-American elderly it means that the difference between those well-off minority elderly and the poor minority elderly is quite distinct (Malveaux, 1993).

Hispanics

The Hispanic elderly constitute one of the fastest-growing minority populations in the United States. According to Table 9–1, the Hispanic elderly will increase from 4.6 percent of the total elderly population in 1995 to 9.8 percent in 2025. This represents a 113 percent increase in the proportion of Hispanic elderly among the total aged population in a 30-year period of time.

Although their histories are different from African Americans, the experiences of Hispanics in the United States have resulted in similar outcomes. Regarding terminology, the term *Hispanic* is used as a rubric identifying individuals from a number of Spanish-speaking countries (Sotomayor, 1989). There is considerable variation regarding income and education levels depending on country of origin. Cuban Americans tend to have higher levels of education and income, whereas Mexican Americans and Puerto Ricans generally rank lowest on these indexes (Feagin & Feagin, 1993).

As a group under the rubric of Hispanic, however, rates of poverty among the elderly are second only to that of African-American elderly. In 1992, 22.0 percent of elderly Hispanics were below the poverty level, compared with 33.3 percent of elderly blacks and 10.9 percent of elderly whites (U.S. Bureau of the Census, 1994).

The social context of aging among Hispanic elderly is unique. For one thing, the Hispanic population is younger; median age is 25.8, compared to 35.5 for whites and 28.6 for blacks (U.S. Bureau of the Census, 1994). In addition, elderly Hispanics have been influenced more by family than by the larger community (Daley, Applewhite, & Jorquez, 1989). Hispanic elderly are more likely to live with their children than are elderly whites or African Americans (Lubben & Becerra, 1987). Any disruption to this family unit may create significant hardship for the elderly member. One such consequence is the increased likelihood of living alone. This type of living arrangement is gender biased. Women constitute almost 70 percent of elderly Hispanics who live alone (Maldonado, 1989). Those elderly Hispanic women who live alone are also characterized as "widowed, but maybe divorced, with an extremely limited educational base and financial resources" (Maldonado, 1989, p. 12).

As a result of language and culture, as well as difficulties assimilating to the larger community among Hispanic elderly, social service agencies must reconsider their provision of service delivery to this population (Arevalo, 1989). Daley et al. (1989, p. 138) cite the concept of *personalismo,* or "relating to others as whole persons and not in an impersonal and/or contractual manner" as an example of what service workers must understand in order to effectively offer and provide needed services.

Hispanic elderly present a unique situation to the aging process. They represent one of the fastest-growing segments of the elderly population and yet they generally remain culturally isolated from the larger elderly population and society. This is not to suggest that their cultural behavior is wrong. Rather, the structure of the support system is likely to overlook and, as a result, not provide the necessary services to those who do not fit the prescribed patterns of behavior. Torres-Gil (1986) reminds us that it is also the responsibility of the larger American society to understand and appreciate the cultural changes that are occurring as a result of increasing numbers of Hispanics and other minority populations.

Asian Americans

As with the term *Hispanic, Asian American* is a rubric within which a number of nationalities are categorized. These nationalities include "Chinese, Japanese, and Korean aged, and some Filipino, and more recently, Vietnamese aged" (Place, 1981, p. 214). Japanese and Chinese elderly are the predominant ethnic groups associated with Asian Americans. According to data from the California Senior Survey of 1982 and 1983, elderly Chinese and Mexicans share considerable similarities. These similarities include being foreign born, living in ethnic enclaves, entering the United States in search of unskilled labor when young and expecting to return to their homeland, living with a relative (generally a child) in a multigenerational environment, and utilizing the informal support network of family (Lubben & Becerra, 1987). Similarities also exist among the Issei. According to Montero (1979), the Issei were the first Japanese to immigrate to the United States in the later 19th and early 20th centuries. The offspring of the Issei are referred to as Nisei, and the third generation (the grandchildren of the Issei) are called Sansei. Historically, the Issei arrived in the United States to work, make money, and return to Japan. Instead, after working for a period of time, in an effort to save money they sent for a potential spouse to join them in the United States, were married, and settled down. Because of age differences at marriage, the Issei alive today are generally women. Montero (1979) found that the Issei selectively disengaged from social interaction. Family ties remained strong, whereas secondary associational ties decreased in importance.

The Asian American elderly population will expand at a very rapid rate over the next 30 years. As a result of earlier immigration and recent arrivals, Asian-American elderly also create new demands on our thinking and treatment of the elderly population. With greater reliance on family and the informal support system, Asian Americans bring a new set of challenges to the current thinking in the provision of services. To best utilize existing resources, it is time for a reexamination of what services are important and how they need to be provided. As the aging population becomes increasingly diverse, policy statements must recognize the multiplicity of circumstances and needs.

Native Americans

One segment of the elderly population that understands its uniqueness relative to the majority white population is that of Native Americans. Although elderly African Americans are generally identified as being the poorest minority, Native-American elderly are the most disadvantaged. One serious problem in attempting to understand the structural and dynamic qualities of Native-American elderly is the lack of adequate data (Place, 1981). Gelfand and Barresi (1987) suggest that data are sparse because the small number of Native-American elderly have not been identified as being particularly important to research. Another reason cited by Gelfand and Barresi (1987) is that Native Americans are suspicious not only of white researchers but also of "apples," that is, people who are "red" on the outside but "white" on the inside. Nonetheless, we do know that there has been some movement of elderly Native Americans from urban areas back to the reservation (Weibel-Orlando, 1988). Although the majority of elderly Native Americans reside in urban areas, a number of misconceptions exist regarding their rights and behavior (Kramer, 1991, pp. 205–207). These misconceptions include the following:

1. *When American Indians get old, they retire to reservations.* Instead, the majority of elderly Native Americans age in place. As Kramer (1991, p. 206) suggests, "this perception has hindered both research on the needs of this population and serious planning efforts to fill these needs."

2. *American Indians are eligible for special services because they are wards of the government.* Native Americans are not wards of the government; they hold U.S. citizenship. If Native Americans move off the reservation for more than 120 days, they lose their medical care benefit through the Indian Health Service (Kramer, 1991). Thus urban Native American elderly are in need of local health services and are not covered by the Indian Health Service.

3. *Title VI of the Older Americans Act provides funds for nutrition and community services to American Indian tribal governments, and therefore Title III providers have limited responsibility to serve older American Indians.* Again, the reality is that half of the elderly Native Americans do not live on reservations. As a result, they are as entitled to provisions of Title III as any other elderly person. Kramer (1991, p. 206) also points out that of the "278 reservations and 209 Alaskan Native Villages . . . only 81 [have] Title VI programs."

4. *American Indians have a homogeneous culture.* The Native American population is quite diverse. There are some 150 languages attributable to Native Americans today. Even the status of the elderly varies depending on the specific tribe. As a result, it is difficult to generalize from research findings (Block, 1979).

Whether elderly Native Americans reside in urban communities or rural reservations, the inescapable fact remains that they are the most disadvantaged aged population in the United States. To illustrate, Kramer (1991) reports that Native Americans in their middle-age years suffer from physical and emotional conditions that are normally experienced among others aged 65 and over. Because their numbers are so small, the conditions of elderly Native Americans are often overlooked. This is unfortunate because their circumstances, more than any other minority population, are the result of direct government intervention.

Following is a reexamination of the conditions that foster discrimination against the elderly in the United States. We know the dynamics and those factors that create and perpetuate inequality within the elderly population. The question is whether there is the will among the elderly as well as the larger population to move beyond group divisiveness.

Critical Connection—Ageism, Sexism, and Racism as Conditions for Discrimination

Throughout this book, the problem of ageism has been addressed. We know that ageist attitudes permeate American culture. Thus being elderly in the land of youth is strike one. This chapter as well as earlier material addressed problems of aging specific to women (income, retirement, and so on). We can conclude that being female in a man's world is strike two. This chapter culminates with the consequences of racial and ethnic prejudice and discrimination. The result is that being a minority (particularly elderly female) in the land of a white male majority (with the power) is strike three.

Is the analogy to baseball a fair one? If the reader is a sports fan, consider the following. I am the pitcher and you are at the plate. Rather than provide you with a bat, you are given a small stick to hit the ball. As the pitcher, I control the tempo of the game. Therefore, I determine when and how I will pitch the ball. If I pitch to you the same way I would pitch to others, regardless of opportunity to hit the ball, you are at a disadvantage. The fact that you had your "turn at bat" will be viewed by society as an equal opportunity to succeed. Never mind that your turn was inherently unequal in potential outcome due to conditions created by others as a result of specific group-level characteristics. Chances are that you will strike out. This is how power influences opportunity and outcome and creates the social problems of age, sex, and racial discrimination.

The consequences of such discrimination will be addressed in the next three chapters. We begin by questioning how living arrangements are differentiated on the basis of age, race, and gender. Living arrangements are inextricably connected to the larger environment within which the person lives. It is within the larger environment that concerns over safety as a result (perceived or real) of crime become an issue. Discrimination follows us even in death. How and when and where we die are, to some extent, discretionary factors determined by social conditions.

Chapter Review

This chapter began by suggesting that the social process of aging was discriminatory. That is, the conditions associated with the aging process are not equitably distributed among the elderly population. For example, economic opportunities throughout life are greater among white males than any other segment of the population. The following questions allow the reader to synthesize information presented not only in this chapter but throughout the book.

1. Discuss why some groups of elderly are better off (in terms of finances, health, and so on) than others.
2. What is meant by the term *double jeopardy?* Do you think double jeopardy will exist 30 years from now? Why or why not?
3. Characterize the elderly woman of today. Based on your knowledge of life expectancy rates, income, and work histories, characterize the elderly woman of the year 2025. Will she be different or roughly the same as today? Explain your answer.
4. What is meant by *triple jeopardy?* Do you think that triple jeopardy will exist 30 years from now? Why or why not?
5. Describe the conditions of life for elderly African-American women. Based on projections in terms of numbers, income, and health status, describe the future of elderly African-American women.
6. Identify one minority group not discussed in the chapter. Conduct library research to determine current economic conditions of the group as well as future economic and population projections. Do these projections differ from those groups discussed in the chapter? If the answer is yes, explain why.
7. Imagine that you are an 80-year-old Hispanic female. Describe yourself. Include not only personal observations, but also your environment, others, your relations with others, financial situation, and so on.

Glossary

Discrimination   The practice of differentiating between groups on the basis of some socially constructed criteria. One group, relative to others, is provided preferential treatment.

Ethnic group   A group defined by similarities in cultural heritage, language, and customs.

Minority group   A group characterized by age, sex, racial, or ethnic identity that is accorded less power and fewer decision-making opportunities over its condition and future.

Prejudice   An attitude of liking or disliking toward member(s) of a group. Although a prejudice can be positive, it generally has a negative connotation.

Racial group   A group characterized by socially defined physical characteristics passed from one generation to the next. These characteristics are temporally, as well as societally, relative.

Suggested Reading

Allen, J., & Pifer, A. (1993). *Women on the front lines: Meeting the challenge of an aging America.* Washington, DC: Urban Institute Press.
This book provides extensive coverage of a large number of issues concerning elderly women today.

Gelfand, D. E., & Barresi, C. M. (Eds.). (1987). *Ethnic dimensions of aging.* Series on Adulthood and Aging, Vol. 5. New York: Springer.
A critical examination of aging and ethnicity in American society.

National Caucus and Center on Black Aged, Inc. (1987). *The status of the black elderly in the United States.* Washington, DC: U.S. Government Printing Office.
A brief, concise statement regarding the state of elderly African Americans. Although dated, the report not only addresses areas of concern but also provides recommendations.

References

Arendell, T., & Estes, C. L. (1991). Older women in the post-Reagan era. In M. Minkler & C. L. Estes (Eds.), *Critical perspectives on aging: The political and moral economy of growing old* (pp. 209–226). Amityville, NY: Baywood.

Arevalo, R. (1989). The Latino elderly. *California Sociologist, 12*(1), 1–7.

Block, M. R. (1979). Exiled Americans: The plight of Indian aged in the United States. In D. E. Gelfand & A. J. Kutzik (Eds.), *Ethnicity and aging: Theory, research, and policy* (pp. 184–192). Series on Adulthood and Aging, Vol. 5. New York: Springer.

Burton, L. M., Dilworth-Anderson, P., & Bengtson, V. L. (1991). Creating culturally relevant ways of thinking about diversity and aging. *Generations, 15*(4), 67–72.

Daley, J. M., Applewhite, S. R., & Jorquez, J. (1989). Community participation of the elderly Chicano: A model. *International Journal of Aging and Human Development, 29*(2), 135–150.

Darnay, A. J. (1994). *Statistical record of older Americans.* Detroit: Gale Research.

Estes, C. L., Gerard, L. E., & Clarke, A. (1984). Women and the economics of aging. In M. Minkler & C. L. Estes (Eds.), *Readings in the political economy of aging* (pp. 209–224). Amityville, NY: Baywood.

Feagin, J. R., & Feagin, C. B. (1993). *Racial and ethnic relations* (4th ed.). Englewood Cliffs, NJ: Prentice-Hall.

Ford, A. B., Haug, M. R., Jones, P. K., Roy, A. W., & Folmar, S. J. (1990). Race-related differences among elderly urban residents: A cohort study, 1975–1984. *Journals of Gerontology: Social Sciences, 45*(4), S163–171.

Gelfand, D. E., & Barresi, C. M. (1987). Current perspectives in ethnicity and aging. In D. E. Gelfand & C. M. Barresi (Eds.), *Ethnic dimensions of aging* (pp. 5–17). New York: Springer.

Gould, K. H. (1989). A minority-feminist perspective on women and aging. *Journal of Women and Aging, 1*(1–3), 195–216.

Harlow, K. S., & McDonald, J. (1991). Aging in Black America: Service needs and utilization patterns. *Evaluation and Program Planning, 14*(4), 233–239.

Hyde, J. C., & Torres-Gil, F. (1991). Ethnic minority elders and the Older Americans Act: How have they fared? *Generations, 15*(3), 57–61.

Jacobs, R. H. (1993). Expanding social roles for older women. In J. Allen & A. Pifer (Eds.), *Women on the front lines: Meeting the challenge of an aging America* (pp. 191–219). Washington, DC: Urban Institute Press.

Jorgensen, L. A. B. (1989). Women and aging: Perspectives on public and social policy. *Journal of Women and Aging, 1*(1–3), 291–315.

Kramer, B. J. (1991). Urban American Indian aging. *Journal of Cross-Cultural Gerontology, 6*(2), 205–217.

Levy, J. A. (1988). Intersections of gender and aging. *Sociological Quarterly, 29*(4), 479–486.

Lewis, M., & Butler, R. N. (1984). Why is women's lib ignoring old women? In M. Minkler & C. L. Estes (Eds.), *Readings in the political economy of aging* (pp. 199–208). Amityville, NY: Baywood.

Lubben, J. E., & Becerra, R. M. (1987). Social support among Black, Mexican, & Chinese elderly. In D. E. Gelfand & C. M. Barresi (Eds.), *Ethnic dimensions of aging* (pp. 130–144). New York: Springer.

Maldonado, D. (1989). The Latino elderly living alone: The invisible poor. *California Sociologist, 12*(1), 8–21.

Malveaux, J. (1993). Race, poverty, and women's aging. In J. Allen & A. Pifer (Eds.), *Women on the front lines: Meeting the challenge of an aging America* (pp. 167–190). Washington, DC: Urban Institute Press.

McDaniel, S. A. (1989). Women and aging: A sociological perspective. *Journal of Women and Aging, 1*(1–3), 47–67.

Montero, D. (1979). Disengagement and aging among the Issei. In D. E. Gelfand & A. J. Kutzik (Eds.), *Ethnicity and aging: Theory, research, and policy* (pp. 193–205). Series on Adulthood and Aging, Vol. 5. New York: Springer.

National Caucus and Center on Black Aged, Inc. (1987). *The status of the black elderly in the United States.* Report for the Select Committee on Aging, House of Representatives, 100th Congress. Washington, DC: U.S. Government Printing Office.

National Center for Health Statistics. (1994). *Health, United States, 1993*. Hyattsville, MD: Public Health Service.

Olson, L. K. (1988). Aging is a woman's problem: Issues faced by the female elderly population. *Journal of Aging Studies, 2*(2), 97–108.

Peterson, S. A., & Somit, A. (1992). Older women: Health and political behavior. *Women and Politics, 12*(4), 87–108.

Pifer, A. (1993). Meeting the challenge: Implications for policy and practice. In J. Allen & A. Pifer (Eds.), *Women on the front lines: Meeting the challenges of an aging America* (pp. 241–252). Washington, DC: Urban Institute Press.

Place, L. F. (1981). The ethnic factor. In F. J. Berghorn & D. E. Schafer (Eds.), *The dynamics of aging: Original essays on the process and experiences of growing old* (pp. 195–226). Boulder, CO: Westview Press.

Sotomayor, M. (1989). The Hispanic elderly and the intergenerational family. *Journal of Children in Contemporary Society, 20*(3–4), 55–65.

Stanford, E. P., & Yee, D. L. (1991). Gerontology and the relevance of diversity. *Generations, 15*(4), 11–14.

Stone, R. I. (1989). The feminization of poverty among the elderly. *Women's Studies Quarterly, 1–2*, 20–34.

Torres-Gil, F. (1986). Hispanics: A special challenge. In A. Pifer & L. Bronte (Eds.), *Our aging society: Paradox and promise* (pp. 219–242). New York: Norton.

Torres-Gil, F. (1987). Aging in an ethnic society: Policy issues for aging among minority groups. In D. E. Gelfand & C. M. Barresi (Eds.), *Ethnic dimensions of aging* (pp. 239–257). New York: Springer.

U.S. Bureau of the Census. (1994). *Statistical abstract of the United States: 1994* (114th ed.). Washington, DC: U.S. Government Printing Office.

Weibel-Orlando, J. (1988). Indians, ethnicity as a resource and aging: You can go home again. *Journal of Cross-Cultural Gerontology, 3*(4), 323–348.

Wilson-Ford, V. (1990). Poverty among black elderly women. *Journal of Women and Aging, 2*(4), 5–20.

Wirth, L. (1945). The problem of minority groups. In Ralph Linton (Ed.), *The science of man in the world crisis*. New York: Columbia University Press.

Wray, L. A. (1991). Public policy implications of an ethnically diverse elderly population. *Journal of Cross-Cultural Gerontology, 6*(2), 243–257.

C h a p t e r *10*

Living Arrangements

The possibilities available to older people seeking to address unsatisfactory housing situations go far beyond merely modifying the physical or financial attributes of their dwellings or changing their neighborhoods. A dwelling is much more than merely shelter, a financial holding, or a type of land use in a particular neighborhood. Judgements of the appropriateness of older people's housing must also consider issues such as family ties and relationships; the availability and quality of caregiving assistance; individual coping styles; the desirability of communal living arrangements; and the cost, availability, and quality of human services and long-term health care.

—GOLANT, 1992, P. 3

The type and location of one's residence provides others with an explanation of who we are. Rightly or wrongly, our social class position is often inferred from our street address. If you live in an urban area, your street address places you within a particular neighborhood and its reputation. A rural address creates residential images replete with particular characteristics of the occupant. The type of dwelling also evokes characterizations. Are apartment dwellers different from homeowners? What about trailer-homeowners or those in SROs (single-room occupants)? We all have an address. Not to have an address implies homelessness, which itself is an example of a particular living arrangement.

Living arrangements imply social condition. Even among the elderly, social class distinctions exist based on availability and range of living options. The greater the living arrangement options, the wealthier the elderly person. Inversely, as wealth declines, so do the options. The relationship of income to other variables such as age, gender, race, or ethnicity is also well known. As a result, living arrangements for women, the oldest-old, and minority elderly are often limited.

This chapter "locates" the elderly within our society. Previous chapters examined differences among the elderly based on some group-level characteristic. Now we can connect the elderly to a location. That location may be a physical location, such as a particular type of dwelling or a geographical location such as the Northeast or the Sunbelt. We will begin with the dynamic qualities associated with migration patterns of the elderly. We then explore spatial locations and finally physical settings. Throughout, the influence of social class position is evident.

Migration

Migration is the movement from one physical location to another. Location changes range from intercommunity and interstate to internation. (An example of internation migration is the movement of Hispanic populations to the United States.) See Angel and Angel (1992) for the effect of age on internation migration.

Migration can be either voluntary or involuntary. Voluntary migration occurs when an elderly couple (or individual) decides to move from location X to location Y. In the case of interstate migration this is usually for retirement or amenity reasons (Hass, 1990). Involuntary migration occurs when an elderly couple (or individual) is forced to relocate because of health or financial reasons.

Migration of elderly persons is the result of a myriad of factors. Attempting to identify a single explanation is neither possible nor worthwhile. Instead, we will examine some patterns associated with the migratory process and characteristics of elderly involved.

Patterns

Discussion of migratory patterns of elderly does not mean that the elderly population is constantly on the move. In fact, when compared with the general population (see Table 10–1), the elderly are less likely to move: "Less than 600,000 people, about 2 percent of

TABLE 10–1 Mobility Status of the Population by Age: 1992

Percent Distribution

| | | Movers (different house in U.S. in 1991) | | | | |
| | | | | Different county | | |
Age	Non-Movers (Same House-hold in 1991)	Total	Same County	Total	Same State	Different State
Total	83	17	11	6	3	3
1–4	78	22	15	7	3	4
5–9	82	18	11	6	3	1
10–14	85	15	10	5	3	3
15–19	83	17	11	6	3	3
20–24	63	35	23	13	7	6
25–29	67	32	21	11	6	5
30–44	82	17	11	6	3	3
45–54	89	10	6	4	2	2
55–64	93	7	4	3	1	2
65–74	95	5	3	3	1	1
75+	96	5	3	3	1	1

Source: U.S. Bureau of the Census. (1994). *Statistical abstract of the United States, 1994.* Table 32. Washington, DC: U.S. Government Printing Office.

all elderly, moved far enough to change their county of residence" (U.S. Bureau of the Census, Current Population Reports, 1992, pp. 5–18).

Among the elderly who do migrate, there are four distinct patterns. First, and most predominant, are those elderly who move from one location to another after retirement or for amenity reasons associated with the host state and community (Hass, 1990). Generally, this is represented by their movement from the Northeast and some Midwest states to Florida or South Central states. This pattern represents the majority of interstate moves made by the elderly. Among the retirement segment of the elderly movers, cost of living in the state of origin, as well as in the host state and community, is perhaps one of the most significant variables in the decision-making process (Fournier, Rasmussen, & Serow, 1988a, 1988b). Secondly, some elderly participate in what is referred to as *return migration,* that is, returning to one's state of birth. Serow and Charity (1988) indicate that the rate of return migration is minimal. However, characteristics of elderly participating in return migration are different from those who migrate for retirement or amenity reasons. Elderly who constitute the third migratory pattern are referred to as *snowbirds,* elderly who leave the cold and snow of the Northeast and Midwest for the sun and warmth of the South or Sunbelt states. In late spring, they return to their home state, where they remain until the next winter. The final migratory pattern is from an independent living arrangement to an institution (Litwak & Longino, 1987).

What do we know about the elderly who migrate? Do the elderly who are return migrants different from those who originally migrated?

Demographic Characteristics

Characteristics of the elderly vary depending on the applicable type of migratory pattern. We know that elderly who migrate for retirement or amenity reasons are younger, wealthier, better educated, and healthier than those who do not move (Serow, 1990). In addition, women are more likely than men to move, particularly as age increases. Whites are more likely than African Americans to move (Watkins, 1989). Finally, Hispanic elderly are less likely to move than other Americans (Biafora & Longino, 1990). Return migrants are more likely to be older, women, and in poorer health relative to those who migrate for retirement (Rogers, 1989). One explanation for the characteristics of the returning migrants is couched in the many demographic differences between men and women. For example, when retirees leave their state of origin, the husband is generally older than the wife. We also know that most husbands die married, leaving a widowed spouse. These widows are likely to be the returning migrants. As these elderly women return to their state of birth, they are likely to be financially less secure than when they left earlier with their husbands.

These migratory patterns affect the states involved as well. When well-to-do young (healthy) elderly move out of a state, they are taking with them considerable disposable income to another location. According to the U.S. Bureau of the Census (1992), Florida gained some $1 billion from in-migration from the state of New York between 1975 and 1980. The returning migration of poorer elderly women reflects an increasing need for medical and social services (Rogers, 1989) within the receiving states. The result is that these states will incur considerable cost providing care and assistance to these elderly.

We now know that the percentage of the elderly who actually migrate is relatively small. The remainder of the elderly remain in the same household in the same community throughout their lifetime. That location can be described as being either in an urban area (where a majority of the elderly are located) or in a rural area. We turn to a brief examination of the elderly within the rural-urban continuum and an accompanying explanation.

Location of the Elderly

Until the 1920 census, the United States was a rural society. Since then, an increasing percentage of the population has migrated to urban areas. Today, over 75 percent of the American population resides in an urban area. The majority of elderly live in urban areas. More specifically, they are most likely to live in central cities or on the urban fringe. Table 10–2 illustrates the urban-rural distribution of elderly and where within urban areas the elderly are most likely to live.

It is evident from the data that the percentage of elderly living in urban areas in general, and the central city in particular, increases with age. This transition to more urban locations may be the result of closer proximity to health care professionals and facilities. Nevertheless, demographic differences continue to persist. Central city elderly are disproportionately women, poor, and minorities. There is a growing differential between one segment of the aging population that is mobile, well-off, and healthy and one that is aging in place because of economics. These class-based differences will become more evident throughout the remainder of the chapter. Table 10–3 illustrates some of the differences

TABLE 10–2   Percentage of Persons Aged 65 and Over Residing in Urban and Rural Locations by Age: 1989

| | Inside Metropolitan Area | | Outside Metropolitan Area | |
| | In Central | Not in | | |
Age	City	Central City	Urban	Rural
65–74	30.3	44.6	9.2	16.0
75+	32.2	40.9	11.5	15.4

Source: U.S. Bureau of the Census. (1993). *Social and economic characteristics.* CP-2-1 Table 39. Washington, DC: U.S. Government Printing Office.

between urban and rural areas regarding rates of poverty. The table also illustrates differences in poverty rates by race and by marital status within urban and rural locations. We know that elderly women are more likely to live alone than elderly men. An examination of the rates of poverty among rural and urban populations indicates that marital status is more significant than age in determining poverty. And, consistent with the data in Chapter 9, growing older, living alone, and being a minority are all related to increased rates of poverty in urban as well as rural locations. The social problems experienced by aging women and minorities are the result not only of prior economic conditions but of normative marriage patterns that increasingly relegate women to societal dependency upon the death of their spouse.

Beyond the statistics, what do we know about aging in urban and rural settings? This section will delineate differences not based on gender, race, or ethnicity but rather on the physical location and its historical significance to the American psyche.

Urban Settings

Historically, Americans have had a love-hate relationship with urban communities. On the one hand, cities have offered a social world with a plethora of activities, cultural diversity, and increased economic opportunities. On the other hand, cities have been viewed with suspicion (Gottdiener, 1994). They have been implicated in the breakdown of the traditional family structure, increased anonymity, and impersonal social relationships.

Broadly speaking, urban areas can be divided into two distinct living areas: the central city and its surrounding suburbs. Until recently, the central city had been like a magnet, attracting people to its stores, factories, and residential neighborhoods. Today, most central cities are losing population to ever-growing suburban communities. There are a number of reasons for this shift of population, including the emergence of the interstate highway system; changing industrial technology that allowed manufacturing to move out of the city; increasing reliance on the automobile; and the concomitant development of suburban living,

TABLE 10–3   **Percentage of Persons Aged 65 and Over Below Poverty by Living Arrangement and Location of Residence by Race: 1989**

| Race, Age, and Living Arrangement | Urban | | | Rural | |
	Central Place	Urban Fringe	Outside Urbanized Areas	Total	Farm
White					
Married-couple families, house holder, 65–74	3.1	2.2	4.0	6.4	5.7
Persons living alone, 65–74	17.5	13.4	23.8	27.0	19.5
Married-couple families, house holder, 75+	4.7	3.8	6.6	11.4	8.7
Persons living alone, 75+	20.7	17.1	27.9	35.1	25.0
African American					
Married-couple families, house holder, 65–74	12.2	9.2	21.9	27.1	31.5
Persons living alone, 65–74	43.1	36.8	60.8	63.2	57.9
Married-couple families, house holder, 75+	16.2	12.9	29.3	39.6	33.5
Persons living alone, 75+	52.0	46.7	70.4	75.4	66.4
American Indian, Eskimo, Aleut					
Married-couple families, house holder, 65–74	7.9	6.1	15.4	24.8	15.2
Persons living alone, 65–74	32.7	25.2	36.5	50.0	31.6
Married-couple families, house holder, 75+	13.3	9.7	17.9	35.6	36.8
Persons living alone, 75+	41.0	28.8	45.7	59.3	23.7

continued

TABLE 10–3 Continued

	Urban			Rural	
Race, Age, and Living Arrangement	Central Place	Urban Fringe	Outside Urbanized Areas	Total	Farm
Asian or Pacific Islander					
Married-couple families, house holder, 65–74	11.1	8.0	5.1	6.0	3.7
Persons living alone, 65–74	27.9	20.1	27.7	21.7	15.6
Married-couple families, house holder, 75+	12.5	10.0	6.0	8.7	3.8
Persons living alone, 75+	34.6	27.3	27.6	37.0	5.5
Hispanic					
Married-couple families, house holder, 65–74	15.0	8.1	20.4	20.0	14.5
Persons living alone, 65–74	47.4	30.4	48.4	46.0	33.3
Married-couple families, house holder, 75+	19.8	12.8	28.1	27.4	15.0
Persons living alone, 75+	54.5	36.7	55.8	56.1	33.1

Source: U.S. Bureau of the Census. (1993). *Social and economic characteristics, United States.* CP-2-1. Tables 100–104. Washington, DC: U.S. Government Printing Office.

replete with shopping malls. As a result, middle-class America moved out of the central city and relocated in the suburbs. Central cities are increasingly home to those with little money but considerable social and economic need. Among those left behind in the central city are the poorer elderly.

Moving is expensive, and people with few resources often cannot afford to move in response to a deterioration in the fiscal condition of their city. Many city residents also may not be able to afford the housing in a jurisdiction with better fiscal health. Moving may be particularly disruptive or even physically difficult for elderly or handicapped city residents. (Ladd & Yinger, 1989, p. 293)

Besides the central city, elderly also reside in suburban communities. Today, in fact, suburbs are home to a greater number of elderly than central cities (Palen, 1995). Suburban communities rely primarily on the automobile rather than public transportation for geographic mobility. Increased physical impairments among suburban elderly or the loss of one's driver's license could seriously impair the mobility of suburban elderly. In addition, the number of children per family has declined, reducing the ability of the informal caregiving community to provide needed services to the suburban elderly. As a result, suburban elderly may experience increasing social isolation. Beyond the central cities and suburban communities, elderly also reside in the small towns and farms of rural America.

Rural Settings

If, historically, urban America represents what is wrong with society, then rural America should represent all that is right. Such a simplistic dichotomy of physical locations does not address the multiplicity of issues that exist within urban and rural settings. Although some may create a romantic and idealistic image of what life was (or should be) like in rural America, it is far from the reality that currently exists for America's rural elderly.

Migration patterns of the elderly and nonelderly have resulted not only in population shifts but also in the concentration of population on the basis of age. Often the concentration of the elderly is greatest in nonmetropolitan areas (Golant, 1992) because of an out-migration of nonelderly from the area (Fuguitt & Beale, 1993).

There are significant differences between rural and urban elderly. According to the poverty rates identified in Table 10–3, rural elderly are poorer than urban elderly. One reason for the increased rates of poverty among rural elderly is their lack of educational attainment, which limits their occupational opportunities (McLaughlin & Jensen, 1993).

Health differences also exist between urban and rural elderly. According to Bane (1991) the health of rural elderly is poorer, particularly among minority populations. It would appear that the double and triple jeopardy examined in Chapter 9 could be extended to quadruple jeopardy: elderly minority women living in rural America.

We began this chapter with two main goals: to understand the geographical location and the physical location of the elderly in the United States. Interwoven within these two goals is the interactive effect of the demographic characteristics of the elderly. We have covered, in depth, the first goal of geographical location. In the process, differentiation on the basis of gender, minority status, and economic condition have been explored in relation to geographical location. We will now examine the second, and more specific, goal of addressing the type of physical locations within which the elderly reside. Once again, differentiation on the basis of gender, minority status, and economic condition is integrated throughout the material.

Physical Settings

Physical settings are material structures that provide a living environment consistent with the occupants' current health and economic status. The physical settings in which we live exist on a continuum ranging from complete independence to total dependence. An example of the relationship between one's age, living environment, and interpersonal relations is presented in Table 10–4. Note how the physical setting changes as ability to maintain social independence decreases.

Notice the range of living arrangement options available in Table 10–4. There is an implication that as a person ages, he or she will be transformed from independent to dependent living with very few options in between. Table 10–5 identifies the range of physical settings that exist for the elderly, depending on their health and economic status. Table 10–5 also identifies a number of other housing options (as well as their advantages and disadvantages) not addressed here.

It is obvious that not all elderly are confined to such a dichotomous living arrangement as rural or urban. Within the defined type of living environment, economic conditions of the elderly significantly influence their range of available physical settings. The physical settings can be arranged on a continuum beginning with complete independence on one end and complete dependence on the other. We begin our examination of this continuum of physical settings with the most common: independent living.

Independent Living Arrangements

Independent living is, by far, the most common living arrangement among the elderly. In addition to independent living, the vast majority of elderly live in households that are free of debt. Racial and ethnic differences continue to persist with regard to the value of homes (Higgins & Folts, 1992). The likelihood of independent living arrangements is also influenced by three specific variables. These variables include health status, economics, and availability of kin (Mutchler, 1990, 1992). Living environments (and options) of the elderly are stratified on the basis of economics. As the financial ability of the elderly increases, their housing options are much greater than for an elderly person who is poor. These differences continue to break down along racial, ethnic, and gender lines, reinforcing societal mechanisms that perpetuate the stratification of age. Consider the impact of double and triple jeopardy relative to living arrangements. Mutschler (1992) identifies a number of basic distinctions between elderly homeowners and renters that reinforce conditions discussed in previous chapters. Elderly renters are more likely to be female, African American, older (a 2-year median age difference), and spending more (as a percentage of income) on their living arrangement.

Although the elderly strive to maintain their independence, they are likely to encounter financial or structural problems, such as the condition of the home or apartment in which they live. According to Golant and LaGreca (1995, p. S13), "substantial percentages of the U.S. elderly population now live in housing with problems. As of 1989, 7 percent of elderly homeowners and 10 percent of elderly renters occupied dwellings having 'severe' or 'moderate' physical problems. . . ." In addition to structural problems, many elderly also experience difficulty paying housing costs (Golant & LaGreca, 1995). More specifically, Keigher and Pratt (1991) state that poor elderly homeowners and renters pay out substantial amounts of their income for housing costs. However, with regard to housing problems, the poor elderly are not any worse off than others who are poor (Golant & LeGreca, 1995). Among those elderly who are mortgage free, the value of their home provides a potential cash resource in times of financial need. This "reverse mortgage" pro-

TABLE 10–4 Age-Related Environmental Changes and Personal Losses

50–64	65–74
Loss of relationships to younger friends and acquaintances of children. Loss of neighborhood role to schools and youth. Home is too large, but payments are low and equity high.	Loss in relation to work environment, loss of mobility due to lessened income. Dissolving of professional work associations and friendships. Move to apartment, smaller home, or struggle with increased maintenance costs of larger home.

75–84	85+
Loss of ability to drive independently. Must rely on bus or relatives and friends. Connections with community, church associations slowly severed. Move to more supportive housing, such as apartment with meals and maid service. Maintanance costs for single-family house unmanageable.	Loss of ability to navigate in the environment. Loss of strong connection with outside neighborhood. Dependence on supportive services. Move to supportive environment necessary, such as nursing home, home for the aged, or sibling's home.

Source: From *Aging: Scientific Perspectives and Social Issues,* by D. S. Woodruff and J. E. Birren. Copyright © 1983, 1975 Brooks/Cole Publishing Company, a division of International Thomson Publishing Inc., Pacific Grove, CA 93950. By permission of the Publisher.

vides elderly homeowners an opportunity to borrow against the value of their home. Various derivations of reverse mortgages exist depending on the needs and circumstances of the elderly (Higgins & Folts, 1992).

In addition to deteriorating housing conditions and financial hardship, many elderly who maintain independent living environments also face the potential risk of *involuntary relocation,* that is, the involuntary removal from their place of residence to another location picked either by the elderly person or by others. The social and psychological effects of a forced relocation can be devastating. When the elderly face involuntary relocation, they generally move to a more structured environment.

For some elderly, independent living means residing in public housing. Public housing in the United States originated during the Depression years of the 1930s. More recently, public housing for the elderly and other populations emerged during the 1960s as the federal government began to establish a private-public partnership of affordable housing (Retsinas & Retsinas, 1993). One issue that has generated considerable research (and controversy) is whether age-integrated or age-segregated housing is best for the elderly residents. Initially, it was believed that an age-integrated environment would democratize living arrangements on the basis of age. Generally speaking, research does not support age-integrated housing as the type of arrangement desired by elderly residents. Early research by Lawton (1976) identified the desire of respondents to be around age peers. However, Winiecke (1976) suggests that those who desire age-segregated housing are bored and lonely. A more recent study by Filinson (1993) builds on earlier explanations. Using six dimensions of environmental quality, Filinson (1993) compared elderly in public

TABLE 10–5 Advantages and Disadvantages of Selected Alternative Housing Options

	Advantages	Disadvantages
Accessory Apartments	Provide additional income for elderly homeowners	Initial construction cost to homeowners
	Companionship and security	Neighborhood concern about lowered property values
	Increase supply of affordable rental housing	Zoning restraints
	Personal support services may be provided in lieu of rent	Possible housing and building code violations
Board and Care Homes	Homelike environment	Not licensed or concerned with standards and treatment of residents
	Afford fragile, isolated elderly opportunity to interact with others	Owner/operators often lack training
	Economical	Little planned social activities
Congregate Housing	Provides basic support services that can extend independent living	Tendency to overserve the needs of tenants, promoting dependency
	Reduces social isolation	Expensive to build and operate
	Provides physical and emotional security	Those without kitchen facilities restrict tenants' independence
		Expensive for most elderly without subsidy
Elder Cottages, Granny flats	Facilitate older persons' receiving support from younger family members	Potential to lower property values
	Option to remain in individual home	Attitude of and impact on neighborhood
	Smaller housing unit, less expensive to operate	Concerns about housing and building code violations
Home Equity Conversion	Converts lifetime investment into usable income	Risk that homeowner will live longer than term of loan

Continued

TABLE 10–5   Continued

	Advantages	Disadvantages
	Allows elderly with marginal incomes to re-main in familiar surroundings	Homes of lower value (often type owned by elderly) may not provide monthly payments large enough to be worth cost of loan
	Can be used to finance housing expenses, i.e., make necessary repairs, utilities, taxes	Reluctance by homeowner to utilize due to lack of information, concern for lien on property, and/or impact on estate for heirs
Life Care Facilities	Offer prepaid health care	Too expensive for many elderly
	Security and protection against inflation and financially draining illness	Questionable protections should the facility go out of business
	Wide range of social activities with health and support systems	Older person receives no deed to property
		No guarantees that monthly payments will not rise
		Location is usually rural, isolated from community services
Shared Housing	Less expensive due to shared costs for household operators	Problems with selection of individual to share home
	Companionship, security	Amount of privacy reduced
		Does not meet medical and personal problems
	Promotes intergenerational cooperation and under-standing	Added income may mean owner is no longer eligible for public benefits
	More extensive use of existing housing Program inexpensive to operate	City zoning ordinances may prohibit

Source: Mutschler, P. "Where Elders Live." Copyright © *Generations* Vol. 16 (2): 7–14. All rights reserved. Reprinted by permission of Baywood Publishing from Callahan, J. J. Jr. (Ed) *Aging in Place* 1993. Pp. 5–18. Copyright © 1993, By Baywood Publishing Company, Inc., Amityville, NY. All rights reserved. No part of this book may be reproduced in any form, by mimeograph or any other means, without permission from the publisher. Printed in the United States of America.

housing and subsidized housing. These dimensions include privacy, stimulation, legibility, accessibility, territoriality, and social networks. Filinson (1993, p. 89) reports that

> the public housing tenants differed (in an unfavorable direction) from their subsidized housing counterparts regarding two dimensions of environmental quality—territoriality and social networks—and on global measures of environmental satisfaction. Without specific prompting, they identified the younger or handicapped (viz. young, mentally ill) residents at their housing site as the source of some of their dissatisfaction.

On a neighborhood level, Sherman (1988, p. 235) argues that "age concentration appears to enhance access to peers but not choice of peers. Thus, it appears that age concentration in neighborhoods is much less influential than that found in specially planned retirement housing."

The issue of age-integrated versus age-segregated housing for the elderly will continue. Remember that this social policy experimentation does not affect all elderly. Instead, this issue, as with many others, affects the most vulnerable and disadvantaged elderly. As with any economically stratified segment of society, those members with the economic means have access to alternative living arrangements.

Utilizing the continuum established at the beginning of the chapter, we will next examine congregate living as an alternative not only to independent living but also to the more structured nursing home environment.

Congregate Living

Congregate living arrangements offer an intermediate living arrangement. In this environment, residents live in their own apartments within the larger facility. The residents are physically independent. They are mobile and can come and go as they wish. However, an activity such as mealtime is a shared experience with the group. From an exchange perspective, the residents receive the companionship of other elderly and freedom from mundane household tasks. The cost to the resident is in terms of privacy and independence in daily life (Golant, 1992). Since the 1980s, congregate care has emerged as a significant money-making enterprise. According to Fairchild, Higgins, and Folts (1991, p. 161), congregate care facilities were developed for the young-old population (65–74) "who required few health or social services."

Congregate care facilities can be characterized as multistory buildings that appear like any other apartment complex. These facilities average around 150 one-bedroom units. Smaller and larger units are generally available but are limited in number. Elderly residents of privately owned facilities pay between $700 and $2,000 per month for a unit. Thus the socioeconomic status of residents is obviously middle and upper-middle class (Golant, 1992).

This type of living arrangement is growing in popularity. By the late 1980s there were some 55,000 units in 400 projects nationwide (Golant, 1992). As an increasing number of elderly retire with the level of income necessary to support an independent lifestyle without the worries of everyday life, the congregate care facility will continue to prosper. Once again, the living environment is defined by the social position of its occupants, even among the elderly.

A special type of congregate care facility is the continuing care retirement community. This is a facility where the elderly person (or couple) pays a significant fee up front plus a monthly maintenance fee. Elderly in this living arrangement are financially secure and quite different from those residing in congregate care facilities or nursing homes. Golant (1992) points out that characteristics of continuing care retirement communities are younger, better educated, wealthier, and healthier. By the late 1980s, more than a quarter of a million elderly were receiving services in some 1,000 facilities (Golant, 1992).

Whereas congregate living arrangements allow residents to maintain their independence, retirement communities require even greater physical mobility among their residents. We now turn to what has emerged as the quintessential image of aging in the past 20 years.

Retirement Communities

In an earlier chapter, we discussed the consequences of voting behavior among the elderly in Arizona. Those elderly were residents of retirement communities. Retirement communities are incorporated areas that provide single-family dwellings occupied by the elderly. In other words, these are very well-defined age-segregated communities.

Retirement communities are located primarily in the South and Southwest areas of the United States. Residents of these communities are not representative of the general elderly population. Residents of retirement communities are younger, wealthier, and in better physical condition. Home ownership in many of these communities requires a significant initial investment and continued capital to maintain the desired lifestyle.

Retirement communities are also quite diverse (Longino, 1981). Golant (1992) categorizes them into retirement new towns, retirement villages, and retirement subdivisions. Retirement new towns are perhaps best known. Names like Sun City or Leisure World are nationally recognized as early entrants into this newly developed industry. New towns are generally the largest (in area and population) of the three types. Retirement new towns are usually located away from, but near, larger metropolitan areas. Access to needed medical facilities is available, but problems of urban living are not. Retirement villages are generally smaller and located within urban communities. These facilities offer many of the same types of amenities that retirement new towns provide. Services, particularly health related, are generally found in the larger community. Finally, retirement subdivisions are the smallest (in area and population) of the three types. They consist of single-family dwellings in what appears to be a suburban development. Retirement subdivisions are less likely to adhere to strict age restrictions. Also, residents must travel away from the subdivision to obtain health-related services or participate in recreational opportunities (Golant, 1992).

Retirement communities provide a range of living arrangements for a significant segment of the elderly population because the need to remain physically and emotionally independent is central to the elderly. Not all elderly have the financial means necessary to afford the luxuries associated with retirement lifestyles. In fact, for some elderly, meeting basic human needs is of primary concern.

SROs

An *SRO* is a hotel that provides for single-room occupancy. This living arrangement offers an environment for single, low-income elderly who reside in inner cities. Although images of SROs have been relatively negative, these facilities have nonetheless provided an environment for a segment of the elderly population (Crystal & Beck, 1995). The impact of budget cuts initiated under President Reagan and continuing through President Bush have all but decimated the availability of SROs (Keigher & Pratt, 1991). These cuts exacerbate the already critical problem of homelessness among the elderly.

Keigher and Pratt (1991) cite a recent study that identifies between 2.5 percent and 9 percent of the homeless aged 60 and over. Although below their percentage of the population, such statistics may be misleading. Survival into old age itself is more difficult for a homeless person. In addition, the elderly have access to Medicare for some coverage of their medical problems. The majority of the elderly also receive some level of economic support through Social Security. These programs are instrumental in keeping increasing numbers of elderly out of the homeless shelters. It is ironic that programs known to produce positive outcomes for their clients have not been considered for further expansion among all age groups. Instead, federal reduction of programs that support the housing needs of this segment of the elderly have been cut. One explanation is that the elderly residing in SROs are considered marginalized when compared with mainstream elderly who maintain independent living arrangements. The marginalization of the elderly continues in the next section of the chapter, in which we examine what many now believe to be the final living arrangement before death.

Institutionalization

The institutionalization of the elderly can be categorized into two broad areas: nursing homes and mental hospitals. We will focus primarily on the nursing home. The role of the mental hospital has decreased in the recent past because of *deinstitutionalization*. Deinstitutionalization is the removal of patients from large, impersonal facilities and placing them in community settings instead. Nursing homes and mental hospitals are what Goffman (1961) called *total institutions*. A total institution is a facility where daily life activities of the patient are determined primarily by staff. According to Goffman (1961), patients in total institutions experience what he referred to as *mortification rituals,* whereby the individual's identity is removed, giving the institution greater control over the activities of the patient. Dunkle and Kart (1990) suggest that the process is dependent on level of care provided by the institution. The institutionalization of the elderly remains one of the more controversial topics of aging.

Nursing Homes   At any given point in time, approximately 5 percent of the elderly are residents in a nursing home. However, as one ages, the likelihood of being institutionalized increases. Golant (1992), citing Kemper and Murtaugh (1991), states that among those aged 65 and over, 43 percent will be institutionalized at some point in their lives. In addition, the cost of nursing home care continues to rise.

The image of nursing homes in American society is still primarily negative. This image is the result of years of very negative publicity regarding conditions in many facilities. In the last two decades, congressional hearings, journalistic exposés, and academic investigations have uncovered serious problems (see, for example, Townsend, 1971; Stannard, 1973; Mendelson, 1975; Kart & Manard, 1976; Moss & Halamandaris, 1977). Today, many elderly continue to view a nursing home environment as their last alternative. In fact, some elderly view going to a nursing home as one's last residence. Why are the images and attitudes so negative? We must first put nursing homes in a historical perspective. Only then can we begin to understand their significance in the lives of the elderly today.

Nursing homes have their origins in the almshouses of colonial America. The almshouse, or poor house, provided shelter and care not only to the poor but to the mentally ill and elderly who were poor. By the early 20th century an increasing percentage of the elderly were being provided care at county poor houses. The eventual passage of the Social Security Act in 1935 was a reaction to the increasing public support of the elderly. Enactment of the Social Security legislation is credited with the establishment of what we now call nursing homes. The connection between these two events is provided by Kayser-Jones (1981, p. 108):

> The 1935 Social Security Act . . . provided the impetus for the beginning development of long-term-care facilities. For the first time in American history, people over the age of 65 had a guaranteed monthly income that enable them to pay, at least in part, for some type of proprietary living accommodations, and this increased the demand for long-term-care facilities.

More recently, the passage of Medicare and Medicaid has resulted in an increased demand for nursing homes (Van Nostrand, Furner, & Suzman, 1992). This demand has resulted in a change in the size and ownership of facilities. Previously, nursing homes were relatively small "mom-and-pop" operations. With the passage of a government subsidy in the form of Medicaid, nursing homes have increased in size and have become chain-based businesses (Matcha, 1985). Beginning in the 1960s, the resident population also experienced rapid growth.

The nursing home industry has been growing at a phenomenal rate. Table 10–6 illustrates recent growth in the rate of residents by age, sex, and race per 1,000 population. Table 10–7 presents the cost of nursing home coverage based on various characteristics of the facility and the resident. According to Schwartz (1987, p. 489), "in 1980, there were 1.5 million nursing and related-care beds, or 60 beds per 1000 aged persons. If average lengths of stay do not change, 2.6 million nursing home beds, or 74 beds per 1000 population 65 years and over, will be required in the United States in the year 2000."

This is equivalent to the construction of one 150-bed nursing home built every day of the year between 1980 and the year 2000. These numbers indicate the magnitude of the nursing home industry in the United States. In the recent past, attempts have also been made to "demedicalize" the nursing home industry by replacing the term *nursing home* with the term *manor* or some other name that evokes a more pleasant and homelike environment. On a much broader level, Bowker (1982) identified 14 recommendations that would "humanize" the nursing home environment.

Historically, nursing homes have had defined levels of care for their residents. Today, these levels consist of intermediate and skilled. An explanation of these levels is provided by the National Center for Health Statistics (1977). A brief structural explanation of each level follows. Later in the chapter we will discuss some of the characteristics associated with nursing home residents. This will provide some explanation of the problems associated with nursing homes as a living environment for the elderly.

TABLE 10–6   Nursing Home Residents 65 Years of Age and Over Per 1,000 Population, According to Age, Sex, and Race: United States, 1963, 1973–1974, 1977, and 1985

Age, Sex, and Race	*Residents per 1,000 population[a]*			
	1963	1973–1974[b]	1977[c]	1985
Age				
All ages	25.4	44.7	47.1	46.2
65–74 years	7.9	12.3	14.4	12.5
75–84 years	39.6	57.7	64.0	57.7
85 years and over	148.4	257.3	225.9	220.3
Sex				
Male	18.1	30.0	30.3	29.0
65–74 years	6.8	11.3	12.6	10.8
75–84 years	29.1	39.9	44.9	43.0
85 years and over	105.6	182.7	146.3	145.7
Female	31.1	54.9	58.6	57.9
65–74 years	8.8	13.1	15.8	13.8
75–84 years	47.5	68.9	75.4	66.4
85 years and over	175.1	294.9	262.4	250.1
Race[d]				
White	26.6	46.9	48.9	47.7
65–74 years	8.1	12.5	14.2	12.3
75–84 years	41.7	60.3	67.0	59.1
85 years and over	157.7	270.8	234.2	228.7
Black	10.3	22.0	30.7	5.0
65–74 years	5.9	11.1	17.6	15.4
75–84 years	13.8	26.7	33.4	45.3
85 years and over	41.8	105.7	133.6	141.5

[a]Residents per 1,000 population for 1973–1974 and 1977 differ from those presented in the original source reports because the rates have been recomputed using revised census estimates for these years.
[b]Excludes residents in personal or domiciliary care homes.
[c]Includes residents of domiciliary care homes.
[d]For data years 1973–1974 and 1977, all people of Hispanic origin were included in the White category. For 1963, "black" includes all other races.
Source: Van Nostrand, J. F., Furner, S. E., & Suzman, R. (Eds.). (1993). *Health data on older Americans: United States, 1992.* National Center for Health Statistics. Table A. *Vital Health Stat.,* 3(27).

Intermediate Level Care Facilities   Intermediate level care facilities are nursing homes in which the resident is in need of minimal level care from the nursing staff. Usually this assistance is because of restricted activities of daily living (ADL) on the part of the resident. Research indicates that a minority of residents in intermediate level care facilities do not need nursing home placement (Lammers, 1983). Many of the residents would be capable of functioning in a more independent facility rather than in an institutional setting such

TABLE 10–7 **Nursing Home Average Monthly Charges Per Resident, According to Selected Facility and Resident Characteristics: United States, 1964, 1973–1974, 1977, and 1985**

Facility and Resident Characteristic	*Average Monthly Charge[a]*			
	1964	1973–1974[b]	1977	1985
All facilities	$186	$479	$689	$1,456
Ownership:				
Proprietary	205	489	670	1,379
Nonprofit and government	145	456	732	1,624
Certification[c]				
Skilled nursing facility	—	566	880	1,905
Skilled nursing and intermediate facility	—	514	762	1,571
Intermediate facility	—	376	556	1,179
Not certified	—	329	390	875
Bed size:				
Less than 50 beds	—	397	546	1,036
50–90 beds	—	448	643	1,335
100–199 beds	—	502	706	1,478
200 beds or more	—	576	837	1,759
Geographic region				
Northeast	213	651	918	1,781
Midwest	171	433	640	1,399
South	161	410	585	1,256
West	204	454	653	1,458
Resident characteristics				
All residents	186	479	689	1,456
Age:				
Under 65 years	155	434	585	1,379
65–74 years	184	473	669	1,372
75–84 years	191	488	710	1,468
85 years and over	194	485	719	1,497
Sex:				
Male	171	466	652	1,438
Female	194	484	705	1,463

[a]Includes life-care residents and no-charge residents.
[b]Data excludes residents of personal care homes.
[c]Medicare extended care facilities and Medicaid skilled nursing homes from the 1973–1974 survey were considered to be equivalent to Medicare or Medicaid skilled nursing facilities in 1977 and 1985 for the purpose of this comparison.
Source: National Center for Health Statistics. (1994). *Health, United States, 1993.* Table 138. Hyattsville, MD: Public Health Service.

as a nursing home. Physical limitations of a resident may eventually require movement from an intermediate care setting to a skilled care setting. For many elderly, this transition in living arrangements represents the last move before death.

Skilled Care Facilities   Skilled care facilities (SCF) provide a more restricted level of health care to its residents. According to Golant (1992, p. 152), these provide "nursing and rehabilitative services, usually based on doctor's orders, that are administered by registered nurses, licensed practical or vocational nurses, physical therapists, and speech pathologists on a frequent and regularly scheduled basis." Not surprisingly, residents in skilled care facilities, compared to those in intermediate level care facilities, are sicker and more likely to die. Research (Lammers, 1983) indicates that a much smaller percentage of residents in skilled care facilities do not need the level of care they are receiving. Rather than offering one level or the other, many nursing homes today are constructed to offer intermediate and skilled nursing care to their residents. Finally, according to the data in Table 10–7, skilled nursing homes are the most expensive.

Nursing Homes and Their Residents

Table 10–6 identifies a number of characteristics of the nursing home residents. For example, we know that as age increases, the likelihood of institutionalization increases. We also know that the majority of nursing home residents are women, white, and alone. However, the rate of institutionalization among elderly African Americans is continuing to increase (Burr, 1990). The characteristics of nursing home residents also identify those elderly most at risk for institutionalization. Roy, Ford, and Folmar (1990) identified elderly who live alone as being at greater risk for nursing home placement. Dolinsky and Rosenwaike (1988, p. 238) identify "income, health status, and race." Zedlewski and McBride (1992, p. 255) state that with an increasing number of elderly living alone, "the demand for formal in-home and nursing-home service will increase . . . because fewer elderly will be living with family caregivers providing significant levels of informal long-term care services."

There are two forces operating in the nursing home environment. First is the demographic reality of aging in America. Not only are we an aging society, but the oldest-old continue to increase most rapidly. This is the demographic category most likely to utilize nursing home services. On the other hand, 71 percent of nursing homes in the United States are operated for profit (U.S. Bureau of the Census, 1994), and, as the data in Table 10–7 indicate, the cost of nursing home care is increasing at a rapid rate. For-profit nursing home corporations understand that when demand for their facilities exceeds availability, costs will increase to those who can afford the services (Harrington, 1991).

Again, with regard to these institutional issues of cost, quality, and type of care the elderly are not the problem. Instead, the problem is socially constructed by government policies that promote and support a for-profit approach to meeting the long-term care needs of an aging population. This argument is perhaps best illustrated by mental hospitalization as the most restrictive living arrangement for the elderly.

Mental Hospitals   In the past, mental hospitals warehoused those who did not adhere to normative standards of behavior. The elderly have been well represented among those hospitalized with a diagnosis of mental illness (Dowd, 1984; Kiesler & Sibulkin, 1987). Explanations vary as to why the elderly are disproportionately represented in mental hospitals. Mechanic (1969) has argued that the lack of applicable alternative arrangements and increased family mobility led to the institutionalization of the elderly in mental hospitals. The political economy approach would question government policy in which class as well as age are used as markers that define normative behavior.

Beginning in the 1950s the United States embarked on an ambitious mission to remove as many mental patients as possible from these hospitals and place them in community environments. Although well intended, the end result was a dumping of many patients into the larger society without the requisite support system necessary to ensure a smooth and therapeutic transition (Gallagher, 1995). This relocation process has been particularly difficult for elderly mental patients. Gallagher (1995), citing Saathoff, Cortina, Jacobson, and Aldrich (1992), states that "elderly patients . . . are more likely to die during the year following discharge than those who remained in the hospital."

The deinstitutionalization of many elderly mental patients has resulted in a shifting of responsibility from one institution to another. Interpretations differ regarding the extent of this population shift. For example, Binney and Swan (1991) suggest that there has been a considerable increase among nursing home residents who were formerly in mental institutions. More specifically, Kiesler and Sibulkin (1987, p. 128) state that "for the elderly, about half or less of the increase of their mentally ill in nursing homes could be accounted for. . . ." Consequently, relocation from a mental hospital to a nursing home results in differential treatment by staff and other residents (Doress & Siegal, 1987). An additional alternative living arrangement for elderly who have experienced deinstitutionalization is that of homelessness. You may wish to reconsider your theoretical explanations of the scenario constructed in Chapter 3 based on the material just presented.

Critical Connection—Integrated or Segregated Living Arrangements: Democratic Ideals or Safety?

Throughout this chapter we have questioned the viability of numerous living arrangements experienced by the elderly. A number of variables consistently arise that influence the range of options available and the likelihood of potential relocation from one arrangement to another. Invariably, the criteria identified as significant relative to living arrangements is similar to that identified in earlier chapters. As a result, the question of whether living arrangements should be integrated or segregated is perhaps secondary to a much larger question: Is the living environment safe? If where one lives is dependent on one's financial ability, then significant differences exist between segments of the elderly population.

The argument over whether a particular living arrangement is democratic or safe is secondary to the more defining question. That is, what is the significance of economic and political policy in determining options? Consider the following scenarios. In the first is an elderly white couple living in a retirement community located in a southwestern state. Between their Social Security, retirement checks from their careers, and interest on stocks, they live a comfortable life. Crime is very low because of the homogeneity of the community and the level of security that the couple and others are willing to pay for to ensure tranquility. In the second scenario, an elderly widowed woman lives in a four-story walk-up in the central section of a metropolitan area. Although her flat is tidy, the building is in need of repair. The owner lives in another state and is using the building as a tax write-off. The woman has difficulty making ends meet every month. She receives a Social Security check that barely covers the cost of rent and groceries. She is afraid to visit a doctor for fear that she will given medication that she cannot afford. Increasingly, she restricts her activity outside the flat because of her fear of being mugged. Her fear is not unfounded. Others residents of the building have already experienced the increasing level of criminal activity, particularly violent offenses. The next chapter considers not only the reality of safety but also its perception. For some elderly, there are considerable discrepancies between the two. For others there is far too much similarity. It is to the consequences of that location that we now turn.

Chapter Review

This chapter examined a multiplicity of living arrangements experienced by the elderly. Many of these arrangements are related to characteristics of the elderly constructed in earlier chapters. Thus where the elderly live is the result of who they are. Many of the following questions not only address material found in this chapter but also connect previous material.

1. Identify the four migration patterns associated with the elderly. Characterize the elderly who fit each pattern. Based on previous material, what is the future for each pattern?
2. If you were to migrate when you retire, which pattern would be most appropriate? Explain why.
3. Are the elderly more likely to live in urban or rural areas of the country? Identify and explain the factors that influence this decision.
4. When (and if) you retire, where would you want to live? Explain your preference based on personal characteristics.
5. Of all the living arrangements discussed, which one is the most appealing to you? Which one is the least appealing? Explain your answer.
6. What are the characteristics of elderly in (pick any two) living arrangements? How do these characteristics differ? What accounts for this difference?

Glossary

Congregate living   A living arrangement in which elderly maintain independence within their own apartment but engage in communal-style eating and activity sharing.

Deinstitutionalization   A governmental policy whereby many patients in mental institutions were released into communities to live and receive treatment. Begun in the 1950s, it was believed to be a more humane method of treating those with mental disorders. Insufficient community resources and unwillingness to accept mental patients has created serious problems for those released.

Intermediate care facility   A nursing home in which the level of nursing care is minimal because of the ability of residents. Residents may be in need of assistance with activities of daily living.

Involuntary relocation   The forced relocation of an elderly person from his or her home or apartment. The person may be forced to move because of health or economic circumstances.

Migration   The movement of elderly populations from one location to another. Migration may occur intrastate as well as interstate.

Mortification ritual   A process by which a person is stripped of his or her identity. This is performed by members of total institutions on new members to ensure acceptance of the rules and regulations of the facility.

Physical settings   The physical environment of an individual. It is determined by economic and health status.

Return migration   Elderly who return to their home state after migrating to another. This usually occurs after the death of one spouse or the onset of a debilitating illness.

Skilled nursing facility   An institutional setting in which around-the-clock nursing services are necessary and prescribed by a physician. Addi-

tional supportive services (such as rehabilitation) may be defined as therapeutic for the resident.

Snowbirds   Elderly who live in a northern climate during the warmer weather and the southern climate during the winter.

SRO   Single-residence occupancy. Generally located in old hotels in the central sections of larger cities, SROs have single rooms rented out on a weekly or monthly basis. In the past, SROs provided a needed option for a segment of the elderly population. In the recent past, SRO units have either been torn down or converted to high-priced townhomes. The result has been an increase in the number of homeless elderly.

Total institutions   A facility that has complete control over its residents. The facility determines all schedules such as eating, activities, and bathing.

Suggested Reading

Goffman, I. (1961). *Asylums.* New York: Anchor Books.
This is the classic study in which Goffman describes the total institution. Must reading for anyone interested in the structure and dynamics of institutions.

Golant, S. M. (1992). *Housing America's elderly: Many possibilities/few choices.* Newbury Park, CA: Sage.
A recent and highly recommended book. The author provides excellent coverage of most types of living arrangements within which elderly reside.

Kayser-Jones, J. S. (1981). *Old, alone, and neglected: Care of the aged in the United States and Scot-*

land. Berkeley: University of California Press.
An excellent comparative study of institutional care for the elderly in the United States and Scotland.

Mendelson, M. A. (1975). *Tender loving greed.* New York: Vintage Books.
A classic exposé of the nursing home industry. Although dated, the book offers the reader a glimpse into the conditions experienced by far too many institutionalized elderly.

References

Angel, J. L., & Angel, R. J. (1992). Age at migration, social connections, and well-being among elderly Hispanics. *Journal of Aging and Health, 4*(4), 480–499.

Bane, S. D. (1991). Rural minority populations. *Generations, 15*(4), 63–65.

Biafora, F. A., & Longino, C. F., Jr. (1990). Elderly Hispanic migration in the United States. *Journal of Gerontology: Social Sciences, 45*(5), S212–219.

Binney, E. A., & Swan, J. H. (1991). The political economy of mental health care for the elderly. In M. Minkler & C. L. Estes (Eds.), *Critical perspectives on aging: The political and moral economy of growing old* (pp. 165–188). Amityville, NY: Baywood.

Bowker, L. H. (1982). *Humanizing institutions for the aged.* Lexington, MA: Lexington Books.

Burr, J. A. (1990). Race/sex comparisons of elderly living arrangements. *Research on Aging, 12*(4), 507–530.

Crystal, S., & Beck, P. (1995). A room of one's own: The SRO and the single elderly. In H. Cox (Ed.), *Annual editions: Aging* (10th ed., pp. 206–214). Sluice Dock, CT: Dushkin.

Dolinsky, A. L., & Rosenwaike, I. (1988). The role of demographic factors in the institutionalization of the elderly. *Research on Aging, 10*(2), 235–257.

Doress, P. B., & Siegal, D. L. (1987). *Ourselves, growing older.* New York: Simon and Schuster.

Dowd, J. J. (1984). Mental illness and the aged stranger. In M. Minkler & C. L. Estes (Ed.), *Readings in the political economy of aging* (pp. 94–116). Amityville, NY: Baywood.

Dunkle, R. E., & Kart, C. S. (1990). Long term care. In K. F. Ferraro (Ed.), *Gerontology: Perspectives and issues* (pp. 225–243). New York: Springer.

Fairchild, T. J., Higgins, D. P., & Folts, W. E. (1991). An offer they could not refuse: Housing for the elderly. *Journal of Housing for the Elderly, 9*(1–2), 157–165.

Filinson, R. (1993). The effect of age desegregation on environmental quality for elderly living in public/publicly subsidized housing. *Journal of Aging and Social Policy, 5*(3): 77–93.

Fournier, G. M., Rasmussen, D. W., & Serow, W. J. (1988a). Elderly migration: For sun and money. *Population Research and Policy Review, 7*(2), 189–199.

Fournier, G. M., Rasmussen, D. W., & Serow, W. J. (1988b). Elderly migration as a response to economic incentives. *Social Science Quarterly, 69*(2), 245–260.

Fuguitt, G. V., & Beale, C. L. (1993). The changing concentration of the older nonmetropolitan population, 1960–1990. *Journal of Gerontology: Social Sciences, 48*(6), S278–288.

Gallager, B. J., III. (1995). *The sociology of mental illness* (3rd ed.). Englewood Cliffs, NJ: Prentice Hall.

Goffman, I. (1961). *Asylums.* New York: Anchor Books.

Golant, S. M. (1992). *Housing America's elderly: Many possibilities/few choices.* Newbury Park, CA: Sage.

Golant, S. M., & LaGreca, A. J. (1995). The relative deprivation of U.S. elderly households as judged by their housing problems. *Journal of Gerontology: Social Sciences, 50B*(1), S13–23.

Gottdiener, M. (1994). *The new urban sociology.* New York: McGraw-Hill.

Harrington, C. (1991). The nursing home industry: A structural analysis. In M. Minkler & C. L. Estes (Eds.), *Critical perspectives on aging: The political and moral economy of growing old* (pp. 153–164). Amityville, NY: Baywood.

Hass, W. H., III. (1990). Retirement migration: Boon or burden? *Journal of Applied Gerontology, 9*(4), 387–392.

Higgins, D. P., & Folts, W. E. (1992). Principles and cash flow expectations of reverse mortgages. *Journal of Applied Gerontology, 11*(2), 187–199.

Kart, C. S., & Manard, B. B. (1976). Quality of life in old-age institutions. *Gerontologist, 16*(3), 250–256.

Kayser-Jones, J. S. (1981). *Old, alone, and neglected: Care of the aged in the United States and Scotland.* Berkeley: University of California Press.

Keigher, S. M., & Pratt, F. (1991). Growing housing hardship among the elderly. *Journal of Housing for the Elderly, 8*(1), 1–18.

Kemper, P., & Murtaugh, C. M. (1991). Lifetime use of nursing home care. *New England Journal of Medicine, 324,* 595–600.

Kiesler, C. A., & Sibulkin, A. E. (1987). *Mental hospitalization: Myths and facts about a national crisis.* Newbury Park, CA: Sage.

Ladd, H. F., & Yinger, J. (1989). *America's ailing cities: Fiscal health and the design of urban policy.* Baltimore: Johns Hopkins University Press.

Lammers, W. W. (1983). *Public policy and the aging.* Washington, DC: Congressional Quarterly Press.

Lawton, M. P. (1976). Social ecology and the health of older people. In C. S. Kart & B. B. Manard (Eds.), *Aging in America* (pp. 315–323). Port Washington, NY: Alfred.

Litwak, E., & Longino, C. F., Jr. (1987). Migration patterns among the elderly: A developmental perspective. *Gerontologist, 27,* 226–273.

Longino, C. F., Jr. (1981). The retirement community. In C. S. Kart & B. B. Manard (Eds.), *Aging in America* (2nd ed., pp. 368–399). Sherman Oaks, CA: Alfred.

Matcha, D. A. (1985). *Determinants of disengagement among nursing home residents.* Unpublished doctoral dissertation, Purdue University, West Lafayette, IN.

McLaughlin, D. K., & Jensen, L. (1993). Poverty among older Americans: The plight of non-metropolitan elders. *Journal of Gerontology: Social Sciences, 48*(2), S44–54.

Mechanic, D. (1969). *Mental health and social policy.* Englewood Cliffs, NJ: Prentice-Hall.

Mendelson, M. A. (1975). *Tender loving greed.* New York: Vintage Books.

Moss, F., & Halamandaris, V. (1977). *Too old, too sick, too bad.* Germantown, MD: Aspen Systems Corporation.

Mutchler, J. E. (1990). Household composition among the nonmarried elderly. *Research on Aging, 12*(4), 487–506.

Mutchler, J. E. (1992). Living arrangements and household transitions among the unmarried in later life. *Social Science Quarterly, 73*(3), 565–580.

Mutschler, P. H. (1992). Where elders live. *Generations, 16*(2), 7–14.

Mutschler, P. H. (1993). Where elders live. In J. J. Callahan, Jr. (Ed.), *Aging in Place* (pp. 5-18). Amityville, NY: Baywood.

National Center for Health Statistics. (1977). Utilization of nursing homes. *Vital and Health Statistics,* Series 13, No. 28. Rockville, MD; U.S. Department of Health, Education and Welfare.

National Center for Health Statistics. (1994). *Health, United States, 1993.* Hyattsville, MD: Public Health Service.

Palen, J. J. (1995). *The suburbs.* New York: McGraw-Hill.

Retsinas, J. M., & Retsinas, N. P. (1993). Subsidized elderly housing: Public-private partnerships on the brink. *Journal of Aging and Social Policy, 5*(3), 55–76.

Rogers, A. (1989). The elderly mobility transition. *Research on Aging, 11*(1), 3–32.

Roy, A. W., Ford, A. B., & Folmar, S. J. (1990). The elderly and risk factors for institutionalization: Evidence from the Cleveland General Accounting Office (GAO) Study 1975–1984. *Journal of Applied Social Sciences, 14*(2), 177–195.

Saathoff, G. B., Cortina, J. A., Jacobson, R., & Aldrich, K. C. (1992). Mortality among elderly patients discharged from a state hospital. *Hospital and Community Psychiatry, 43*(3), 280–281.

Schwartz, H. D. (1987). Irrationality as a feature of health care in the United States. In H. D. Schwartz (Ed.), *Dominant issues in medical sociology* (2nd ed., pp. 475–490). New York: Random House.

Serow, W. J. (1990). Economic implications of retirement migration. *Journal of Applied Gerontology, 9*(4), 452–463.

Serow, W. J., & Charity, D. A. (1988). Return migration of the elderly in the United States. *Research on Aging, 10*(2), 155–168.

Sherman, S. R. (1988). A social psychological perspective on the continuum of housing for the elderly. *Journal of Aging Studies, 2*(3), 229–241.

Stannard, C. (1973). Old folks and dirty work: The social conditions for patient abuse in a nursing home. *Social Problems, 20,* 329–342.

Townsend, C. (1971). *Old age: The last segregation.* New York: Grossman.

U.S. Bureau of the Census. (1992). Current Population Reports, Special Studies, P23–178, *Sixty-five plus in America.* Washington, DC: U.S. Government Printing Office.

U.S. Bureau of the Census. (1994). *Statistical abstract of the United States.* Washington, DC: U.S. Government Printing Office.

Van Nostrand, J. F., Furner, S. E., & Suzman, R. (1992). *Health data on older Americans: United States, 1992.* National Center for Health Statistics. *Vital Health Statistics, 3*(27), 143–159.

Watkins, J. F. (1989). Gender and race differentials in elderly migration. *Research on Aging, 11*(1), 33–52.

Winiecke, L. (1976). The appeal of age segregated housing to the elderly poor. In C. S. Kart & B. B. Manard (Eds.), *Aging in America* (pp. 331–346). Port Washington, NY: Alfred.

Zedlewski, S. R., & McBride, T. D. (1992). The changing profile of the elderly: Effects on future long-term care needs and financing. *Milbank Quarterly, 29*(2), 247–275.

Chapter *11*

Victims and Criminals

The older person's subjective sense of risk and subsequent act of self-confinement, to some extent, help to break the chain of events that would otherwise set the stage for his or her risk of victimization outside the protective confines of home. Unfortunately, however, self-confinement is not fool-proof. . . . Elder abuse, which is inflicted most frequently behind closed doors of private homes by a member of the elder's family or a nonfamily caregiver, is a well-known example of this kind of victimization.

—WATSON, 1991, P. 55

As with any age group, the elderly are not only the victims, but also the perpetrators, of criminal acts. When the elderly are the victims of crime and abuse, we as a society feel sorry for them. Unfortunately, we too often think of the elderly as being helpless. This paternalistic attitude reinforces the belief that the elderly are dependent on society.

We will discover in this chapter that once again what is assumed to be fact is not necessarily supported by the reality. An example is crime against the elderly. The consequence of this myth is an ongoing belief by the elderly that they (as a group) are more likely to be victimized. As a result, they feel dependent on others for support and protection from this created fear. For some elderly, however, crime is all too real. This is particularly true for the most disadvantaged elderly: those who live in central cities, are poor, and have few alternatives.

The most insidious crime against the elderly is that of physical, emotional, sexual, or financial abuse. Here all elderly are potential victims. We will examine this problem and the characteristics of those elderly most likely to be abused and the characteristics of their abuser.

Although the elderly are more likely to be the victim of crime, they also commit crimes. We examine who is most likely to become criminals and the types of crimes they are likely to commit, and discuss the consequences of their actions. Throughout the chapter, the social construction of crime as reality is addressed as a major problem experienced by the elderly today.

Victimizing the Elderly

Although the elderly are vulnerable to the violence associated with American society, they are not, relative to other age groups, more likely to be a victim of a criminal act. The elderly, however, report considerable fear of the world outside. This difference between perception and reality will be addressed in the following section.

Reality Versus Myth

We know that *victimization* rates among the elderly are lower than other age groups. These differences are presented in Table 11–2. Although the extent of crime against the elderly is challenged by the statistics in Table 11–2, a sobering reality exists. If, as Janson and Ryder (1983) suggest, the quality of life for the elderly is diminished out of fear of crime, then the numbers are not particularly important. This view is also shared by Khullar and Wyatt (1989, p. 101) who point out that "there are two levels of crime as it affects the elderly person: 1) the actual crime committed and 2) the fear or perception that one will be a victim of crime." The classic study demonstrating this point was published in 1975. According to the findings, fear of crime was identified over health and money as a "very serious problem experienced by public 65 and over" (Harris, 1976). The results of that survey are presented in Table 11–1. Others (Ferraro & LaGrange, 1988, p. 278) suggest that "fear of crime among the elderly has been exaggerated, principally because of conceptual cloudiness and operational obfuscation of the fear of crime concept."

The data in Table 11–1 are straightforward. Although the elderly are fearful of crime, the difference between what the elderly have experienced and what others think is significant. At the same time, the data in Table 11–2 identify the differences in victimization rates

TABLE 11–1   Personal Experience Versus Public Expectation: "Very Serious" Problems of Public 65 and Over Compared With "Very Serious" Problems Attributed to "Most People Over 65" by Total Public

	Personal Experience: "Very Serious" Problems Experienced by Public 65 and Over (%)	Public Expectation "Very Serious" Problems Attributed to "Most People Over 65" by Total Public (%)	Net Difference
Fear of crime	23	50	+27
Poor health	21	51	+30
Not having enough money to live on	15	62	+47
Loneliness	12	60	+48
Not enough medical care	10	44	+34
Not enough education	8	20	+12
Not feeling needed	7	54	+47
Not enough to do to keep busy	6	37	+31
Not enough friends	5	28	+23
Not enough job opportunities	5	45	+40
Poor housing	4	35	+31
Not enough clothing	3	16	+13

Source: Louis Harris and Associates. (1975). *The myth and reality of aging in America.* Washington, DC: National Council on Aging. P. 31. Copyright by and reprinted with permission of the National Council on the Aging, Inc., 409 Third Street SW, Washington, DC 20024.

TABLE 11–2   Personal Crimes—Victimization Rate, by Type of Crime and by Age: 1992 (Rate per 1,000 Persons Aged 12 Years and Older)

	Total	Rape	Robbery	*Assault* Total	Aggravated	*Larceny* Simple	Theft
Total	91.2	0.7	5.9	25.5	9.0	16.5	59.2
12–15 years old	171.0	1.1	9.8	64.8	20.1	44.7	95.3
16–19 years old	172.7	1.6	15.4	60.9	26.3	34.5	94.8
20–24 years old	177.0	2.6	11.4	56.0	18.1	38.0	106.9
25–34 years old	111.1	0.5	7.7	29.4	9.3	20.1	73.4
35–49 years old	75.1	0.4	3.8	17.1	6.8	10.2	53.9
50–64 years old	43.3	0.1	2.8	7.1	2.3	4.8	33.3
65 years and older	21.1	0.2	1.5	3.1	1.3	1.8	16.3

Source: U.S. Bureau of the Census. (1994). *Statistical abstract of the United States* (114th ed.). Table 311. Washington, DC.

by age. According to the data the elderly, relative to other age groups, experience the lowest rates of victimization.

Types of Criminal Activity Against the Elderly

Although the elderly experience the lowest rates of victimization, they continue to fear being the victim of crime. Perhaps one reason is the result of where crimes of violence against the elderly tend to occur. A cursory examination of Table 11–3 indicates that crimes of violence against the elderly are more likely to occur in the victim's home rather than in a less well-known area. As a result, fear of being victimized within one's place of residence is quite real for the elderly. Additional tables will provide further evidence of the discriminatory effect of crime against the elderly.

Among the elderly, crimes of violence are more likely to occur either at or near the home. This personalization of the crime environment is related to the elderly's increased fear of becoming a crime victim. If people cannot feel safe within their residences, how will they feel about going out in public? The consequence is an increasing social isolation of the elderly within their living environment. As a result, Miethe and Lee (1984, p. 412) "suggest that future attempts to explain fear of crime should also consider an individual's perception of risk of victimization and vulnerability to crime."

The next question is, What are the characteristics of crime victims? In other words, are the concepts from previous chapters relevant to understanding who among the elderly is likely to be victimized? An examination of the data in Table 11–4 indicates considerable support for earlier claims of differentiation on the basis of sex, race, marital status, location of residence, and social class position.

TABLE 11–3   Place of Occurrence of Crimes of Violence by Age of Victim and Type of Crime: 1987 to 1990

			Place of Occurrence			
	Total	At Home	Near Home	On the Street	In Commercial or Public Establishment	Else-where
Crimes of violence						
Under 65	100%	14%	11%	39%	21%	15%
65 or older	100%	25	25	31	9	10
Robbery						
Under 65	100%	13	9	52	16	10
65 or older	100%	20	21	37	13	10
Assault						
Under 65	100%	14	12	36	21	15
65 or older	100%	27	29	27	7	10

Source: Reprinted from the *Statistical handbook on aging Americans, 1994 edition* by Frank L. Schick and Renee Schick. Used with permission from the Oryx Press, 4041 N. Central Ave., Suite 700, Phoenix, AZ, 85012. Table B5-5.

TABLE 11–4   Average Annual Victimization Rates of Persons Age 65 and Over by Sex, Race, Marital Status, Location of Residence, Home Ownership, and Family Income by Type of Crime: 1987 to 1990

Number of victimizations per 1,000 persons or households

	Sex		Race		Marital Status			
	Male	Female	White	Black	Never Married	Widowed	Married	Divorced/ Separated
Crimes of violence	4.9	3.4	3.6	7.6	3.0	4.2	7.6	11.3
Robbery	2.0	1.2	1.2	4.4	1.2	1.7	5.1	1.7
Aggravated assault	1.4	.8	1.1	1.4	.8	.9	1.5	4.8
Simple assault	1.4	1.2	1.2	1.4	.9	1.4	.7	4.4
Crimes of theft	19.8	19.4	19.5	19.6	18.2	4.2	26.3	35.4
Personal larceny with contact	1.8	3.2	2.3	5.7	1.8	2.9	6.1	6.4
Personal larceny without contact	17.9	16.2	17.2	13.9	16.4	15.1	20.2	30.0
Household crimes*	82.2	74.3	70.9	154.1	77.6	75.1	71.1	110.4
Burglary	32.8	31.9	29.1	63.8	28.7	33.7	35.2	46.3
Household larceny	41.6	37.1	36.5	71.9	41.6	35.7	34.1	37.8
Motor vehicle theft	7.7	5.2	5.3	18.3	7.2	5.7	1.8	10.5

*Household crimes are categorized by sex, race, and marital status of head of household.

	Locality of Residence			Tenure	
	City	Suburb	Rural	Own	Rent
Crimes of violence	7.1	2.9	2.2	3.1	7.7
Robbery	3.5	.9	.4	1.1	3.6
Aggravated assault	1.4	.8	1.0	1.0	1.6
Simple assault	1.9	1.1	.7	1.0	2.2
Crimes of theft	26.4	19.6	11.4	17.8	26.7
Personal larceny with contact	6.5	1.2	.4	1.9	5.5
Personal larceny without contact	19.9	18.4	10.9	16.0	21.1
Household crimes	112.6	61.2	64.5	82.0	66.8
Burglary	42.4	25.6	30.7	33.6	28.3
Household larceny	57.3	31.2	31.3	42.1	30.9
Motor vehicle theft	12.8	4.3	2.5	6.2	7.5

(continued)

TABLE 11–4   Continued

	Less Than $7500	$7500–$14,999	$15,000–$24,999	$25,000 or More
Crimes of violence	12.0	8.4	6.5	6.1
Robbery	4.4	2.6	1.5	3.9
Aggravated assault	3.4	3.3	1.5	.6
Simple assault	3.9	2.3	3.3	1.5
Crimes of theft	29.1	30.4	40.3	60.8
Personal larceny with contact	7.1	4.2	5.7	4.3
Personal larceny without contact	22.0	26.2	34.6	56.5
Household crimes	76.3	70.2	81.3	96.0
Burglary	37.9	29.3	30.7	34.2
Household larceny	35.1	35.0	43.0	51.6
Motor vehicle theft	3.3	5.8	7.5	10.2

Note: It should be remembered that this measure represents only annual family income, not total assets.
Source: Reprinted from the *Statistical handbook on aging Americans, 1994 edition,* by Frank L. Schick and Renee Schick. Used with permission from The Oryx Press, 4041 N. Central Ave., Suite 700, Phoenix, AZ, 85012. Tables B5–6,7, and 8.

The data in Table 11–4 support many of the arguments stated in previous chapters. For example, African-American elderly are much more likely to be victimized than whites. Although elderly men are more likely to be victimized than elderly women, personal larceny with contact is directed at women. The result is increased isolation of elderly women. This is supported by the location of victimization. Regardless of the type of crime, residence in the city results in a heightened risk for victimization, particularly if the person is renting. However, elderly homeowners are at greater risk for household crimes. Although increased income is related to increased risk of victimization from crimes of theft and household crimes, the method of committing the crime is related to income. Note that the elderly with the lowest income are more likely to be the victim of personal larceny with contact and crimes of violence. Zopf (1986, p. 289) states that "many elderly, especially the poor and the less educated, are easy victims of hoodlums, confidence artists, and unscrupulous salespeople, and are unable to get protection or help after a crime occurs." In addition, elderly crime victims are more likely to be hospitalized as a result of the crime (Darnay, 1994).

The final statistical example of crime against the elderly is also the most deadly: the number of murders committed against those aged 65 and over. In 1992 there were 1,051 elderly Americans murdered. In other words, the elderly constituted 4.7 percent of all murder victims for that year. Elderly murder victims are disproportionately male (56.4 percent) and African American (30.5 percent) (U.S. Bureau of the Census, 1994). Perhaps the most disturbing part of these statistics is how the elderly are killed. Table 11–5 differentiates murders in 1990 by the type of weapon used against the general population and those aged 65 and over.

TABLE 11–5   Age of Murder Victim by Type of Weapon: 1993

Weapon	All Ages[3]	Age 65 and Over
Firearm	69.6%	36.6%
Knives or Cutting instruments	12.7	20.2
Blunt objects (clubs, hammers, etc)	4.4	12.7
Personal[1] weapons (hands, fists, feet, etc)	5.0	12.2
Poison	0.00	0.2
Explosives	0.1	0.3
Fire	0.9	2.9
Narcotics	0.1	0.0
Strangulation	1.4	3.1
Asphyxiation	0.5	1.6
Other weapon or weapon not stated[2]	5.2	10.0

[1] "Pushed" is included in personal weapons.
[2] Includes drowning.
[3] Because of rounding, percentages may not add to totals.
Source: Uniform Crime Reports. (1994). Table 2.11. U.S. Department of Justice, Federal Bureau of Investigation, Washington, DC: U.S. Government Printing Office.

Among the general population, murder occurs predominantly as the result of firearms. However, among the elderly population, the use of firearms is much less frequent. Instead, the method is generally much more personal. That is, the methods require the perpetrator to come in physical contact with the victim. As the statistics indicate, the elderly are two to three times more likely to be murdered by being stabbed or beaten than the general population. This personalization of the act of murder reveals the physical vulnerability of the elderly to their environment.

From the data presented, it would appear that the fear expressed by the elderly is directed at becoming a victim of crime (a personal trouble) rather than toward crime as a public issue (Clemente & Kleiman, 1976). As Lawton and Yaffe (1980, p. 773) report, "fear was higher (and independently so) in age-integrated settings, in high-crime areas, in larger communities, and among those who had been victimized." In addition to victimization by those unknown to them, the elderly are also targets of abuse and neglect by those they trust and love.

Elder Abuse

Elder abuse consists of a multiplicity of behaviors, ranging from physical and sexual to financial and emotional. We will define the problem, address the extent of elder abuse in this country, and examine various consequences of abuse to the victim as well as society.

It is important to realize that elder abuse is not a recent phenomenon. Stearns (1986) suggests that abuse predates modernity and may, in fact, have been worse in the past.

Because conclusive evidence does not exist, considerable speculation continues regarding the extent of elder abuse in earlier historical periods. Rather than engage in speculation, this section will address what is known today regarding the extent of the problem. We will also examine who among the elderly are most at risk for victimization. Throughout this discussion, the elderly are the victims, and in some instances the perpetrators, of this social problem. This is a particularly difficult social problem for many to address because of family involvement (Lucas, 1989).

How do we define elder abuse and neglect? The variation among states has created difficulty in the establishment of a single definition. As a result, it is difficult to ascertain the extent of elder abuse (Wolf, 1988). The following is but one definition that will serve as an example.

> Neglect is seen as an act of omission, of not doing something, of withholding goods or services, perhaps due to ignorance or stress on the part of the caregiver. . . . Abuse is generally viewed as being more serious. This is seen as a deliberate act of the caregiver, an intentional act, an act of commission. The caregiver means to inflict injury. (Douglass & Hickey, 1983, in Quinn & Tomita, 1986, p. 34)

Definitions vary, but there are five categories basic to explaining elder abuse and neglect: (1) physical abuse, (2) psychological abuse, (3) financial abuse, (4) violation of rights, and (5) self-neglect (Perrin, 1993, p. 162). Consider the extent of elder abuse: Perrin (1993), citing data from the Select Committee on Aging (1981), estimates that 1 in every 25 elderly persons (4 percent) is the victim of abuse annually. Other estimates range upward to 10 percent of the elderly (Pedrick-Cornell & Gelles, 1982, as cited in Perrin, 1993). As Hansson and Carpenter (1994, p. 58) point out, "estimates of elder abuse have been difficult to verify." Unfortunately, the rate of reporting elder abuse is low (Heisler, 1991). As of 1990 four states had statutes that allowed for voluntary reporting of elder abuse and neglect. The remaining 46 states and the District of Columbia had mandatory reporting (Schick & Schick, 1994). Olinger (1991) reports that some opposition exists to mandatory reporting. Those in opposition include service providers and the elderly. The reason for this opposition is the potential loss of control by the elderly over their lives. Thus what may appear to be in the best interest of some elderly may instead exacerbate the issue of aged dependency. We will move from a discussion of abuse in a political context to a societal-level analysis.

What are some of the characteristics of elderly who are abused? We know that they are twice as likely to be female. Pillemer and Finkelhor (1988) dispute this argument and report that among the elderly, males represented a greater percentage of those abused. We also know that the likelihood of abuse increases with the age of the elderly person (Schick & Schick, 1994). Theoretically, "exchange theory would suggest that as the elderly become more dependent and impaired, an imbalance in the exchange of positive reinforcements occurs in their relationships with their Caregivers" (Godkin, Wolf, & Pillemer, 1989, p. 209). Anetzberger (1990) attempts to broaden the range of factors associated with abuse. She identifies personal, situational, environmental, and cultural factors that contribute to elder abuse, as well as characteristics of the system. In addition to the victim, what do we know of the abuser? Perrin (1993) states that the abuser is often under considerable stress and may be abusing drugs or alcohol as well. More specifically, the relationship between the victim and the abuser is one of kinship (see Table 11–6).

TABLE 11–6   Abusers of the Elderly: 1990 and 1991 (Reports from 21 States)

Type of Abuser	*Percentage* FY90 (N = 21)	FY91 (N = 21)
Adult children	31.9%	32.5%
Grandchildren	4.0%	4.2%
Spouse	15.4%	14.4%
Sibling	2.6%	2.5%
Other relatives	13.0%	12.5%
Service provider	6.6%	6.3%
Friend/neighbor	7.3%	7.5%
All other categories	16.7%	18.2%
Unknown/missing data	2.5%	2.0%
Totals	100.0%	100.1%*

*Due to rounding errors, the total is not exactly 100.0%.
States reporting for 1990: Arizona, California, the District of Columbia, Florida, Illinois, Iowa, Kentucky, Michigan, Missouri, Montana, Nebraska, New Hampshire, New Jersey, New York, Pennsylvania, Rhode Island, South Dakota, Texas, Utah, Wisconsin, and Wyoming.
States reporting for 1991: Arizona, Arkansas, California, Delaware, the District of Columbia, Florida, Illinois, Kentucky, Michigan, Missouri, Montana, Nebraska, New Hampshire, New Jersey, New York, Pennsylvania, Rhode Island, South Dakota, Texas, and Utah.
Source: Reprinted from the *Statistical handbook on aging Americans, 1994 edition,* by Frank L. Schick and Renee Schick. Used with permission from The Oryx Press, 4041 N. Central Ave., Suite 700, Phoenix, AZ, 85012. Table B5–22.

As the data in Table 11–6 indicate, the person most likely to abuse the elderly is an adult child. The spouse of the elderly person is a distant second. Together, adult children and spouse account for roughly one-half of the elder abusers in this country. Other research, however, identifies the spouse as the most likely abuser (Pillemer & Finkelhor, 1988; Pillemer & Suitor, 1992). One explanation offered by Pillemer and Suitor (1992, p. S166) states that "violence by caregiving spouses may be more likely than by caregiving children or other relatives, as it is a relatively more socially acceptable response to the care recipient's behaviors." Because the caregiver role in American society has been assigned primarily to women, it is not surprising that the majority of abusers are women (Milner, 1990; National Center on Elder Abuse, 1995). The explanation of this gender-specific behavior is, in itself, an indictment of the status of women in American society (Williamson, Shindul, & Evans, 1985). Others (for example, Pillemer & Suitor, 1994) suggest that violence is gender neutral. This section concludes with an extended discussion of the various forms of abuse; the material in this section draws extensively on the work of Quinn and Tomita (1986).

Physical Abuse and Neglect   Among all the forms of elder abuse, this is perhaps the easiest to detect because the outcomes of this abuse are likely to be the most visible. This form can also be the most deadly. Examples of physical abuse and neglect include bruises, burns, pressure sores, ulcers, and malnutrition. Additionally, "deprivation of appliances such as glasses, hearing aids, and walkers can be abusive" (Quinn & Tomita, 1986, pp. 37–42).

Sexual Abuse   Research of sexual abuse among the elderly has not been as extensive as other forms of abuse and neglect. According to Ramsey-Klawsnik (1993, pp. 5–6) "little research, literature, or training on elder sexual abuse exists." Ramsey-Klawsnik (1993, p. 7) identifies a number of possible symptoms that may be associated with sexual abuse:

> Genital or urinary irritation, injury, infection, or scarring
>
> Presence of sexually transmitted disease
>
> Intense fear reaction to an individual or to people in general
>
> Nightmares, night terrors, sleep disturbance
>
> Phobic behavior
>
> Mistrust of others
>
> Extreme upset when changed, bathed, or examined
>
> Regressive behaviors
>
> Aggressive behaviors
>
> Disturbed peer interactions
>
> Depression or blunted affect
>
> Poor self-esteem
>
> Self-destructive activity or suicidal ideation
>
> Coded disclosure of sexual abuse

Psychological Abuse   Indicators of psychological abuse range from passivity to suicide. Psychological abuse is much more difficult to prove because the injury is not an obvious bruise or broken bone. Instead of a physical injury, the elderly person experiences emotional trauma, which may not lend itself to a simple medical model explanation and cure.

Financial Abuse   This type of abuse relates to the mismanagement of an elderly person's financial affairs. Activity that would qualify as financial abuse ranges from "stealing small amounts of cash from an impaired elder or shortchanging him at the grocery store to inducing him to deed over his house" (Quinn & Tomita, 1986, p. 47). Trapp (1987, pp. 11–12) identifies a number of indicators suggesting financial abuse:

1. There is unusual or inappropriate activity in the client's bank accounts.
2. Bank statements and canceled checks no longer come to the elder's home.
3. The caregiver expresses unusual interest in the amount of money being expended.
4. Personal belongings are missing.
5. The elder appears isolated from family and friends.
6. Signatures on checks or other documents appear suspicious.
7. There are implausible explanations about the finances of the elder.

Violation of Rights   This form of abuse and neglect is grounded in theoretical arguments basic to the structure of American society. For example, Americans have the "right to personal liberty, the right to adequate appropriate medical treatment, the right not to have one's property taken without due process of law, the right to freedom of assembly, speech, and religion, the right to freedom from forced labor, the right to freedom from sexual abuse, the right to freedom from verbal abuse, the right to privacy, the right to a clean, safe living environment, the right not to be declared incompetent and committed to a mental institution without due process of law, the right to complain and seek redress of grievances, the right to vote and exercise all the rights of citizens, the right to be treated with courtesy, dignity, and respect" (Quinn & Tomita, 1986, p. 50).

Self-Neglect   This type of abuse and neglect occurs as a result of action(s) taken by the elderly individual toward themselves. As a result, there are legitimate questions whether this should even be included. Quinn and Tomita (1986) raise the issue of free will in the determination of one's own outcome. For example, does an elderly person have the right to knowingly stop taking medication necessary to sustain life?

It is evident from the descriptions just presented that elder abuse and neglect occur within a multiplicity of circumstances and relationships. The consequence is that elderly in America become victims of abuse and neglect because they live in a social system that fosters an environment that creates the circumstances for victimization to emerge.

Finally, with regard to criminal behavior, the elderly are not without guilt. We will next examine the role of the elderly as perpetrators of crime rather than its victims.

The Elderly as Criminals

Relative to other age groups, the elderly engage in fewer acts of criminal behavior. The relationship between age and rate of criminal activity is negative. What we know is that according to the 1990 statistics from the Uniform Crime Report, those aged 65 and over accounted for 0.7 percent of all arrests. Interestingly, there is little differentiation between elderly males and females. Elderly women accounted for 0.7 percent of all women arrested, whereas elderly men constituted 0.8 percent of all men arrested. The lack of significant differentiation between the percentage of crimes arrested for by sex is of interest. The question is, Are elderly men and women arrested for the same types of crimes?

Types of Criminal Activity Perpetrated by the Elderly

According to the data in Table 11–7, elderly women are more likely to be arrested for property crimes, whereas elderly men are more likely to be arrested for violent crimes. Interestingly, compared to men, elderly women were responsible for a greater proportion of all murders. One explanation would suggest that because elderly women are more likely to be in a caregiver role toward their spouse, they may have opportunity and motive to engage in what the state defines as murder. Overall, however, elderly men were more likely to be arrested for violent crimes.

TABLE 11–7　Arrests of Perpetrators Age 65 and Over by Gender: 1993 (Selected Offenses)

Offenses Charged	*Percentage of Total*	
	Women	Men
Murder and nonnegligent manslaughter	1.1%	0.9%
Larceny-theft	1.4	0.9
Violent crime[1]	0.5	0.7
Property crime[2]	1.2	0.6
Liquor laws	0.3	0.5
Drunkenness	0.7	1.6
Vagrancy	0.9	0.9

[1] Violent crimes are offenses of murder, forcible rape, robbery, and aggravated assault.
[2] Property crimes are offenses of burglary, larceny-theft, motor vehicle theft, and arson.
Source: Uniform Crime Reports. (1994). Tables 39 & 40. U. S. Department of Justice, Federal Bureau of Investigation, Washington, DC: U.S. Government Printing Office.

Elderly men were also more likely to be arrested for drunkenness. This is an increasing problem for some elderly, particularly males. With retirement, some elderly males experience not only increased free time but also a considerable loss of social significance. Although differences exist between elderly men and women regarding the types of crimes they commit, Kercher (1987) reports few causes and correlates with crime by the elderly. For example, Kercher (1987, p. 294) states that "a number of factors hypothesized to influence crime by the elderly seemingly do not. These variables include marital status, income, occupation, and less certainly, residential mobility, education, and unemployment."

The Elderly in Prison

The consequence of committing a crime and being arrested is serving time in prison. Growing older in prison is not the "Norman Rockwell" image that we have created of the aging process. What we know is that the number and percentage of elderly prison convicts is relatively minor. However, data indicate that the numbers could increase. Table 11–8 provides a historical context within which middle-aged convicts continue to increase numerically and as a percentage of the total inmate population. Depending on the length of their prison sentence, these middle-aged prison inmates could become elderly convicts or ex-convicts. As American society continues to incarcerate an increasing number of its population for extended periods of time, the potential exists for the emergence of an elderly prison population. Unfortunately, there is little research that addresses this issue (Johnson, 1989).

TABLE 11–8   State Prison Inmates by Age: 1986 and 1991

	Percentage of Prison Inmates	
Age	1986	1991
Under 18 years old	0.5	0.6
18–24 years old	26.7	21.3
25–34 years old	45.7	45.7
35–44 years old	19.4	22.7
45–54 years old	5.2	6.5
55–64 years old	1.8	2.4
65 years old and over	0.6	0.7

Source: U.S. Bureau of the Census. (1994). *Statistical abstract of the United States* (114th ed.). Table 340. Washington, DC: U.S. Government Printing Office.

Following is my personal evaluation of this social phenomenon. I spent 5 years teaching at least one course per semester in a medium-security prison. Among the hundreds of student inmates enrolled in the various courses, there were only a few that I would categorize as nearing "old age" (perhaps age 50–55). In fact, elderly inmates were incarcerated in a separate facility in the state. The reason for the segregation is unknown, although the potential for victimization by other inmates would appear quite real.

Critical Connection: Victimization Is Not Just Physical

This chapter demonstrates serious consequences of aging for some segments of the elderly population. For example, being female increases the risk of victimization by strangers as well as relatives. Victimization, however, involves more than crime, abuse, or neglect. The elderly are also victims of the social structure, even in death. As this chapter and others have demonstrated, how and when we die is, to an extent, dependent on group-level characteristics.

Society differentiates among the elderly based on these group-level characteristics and creates the conditions within which they function. That is, married white males are unlikely to experience the victimization of death by strangers or a loved one. However, widowed women, particularly minorities, face an increased risk of living isolated from the larger society and are dependent on others for financial and physical support. The result is the potential for abuse, neglect, or other criminal behavior. Thus the physical and social environment provides the conditions within which specific outcomes may occur. The most permanent outcome is that of death. The next chapter examines the sociology of death and dying among the elderly chapter.

Chapter Review

This chapter addressed a number of basic, yet sensitive, issues relevant to the elderly. Problems of abuse and neglect are not always easy to confront because the abuser is generally known to the victim. The result is a cognitive conflict between believing in the role of kin and the reality of their behavior. For many elderly, the fear of crime is more real than the actual commission of the act. The following questions address many of these issues. Questions also extrapolate from earlier material in an attempt to link meanings between chapters.

1. Identify the myth and reality of crime for the elderly. Why is there such discrepancy between the two?
2. Are there particular segments of the elderly population that are more at risk as victims of crime? If so, who are they? Why?
3. Are there particular segments of the elderly population more at risk as victims of elder abuse? If so, who are they? Why?
4. Are those elderly most at risk as victims of crime the same elderly who are most at risk as victims of elder abuse? Explain this apparent relationship.
5. What would you propose as a deterrent to elder abuse? Think of this not on the individual but on the societal level.
6. The elderly engage in fewer acts of criminal behavior than any other age group. However, the elderly do commit acts of violence toward others. Discuss the role of the elderly as perpetrators of crime and their eventual incarceration.

Glossary

Elder abuse A general term that implies one or more types of abuse against an elderly person.

Financial abuse Any attempt to relieve an elderly person of his or her income or wealth. This may occur illegally in the form of deception or a scam or legally through guardianship of a person's estate.

Neglect A general term suggesting a lack of care directed toward an elderly person. Neglect can occur as a result of others responsible for an elderly person or through self-neglect initiated by aging persons toward themselves.

Physical abuse Behavior that inflicts physical pain and suffering upon another individual.

Psychological abuse Manipulation of an elderly person's feelings and emotions that causes distress.

Self-neglect Behavior by elderly people toward themselves that places their health or well-being in jeopardy.

Sexual abuse Forced sexual activity or actions that involve involuntary manipulation of another's genitalia.

Victimization A general term indicating the loss of rights because of others' actions toward a person.

Violation of rights The involuntary loss of rights guaranteed by law to all citizens.

Suggested Reading

Harris, L. (1976). *The myth and reality of aging in America.* Washington, DC: National Council on the Aging.
A classic that is must reading for anyone interested in the sociology of aging.

Krassen Maxwell, E., & Maxwell, R. J. (1992). Insults to the body civil: Mistreatment of elderly in two Plains Indian tribes. *Journal of Cross-Cultural Gerontology, 7*(1), 3–23.
A cross-cultural examination of elder abuse. This article also addresses the applicability of exchange theory.

Pillemer, K. A., & Wolf, R. S. (Eds.). (1986). *Elder abuse: Conflict in the family.* Dover, MA: Auburn House.
Although dated, this work offers a historical as well as a theoretical view of abuse.

Quinn, M. J., & Tomita, S. K. (1986). *Elder abuse and neglect.* New York: Springer.
A good source book identifying and defining the types of abuse and associated characteristics.

References

Anetzberger, G. (1990). Abuse, neglect, and self-neglect: Issues of vulnerability. In Z. Harel, P. Ehrlich, & R. Hubbard (Eds.), *The vulnerable aged* (pp. 140–148). New York: Springer.

Clemente, F., & Kleiman, M. B. (1976). Fear of crime among the aged. *Gerontologist, 16*(3), 207–210.

Darnay, A. J. (Ed.). (1994). *Statistical record of older Americans.* Detroit: Gale Research.

Douglas, R. L., & Hickey, T. (1983). Domestic neglect and abuse of the elderly: Research findings and systems perspective for service delivery planning. In J. I. Kosberg (Ed.), *Abuse and maltreatment of the elderly: Causes and interventions* (pp. 115–133). Littleton, MA: John Wright-PSG.

Ferraro, K. F., & LaGrange, R. L. (1988). Are older people afraid of crime? *Journal of Aging Studies, 2*(3), 277–287.

Godkin, M., Wolf, R. S., & Pillemer, K. (1989). A case-comparison analysis of elder abuse and neglect. *International Journal of Aging and Human Development, 28*(3), 207–225.

Hansson, R. O., & Carpenter, B. N. (1994). *Relationships in old age: Coping with the challenge of transition.* New York: Guilford Press.

Harris, L. (1976). *The myth and reality of aging in America.* Washington, DC: National Council on the Aging.

Heisler, C. J. (1991). The role of the criminal justice system in elder abuse cases. *Journal of Elder Abuse and Neglect, 3*(1), 5–33.

Janson, P., & Ryder, L. K. (1983). Crime and the elderly: The relationship between risk and fear. *Gerontologist, 23*(2), 207–212.

Johnson, H. W. (1989). If only: The experience of elderly ex-convicts. *Journal of Gerontological Social Work, 14* (1/2), 191–208.

Kercher, K. (1987). Causes and correlates of crime committed by the elderly: A review of the literature. In E. F. Borgatta & R. J. V. Montgomery (Eds.), *Critical issues in aging policy* (pp. 254–306). Newbury Park, CA: Sage.

Khullar, G. S., & Wyatt, B. (1989). Criminal victimization of the elderly. *Free Inquiry in Creative Sociology, 17*(1), 101–105.

Lawton, M. P., & Yaffe, S. (1980). Victimization and fear of crime in elderly public housing tenants. *Journal of Gerontology, 35*(5), 768–779.

Lucas, E. T. (1989). Elder mistreatment: Is it really abuse? *Inquiry in Creative Sociology, 17*(1): 95–99.

Miethe, T. D., & Lee, G. R. (1984, Summer). Fear of crime among older people: A reassessment of the predictive power of crime-related factors. *Sociological Quarterly, 25,* 397–415.

Milner, J. S. (1990). Elder abuse and neglect. In K. F. Ferraro (Ed.), *Gerontology: Perspectives and issues* (pp. 316–332). New York: Springer.

National Center on Elder Abuse. (1995). *Understanding the nature and extent of elder abuse in domestic settings.* Washington, DC: Author.

Olinger, J. P. (1991). Elder abuse: The outlook for federal legislation. *Journal of Elder Abuse and Neglect, 3*(1), 43–52.

Pedrick-Cornell, C., & Gelles, R. J. (1982, July). Elder abuse: The status of current knowledge. *Family Relations, 31,* 457–465.

Perrin, N. (1993). Elder abuse: A rural perspective. In C. Neil Bull (Ed.), *Aging in rural America* (pp. 161–170). Newbury Park, CA: Sage.

Pillemer, K., & Finkelhor, D. (1988). The prevalence of elder abuse: A random sample survey. *Gerontologist, 28*(1), 51–57.

Pillemer, K., & Suitor, J. J. (1992). Violence and violent feelings: What causes them among family caregivers? *Journals of Gerontology: Social Sciences, 47*(4), S165–172.

Quinn, M. J., & Tomita, S. K. (1986). *Elder abuse and neglect.* New York: Springer.

Ramsey-Klawsnik, H. (1993). Interviewing elders for suspected sexual abuse: Guidelines and techniques. *Journal of Elder Abuse and Neglect, 5*(1), 5–18.

Schick, F. L., & Schick, R. (Eds.). (1994). *Statistical handbook on aging Americans.* Phoenix, AZ: Oryx Press.

Select Committee on Aging, U.S. House of Representatives. (1981). *Elder abuse: An examination of a hidden problem.* Washington, DC: U.S. Government Printing Office.

Stearns, P. (1986). Old age family conflict: The perspective of the past. In K. A. Pillemer & R. S. Wolf (Eds.), *Elder abuse: Conflict in the family* (pp. 3–24). Dover, MA: Auburn House.

Trapp, L. (1987). Financial abuse. In L. Nerenberg (Ed.), *Serving the victim of elder abuse* (pp. 11–24). San Francisco: San Francisco Institute on Aging and San Francisco Consortium for Elder Abuse Prevention.

U.S. Bureau of the Census. (1994). *Statistical abstract of the United States* (114th ed.). Washington, DC.

Watson, W. H. (1991). Ethnicity, crime, and aging: Risk factors and adaptation. *Generations, 15*(4), 53–57.

Williamson, J. B., Shindul, J. A., & Evans, L. (1985). *Aging and public policy: Social control or social justice?* Springfield, IL: Charles C. Thomas.

Wolf, R. S. (1988). Elder abuse: Ten years later. *Journal of the American Geriatrics Society, 36*(8), 758–762.

Zopf, P. E., Jr. (1986). *America's older population.* Houston: Cap and Gown Press.

Chapter *12*

Death and Dying

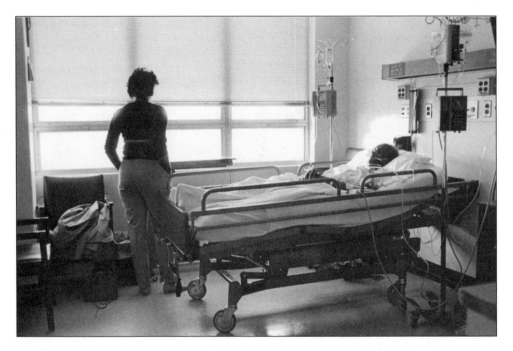

The dying process, like any other stage in human development, is influenced by numerous decisions. Although we often perceive the events that surround dying as automatic, inevitable, or beyond our control, in actuality they are constantly affected by cultural traditions and human decision makers.

The decisions "who," "where," "when," and "how" are part of the dying process of each individual. . . . We will deal with such decisions as who lives and who dies, where death occurs, how and when death comes about, who is to be with the dying patient, and how he is to learn of his imminent dying.

—KALISH, 1981, P. 519

This chapter will address the most personal, and yet one of the most social, acts we will ever perform: that of dying. On the one hand, death is an intensely personal process. Its experience on the individual level relieves society of the intimacy associated with the loss of a life. One is literally forced to "die alone." On the other hand, death and dying is a social process and event that incorporates a plethora of others who are directly and indirectly related to the dying person (Aries, 1981; see, for example, the position statement prepared by the Ethics Committee of the American Geriatrics Society [1995a] regarding the care of dying patients).

The dichotomy between the individual and social contexts of death and dying is perhaps best illustrated by the elderly. Because of advanced age and societal expectations of death on the basis of age, we generally identify death as a phenomena of old age. Yet the elderly engender familial images that reflect their connection to the kin network as well as the larger community.

This chapter will address death and dying as a process and an event. The chapter begins with a brief historical examination and definition of death and dying. We will then examine death and dying from a sociological perspective. Specifically, we will investigate the structure, methods, and organization of dying relative to the elderly.

This chapter examines death and dying as general concepts that are not necessarily related to the aging process. However, we know that the majority of deaths occur among the elderly. Thus, although we may not specify a relationship between death and aging, we know that death is more age specific to the elderly than to any other age category. We also know that the dying process can be described as a medical social problem (Levine & Scotch, 1970).

The Historical Context of Death and Dying

Our image of death has undergone considerable change. Illich (1976), drawing on the work of Aries (1975), presents six stages in the historical development of the image of death:

1. *The 15th-century "dance of the dead."* During this period death was an occasion for reveling in life. Dancing on the tombs of the dead occurred as an affirmation of the joy of life.
2. *The Renaissance dance at the bidding of the skeleton man, the so-called Dance of Death.* Here the image of death emerged as marking the end of life and the beginning of eternity. One indication of the switch between images was the proliferation of clocks, symbolizing the new time-bound perspective. During this period, the human body became an object for dissection. Increasingly, the concept of "natural death" emerged.
3. *Bourgeois death.* The industrial revolution led to the emergence of a new class structure that included the bourgeois. One of the new and developing set of services this class could afford to pay for was that of physician. The purpose of hiring a physician was to keep death away. This marked the first use of physicians as death delayers or preventers.
4. *Clinical death.* During this period (the 19th century), death was defined as the result of specific diseases identified by the physician. The role of the physician increased as those with the ability to pay continued to expand.

5. *The mid-20th-century doctor who steps between the patient and death.* The physician (and society) are responsible for ensuring that the patient be kept alive. The prevention of death is the paramount purpose of the physician.

6. *Death under intensive care.* We have created the conditions within which "unnecessary deaths" are to be prevented at all costs using every medical technique available. In essence, an attempt to deny death has emerged.

The progression through these six stages suggests that we have transformed the interpretation of death. Historically, we began by embracing death, but eventually the modernization of society created the technology necessary to combat death. As a result, death is now feared because we assume it to be avoidable (at least until old age). As Carpenter and Wylie (1977, p. 329) state, "modern society defies age and denies death," and McCue (1995) addresses the movement of death from a natural event to an enemy of medicine. Kastenbaum (1979, pp. 70–78) identifies four generalizations of death and aging that remain with us today: (1) there is a cultural gender bias in favor of males; (2) respect of the elderly is not a universal concept; (3) most people died in early age; and (4) societies have expressed mixed messages regarding aging and death. What Kastenbaum is able to identify in these four points is the historical position of the elderly within society relative to the issue of dying. Fear of aging and of dying become transformed into a single, undistinguishable image.

An example of our fear of death is the inability to define adequately what constitutes death. A number of attempts to clarify the definition have resulted in a increasing reliance on technology rather than physicians or others to make that determination. The following section addresses the issue of definition and attendant criteria of death.

Death Defined

In its most logical definition, *death* is the cessation of life-sustaining functions within a previously viable organism. Whatever the definition, a number of highly specific and testable hypotheses are inherent. This effort to establish criteria defining when death occurs has profound implications for the sociology of aging.

In 1968 an ad hoc committee of the Harvard Medical School identified four "characteristics of a permanently nonfunctioning brain" (Ad Hoc Committee, 1968, p. 85): (1) unreceptivity and unresponsivity, which is associated with "a total unawareness to externally applied stimuli and inner need and complete unresponsiveness. . . ."; (2) no movements or breathing, which is satisfied if there is "no spontaneous muscular movements or spontaneous respiration or response to stimuli such as pain, touch, sound, or light"; (3) no reflexes, which is satisfied when "the pupil [is] fixed and dilated and will not respond to a direct source of bright light"; and (4) flat electroencephalogram, which is satisfied when the technology is functioning and applied properly by trained personnel and the result is a flat EEG. The Ad Hoc Committee states that the four tests should be repeated 24 hours later. They also identify two conditions that must be excluded: hypothermia and "central nervous system depressants, such as barbiturates" (Ad Hoc Committee, 1968, pp. 85–86).

In 1970 the state of Kansas attempted to legislate a definition of death. This decision was based on the increase in organ transplants. Capron and Kass (1977, pp. 117–118, citing Law of Mar. 17, 1970, ch. 378, Kan. Laws 994) state that the Kansas definition is really two definitions. The first definition states that "a person is considered 'medically and legally dead' if a physician determines 'there is the absence of spontaneous respiratory and cardiac function and . . . attempts at resuscitation are considered hopeless.' In the second 'definition,' death turns on the absence of spontaneous brain function if during 'reasonable attempts' either to 'maintain or restore spontaneous circulatory or respiratory function,' it appears that 'further attempts at resuscitation or supportive maintenance will not succeed.' The purpose of the latter 'definition' is made clear by the final sentence of the second paragraph: 'Death is to be pronounced before artificial means of supporting respiratory and circulatory function are terminated and before any vital organ is removed for the purpose of transplantation.'"

Capron and Kass suggest that the Kansas definition does not adequately clarify the distinction between when a person is dead and when artificial life support systems can be terminated. Capron and Kass (1977, p. 119) offer an alternative definition of death:

> A person will be considered dead if in the announced opinion of a physician, based on ordinary standards of medical practice, he has experienced an irreversible cessation of spontaneous respiratory and circulatory functions. In the event that artificial means of support preclude a determination that these functions have ceased, a person will be considered dead if in the announced opinion of a physician, based on ordinary standards of medical practice, he has experienced an irreversible cessation of spontaneous brain functions. Death will have occurred at the time when the relevant functions ceased.

In an attempt to further refine the definition of death, the Task Force on Death and Dying (1972, p. 49) suggested that any criteria used in defining death should have the following characteristics.

1. The criteria should be clear and distinct, and the operational tests that are performed to see if the criteria are met should be expected to yield vivid and unambiguous results. Tests for presence or absence are to be preferred to tests for gradations of function.

2. The tests themselves should be simple, both easily and conveniently performed and interpreted by an ordinary physician (or nurse), and should depend as little as possible on the use of elaborate equipment and machinery. The determination of death should not require special consultation with specialized practitioners.

3. The procedure should include evaluation of the permanence and irreversibility of the absence of functions and a determination of the absence of other conditions that may be mistaken for death (e.g., hypothermia, drug intoxication).

4. The determination of death should not rely exclusively on a single criterion or on the assessment of a single function. The more comprehensive the criteria, the less likely will be the occurrence of alleged or actual errors in the final determination.

5. The criteria should not undermine but should be compatible with the continued use of the traditional criteria (cessation of spontaneous heartbeat and respiration) in the vast majority of cases where artificial maintenance of vital functions has not been in use. The revised criteria should be seen as providing an alternative means for recognizing the same phenomenon of death.

6. The alternative criteria, when they are used, should determine the physician's actions in the same way as the traditional criteria; that is, all individuals who fulfill either set of criteria should be declared dead by the physician as soon as he discerns that they have been fulfilled.

7. The criteria and procedures should be easily communicable, both to relatives and other laymen as well as to physicians. They should be acceptable by the medical profession as a basis for uniform practice, so that a man determined to be dead in one clinic, hospital, or jurisdiction would not be held to be alive in a different clinic, hospital, or jurisdiction, and so that all individuals who equally meet the same criteria would be treated equally, that is, declared dead. The criteria and procedures should be acceptable as appropriate by the general public, so as to provide the operational basis for handling the numerous social matters which depend upon whether a person is dead or alive, and so as to preserve the public trust in the ability of the medical profession to determine that death has occurred.

8. The reasonableness and adequacy of the criteria and procedures should be vindicated by experience in their use and by autopsy findings. (Task Force on Death and Dying of the Institute of Society, Ethics, and the Life Sciences, *Journal of the American Medical Association, 221*(1), 48–53. Copyright 1972, American Medical Association.)

These criteria provide the framework necessary for an adequate definition of death. Today, death is legally defined as

> The cessation of life; permanent cessations of all vital functions and signs. Numerous states have enacted statutory definitions of death which include brain-related criteria. For example, many states have adopted, sometimes with variations, the Uniform Determination of Death Act definition: "An individual who has sustained either (1) irreversible cessation of circulatory and respiratory function, or (2) irreversible cessation of all functions of the entire brain, including the brain stem, is dead. A determination of death must be made in accordance with accepted medical standards." (Nolan & Nolan-Haley, 1990, p. 400)

The brain-related criteria alluded to in the definition are the Harvard Medical School criteria discussed earlier. Readers interested in the legal construction of death are encouraged to read the article by the President's Commission for the Study of Ethical Problems in Medicine and Biomedical and Behavioral Research (1984). More recently, Halevy and Brody (1993) have suggested that there are three essential questions that must be asked regarding death: "When is a patient ready for the services of the undertaker rather than those of the clinician? . . . When is it appropriate to unilaterally stop supporting patients (as opposed to stopping support at the request of a patient or surrogate)? and When can organs be obtained for transplantation" (Halevy & Brody, 1993, p. 523). One of the answers that Halevy and Brody (1993, p. 524) provide is that "appropriate use of social resources should serve as the justification for the unilateral withholding or withdrawing of care." The emphasis on economics as the primary consideration in the maintenance of life creates significant problems for the elderly. As we know from previous chapters, the elderly are devalued in American society. If unilateral decisions are allowed on the basis of social resources (money), the elderly could potentially experience discriminatory lifesaving decisions. This historical context of defining death is fundamental to understanding the socio-logical explanation associated with death and dying.

The Sociology of Death and Dying

Now that we understand what constitutes death, we can begin to examine who dies, where, and how. The sociological explanation of death and dying addresses the relationship between the social structural framework of society and the group-level characteristics of the individuals involved in the process.

Who Dies and How

We know that death occurs primarily among the elderly. Table 12–1 disaggregates the data and presents a comprehensive view of mortality by cause among the elderly in America.

The data in Table 12–1 indicate that death among the elderly is dependent on a num-ber of characteristics. First of all, as stated earlier, the majority of deaths occur among those aged 65 and over. A comparison of men and women indicates that women are more likely to die in old age than are men. This is consistent with our knowledge that men die younger, leaving women as widows. With regard to specific causes of death, cancer deaths after age 65 are roughly equivalent between men and women. However, gender differences are evident with regard to the other diseases specified in the table. That is, women, when compared to men, aged 65 and over are more likely to die from these diseases. Racial dif-ferences are also evident in Table 12–1. Elderly whites are more likely to die as a result of these diseases than are elderly blacks. This is true not only in terms of overall percentages but also for diseases specified in the table.

TABLE 12–1   Percentage of Selected Causes of Death by Age, Race, and Sex: 1991

	All Elderly	Elderly Males	Elderly Females	White Elderly	Black Elderly
Total deaths	72.1%	65.2%	79.4%	75.0%	53.3%
Heart disease	82.9	75.7	89.9	84.6	69.6
Cancer	68.9	69.0	68.8	70.3	59.6
Cerebrovascular diseases	87.2	82.5	90.1	85.6	67.2
Pneumonia, flu	88.4	85.1	92.1	90.9	66.2
Chronic liver disease, cirrhosis	40.9	35.6	50.0	44.4	22.9
Diabetes mellitus	74.5	69.7	78.9	77.0	64.7

Source: U.S. Bureau of the Census. (1994). *Statistical abstract of the United States* (114th ed.). Table 126. Washington, DC: U.S. Government Printing Office.

The findings in Table 12–1 confirm earlier research by Kalish (1981, p. 562). Kalish identified five factors that he believed were related to the decision-making process regarding death:

Age. Relative to other age groups, the elderly are considered less "valuable" and accorded a lower social status (Blauner, 1976). As a result, less medical effort is directed toward lifesaving measures. A classic example of this is found in the work of Sudnow (1967).

Race. Minorities die at younger ages as a result of a lifetime of discrimination. This social differentiation on the basis of race creates economic and social disadvantages that prohibit access to health care coverage.

Sex. Women live longer than men. The influence of culture is unknown but is believed to be significant. In American culture, women are accorded greater latitude in seeking medical assistance throughout their lifetime. Because that opportunity is less available to males, the phrase "women get sick, but men die" is an indication of the general outcome experienced on the basis of gender.

Finances. Access to medical care in the United States is related to ability to pay (as well as the method of payment). For many elderly, Medicare offers access to the health care system. Because Medicare does not cover all health care costs (in actuality, less than half), the financial position of the elderly individual influences health outcomes.

Personality. This refers to how we interact with others. For example, elderly who are pleasant toward caregivers are likely to receive better treatment. Those elderly who are mean or antagonistic toward others are generally responded to in kind by caregivers.

If cause of death is related to age, then at what age is death likely to occur? Table 12–2 identifies various causes of death, the total number of deaths by cause, and the percentage of these deaths among the aged-65-and-over population. The data indicate that the majority of deaths occur after the age of 65.

These group-level characteristics establish the significance of a sociological interpretation of death and dying. Although the event is ultimately an individual act, the circum-

**TABLE 12–2   Cause of Death, Total Number of Deaths, and
Percentage of Deaths Among 65 and Over: 1990**

Cause of Death	Total Number of Deaths	Percentage of Deaths Among 65+
Major cardiovascular diseases	916,007	83.6%
Pneumonia	77,415	88.6
Chronic liver disease and cirrhosis	25,815	40.3
Malignant neoplasms, including neoplasms of lymphatic and hematopoietic tissues	505,322	68.3

Source: National Center for Health Statistics. (1994). *Vital statistics of the United States, 1990,* vol. II, Mortality, part B. Table 8.5. Washington DC: Public Health Service. 1994a.

stances leading to its culmination, that is, the process, is openly social. The sociology of death and dying places the event and process within a conceptual framework that requires an empirical base for substantiation. (Refer to Vernon [1970] and Bendiksen [1976] as examples of differing early empirical interpretations addressing the sociology of death; see also Lerner [1970].) Death occurs as a result of various circumstances. In particular, death as a result of suicide is of significant interest to the sociology of death and dying.

Suicide and Euthanasia

Suicide is the taking of one's own life. However, "it is very much influenced by the location of a person in social space and time" (Havighurst, 1969, p. 54). Suicide should be distinguished from *euthanasia,* which is "the allowance of death through the removal or withholding of treatments that prolong life" (Hardt, 1979, p. 68). The difference between suicide and euthanasia should be apparent. Suicide involves a person taking his or her own life. Euthanasia requires the presence and at least tacit involvement of another person in the voluntary taking of a life. There are two basic forms of euthanasia: active and passive. Active euthanasia (also referred to as mercy killing by some) refers to the direct involvement of the person assisting in the death of another person (Dr. Jack Kevorkian, for example). Passive euthanasia involves less direct means of aiding in death. For example, withholding feeding or removing a respirator would constitute passive euthanasia (Fletcher, 1977). Also used are the terms *physician-assisted suicide* and *voluntary active euthanasia.* Finn and Bacchetta (1995, p. 563) define "physician-assisted suicide (PAS) as a physician's knowingly providing the means to commit suicide to a competent patient who voluntarily makes this request and then uses those means independently to take his own life. Voluntary active euthanasia (VAE) occurs when a physician intentionally provides and administers the means to directly cause death in a patient who voluntarily requests this service." Because the majority of people who are seriously ill and die are elderly, it is not surprising that suicide and euthanasia (right-to-die issues) are topics of debate (Glick, 1991) within the legal, medical, and ethical communities (see, for example, the work of Sachs, Abronheim, Rhymes, Volicer, and Lynn [1995] or the Position Statement by the American Geriatrics Society Ethics Committee [1995b]). Leinbach (1992) presents research findings that do not support earlier data that attitudes toward euthanasia become increasingly negative with age. Montalvo (1991) discusses the need for development of choice-clarification skills among health care providers. Such skills help patients understand and address their medical condition. Trammell (1990, pp. 496–497) points out that if euthanasia were legal, some elderly might experience "unhappiness [that] will stem from guilt, or from resentment of friends or family, or from neglect by other people generated by the attitude that if a person could choose euthanasia and does not, then things must not really be so bad for that person. Even today, when those confined to bed or home have little or no choice but to accept their restricted conditions, most of us find it very easy to neglect doing simple things which could make their lives more meaningful and happy."

An example of euthanasia as an ethical issue is raised by Laney (1969), who argues that a mistake in judgment by the medical profession could result in an unwanted death of a patient. Although such an outcome is recognized as rare, raising such an issue creates immediate debate regarding the fallibility of life-and-death decision making.

Sociologically, the most famous work on suicide was published almost 100 years ago by Emile Durkheim (1951 [1897]). In this seminal work,

> suicide was hypothesized to be common in societies in which the degree of social integration (that is, the strength of the individual's social network) was very low (egoistic suicide) or very high (altruistic suicide). Similarly, suicide was hypothesized to be very common where the degree of social regulation (that is, the degree to which the individual's attitudes and desires are regulated by the society) was very low (anomic suicide) or very high (fatalistic suicide). (Lester & Yang, 1992, p. 38)

Relative to the elderly, suicide is a significant method by which death occurs. Suicide, as a cause of death, was not listed in Table 12–1 because it is of sufficient importance to be presented separately. Table 12–3 identifies death rates for suicides by sex, race, and age. Because the rates are consistently below 1 per 100,000, ages 1–14 are excluded.

The data in Table 12–3 indicate some rather significant findings. First, the highest rate of suicide is among elderly white males. In general, suicide rates among white males is directly related to age. That is, as white males age, their rate of suicide increases (Altergott, 1988). The data do not indicate similar trends among white females or black males. The most obvious question is, Why are elderly white males so much more likely to commit suicide than any other group?

What we know about suicide in general is that although females are more likely to attempt suicide, males are more likely to succeed. The reason is the method employed. That is, women are more likely to use measures that are less lethal (such as pills), whereas men are more likely to utilize methods such as firearms. In fact, nearly 80 percent of males aged 65 and over who committed suicide in 1988 used a firearm (Kaplan, Adamek, & Johnson, 1994). We also know that relative to other age groups, the elderly are more "successful" when they attempt suicide. As Schneidman (1973, p. 29) points out, "with people of increasing age, one sees an increasing number and percentage of subintentional deaths." *Subintentional death* refers to "deaths in which the decedent plays some partial, covert, latent, sub-manifest, or unconscious role in hastening his own demise" (Schneidman, 1973, p. 29).

To understand why elderly males are more likely to commit suicide, we need to remember some basic demographic data. We know that men die at younger ages than do women. However, men who survive into the oldest-old age category are likely to find themselves widowed. In Chapter 5 we found out that men are also more likely to identify their spouse as their best friend. Thus, with her death, the older male loses more than a spouse; he loses his closest (and in many cases his only) friend. In addition to the loss of spouse, advanced age also brings with it increased susceptibility to chronic and debilitating diseases. Glass and Reed (1993, p. 770) question whether "the losses of social status, power, and money that often accompany old age to be severe enough to suggest suicide as a welcome outlet." The apparent answer for a disproportionate number of elderly white males would seem to be yes. In an effort to specify the types of expected losses by the elderly, Glass and Reed (1993, pp. 771–772) identify eight broad categories:

1. Social roles at work, in the family, and in the community generally become more constricted as persons age.

TABLE 12–3   Death Rates for Suicide According to Sex, Race, and Age: United States, Selected Years

Sex, Race, and Age	Deaths per 100,000 resident population					
	1950[1]	1960[1]	1970	1980	1990	1991
All races						
15–24 years	4.5	5.2	8.8	12.3	13.2	13.1
25–34 years	9.1	10.0	14.1	16.0	15.2	15.2
35–44 years	14.3	14.2	16.9	15.4	15.3	14.7
45–54 years	20.9	20.7	20.0	15.9	14.8	15.5
55–64 years	27.0	23.7	21.4	15.9	16.0	15.4
65–74 years	29.3	23.0	20.8	16.9	17.9	16.9
75–84 years	31.1	27.9	21.2	19.1	24.9	23.5
85 years and over	28.8	26.0	19.0	19.2	22.2	24.0
White male						
15–24 years	6.6	8.6	13.9	21.4	23.2	23.0
25–34 years	13.8	14.9	19.9	25.6	25.6	26.1
35–44 years	22.4	21.9	23.3	23.5	25.3	24.7
45–54 years	34.1	33.7	29.5	24.2	24.8	25.3
55–64 years	45.9	40.2	35.0	25.8	27.5	26.8
65–74 years	53.2	42.0	38.7	32.5	34.2	32.6
75–84 years	61.9	55.7	45.5	45.5	60.2	56.1
85 years and over	61.9	61.3	45.8	52.8	70.3	75.1
Black male						
15–24 years	4.9	4.1	10.5	12.3	15.1	16.4
25–34 years	9.3	12.4	19.2	21.8	21.9	21.1
35–44 years	10.4	12.8	12.6	15.6	16.9	15.2
45–54 years	10.4	10.8	13.8	12.0	14.8	14.3
55–64 years	16.5	16.2	10.6	11.7	10.8	13.0
65–74 years	10.0	11.3	8.7	11.1	14.7	13.8
75–84 years	—	6.6	8.9	10.5	14.4	21.6
85 years and over	—	6.9	8.7*	18.9*	19.6*	17.4*
White female						
15–24 years	2.7	2.3	4.2	4.6	4.2	4.2
25–34 years	5.2	5.8	9.0	7.5	6.0	5.8
35–44 years	8.2	8.1	13.0	9.1	7.4	7.2
45–54 years	10.5	10.9	13.5	10.2	7.5	8.3
55–64 years	10.7	10.9	12.3	9.1	8.0	7.1
65–74 years	10.6	8.8	9.6	7.0	7.2	6.4
75–84 years	8.4	9.2	7.2	5.7	6.7	6.0
85 years and over	8.9	6.1	5.8	5.8	5.4	6.6
Black female						
15–24 years	1.8*	1.3*	3.8	2.3	2.3	1.6
25–34 years	2.6	3.0	5.7	4.1	3.7	3.3
35–44 years	2.0	3.0	3.7	4.6	4.0	2.9
45–54 years	3.5	3.1	3.7	2.8	3.2	3.0
55–64 years	1.1*	3.0	2.0*	2.3	2.6	2.1
65–74 years	1.9*	2.3*	2.9*	1.7*	2.6	2.4
75–84 years	—	1.3*	1.7*	1.4*	0.6*	1.4*
85 years and over	—	*—	2.8*	*—	2.6*	1.2*

[1] Includes deaths of nonresidents of the United States.
*Based on fewer than 20 deaths.
Source: National Center for Health Statistics. (1994). *Health, United States, 1993.* Table 52. Hyattsville, MD: Public Health Service. 1994b.

2. Retirement leads to reduced income and may result in lowered status, prestige, and influence.

3. In a society that values youth and health, older persons may come to feel devalued and useless.

4. Elderly persons often experience sensory and perceptual losses, such as hearing and visual impairments, that can limit their mobility and their ability to interact with other people.

5. As persons age, they are more likely to develop chronic illnesses. These illnesses can be painful and expensive, and they can lead to increasing dependence and confinement and greater isolation from others.

6. As elderly persons lose physical strength and stamina, experience sensory losses, and develop chronic illnesses, they may lose self-esteem and develop negative body images.

7. Elderly persons also experience loss through the deaths of their loved ones, including spouses, parents, children, and friends.

8. If their physical and social circumstances necessitate institutionalization, elderly persons face losses resulting from leaving familiar homes and communities. They lose their freedom, and they must adjust to dependence, restricted mobility, and smaller life space. (From *Educational Gerontology,* Vol. 19 (8), pp. 771–772, J. Conrad Glass Jr. and Susan E. Reed, Taylor & Francis 1101 Vermont Ave. N.W. Ste. 200, Washington, DC. Reproduced with permission. All rights reserved.)

What we know then, is that age alone is not the only reason why elderly commit suicide. Other risk factors must also be examined (Blazer, 1991) such as medical condition (Grollman, 1971) or vulnerability (Weisman, 1991). Vulnerability emerges when the elderly person feels dependent on others for support (financial, emotional, physical) and is unable to reciprocate. Increasingly, such dependence is the result of "where" death occurs: within an institutional setting. The significance of this shift in the location of death will be explored in the next section. Before we explore the location of death, we briefly examine the ethics of suicide. Society generally abhors the use of suicide as an individual means of controlling one's life and death. However, Carpenter (1993) raises a particularly compelling argument. Carpenter (1993, p. 362) argues that "one reason our blanket condemnation of geriatric suicide is so puzzling is that it contradicts the pervasive American ethic of self-determination." Carpenter (1993, p. 365) argues that "the elderly deserve autonomy and, thus, the privilege of suicide because of a lifelong pattern of learning that gives them the necessary perspective to decide what kind of life they want and what kind of life they don't want." How would you respond to this argument? Can you defend the right of society to define suicide as illegal? Is suicide rational behavior for an elderly person with a terminal illness who is capable of making informed decisions? Is there a "slippery slope" that could result in the death of elderly solely on the basis of age? These are the types of questions that our society must continue to address. Are there other sociological issues that should be examined relative to suicide?

The Institutionalization of Death

One of the most dramatic changes in death and dying has been in terms of location. Until recently, the majority of deaths in the United States occurred in the home (Feifel, 1973). Today death is most likely to occur within some type of institutional setting: primarily a

**TABLE 12–4   Distribution and Location of Deaths
Among Those Aged 65 and Over: 1990**

Percentage of Total Deaths 65 and Over

Age	Hospital[1]	Nursing Home	Residence	Other/ Unknown
65–74	68.5%	8.8%	20.1%	2.7%
75–84	61.6	19.5	16.9	2.0
85+	47.6	38.1	12.7	1.6
65+	59.6	21.7	16.6	2.1

[1] Hospital includes inpatient/outpatient or emergency room/death on arrival and status unknown.
Source: National Center for Health Statistics. (1994). *Vital statistics of the United States, 1990,* vol. II, Mortality, Part A. Washington DC: Public Health Service. 1994c.

hospital, nursing home, or, increasingly, a hospice. Table 12–4 identifies the location of death among persons over the age of 65 in the United States in 1990.

Based on Table 12–4, we know that the majority of deaths among the elderly occur within institutional settings, although the type of institutional structure changes with increased age. The following section will examine the dying process within the institutional setting, primarily the hospital.

The Setting

The transformation of death as a family affair to a public event has changed the dynamic interrelationship between the dying person and those who minister care. As a result, there have been various attempts to explain the dying process. One of the earliest is the stage theory of dying advanced by Kubler-Ross (1969). In her description of some 200 patients, Kubler-Ross suggests that the dying patient proceeds through a series of stages. Since the publication of her book *On Death and Dying,* considerable criticism of a stage approach to dying emerged (see, for example, Schulz & Aderman, 1974). Corr (1993, p. 72) identifies a number of limitations associated with Kubler-Ross. These limitations include the fact that "it is drawn from a particular social population dying in particular ways and in a particular time and location. It is organized around one author's clinical impressions, not around empirical data. Thus, this model depends very much upon the validity of a single author's interpretations." More specifically, Retsinas (1988) questions whether the work of Kubler-Ross is even applicable to the elderly. Retsinas (1988) discusses four possible differences between the elderly and middle-aged patients studied by Kubler-Ross. The argument by Retsinas (1988) offers a more thorough sociological investigation of death and the dying process among elderly patients. Here the dying process is understood within the context of society's norms, values, and role expectations. For example, Retsinas (1988, p. 211) argues that "illness forces a redefinition of role, especially if medical intervention cannot enable the individual to overcome the illness." Finally, as Fulton and Metress (1995, p. 314) point out, "effects of age, gender, religion, ethnic background, and life expectancy have not been systematically studied as they apply to Kubler-Ross's stage theory." At the same time, Fulton and Metress (1995, p. 314) recognize the influence of Kubler-Ross's work "in sensitizing us to the needs and rights of the dying."

Continuing within a sociological analysis of death and dying, Glaser and Strauss (1965, p. ix) examined what they identified as "awareness contexts," which "refers to who, in the dying situation, knows what about the probabilities of death for the dying patient." These awareness contexts will be examined individually as they operate within the structural confines of an institutionalized death system. (The following excerpts are reprinted with permission from Glaser, Barney G. and Strauss, Anselm L. *Awareness of Dying.* New York: Aldine de Gruyter. Copyright © 1965 Barney G. Glaser and Anselm L. Strauss.)

Closed Awareness   A closed awareness context means that the doctor and hospital staff are aware of the impending death of the patient. The patient, however, has not been made aware of the situation. In addition, the doctor and staff attempt to keep this information from the patient. Glaser and Strauss (1965, pp. 29–32) identify a number of

> structural conditions which contribute to the existence and maintenance of the closed awareness context. First, most patients are not especially experienced at recognizing the signs of impending death. . . . A second structural condition is that American physicians ordinarily do not tell patients outright that death is probable or inevitable. . . . A third structural condition is that families also tend to guard the secret. . . . A fourth structural condition is related both to the organization of hospitals and to the commitments of personnel who work with them. Our hospitals are admirably arranged, both by accident and by design, to hide medical information from patients. . . . A fifth structural condition, perhaps somewhat less apparent, is that ordinarily the patient has no allies who reveal or help him discover the staff's knowledge of his impending death.

This context is often preferred by hospital staff and doctors. If the patient is unaware of an impending death, then control of the patient is considerably easier. The lack of interaction requiring communication of death is also welcome by many in the hospital setting. Whereas closed awareness offers control to the hospital staff, the next creates considerable game-playing between patient and staff.

Suspicion Awareness   In a suspicion awareness context, the relationship between the patient and hospital staff is strained. Here the patient suspects that death is likely. If staff will not directly confirm this suspicion, then the patient attempts to gain access to this information through manipulation of interaction with others. Glaser and Strauss (1965, p. 47) refer to this "as a fencing match, wherein the patient is on the offensive and staff members are carefully and cannily on the defensive." This awareness context has ramifications not only for the patient but also for family and hospital staff. For example, hostility between patient and staff may increase because of less-than-candid communication. The more the patient suspects that death is imminent but does not receive direct information that would either confirm or deny the suspicion, the greater the frustration with those withholding knowledge.

Mutual Pretense   According to Glaser and Strauss (1965, p. 64), a mutual pretense awareness context exists "when patient and staff both know that the patient is dying but pretend otherwise—when both agree to act as if he were going to live. . . . Either party can initiate his share of the context; it ends when one side cannot, or will not, sustain the pretense any longer." The difficulties of sustaining this pretense are considerable. To begin, a mutual pretense is grounded in subtlety. For example, the extent of patient/staff interaction and the content of information discussed must always be guarded. Death as a topic of conversation must be either circumvented or restructured so that it does not address the known impending death of the patient. If the patient or staff is willing to openly acknowledge the impending death of the patient, then they have emerged into the last awareness context.

Open Awareness   This awareness context exists when the patient and staff openly acknowledge that the patient will die. For example, Foley, Miles, Brock, and Phillips (1995, p. 120) report that "42% of the informants reported that a physician told either the patient directly or someone else close to the patient that he/she was dying and 34% of the informants indicated that the decedents themselves had spoken or behaved as if they knew they were dying." However, even within this context, differences in information may lead to some ambiguity. For example, the patient may know that death will occur, but not when or how. If staff are aware of a time frame, they may withhold such information. Timmermans (1994, p. 329) argues that the open awareness context "should be split up into three different contexts. . . ." Timmermans (1994, p. 330) identifies these three contexts as "the context of suspended open awareness . . . the context of uncertain open awareness . . . [and] the active open awareness context."

Within an open awareness context, expectations arise regarding roles. Glaser and Strauss (1965, p. 83) identify two obligations of the patient. These obligations are that, first, "they should not act to bring about their own deaths. Second, there are certain positive obligations one has as a dying patient." The first obligation is quite obvious: that the patient should not commit suicide. The second obligation, however, suggests that there are standards for dying. Glaser and Strauss (1965, p. 86) enumerate these standards as the following:

> The patient should maintain relative composure and cheerfulness. At the very least, he should face death with dignity. He should not cut himself off from the world, turning his back upon the living; instead he should continue to be a good family member, and be "nice" to other patients. If he can, he should participate in the ward social life. He should cooperate with the staff members who care for him, and if possible he should avoid distressing or embarrassing them. A patient who does most of these things will be respected. He evinces what we shall term "an acceptable style of dying," or, more accurately, "an acceptable style of living while dying."

The awareness contexts provide further explanation to the intricacies of the patient-staff relationship. This is of particular importance to the elderly as they, relative to any other age group, are most likely to experience this relationship. For example, when a patient is near death, staff may begin to treat the individual as if they are already dead. This designation of "social death" allows staff to remove themselves from interaction with the patient (Cook & Oltjenbruns, 1989). Such institutional practices create an impersonal death arrangement for the dying patient (Blauner, 1976). Recently, attempts have been made to allow patients to "die with dignity," that is, providing patients with an environment within which death is more humane. This environment is known as hospice.

Hospice   *Hospice* is a physical environment within which a dying patient is allowed to die with dignity as defined by the patient and family. A hospice allows the patient to structure the dying process to fit his or her needs rather than the needs of the institution (Howell, Allen, & Doress, 1987). Although hospice is structurally distinct from hospitals, they do share a linguistic similarity regarding the meaning of their name (Cohen, 1979). Considering that the elderly are more likely to die than any other age group, hospice is particularly important. However, as a population, the elderly are underserved by hospice (Kalish, 1985).

Historically, hospice began in England with the opening of St. Christopher's in 1967 (DuBois, 1980). The first American hospice opened in the early 1970s in New Haven, Connecticut, as Hospice, Inc. (Dubois, 1980). DuBois (1980, p. 85) quotes the philosophy of Hospice, Inc.:

> We care for those suffering from advanced cancer or similar disease. We plan to show this concern in a program designed to meet the physical and spiritual needs of those, of all ages, who are unlikely to recover from illness. These needs can be met with skilled medical and nursing care, in the use of every scientific means of relieving distress and controlling pain. . . .
>
> This specialized attention focuses on the family as the unit of care. The unique needs of relatives will be our concern as well as the direct welfare of the patients.
>
> We maintain that this can best be achieved by providing the finest available skills of the medical, nursing and health-related professions, together with available community resources. Our aim is to provide a creative approach to meet the total health needs—physical, psychological, and spiritual—of each patient and family.

Thus hospice developed from the belief that death should be meaningful to the patient. At the same time, the patient should be directly involved in the control of the dying process. Sociologically, the hospice movement is an example of a social movement in the tradition of C. Wright Mills (Levy, 1994).

Mesler and Miller (1995) report a shift in hospice toward an increasingly business philosophy. They argue that this shift occurred with the advent of Medicare and Medicaid. As a consequence, hospice units are no longer confined to noninstitutionalized settings. For example, Mesler and Miller (1995) report that hospice units have been established in nursing homes. Generally speaking, however, the type of care provided by hospice is usually confined to the following environments: (1) home care, (2) inpatient care, (3) continuous care, and (4) respite care (Mesler & Miller, 1995). Another argument regarding growth of hospice comes from the work of Mor, Greer, and Kastenbaum (1988). They cite issues such as consumerism, naturalism, holism, discovering the total life span, and cost containment that have influenced the extensive growth of the hospice industry. Attempting to integrate the broader context of the health care industry with an aging population, Levy (1994, p. 355) argues that the growth of hospice was the result of "a collective response to strain in the personal and institutional arrangements of an aging society resulting from demographic change. Shifts in patterns of disease produced the necessary ingredients for a movement: constituency, ideology, resources, and tentative support from powerful interest groups. By 1984 over 1500 hospice programs existed in the United States. . . ." According to Brower (1995) these programs provide services to some 200,000 patients.

Regardless of the reason, the hospice movement has had a significant impact on how some people die. Those most likely to utilize hospice are generally "white, middle or working class patients from reasonably intact families" (Levy, 1994, p. 358). Unfortunately, because of requirements regarding availability of a caregiver, patients with other terminal diseases may not have access to hospice.

Nevertheless, once a patient is admitted, hospice units are regulated through the National Hospice Organization (NHO). Guidelines for hospice care include the following:

1. Include both the patient and the family as the unit of care
2. Be provided by an interdisciplinary team that includes the patient and family
3. Be directed by a qualified physician
4. Focus on social, psychological, emotional, and spiritual needs in addition to medical needs
5. Include bereavement follow-up services for the family
6. Be available 24 hours per day, 7 days a week
7. Involve volunteer assistance
8. Provide palliative care (that is, comfort care rather than curative care) (Cook & Oltjenbruns, 1989, p. 31)

As a location for death, hospice provides an alternative to the institutional structure of hospitals. However, hospice does not alleviate the differentiation in how elderly die or who among the elderly dies. According to Rhymes (1995) the average length of stay in hospice is 59 days and the average age of a hospice patient is just over 71 years old. As stated earlier, the availability of family and social class position also appear to be important considerations in the ability to provide care to a hospice patient (Rhymes, 1995). These concerns continue to raise the specter of societal involvement in the dying process.

Finally, death and the dying process inevitably leave others who grieve for the loss of a loved one. Based on demographic characteristics, we know that husbands are more likely to die before their wives than vice versa, and that as the elderly age, the likelihood of widowhood increases for women. Thus bereavement is primarily experienced by elderly women. These experiences include various emotional states as well as a removal from social interaction (Lund et al., 1985–86). Among the elderly, these experiences may be exacerbated by "deteriorating physical health and social relationships" (Lund et al., 1985–86, p. 214). Horacek (1991, p. 469) points out that "the elderly are more likely to experience multiple losses, such as the deaths of a spouse, friends, or relatives or the loss of roles, health, or income, over relatively short periods of time." In such instances, the elderly are reportedly experiencing "bereavement overload" (Horacek, 1991). Steele (1992, p. 394) found that in addition to young surviving spouses, "the elderly (66–85) should be carefully observed for despair, hopelessness, and loss of meaning in life . . . the elderly may also feel they are approaching the end of their own life and have nothing to live for anymore." The experience of bereavement is especially relevant to the elderly, and Horacek (1991, pp. 469–470) identified three societal trends that may influence the elderly as they attempt to cope with their loss. The first is that "losses should be anticipated with age. . . . Second . . . [society increasingly expects] people to do their serious grief work in private. . . . Third, there is a growing trend toward deritualizing the mourning process." These trends do not bode well for an aging population. Role expectations of participants in death and the dying process change as death is institutionalized and bereavement becomes a private matter.

Throughout this chapter we have addressed what is perhaps the most significant, personal, and yet socially defined process and event: the dying process and one's death. The final chapter will draw together the common threads that have become interwoven throughout the chapters of this book. We will also examine the future of aging in American society today and offer suggestions regarding social policy toward the elderly.

Critical Connection: There Is More to Growing Older Than Dying

One of the reasons why many fear the aging process is that it reminds them of their own mortality. In other words, aging has become a metaphor for dying. This chapter reminds us that although the elderly are the one age group most likely to experience death, the process of dying is quite varied. Thus we can understand death and dying as sociological concepts and address the differential outcomes as an expression of the status accorded various group-level characteristics within a given society.

The sociology of aging offers its adherents the knowledge to dispel the myths associated with death and the aging process. Death is the final outcome of life, but understanding death as a social construct allows us to reexamine our views and fears associated with this process. For example, the issues surrounding euthanasia generally examine the ethical and moral dilemmas associated with its outcome. What is generally overlooked are the sociological questions of why and how the economics of life dictate the realities of death. It is this promise of affecting change that provides the excitement associated with the next chapter. The application of the sociological imagination increasingly becomes a reality. The next chapter explores how the social construction of age creates social policies that inhibit the elderly from becoming fully engaged within the larger society. It also examines how social policy detracts from the real social problems that create the images and myths of aging. Finally, we will explore the future of aging in America. As we enter this final chapter, we should appreciate the aging process as a gift, rather than a burden, to society.

Chapter Review

This chapter addressed a number of significant issues regarding death and dying. In many respects, the chapter is an embodiment of the book itself. That is, the social construction of death and dying is illustrated as characteristic of aging itself. Although as a group, the elderly are the most likely to experience death, it does not mean that all elderly should be viewed as dying. Death and dying among the elderly are again differentiated on the basis of social class position, sex, and race. The following questions address the specific aspects of death and dying as well as the more general conceptual relationships evident throughout the material.

1. Chronicle the historical development of the image of death. Speculate on the possible emergence of a seventh stage. What would you call this stage? Why?
2. Identify the criteria established by the 1968 ad hoc committee used in defining death. Do you agree with these criteria? Explain your answer.
3. Reexamine the questions addressed by Halevy and Brody (1993). Are these questions appropriate or do they create an anti-aging bias in defining death? Explain your answer.
4. Identify and discuss the five factors that Kalish described as related to the decision-making process regarding death.
5. Suicide is of particular concern to elderly white males. Why is this group more likely to commit suicide than any other elderly group?
6. Should euthanasia be legalized for elderly diagnosed with a terminal disease? Beyond the ethical issues, explain your answer.
7. The institutionalization of death is illustrated with the work of Glaser and Strauss. With an increasing number of elderly in society, will this location and process of death continue? Explain your answer.

Glossary

Awareness context   Relative to the dying process, a context within which interaction occurs regarding one's own and others' knowledge of impending death.

Closed awareness   A context in which the doctor and hospital staff are aware of the impending death of a patient. The patient, however, is not aware of his or her impending death.

Death   An event in which specific biological functions cease within the human body as determined by a defined set of criteria.

Dying   A process by which an individual experiences physical, psychological, and social distinctions as a result of a terminal disease.

Euthanasia   An action whereby an individual wishes to die and is provided assistance, actively or passively, by someone else in the completion of the wish.

Hospice   An alternative to the institutionalization of death. Patients are accorded greater control of their impending death, and death occurs either within one's home or in a noninstitutionalized setting with family and friends available.

Mutual pretense   In which the patient as well as the physician and hospital staff are all aware of impending death. However, they hide their knowledge from each other and act as if the patient will live.

Open awareness   A context in which the patient and staff openly acknowledge that the patient is going to die. The staff may know how long the patient has to live, but the patient is not aware of this information.

Suicide   An action whereby a person takes his or her own life. The highest rate of suicide is found among elderly white males.

Suspicion awareness   A context in which the patient suspects that he or she is going to die. If staff will not confirm the patient's suspicions, there is an ongoing attempt to manipulate information from the other to find out what the other knows.

Suggested Reading

Gervais, K. G. (1986). *Redefining death.* New Haven, CT: Yale University Press.
Although the author is a philosopher, the book addresses the basic foundations of death. The chapter on the contemporary history of the problem is of particular significance.

Glaser, B. G., & Strauss, A. L. (1965). *Awareness of dying.* Chicago: Aldine.
A sociological classic in which a number of awareness contexts of dying were assessed. The authors address the social context within which dying occurs. Must reading for anyone interested in death and dying.

Kubler-Ross, E. (1969). *On death and dying.* New York: Macmillan.
A classic among those interested in death and dying. Although later criticized, this book established the framework for discussion on death and dying for a considerable period of time.

Sudnow, D. (1967). *Passing on: The social organization of dying.* Englewood Cliffs, NJ: Prentice-Hall.
A classic examination of the structural influences on who dies and why. This is must reading for any student seriously considering a career in sociology in general and aging in particular.

References

Ad Hoc Committee of the Harvard Medical School to Examine the Definition of Brain Death. (1968, August). A definition of irreversible coma. *Journal of the American Medical Association, 205,* 85–88.

Altergott, K. (1988). Qualities of daily life and suicide in old age: A comparative perspective. *Journal of Cross-Cultural Gerontology, 3*(4), 361–376.

American Geriatrics Society Ethics Committee. (1995a). The care of dying patients: A position statement from the American Geriatrics Society. *Journal of the American Geriatric Society, 43*(5), 577–578.

American Geriatrics Society Ethics Committee. (1995b). Physician-assisted suicide and voluntary active euthanasia. *Journal of the American Geriatrics Society, 43*(5), 579–580.

Aries, P. (1975). *Western attitudes toward death: From the Middle Ages to the present.* Baltimore: Johns Hopkins University Press.

Aries, P. (1981). *The hour of our death.* New York: Alfred A. Knopf.

Bendiksen, R. (1976). The sociology of death. In R. Fulton (Ed.), *Death and identity* (rev. ed., pp. 59–81). Bowie, MD: Charles Press.

Blauner, R. (1976). Death and social structure. In C. S. Kart & B. B. Manard (Eds.), *Aging in America: Readings in social gerontology* (pp. 529–561). Port Washington, NY: Alfred.

Blazer, D. (1991). Suicide risk factors in the elderly: An epidemiological study. *Journal of Geriatric Psychiatry, 24*(2), 175–190.

Brower, V. (1995). The right way to die. In H. Cox (Ed.), *Annual Editions: Aging* (10th ed., pp. 163–166). Guilford, CT: Dushkin.

Capron, A. M., & Kass, L. R. (1977). A statutory definition of the standards for determining human death: An appraisal and a proposal. In R. F. Weir (Ed.), *Ethical issues in death and dying* (pp. 103–124). New York: Columbia University Press.

Carpenter, B. D. (1993). A review and new look at ethical suicide in advanced age. *Gerontologist, 33*(3), 359–365.

Carpenter, J. O., & Wylie, C. M. (1977). On aging, dying, and denying: Delivering care to older dying patients. In J. P. Carse & A. B. Dallery (Eds.), *Death and society: A book of readings and sources* (pp. 327–335). New York: Harcourt Brace Jovanovich.

Cohen, K. P. (1979). *Hospice: Prescription for terminal care.* Germantown, MD: Aspen Systems Corporation.

Cook, A. S., & Oltjenbruns, K. A. (1989). *Dying and grieving: Lifespan and family perspectives.* New York: Holt, Rinehart and Winston.

Corr, C. A. (1993). Coping with dying: Lessons that we should and should not learn from the work of Elisabeth Kubler-Ross. *Death Studies, 17,* 69–83.

DuBois, P. M. (1980). *The hospice way of death.* New York: Human Sciences Press.

Durkheim, E. (1951). *Suicide.* New York: Free Press.

Feifel, H. (1973). The meaning of dying in American society. In R. H. Davis (Ed.), *Dealing with death* (pp. 1–8). The Ethel Percy Andrus Gerontology Center: University of Southern California.

Finn, J., & Bacchetta, M. D. (1995). Framing the physician-assisted suicide and voluntary active euthanasia debate: The role of deontology, consequentialism, and clinical pragmatism. *Journal of the American Geriatrics Society, 43*(5), 563–568.

Fletcher, J. (1977). Ethics and euthanasia. In R. F. Weir (Ed.), *Ethical issues in death and dying* (pp. 348–359). New York: Columbia University Press.

Foley, D. J., Miles, T. P., Brock, D. B., & Phillips, C. (1995). Recounts of elderly deaths: Endorsements for the Patient Self-Determination Act. *Gerontologist, 35*(1), 119–121.

Fulton, G. B., & Metress, E. K. (1995). *Perspectives on death and dying.* Boston: Jones and Barlett.

Glaser, B. G., & Strauss, A. L. (1965). *Awareness of dying.* Chicago: Aldine.

Glass, J. C., Jr., & Reed, S. E. (1993). To live or die: A look at elderly suicide. *Educational Gerontology, 19*(8), 767–778.

Glick, H. R. (1991). The right-to-die: State policymaking and the elderly. *Journal of Aging Studies, 5*(3), 283–307.

Grollman, E. A. (1971). *Suicide: Prevention, intervention, postvention.* Boston: Beacon Press.

Halevy, A., & Brody, B. (1993). Brain death: Reconciling definitions, criteria, and tests. *Annals of Internal Medicine, 119*(6), 519–525.

Hardt, D. V. (1979). *Death: The final frontier.* Englewood Cliffs, NJ: Prentice-Hall.

Havighurst, R. J. (1969). Suicide and education. In E. S. Shneidman (Ed.), *On the nature of suicide* (pp. 53–67). San Francisco: Jossey-Bass.

Horacek, B. J. (1991). Toward a more viable model of grieving and consequences for older persons. *Death Studies, 15,* 459–472.

Howell, M. C., Allen, M. C., & Doress, P. B. (1987). Dying and death. In P. B. Doress & D. L. Siegel (Eds.), *Ourselves, growing older* (pp. 392–403). New York: Simon and Schuster.

Illich, I. (1976). *Medical nemesis.* New York: Pantheon Books.

Kalish, R. A. (1981). The aged and the dying process: The inevitable decisions. In C. S. Kart & B. B. Manard (Eds.), *Aging in America* (2nd ed., pp. 519–530). Sherman Oaks, CA: Alfred.

Kalish, R. A. (1985). The social context of death and dying. In R. H. Binstock & E. Shanas (Eds.), *Handbook of aging and the social sciences* (2nd ed., pp. 149–170). New York: Van Nostrand Reinhold.

Kaplan, M. S., Adamek, M. E., & Johnson, S. (1994). Trends in firearm suicide among older American males: 1979–1988. *Gerontologist, 34*(1), 59–65.

Kastenbaum, R. (1979). Exit and existence. In D. D. Van Tassel (Ed.), *Aging, death, and the completion of being* (pp. 69–94). Case Western University: University of Pennsylvania Press.

Kubler-Ross, E. (1969). *On death and dying.* New York: Macmillan.

Laney, J. T. (1969). Ethics and death. In L. O. Mills (Ed.), *Perspectives on death* (pp. 231–252). Nashville: Abingdon Press.

Leinbach, R. M. (1992). Euthanasia attitudes of older persons. *Research on Aging, 15*(4), 433–448.

Lerner, M. (1970). When, why, and where people die. In O. G. Brim, Jr., H. E. Freeman, S. Levine, & N. A. Scotch (Eds.), *The dying patient* (pp. 5–29). New York: Russell Sage Foundation.

Lester, D., & Yang, B. (1992). Social and economic correlates of the elderly suicide rate. *Suicide and Life-Threatening Behavior, 22*(1), 36–47.

Levine, S., & Scotch, N. A. (1970). Dying as an emerging social problem. In O. G. Brin, H. E. Freeman, S. Levine, & N. A. Scotch (Eds.), *The Dying Patient* (pp. 211–224). New York: Russell Sage Foundation.

Levy, J. A. (1994). The hospice in the context of an aging society. In H. D. Schwartz (Ed.), *Dominant issues in medical sociology* (3rd ed., pp. 351–361). New York: McGraw-Hill.

Lund, D. A., Diamond, M. F., Caserta, M. S., Johnson, R. J., Poulton, J. L., & Connelly, J. R. (1985–86). *Omega, 16*(3), 213–224.

McCue, J. (1995). The naturalness of dying. *Journal of the American Medical Association, 273*(13), 1039–1043.

Mesler, M., & Miller, P. J. (1995). *Incarnating heaven: Making the hospice philosophy mean business.*

Paper presented at the Eastern Sociological Society Annual Meetings, Philadelphia, PA, March 31.

Montalvo, B. (1991). The patient chose to die: why? *Gerontologist, 31*(5), 700–703.

Mor, V., Greer, D. S., & Kastenbaum, R. (1988). The hospice experiment: An alternative in terminal care. In V. Mor, D. S. Greer, & R. Kastenbaum (Eds.), *The hospice experiment* (pp. 1–15). Baltimore: Johns Hopkins University Press.

National Center for Health Statistics. (1994a). *Vital statistics of the United States, 1990* (vol. II, part B). Washington, DC: Public Health Service.

National Center for Health Statistics. (1994b). *Health, United States, 1993*. Hyattsville, MD: Public Health Services.

National Center for Health Statistics. (1994c). *Vital statistics of the United States, 1990* (vol. II, part A). Washington, DC: Public Health Service.

Nolan, J. R., & Nolan-Haley, J. M. (1990). *Black's law dictionary* (6th ed.). St. Paul, MN: West.

President's Commission for the Study of Ethical Problems in Medicine and Biomedical and Behavioral Research. (1984). Model legislation and statutes on the definition of death. In E. S. Shneidman (Ed.), *Death: Current perspectives* (3rd ed., pp. 130–143). Palo Alto, CA: Mayfield.

Retsinas, J. (1988). A theoretical reassessment of the applicability of Kubler-Ross's stages of dying. *Death Studies, 12,* 207–216.

Rhymes, J. A. (1995). Hospice care—too little, too late? *Journal of the American Geriatrics Society, 43*(5), 553–562.

Sachs, G. A., Abronheim, J. C., Rhymes, J. A., Volicer, L., & Lynn, J. (1995). Good care of dying patients: The alternative to physician-assisted suicide and euthanasia. *Journal of the American Geriatrics Society, 43*(5), 553–562.

Sager, M. A., Easterling, D. V., Kindig, D. A., & Anderson, O. W. (1989). Changes in the location of death after passage of Medicare's prospective payment system. *New England Journal of Medicine, 320*(7), 433–439.

Schneidman, E. S. (1973). Suicide in the aged. In R. H. Davis (Ed.), *Dealing with death* (pp. 25–32). The Ethel Percy Andrus Gerontology Center: University of Southern California.

Schulz, R., & Aderman, D. (1974). Clinical research and the stages of dying. *Omega, 5*(2), 137–143.

Steele, L. (1992). Risk factor profile for bereaved spouses. *Death Studies, 16,* 387–399.

Sudnow, D. (1967). *Passing on: The social organization of dying*. Englewood Cliffs, NJ: Prentice-Hall.

Task Force on Death and Dying. (1972, July 3). Refinements in criteria for the determination of death: An appraisal. *Journal of the American Medical Association, 221,* 48–53.

Timmermans, S. (1994). Dying of awareness: The theory of awareness contexts revisited. *Sociology of Health and Illness, 16*(3), 322–339.

Trammell, R. L. (1990). Euthanasia and the law. In N. F. McKenzie (Ed.), *The crisis in health care: Ethical issues* (pp. 493–500). New York: Meridian.

U.S. Bureau of the Census. (1994). *Statistical abstract of the United States* (114th ed.). Washington, DC.

Vernon, G. M. (1970). *Sociology of death: An analysis of death-related behavior*. New York: Ronald Press.

Weisman, A. D. (1991). Vulnerability and suicidality in the aged. *Journal of Geriatric Psychiatry, 24*(2), 191–201.

Chapter 13

A Reassessment

Aging in America

We believe that the challenge to aging societies lies not only in creating a just distribution of resources between and within age groups but also in forcing us to move beyond the alienated form of old age common in advanced industrial society, where old people are pressured into retirement and encouraged to opt for trivialized leisure or the consumption of professional services. . . . A new moral economy of later life will require attention to quality of life issues in education, work, productivity, and health care at each stage of the life course. It will require social support for higher forms of activity: education, new forms of paid and unpaid work, and new arenas that bring old and young together. It will require too a vision of the whole life course which reaffirms the intimate interdependence of generations.
—MINKLER & COLE, 1991, P. 47

This book began with an observation: that individuals lose sight of the social environment within which aging occurs. The purpose of this book was to examine that social environment and its impact on the aging process, in other words, the sociology of aging. Olson (1994, p. 49) describes the relationship this way: "While aging is a universal phenomenon, the way we age is linked to the social context."

This chapter reexamines the basic threads that interconnect the aging process to the social environment. In addition, we explore the future of aging in America. More than the demographic imperative, how will the next generation of elderly cope with impending health and social policy changes, particularly at the federal level of government? Will those who have pursued "generational equity" be given legitimacy in an era of limited resources? We conclude with an examination of what is described as a "window of opportunity" in the formulation of social policy. Throughout, as in previous chapters, we address the influence of social forces impinging on and influencing the aging process. The Presidential Address to the 1995 White House Conference on Aging is an example of what role government should play with regard to Medicare and Social Security (Clinton, 1995). We will return to issues of policy. First, we begin with a reexamination of the social context of aging.

Growing Old in America: The Sociology of Aging

By now we have some familiarity with the demographics of aging in America. Specifically, when addressing the demographics of aging, we are concerned with the following:

> (1) the state of the older population, (2) changes in the numbers, proportionate size, and composition of this subpopulation, (3) the component forces of fertility, mortality, migration, and status changes that brings these changes about, and (4) the impact of these demographic changes on such issues as modified family and household structures, intergenerational relations and exchange, and policies on allocation of social, economic, and health-care resources. (Myers, 1990, p. 19)

Relative to the United States, the current 37 million elderly will eventually reach 68 million by the year 2040. As a percentage of the population, the population aged 65 and over will increase from the current 12.7 percent to approximately 22.6 percent of the total population. In addition, the distribution of the elderly population will continue to shift toward an increasingly older population. The consequence will be a threefold increase in the number of elderly aged 85 and over in the next 50 years (U.S. Bureau of the Census, 1989). Although significant, these numbers must be kept in context. That is, growth in the size of the elderly population alone is an insufficient basis for the construction of popular mythology or public policy on aging. Although population aging provides a framework within which policy analysis can make predictions, "we cannot at this stage comprehend its full impact as it extends into the next century" (Pifer, 1986, p. 391). Used here, "public policies are formal statements regarding a society's strategies or goals concerning the allocation of social positions, roles, and resources" (Gonyea, 1994, p. 238). Unfortunately, aging policy is all to often designed and implemented based on the misguided interpretation of available data. For example, Borgatta and Montgomery (1987, p. 25) state that "when analysis of aging policy is confined to options within existing frameworks and prevailing values, limits are placed upon the research questions and the research that is undertaken."

The aging process is constructed from a variety of sources. One source is that of the popular press, which would include newspapers and weekly newsmagazines. Vesperi (1994) and Cirillo (1994) illustrate how pictures as well as the written word can create images detrimental to the elderly. These images are converted to perceptions that are then used to interpret the aging process. As discussed in previous chapters, this results in a societal-level perpetuation of stereotypic gender-based norms of aging. Examples of how elderly are labeled can be found in the work of Johnson and Slater (1993). The media create an image within which a social context of aging is defined, and the structured inequality of society creates the framework for implementation of that definition.

We revisit the effects of social inequalities to illustrate the long-term impact of social policy. It is the development and implementation of such social policy that ultimately is identified as responsible for many of the social problems that the elderly continue to experience. As Johnson and Williamson (1980, p. 2) suggest, the elderly must deal with "four categories of injustice: exploitation, oppression, discrimination, and victimization." The relationship between social problems, social policy, and social structure is illustrated by Miller (1976, p. 131), who contends that

> economic pressures and political stresses mold the emergence and treatment of social problems. We should be more aware of this influence. Our analysis of problems and policies should not remain so narrow. They should include consideration of broader structural forces which shape general ideas and actions on social problems, recognition of common issues underlying many particular problems, and identification of concerns not currently regarded as social problems.

Specific to the aging process, the impact of social policy on economic opportunity is best illustrated by examining the traditional and the structural explanations of this relationship. The traditional explanation is grounded in the various programs that currently exist to provide assistance to the elderly population. American culture is dominated by values that stress individualism and a market explanation of economic outcomes. An outcome of this approach is the creation of old-age dependency on the programs and services established by the government. The result of such policy is to "promote age-segregated policies and services for a detached and dependent minority" (Estes, 1983, p. 247).

The structural explanation "starts with the proposition that the status and resources of the elderly, and even the trajectory of the aging process itself, are conditioned by one's location in the social structure and the economic and political factors that affect it. . . . Policy intervention from this perspective would be directed toward various institutionalized structures of society, in particular the labor market" (Estes, 1983, p. 247). Thus, on one level, the social context of aging is defined by the interpretation given legitimacy within the social system. Generally, that interpretation has been the traditional explanation. In addition to societal-level explanations of the social context of aging, other variables also result in differential outcomes for the elderly.

One relationship that has been stated repeatedly throughout this book is that men and women experience the aging process differently. This is particularly true in contemporary

America. Gonyea (1994) uses poverty as an example of recent changes between elderly men and women. Thirty-five years ago elderly men and women were equally as likely to be in poverty. Today elderly women are twice as likely to be living below the poverty line. Some of the reasons for this change are outlined by Gonyea (1994), who identifies four variables that affect elderly men and women equally but have significantly greater impact on women than men. These variables include (1) life expectancy, (2) marital status, (3) living arrangements, and (4) work-life experiences. Based on earlier material, we know that women outlive men, but men are more likely to be married and living with their spouse, and have held a full-time job (in the primary labor market) throughout their lifetime. The result is that although men die earlier than women, they are more likely to be financially secure.

A second reason for differences in outcome in the workplace is related to the allocation of job-related benefits. Social Security offers a classic example of discriminatory practices against women, particularly those who have worked. Gonyea (1994, p. 246) identifies three underlying assumptions of Social Security:

1. Only a small percentage of Americans would survive to old age to collect benefits, and those who did would receive benefits only for a brief time period. In fact, in the 1930s, for men who survived to the age of 20, their remaining life expectancy was approximately 42 years (Torrey, 1982).
2. Social Security would be only one of several sources of support—in addition to personal savings, pensions, interest and dividends, and other assets—in securing an economically viable future for the elderly. Social Security was never envisioned to be the sole source of financial support to older citizens.
3. The family would be the economic unit that receives the Social Security benefit. The typical family was viewed as being composed of a wage-earner husband and a homemaker wife, and marriage was regarded as a lifelong commitment. Women were seen as economically dependent on their husbands.

These three points clearly reflect a traditional family arrangement as well as the relationship between the individual and the federal government. Elderly males continue to gain financially from the current pension structure of Social Security, while women continue to lose.

The aging process also differs by race, socioeconomic status, and marital status and the interactive effects of these variables (see Crown, Longino, & Cutler, 1993). As a result, we know that elderly black women living alone are much more likely to suffer considerable economic hardships. On the other hand, married young-old white males have relatively low poverty rates and are in reasonably good health. The central variable within this argument is that of class. Increasingly, even more than age itself, one's social class position influences how we interpret the process (see, for example, Arber and Ginn [1991] for the relationship between gender, health, and class). Differentiation between elderly on the basis of social class has been evident throughout the preceding chapters. Elderly with the financial means are better able to provide the necessary health care, live in safer physical environments, and maintain their needs without becoming dependent on the larger society.

Growing old(er) may be an individual process whereby one progresses chronologically from one age to the next. However, in keeping with the knowledge provided by Mills

(1959), we must look beyond the personal troubles of the individual and understand how those troubles are reflective of larger public issues. This is particularly true of aging. Within American culture, age is a private matter. At the same time, industries abound trying to keep us from "looking our age." Two short but poignant expressions of this problem can be found in Macdonald (1993) and Myers (1993).

Beyond the individual level of analysis is the social construction of age. In other words, "old age . . . is socially constructed by the attributions and imputations of others" (Estes, 1991, p. 28). These "others" have the political and economic power to define and explain aging within society. Thus what is defined as a "problem" is constructed in an attempt to manipulate facts and analysis. The result is that "those who control definitions of aging in effect control access to old age benefits" (Estes, 1991, p. 28).

It is the interrelationship between the individual and society that provides for a critical analysis of the process of aging. We can now understand aging as more than a chronological advancement or a biological transformation. Aging is a social process that involves the individual in relationship with a societal-level analysis of the definition and explanation of age. From this relationship, we can discover the influence of our location in the social system and its influence on our aging process. This is the promise and value of the sociological imagination.

We turn to a set of relationships that provide significant meaning to the aging process and serve as an example of how the sociological imagination is applied. We are referring here to intergenerational relations.

Intergenerational Relations

Intergenerational relations exist at the family as well as at the societal level. Chapter 5 addressed many of the issues between elderly parents and adult children. Here we examine intergenerational relations on a societal level. The importance of this topic can be understood by reexamining the impending number of elderly. As the baby boom generation reaches age 65 and beyond, an increasing percentage of the population will be considered old and a decreasing percentage will be defined as young. In between, a decreasing number of work-age adults are paying into social and health care programs that provide support and leisure for the elderly. This perceived economic inequality between generations has resulted in increased resentment of the elderly and the creation of the "greedy geezer" image. However, an "age war" between generations is not only unlikely but an oversimplification of the issue. The organization most identified with the belief that economic inequality is the result of intergenerational inequity is known as Americans for Generational Equity (AGE). The empirical basis for AGE is the work of "Samuel Preston, then president of the Population Association of America . . . [and] the [former] President's [Reagan] Council of Economic Advisors" (Minkler, 1991, pp. 68–69). The argument put forth by AGE is simple yet deceiving. The Americans for Generational Equity portray the elderly as financially secure and disproportionately receiving income and services that could be better spent on children. AGE identifies Medicare and Social Security as the two major programs that benefit the elderly at the expense of others. What AGE does not address, however, is the fact that "one out of eight Social Security recipients is under the age of eighteen" (Achenbaum, 1986, pp. 29–30). In addition, the availability of Social Security frees younger generations from incurring economic responsibility for parents (Minkler, 1991). The argument put forth by AGE is also flawed because "the call for intergenerational equity represents a convenient smokescreen for more fundamental sources of inequality in American society" (Minkler, 1991, pp. 78–79). The elderly are not "stealing" from the children. Rather, the problems of poverty among children is the result of national policy (Neugarten & Neugarten, 1986), not how money is distributed between various age groups. For example, health care spending on the elderly pays the health care profession for their services. It is the cost of these services (dictated by the health profession) that makes health care for the elderly (and all groups) expensive. In addition, a sizable minority of the elderly live either below or near poverty. As a result, there is significant need among the elderly population for programs and services that assist the elderly in maintaining a modicum of basic existence. The following quotation illustrates the extent to which some are questioning intergenerational responsibility toward the elderly: "What is the proper—or at least the acceptable—proportion of public resources that should be devoted to the elderly, both in relationship to the health needs of other age groups and to other social requirements as a whole?" (Callahan, 1986, pp. 327–328).

Creating intergenerational differences between the young and the old is presented in the following by Richman and Stagner (1986). Consider the emotional context of this statement and how policy formulation might be influenced by it.

> The decrease in the percentage of children may have profound consequences for their public support. A society that requires young workers to help support an aging population may find itself demanding earlier entry into the labor market, forcing the shortening of childhood for some Americans. As other groups compete for resources, public expenditures for children may be cut back, and the tendency to consider children as special dependents, who deserve protection from adult pressures may be reversed. In short, as society ages, it may become easier to ignore the special needs of children. (Richman & Stagner, 1986, p. 166)

The problems of adequate funding for the youth of this society is very real. However, attempting to improve one generation at the expense of the other, or to assume that the elderly have benefited at the expense of children, misses the larger public issue of how much money is spent on all public programs in this country.

Finally, research does not support the argument that younger generations do not want to support the elderly (Street & Quadagno, 1993). This argument has been challenged, however, by the findings of Rosenbaum and Button (1995, p. 238), who point to a "statistically significant association between critical appraisals of the aging and the size of the aging population in the respondent's home counties." Thus the extent to which the elderly demographically dominate a particular geographical location may influence how the larger population responds to the needs of the elderly.

Although intergenerational relations have not deteriorated into an "age war," there appear to be areas of potential conflict. This conflict is fueled by an ideological belief in reducing the responsibility of government toward its citizens. The future of this conflict is uncertain. It is known that continued reversal or elimination of government programs will increase conflict between those receiving any form of governmental assistance. Considering the direction of the 104th Congress in general and the Contract with America specifically, there is the potential for increased intergenerational tension. Congressional efforts to divert monies from social programs will only intensify debate over what remains. Attempts to reduce Medicare and Medicaid could leave the elderly in a precarious position. If the general public supports efforts to reduce the cost of health care, the elderly will appear as "greedy geezers" if they fight against cuts in Medicare and Medicaid. If the present does not appear particularly optimistic, what is the future of aging in America? This chapter concludes with an exploration of some possible explanations.

A Window of Opportunity for the Future: The Importance of Social Policy

American history is replete with instances of opportunity for some particular segment of society. The elderly have been the recipients of a number of such opportunities in the past. In 1935 the passage of the Social Security Act established the beginnings of a new contractual relationship regarding retirement benefits between the federal government and its people. In 1965 Medicare and Medicaid began a similar relationship in the area of health care coverage. In both instances, the elderly, as well as other age groups, benefited from the passage of these legislative bills. Although Social Security and Medicare were major legislative benchmarks, they do not establish a public policy on aging in America (Rich & Baum, 1984). Rather, in each instance, there was a window of opportunity through which such legislation could be relatively assured of passing. As in the past, another window of opportunity currently exists for the creation of public policy that will benefit not only the elderly but the population in general. To continue with this metaphor, the window will remain open only so long. Although exact dates are impossible to predict, we know that the passage of the baby boomers into "old age" (65) will begin in the year 2011. This will mark the beginning of a significant shift in the population of this country. Differences exist regarding public policy implications of such an event, but it will nonetheless require a reexamination of the aging process. Political and social actions taken today will have ramifications over an extended period of time and will influence the lives of millions of elderly.

First, what is public policy? Williamson, Shindul, and Evans (1985, p. 6) point out that *public policy* "not only includes laws and regulations made by federal, state and local government, it also includes certain policies made by private industry because these decisions can have as significant an impact on the aged as those made by the government." Transferring these ideas more specifically to aging policy, Gold, Kutza, and Marmor (1981, p. 557) suggest that "if aging policy means an intentional, coherent, overall plan about what the United States should do about aged citizens, then the United States does not have a social policy on old age." The White House Conference on Aging is perhaps the one event that generally does produce social policy on aging (Pillemer, Moen, Krout, & Robison, 1995). More broadly, social policy on aging currently does exist on the issue of retirement. This is one area within which the federal government, business, and age are most intertwined. Because Social Security was never intended as the sole source of pension revenue, employees have had to rely on work and the workplace to supplement pension needs. Recent public policy has generally supported the notion of a timely removal of workers from the workplace. We know from earlier chapters that workers are accommodating this policy by retiring at an earlier age. Whether such a process is in the best interests of the worker or the workplace continues to be questioned. In a critical examination of retirement, Atchley (1993, p. 4) suggests that "the ways we conceive of retirement need to be conjoined with our more abstract ways of thinking about social life in general so both areas of thought can be enriched. Ideas of retirement can be broadened and deepened, and abstract social thought can be made more concrete, which may allow its improvement." Employing the critical perspective, Atchley (1993) continues his explanation by examining two significant shifts in the relationship between the individual and society. The first shift is that of *demassification,* which refers to "the breakup of large-scale social organizations and the mass culture that supported them . . . and is nothing short of a rediscovery of interactive community within various social institutions" (Atchley, 1993, pp. 15–16). *Status groups* (a group whose members consider one another equals) are replacing organizational structures as the basis for identification. The second shift is that of *post-modernism,* which is explained as "a philosophical shift that gives validity to the diverse normative results of culture making in status groups . . . with [an] antipositivist stance towards knowledge, [which] encourages anarchy in the marketplace of ideas" (Atchley, 1993, p. 16). Given an increase in status groups within post-modernism, an event (and process) such as retirement would have quite different functions compared to the present. As society changes, social policy regarding the most fundamental relationships between social institutions would be reexamined.

This analysis of social (aging) policy change assumes that the significance of major social institutions will, in fact, decline. Before we abrogate our social responsibility, however, it is instructive to understand what issues associated with aging policies have been identified in the past, as well as expectations for the future. Gold et al. (1981, pp. 579–580) identify a number of "issues . . . as significant in the prediction of future policy directions:

1. With the introduction of the SSI program, a reevaluation of the welfare function of OASI is needed.
2. Future policymakers must question the wisdom of programming around a constituency group rather than around a problem area.
3. Policy which is age-targeted results in a statistical artifact that misrepresents reality. Once a category of need is defined, it tends to be measured and analyzed by averaging the need only across the needy group. One argument in support of a national health insurance for older persons (Medicare), for example, has been that, on average, the elderly have medical costs that are twice those of younger groups. Would the same program have been supported if, instead of counting average costs across the aged population, one counted the number of all people who actually sustain large medical bills relative to their income? Given the latter statistic, the program might have been quite differently designed.
4. It is essential for future policymakers to acknowledge that there are costs associated with all policy decisions. There are political costs that may be sustained by the decision maker himself, but there are also costs to the intended beneficiary group, frequently in the form of unintended consequences.

5. A government that aims to better the lives of its older citizens cannot neglect the impact of its policies on family stability.

6. A final issue that will affect old-age policy focuses on the general question of public versus private responsibility. How much is the government responsible for supporting an older person in the manner to which he has become accustomed, and how much of that responsibility falls upon the individual himself or his relatives?"

These issues were identified in the late 1970s as significant to the needs of the elderly within the larger society. How many of these issues have been addressed (resolved) in the past 20 years? Although many of these points have resulted in political debate and academic research, enactment of findings into policy is much more difficult. Perhaps that is why policy issues may change somewhat but essentially remain quite similar in terms of the expected outcome.

The most recent example of the development of aging policy is the 1995 White House Conference on Aging. Here thousands of individuals from diverse backgrounds and from all 50 states converged on Washington, DC, to identify, discuss, and vote on those issues believed to be important to the aging community today and in the future. The theme for this conference is indicative of the future orientation of policy development. The 1995 conference was entitled "Preparing for Aging in the 21st Century." The panel (Pillemer et al., 1995, p. 259) who constructed the conference title also cite a number of examples that illustrate its significance. Consider the breadth of these examples, not only among the elderly, but all age levels:

1. Individuals must become more aware of their own future as older persons. They must consider the impact that choices they make earlier in life will have on their well-being in later years, including decisions about savings, health behaviors, residence, and other areas.

2. Our nation must prepare for changes in family life. Increases in the life span mean that most people will spend a longer period of time in a three-or-four-generation family. Spouses and children will increase in importance as major sources of support for disabled elders.

3. The health and social services systems must prepare for new demands for their resources. Dramatic growth in the population of the "oldest-old" will lead to increased numbers of older people with multiple chronic conditions and functional limitations. The demographic imperative will increase the demand for long-term care. At the same time, states and the federal government are operating with constrained resources.

4. Businesses must also prepare for an aging society. They need to consider the implications of the aging workforce, the increase in early retirement, and the security of pension plans, among other issues.

5. The voluntary sector must plan for an increased role by providing opportunities for meaningful community participation for senior citizens.

6. Government at all levels bears special responsibility to ensure that all of the above institutions are prepared to meet the challenges of aging in the 21st century. (Karl Pillemer et al., "Setting the White House Conference on Aging Agenda: Recommendations from an Expert Panel." *The Gerontologist* Vol. 35, No. 2, p. 259, 1995. Copyright © The Gerontological Society of America.)

Although these points do not identify specific policy initiatives, they do address those issues that are fundamental to aging policy. These issues represent the most ideal in American society. More realistically, aging policy will attempt to optimize the strengths of the increased size of the aging population and minimize the serious financial costs of benefits and services to this population. Future aging policy will also be constrained by decreased governmental assistance. As a consequence, the future for aging Americans is not particularly optimistic. The current political and economic climate envisions greater individual responsibility at all age levels. At a time when individual needs are increasing, the ability of others to provide assistance will be limited. The result will be an increasing polarization of the elderly population. This polarization will emerge between those who are financially capable of providing for themselves and those who are unable to maintain a minimum standard of living. This differentiation on the basis of socioeconomic status reflects the historical differences that exist throughout the lifetime of those involved. Table 13–1 illustrates class differences by defining the "deserving" and "undeserving" elderly. Data in Table 13–1 represent dollar amounts reflective of the early 1980s rather than the present. Nevertheless, the use of class as a qualifier for services highlights the disparity existing in American aging policy. The fact that aging policy differentiates between elderly who are "deserving" and those who are "undeserving" reflects deep-seated cultural values regarding the role of government toward its citizens.

TABLE 13–1   Class Basis of Policies for the Aged

Policy Area	"Deserving Poor" (Upper Class/Middle Class)	"Undeserving Poor" (Lower Class)
Income	Highest social security payments to upper and middle class Regressive taxation—no social security Tax after $32,400 salary level Pensions Tax credits	$6,000 retirement test for social security hurts this group the most Supplemental security income payment levels are below poverty
Medical care	Medicare—hospital and medical expenditures are highest for upper and middle classes Private health insurance	Medicaid—approximately 50% of those below poverty level are not covered; states may have more restrictive eligibility than the federal government
Social services	Social services block grant (formerly Title XX of the Social Security Act)—$2.4 billion ceiling in 1983; no federally mandated priority to Aid for Dependent Children, Supplemental Security Income, or Medicaid recipients Older Americans Act access/socialization services—limited resources; all aged are eligible, but provides services most needed by the middle class (e.g., access)	

Note: There is one federal policy covering the "deserving poor," in contrast to 50 state variable policies covering the "undeserving poor." State variable policies emerge primarily from state-federal programs in which states have much discretion over eligibility and the scope of available services. State discretionary programs are fiscally vulnerable, unstable, and highly vulnerable to swings in state-level political and economic factors.
Source: Estes, C. L. (1984). Austerity and aging: 1980 and beyond. Pp. 241–253. In M. Minkler and C. L. Estes (Eds.), *Readings in the political economy of aging.* (pp. 241–253). Amityville, NY: Baywood Publishing Company. Copyright © 1984, by Baywood Publishing Company, Inc., Amityville, New York. All rights reserved. No part of this book may be reproduced in any form, by mimeograph or any other means, without permission from the publisher. Printed in the United States of America.

In addition to economic polarization, aging policy must counter continued generational differences by identifying funding mechanisms for services that are based on cooperative measures and include the widest possible pool of supporters. These generational differences detract from the real cause of economic and social inequality within society: those in positions of power create the conditions that define opportunities not only for the elderly but for all age levels. An example of this difference can be found in health policy. Moody (1991, p. 190) states that "policy proposals for reordering health care priorities actually appear to have some significant support among elite groups such as bioethicists, health care policy analysts, and perhaps national policy makers. However, public opinion data show that the public at large strongly rejects age-based rationing, or even the need, accepted by elites, to make harsh priority choices."

Although the future of aging policy does not appear optimistic, opportunity for change does exist. As mentioned earlier, a window of opportunity is available for a brief period of time (even if congressional efforts continue to undermine implementation). To a great extent, conditions for change will come from the elderly themselves. For example, with the rapid democratization of technology, there has been an increasing number of elderly using computers. There is now a SeniorNet Network available for communication of ideas (Furlong, 1989). The efforts of many elderly to remain intellectually connected to the larger society provides a new image of a competent and capable aging individual. Because of the diversity that exists among the aging population, it will take the intelligence and efforts of many to ensure that an effective and equitable aging policy is developed and implemented. The future of aging policy lies with those who decide that the field of aging offers them an opportunity to make a difference. Whether it is in providing assistance to an elderly shut-in, working at the local senior citizen center, or creating policy at the state or federal level, serious work exists for those who believe that the elderly are a vital segment of American society. We will conclude this section with a brief glimpse into employment opportunities in aging.

Employment Opportunities in Aging

Aging is a relatively young field of study. The reader can refer to Chapter 1 for an overview of the history of gerontology in America. The recent past has witnessed significant growth in the number of courses in gerontology, geriatrics, and aging studies (referred to as GGA) offered on college and university campuses (Peterson, Wendt, & Douglass, 1994). This increase in coursework has resulted in a concomitant growth in the number of programs offering majors or some form of credential by the institution (Peterson et al., 1994). Coursework on aging is found at all levels (from community college to research university) of the academy. Because coursework and credentials differ depending on the level of the academic institution, employment opportunities are also quite distinct. For those interested in pursuing graduate and professional training, career opportunities exist in the traditional fields such as sociology, psychology, and social work. In addition, consider the following E-mail response to a new graduate student who had requested information on careers in gerontology.

> One field would be Gerontology Information Specialist or Librarian. Gerontology can also be connected to degrees in the humanities, such as English, Art, History. This person would be a Humanistic Gerontologist. In English, you would study the impact of literature

which discusses aging or the [effect] of aging on the creativity of older writers and artists. For historians, they can participate or develop oral history programs to get the biographies or memories of elderly people in their community or state. . . . (Shumway, 1995)

Gerontology is increasing its presence in the biological sciences as well. Mullins (1992, p. 10) identifies areas such as "nursing, medicine, dentistry, public health . . . [and] increasingly adjunctive to more traditional disciplinary or professional degrees, such as law and pharmacology. . . ." Mullins (1992, p. 11) continues this list of professional programs by stating that "colleges and universities will need to produce more geriatric psychiatrists, geropsychologists, mental health counselors, and social workers to work with the elderly."

On the professional level, there will be continued growth in the number and diversity of careers centered on aging. These careers will provide economic and professional status. There are additional employment opportunities that do not require advanced degrees. For example, directors of Area Agencies on Aging, senior citizen centers, local aging offices, and the like will continue to rely on those with an undergraduate degree. Jobs that involve considerable contact with the elderly will require far less training. A serious problem with many of these jobs is the lack of adequate pay, minimal job security, and considerable turnover of personnel. It is at this level that the greatest number of workers will be needed. Thus, even in the provision of care to the elderly, there is (and will continue to be) considerable economic differentiation.

Critical Connection: Demographic Realities and the Power of Definition

There are two contradictory schools of thought regarding the growth of the aging population. One school argues that the demographic imperative cannot be stopped and we, as a society, must prepare for a rapid aging of our numbers. Because of these population changes, social policy toward the elderly must also be altered to reflect their increased presence, cost, and a decreased societal commitment. This argument, although factual regarding population aging, continues to define the aging process in homogeneous stereotypes. Because of the images and definitions of aging that have been constructed, this argument perpetuates the belief that social problems experienced by the elderly are the result of aging itself. The second school argues that society must understand and appreciate the diversity of the aging population. As a result, we need to address this mosaic of needs based on characteristics other than age. This school of thought would examine the aging process as a consequence of various social forces. These social forces construct not only the image of aging but also the political, economic, and social framework within which the process will be defined. This school also recognizes that significant demographic changes are about to occur. The consequences of these demographic alterations are of less concern than attempts by those in positions of power to manipulate the formulation and implementation of aging policy that will affect an increasing number of elderly.

Although these two schools of thought are diametrically opposed to one another, they do share one common bond: the belief that the aging process is defined. Their differences lie in who defines aging and how definitions of aging should be created. This is an issue of who has the power and influence to have their arguments accepted. Aging in America is at a historical juncture. It is quite possible that the aging process will experience a redefinition. Whatever the new definition, it appears grounded in the social Darwinist rhetoric of the 104th Congress. If this concern is valid, then the aging process will become increasingly differentiated on the basis of social class. It is hoped that such concern is premature and overstated.

Chapter Review

The purpose of this chapter is a reminder of the basic foundation on which this book is constructed. With a brief reiteration of the demographic expectations and a realization of the significance of economics in the aging process, the intellectual breadth of the sociology of aging is illustrated. The following questions not only address material in this chapter but require knowledge acquired throughout the book.

1. Define aging policy. Identify one area within aging policy that you would like to restructure. Explain why and how you would restructure that particular area. What are some consequences of your actions?
2. Reexamine the demographic changes expected in the next 30 years in the United States. Based on your knowledge, what is the most significant aging policy that must be examined to accommodate this change? Explain your answer.
3. Respond to the argument by Americans for Generational Equity (AGE) that the monies spent by government should be distributed more evenly. In other words, governmental action should target efforts to assist children as much as the elderly.
4. Throughout this chapter and the book, economic inequality was continually identified as the primary problem resulting in differential treatment and outcome for the elderly in America. Do you agree with this assessment? If so, explain why. If you do not, explain why.
5. Using resources at your library, investigate employment opportunities, salary scale, and level of education needed for a high-status position and a low-status position in the field of aging.

Glossary

Demassification　The attempt to reduce the significance of large institutional structures as support mechanisms for mass society.

Post-modernism　A philosophical explanation given to the demassification of society and the rise of status groups.

Public policy　Consists of statements that define a strategy regarding some specific component of society (such as aging).

Status groups　a group within which everyone considers everyone else an equal. Within a postmodernist perspective, status groups, rather than institutional structures, provide identity for individuals.

Suggested Reading

Cole, T. R., et al. (Eds.). (1993). *Voices and visions of aging: Toward a critical gerontology.* New York: Springer.
This book is a forum in which discussion of a critical perspective of gerontology is examined relative to the growth of a post-modernist explanation of social life.

Lobenstine, J. C., et al. (1994). *National directory of educational programs in gerontology and geriatrics* (6th ed.). Washington, DC: Association for Gerontology in Higher Education.
As the title implies, this is a directory of gerontological programs that responded to an AGHE request for inclusion. This list covers primarily the United States, but it does identify AGHE member institutions in other countries. If a reader is seriously considering a career in aging, this directory is a valuable tool in identifying possible graduate-level programs.*

Olson, L. K. (Ed.). (1994). *The graying of the world: Who will care for the frail elderly?* New York: Haworth Press.
A most welcome book. The author addresses a real need by engaging in an intercountry examination of nursing home care.

Shenk, D., & Achenbaum, W. A. (Eds.). (1994). *Changing perceptions of aging and the aged.* New York: Springer.
As the title implies, the editors of this book offer articles that provide explanations for the images that are created of aging. The articles range from an emphasis on individual experiences to the influence of institutional structures.

References

Achenbaum, W. A. (1986). The aging of "the first new nation." In A. Pifer & L. Bronte (Eds.), *Our aging society: Paradox and promise* (pp. 15–32). New York: Norton.

Arber, S., & Ginn, J. (1991). *Gender and later life.* London: Sage.

Atchley, R. C. (1993). Critical perspectives on retirement. In T. R. Cole, W. A. Achenbaum, P. L. Jakobi, & R. Kastenbaum (Eds.), *Voices and visions of aging: Toward a critical gerontology* (pp. 3–19). New York: Springer.

Borgatta, E. F., & Montgomery, R. J. V. (1987). Aging policy and societal values. In E. F. Borgatta & R. J. V. Montgomery (Eds.), *Critical issues in aging policy* (pp. 7–27). Newbury Park, CA: Sage.

Callahan, D. (1986). Health care in the aging society: A moral dilemma. In A. Pifer & L. Bronte (Eds.), *Our aging society: Paradox and promise* (pp. 319–339). New York: Norton.

Cirillo, L. (1994). Verbal imagery of aging in the news magazines. In D. Shenk & W. A. Achenbaum (Eds.), *Changing perceptions of aging and the aged* (pp. 173–178). New York: Springer.

Clinton, William J. (1995). *Remarks by the President to the White House Conference on Aging.* Washington, DC: Office of the Press Secretary, The White House.

Crown, W. H., Longino, C. F., & Cutler, N. E. (1993). Net worth and the economic diversity of the elderly. *Journal of Aging and Social Policy, 5*(4), 99–118.

Estes, C. L. (1983). Austerity and aging: 1980 and beyond. In M. Minkler & C. L. Estes (Eds.), *Readings in the political economy of aging* (pp. 241–253). Amityville, NY: Baywood.

Estes, C. L. (1991). The new political economy of aging: Introduction and critique. In M. Minkler & C. L. Estes (Eds.), *Critical perspectives on aging: The political and moral economy of growing old* (pp. 19–36). Amityville, NY: Baywood.

Furlong, M. S. (1989). An electronic community for older adults: The SeniorNet network. *Journal of Communication, 39*(3), 145–153.

Gold, B., Kutza, E., & Marmor, T. R. (1981). United States social policy on old age: Present patterns and predictions. In C. S. Kart & B. B. Manard (Eds.), *Aging in America* (2nd ed., pp. 557–582). Sherman Oaks, CA: Alfred.

Gonyea, J. G. (1994). Making gender visible in public policy. In E. H. Thompson (Ed.), *Older men's lives* (pp. 237–255). Thousand Oaks, CA: Sage.

Johnson, E. S., & Williamson, J. B. (1980). *Growing old: The social problems of aging.* New York: Holt, Rinehart and Winston.

Johnson, J., & Slater, R. (Eds.). (1993). *Ageing and later life.* London: Sage.

Macdonald, B. (1993). Look me in the eye. In J. Johnson & R. Slater (Eds.), *Ageing and later life* (pp. 5–8). London: Sage.

Miller, S. M. (1976). The political economy of social problems: From the sixties to the seventies. *Social Problems, 24*(1), 131–141.

Mills, C. W. (1959). *The sociological imagination.* New York: Oxford University Press.

Minkler, M. (1991). "Generational equity" and the new victim blaming. In M. Minkler & C. L. Estes (Eds.), *Critical perspectives on aging: The political and moral economy of growing old* (pp. 67–80). Amityville, NY: Baywood.

Minkler, M., & Cole, T. R. (1991). Political and moral economy: Not such strange bedfellows. In M. Minkler & C. L. Estes (Eds.), *Critical perspectives on aging: The political and moral economy of growing old* (pp. 37–49). Amityville, NY: Baywood.

Moody, H. R. (1991). Allocation, yes; Age-based rationing, no. In R. H. Binstock & S. G. Post (Eds.), *Too old for health care?* (pp. 180–203). Baltimore: Johns Hopkins University Press.

Mullins, L. C. (1992). Reflections on gerontological education into the twenty-first century. In *Gerontology: The next generation* (pp. 9–12). Proceedings of a plenary session presented at the Annual Meeting of the Association for Gerontology in Higher Education, Baltimore, MD, March 1.

Myers, G. C. (1990). Demography of aging. In R. H. Binstock & L. K. George (Eds.), *Handbook of aging and the social sciences* (3rd ed., pp. 19–63). San Diego: Academic Press.

Myers, M. (1993). Coming out of the age closet. In J. Johnson & R. Slater (Eds.), *Ageing and later life* (pp. 9–11). London: Sage.

Neugarten, B. L., & Neugarten, D. A. (1986). Changing meanings of age in the aging society. In A. Pifer & L. Bronte (Eds.), *Our aging society: Paradox and promise* (pp. 33–51). New York: Norton.

Olson, L. K. (Ed.). (1994). *The graying of the world.* Binghamton, NY: Haworth Press.

Peterson, D. A., Wendt, P. F., & Douglass, E. B. (1994). *Development of gerontology, geriatrics, and aging studies programs in institutions of higher education.* Washington, DC: Association for Gerontology in Higher Education.

Pifer, A. (1986). The public policy response. In A. Pifer & L. Bronte (Eds.), *Our aging society: Paradox and promise* (pp. 391–413). New York: Norton.

Pillemer, K., Moen, P., Krout, J., & Robison, J. (1995). Setting the White House Conference on Aging agenda: Recommendations from an expert panel. *Gerontologist, 35*(2), 258–261.

Rich, B. M., & Baum, M. (1984). *The aging: A guide to public policy.* Pittsburgh: University of Pittsburgh Press.

Richman, H. A., & Stagner, M. W. (1986). Children: Treasured resource or forgotten minority? In A. Pifer & L. Bronte (Eds.), *Our aging society: Paradox and promise* (pp. 161–179). New York: Norton.

Rosenbaum, W. A., & Button, J. W. (1995). The unquiet future of intergenerational politics. In H. Cox (ed.), *Aging: Annual editions* (10th ed., pp. 231–240). Guilford, CT: Dushkin.

Shumway, V. (1995, March 16). Electronic mail message posted on geriatric health care discussion group.

Street, D., & Quadagno, J. (1993). The state, the elderly, and the intergenerational contract. In K. W. Schaie & W. A. Achenbaum (Eds.), *Societal impact on aging: Historical perspectives* (pp. 130–150). New York: Springer.

Torrey, B. (1982). The lengthening of retirement. In M. W. Riley, R. P. Abeles, & M. Teitelbaum (Eds.), *Aging from birth to death* (vol. 2, pp. 178–205). Boulder, CO: Westview.

U.S. Bureau of the Census. (1989). Current population reports, Series P-25, No. 1018, *Projections of the population of the United States, by age, sex, and race: 1988 to 2080.* Washington, DC: U.S. Government Printing Office.

Vesperi, M. D. (1994). Perspectives on aging in print journalism. In D. Shenk & W. A. Achenbaum (Eds.), *Changing perceptions of aging and the aged* (pp. 163–171). New York: Springer.

Williamson, J. B., Shindul, J. A., & Evans, L. (1985). *Aging and public policy: Social control or social justice?* Springfield, IL: Charles C. Thomas.

Photo Credits

Author Index

Abraham, L., 150
Achenbaum, W., 3, 4, 8, 33, 34, 43, 260
Adams, B., 89
Aday, R., 70
Adelman, M., 87
Ad Hoc Committee, 236
Allen, J., 191
Altergott, K., 242
Amenta, E., 156
American Geriatrics Society, 235, 241
Anderson, M., 28
Anderson, W., 173
Anetzberger, G., 225
Angel, J., 195
Angell, M., 132
Arber, S., 73, 76, 82–3, 90, 258
Arendell, T., 86, 181
Arevalo, R., 188
Aries, P., 235–236
Atchley, R., 58, 70, 113–114, 119–120, 128, 262
Austin, D., 70
Avorn, J., 73–74, 145–146

Babbie, E., 13–16, 18, 21
Bane, S., 201
Barrow, G., 70
Battin, M., 146
Bazargan, M., 164
Beauvoir, S., 24
Bell, J., 75
Bendiksen, R., 241
Bengtson, V., 13, 57, 63, 85, 89
Bernstein, V., 157
Biafora, F., 197

Binney, E., 35, 213
Binstock, R. 21, 73–74, 76, 78, 98, 133, 145, 150, 158
Birren, J., 63
Bishop, J., 75
Blauner, R., 240, 247
Blazer, D., 244
Block, M., 189
Blumer, H., 49
Booth, P., 157
Borgatta, E., 256
Bowker, L., 209
Breen, L., 3
Briggs, D., 163
Brigham, J., 71
Brower, V., 249
Brubaker, T., 71–72, 84, 86
Burgess, E., 68
Burr, J., 212
Burton, L., 185
Busse, E., 86
Butler, R., 73
Button, J., 173–174

Callahan, D., 74, 133, 143, 145, 150, 260
Cantor, M., 92, 96–97
Capron, A., 236–237
Carpenter, B., 244
Carpenter, J., 236
Cassel, C., 146, 160
Catania, J., 87–88
Cavan, R., 53
Charon, J., 70
Chen, Y., 105, 117
Cherlin, A., 95

Christensen, H., 84–85
Cicirelli, V., 95–96
Cigler, A., 167
Cirillo, L., 257
Clark, R., 116
Clemente, F., 224
Clinton, W., 256
Cockerham, W., 133
Cohen, K., 248
Cole, T., 268
Coles, C., 17
Comfort, A., 72
Cook, A., 247, 249
Cook, F., 158
Copper, B., 87, 101
Corr, C., 245
Coser, L., 109
Covey, H., 26
Cowdry, E., 3
Cowgill, D., 4, 25, 30–32, 43
Craib, I., 49
Crown, W., 258
Crystal, S., 207
Cumming, E., 52, 63
Cutler, N., 164

Daley, J., 187–188
Darney, A., 158, 180, 223
Davis, K., 132, 148
Davis, R., 75
Derthick, M., 159
Dobelstein, A., 34–35, 96,98, 161, 170–171
Dolan, T., 74, 146–147
Dolinsky, A., 212
Doob, C., 69

271

Subject Index